PASSING THE TORCH OF LIBERTY TO A NEW GENERATION

PASSING THE TORCH OF LIBERTY TO A NEW GENERATION

AMERICAN VISION PRESS
POWDER SPRINGS, GEORGIA

PASSING THE TORCH OF LIBERTY TO A NEW GENERATION

Copyright © 2009 by The American Vision, Inc.
    The American Vision, Inc.
    3150 Florence Road
    Powder Springs, Georgia 30127-5385
    www.AmericanVision.org
    1-800-628-9460

Printed in the United States of America.
Cover and interior layout design by Luis Lovelace

ISBN-13: 978-0-915815-97-5
ISBN-10: 0-915815-97-4

Dedicated to the memory of

CHRISTOPHER RORY HOOPS

Faithful Christian, husband, and father

JANUARY 29, 1950 – JULY 17, 2008

CONTENTS

CONTENTS

FOREWORD

"As long as the people of the United States are well informed and virtuous, so long they will be free and their government uncorrupted. It is in their power to remedy the evils arising from having wicked and designing men at the head of government—they can lift up and pull down at pleasure. If government be not wisely administered, the fault must be in the people; for the frequent election of every branch of the national legislature, if wisely executed is a sufficient remedy to all the mischiefs arising from a corrupt administration."

—*Cyprian Strong* (1799)

"Let us implore the forgiveness of our national and private transgressions; beseech the Almighty to smile on the United States of America; to diffuse knowledge and political and religious liberty, free from licentiousness, to all mankind; and manifest the gratitude of our hearts by lives conformed to the revealed will of God, and holy anticipations of the blessedness prepared for his children, in the world of eternal praise."   —*Henry A. Rowland* (1800)

I was driving north on I-75 toward Knoxville in late May 2008 on my way to a speaking engagement in Morgantown, West Virginia, when I received a phone call from my office. "Gary, a man just called. He said that he was dying and that he had to talk with you." I knew it was Chris Hoops. He had been ill for some time from a failing liver. Chris was a godly man who understood the Christian heritage of our nation and how it had been forgotten. Not only had he been fighting for his life for more than 25 years, he was fighting to return this nation back to its Christian foundation. When I got Chris' message, I immediately called him.

He told me that he had a 200-year-old book in his possession that he wanted American Vision to publish. He entrusted me with the only copy, and I assured him that we would reprint it if funds became available. A few weeks after Chris' call, the book arrived. It had a worn leather binding but did not have a title page.

After some research, I came to realize that the book I was holding in my hands was a one-of-a-kind discovery. It's what librarians describe as a "bound-with" book. Dr. Stephen Crocco, the James Lenox Librarian at Princeton Theological Seminary, offered this helpful explanation after I described the content of the book to him and sent him a scanned copy:

> It was common practice to take a group of sermons or pamphlets and have them bound together for the convenience of the owner. Libraries are full of these things and no two "bound-with" volumes are the same. That's why they don't have title pages for the whole and why the pagination is on a pamphlet by pamphlet basis. While they are rich resources, they require that each title be separately cataloged. Some libraries "disband" these collections to protect the individual items. What is different about this collection is that the pamphlets appear to be published by the same printer and they seem to be of a uniform size.

As a result, you won't find this book anywhere, not even in the Library of Congress. Its 500 pages consist of messages delivered on various occasions and on a variety of subjects dating from 1799 to 1802. The pamphlets are originals that were handled more than 200 years ago! While the individual chapters exist in pamphlet form and can be found in private collections and libraries, it would take someone years to find original copies and a small fortune to procure them. Most libraries only have digital copies of these pamphlets.

The makeup of the pamphlets is interesting. In addition to Election Sermons, there are messages on the anniversary of "American Independence" and tributes to the late George Washington delivered soon after his death. One of special note was delivered by Timothy Dwight, President of Yale-College, on February 22, 1800, on what would have been Washington's 68th birthday. The title of Dwight's discourse—"On the Character of George Washington"—is instructive considering that so many scandal-ridden officials get elected. Also included in this volume is President Washington's Farewell Address of September 17, 1796 in which he stated, "Of all the dispositions and habits which lead to political prosperity, Religion and Morality are indispensable supports."

Another unique feature of these messages is the historical value of the Century Sermons. They were designed by their authors to remind people of God's work of providence in history. Moses C. Welch writes:

> Who can view the great things God has done among the inhabitants of the earth and not have exalted conceptions of him? He has overturned, and overturned, the nations at his pleasure. When it was nec-

essary for the accomplishment of his purposes, he has raised up and exalted a nation—suffered them to continue in power, and bear down all before them, for a season, and, by and by, has caused them to fall in their turn, and crumble to pieces. The Babylonian, Persian, and Grecian monarchies rose in succession, flourished and conquered; and in succession were conquered, and overcome. The last of these gave way to the greater power of the Romans. In these overturnings God was displaying himself, and making way for the introduction of Christianity in the greatest glory of the greatest pagan monarchy that ever existed. The rise and fall of empires, and overturning powerful monarchies, gives a serious, contemplative mind exalted ideas of God.... We all begin the new century with new resolutions in favor of Godliness. May we gird up our loins, and be strong in the Lord. May we set up our Ebenezer, strongly impressed with this idea that hitherto hath the Lord helped us.

What would happen if America's pulpits once again proclaimed the "whole counsel of God" (Acts 20:27) like these ministers of two centuries ago? Not only would atheists be upset, many ministers would object to their content as well. Today's clergy have tried to remain neutral in their pulpits by claiming that religion and politics do not meet on any point. I'm sure you've heard ministers tell their congregations to stay out of politics using some of the following unsupported claims:

- "Politics is dirty." (So what isn't?)
- "Jesus didn't get mixed up in politics." (He didn't get married either.)
- "There's a separation between Church and State." (There's no separation between God and the State.)
- "Our citizenship is in heaven." (It didn't stop Paul from using his Roman citizenship and appealing to Caesar.)
- "We're not supposed to judge." (We are to judge consistently and righteously.)
- "You can't impose your morality on other people." (Every law is the imposition of someone's view of morality.)

The men who penned these pamphlets would recoil in disbelief and despair if they heard these excuses coming from ministers of the gospel. Joseph Strong stated in 1802 that our founding fathers adhered to the principle "that none ought to be elevated to public office except those whose opinions and behavior were strictly Christian" and that "righteousness exalts a nation." Such claims would be considered "intolerant" and "non-inclusive," or worse, "hate speech." These ministers were not afraid to proclaim the truth:

- "In the judicial department, a high regard to law and justice must never be subordinated to party interest or a fear of rejection from office." (23)

- "Religion promotes union and confidence, and thus gives strength to a nation." (51)

- "Religion will make good rulers and good citizens." (52)

- "Any good order is but the political name for religion." (52)

- "[N]o religion has been so favorably calculated for the rectitude, support and comfort of the individual, or for the order, improvement and honor of society, as the Christian." (52-53)

These are principles that many Christians have long forgotten. We're not in a mess today solely because of unbelievers; we're in a mess because we are a nation that has lost its memory of its Christian beginnings and the biblical injunction that civil governors are "ministers of God" (Rom 13:4). It seems also that many Christians have lost their courage.

The public political sermons found in this book are just a few of thousands of such sermons preached from colonial times until well after the framing and ratification of the U.S. Constitution. Prof. Ellis Sandoz has read more than 8,000 of them and edited *Political Sermons of the American Founding Era, 1730–1805*. These public sermons, some of which were preached in the halls of Congress, are a vast mountain of evidence that (1) the church used to preach and teach the whole counsel of God, including what God's Word says about civil government, law, public life, and the political issues of the day; (2) that Christianity was predominant in early American political thought before, during, and after the framing and ratification of the Constitution; (3) that early Americans—and their pastors—did not believe that either the Constitution or the First Amendment imposed a "separation of church and state" which required a secularization or de-Christianization of civil government, its laws, or a "religious neutrality" among all the religions of man concerning civil government, law, and public life.

The church in early America preached and taught the whole counsel of God. It spoke from Scripture to the ministry of civil government—a crucially important ministry which the church today (and for many decades now) has turned over to the enemies of Jesus Christ. Today's church needs to get back to doing what the Great Commission commands: preaching, teaching, and acting to influence the ministry of civil government for Jesus Christ and His righteousness. Many in the church have failed to honor God because of their colossal neglect of their duty to teach about and speak to the ministry of civil government!

In addition to the political messages found in this rare volume, there are sermons that express optimism about the future in the midst of surrounding evil. While these ministers did not deny that their new century had its troubles, they continued to preach about the success of the gospel in the world. Consider these words from Nathan Strong, Pastor of the North Presbyterian Church in Hartford Connecticut, which he preached on the "first Sabbath of the nineteenth century of the Christian era":

> If the present state of things among the nations, and the changes that have happened in the past century, are a train of events, that do, in a most astonishing degree, prepare for the fulfilment of the divine promise, that the kingdom of Christ shall fill the world; and if viewed on a large scale, they have a most propitious aspect for the gospel, then, surely pious minds will rejoice; and as surely infidels ought to tremble for themselves, and for the vain contest in which they are engaged with the king in Zion.

While Strong misinterpreted passages from Daniel and followed the Reformation view that the antichrist was the Papacy of his day, even so, there is no preoccupation with "last days madness." He believed in the "Universal Spread of the Gospel."

To read these sermons is to be transported back to a time where God was acknowledged as the Creator and Sustainer of all things, where history was important and under His sovereign control, and the character of civil officials was indispensable for the survival of a nation. It was Chris Hoops' prayer that in some small way this book would recapture these biblical truths and return America to real liberty: "Now the Lord is the Spirit, and where the Spirit of the Lord is, there is liberty" (2 Cor. 3:17). I have reproduced the note that Chris sent to me which expresses his desire to see this book reprinted.

Gary DeMar
January 29, 2009

Original letter from Chris Hoops to Gary DeMar

Dear Gary

I Can not begin to tell you
how much your ministry has ment
to me,
I have you yu to be a man of honesty,
litegrety Knaokess American
Christein History.

You are a Christian PeaceMaker
without Compromise of Principle
of Gods word,
So of all the men I have
know over the years I have
appreiated you and your work the
Most,

the Doc's have not given me much
Time to live – for the grave have
no fear to me no the grave
a my victory – Men I fear even less

God must be our of fear
our only master our God
Lord,

This Book inclose I bought in
1982 hoping then one day to get some
of the Sermons Published — to no
avail I wanted to leave it to
someone who would appreciate its
content and Message to a the
Christian Church today —
God Is calling us to
Action,
We can be reluctant but we must
act as an obedient Soldier of
the Cross,

I hope you enjoy the Book,
I can think of know one else I would rather
have it, God Bless
Chris Aoor

Transcription of Mr. Hoops' letter:

Dear Gary,

I can not begin to tell you how much your ministry has meant to me. I have known you to be a man of honesty and integrity and knowledgeable of America's Christian History. You are a Christian peacemaker without compromise of principle or God's Word. So of all the men I have known over the years, I have appreciated you and your work the most.

The Doc's have not given me much time to live… the grave holds no fear over me nor the grave any victory… Man I fear even less than God—He must be over fear, our only Master our Lord.

This book enclosed I bought in 1982. Hoping that one day to get some of the sermons published—to no avail. I wanted to leave it to someone who would appreciate its content and meaning to the Christian Church today.

God is calling us to action.

We can be reluctant but we must act as an obedient soldier of the Cross.

I hope you enjoy the book, I can think of no one else I would rather have it.

God Bless,

Chris Hoops

Spelling and Punctuation

The reader will notice that some of the sermons in this volume contain words where an "s" within a word looks like an "f" but without the short horizontal line. These "long esses," as they are called, can be seen in the following example:

> GREAT and interefting events have ever been confidered, as meriting a particular memorial. It has not been uncommon, to perpetuate fuch a memorial, by the inftitution and obfervation of annual rites and feftivals.——The meffengers which God fent to the Hebrews, his ancient covenant people, very frequently called their attention, to great and fignal national events ; as appears from the facred writings. How frequently did they recapitulate, the various deliverances which that people had experienced ? A recollection of fuch events was con-
> fidered, as being eminently calculated to folemnize

"Long esses" can be found in most printed documents from the 18th century, including the Declaration of Independence and the Constitution. Because Passing the Torch of Freedom to a New Generation is a facsimile reprint, the "long esses" have not been corrected for the modern reader. While they take some getting used to, after a few minutes of reading, they are easy to spot. "Short esses" (s) appear at the end of words, and "long esses" are never used for an upper case S. This can be seen in the heading of the Declaration of Independence where there are no "long esses" because there are no lower case letters:

In CONGRESS, JULY 4, 1776.

A DECLARATION
BY THE REPRESENTATIVES OF THE
UNITED STATES OF AMERICA,
IN GENERAL CONGRESS ASSEMBLED.

In addition to "long esses," many early printed pamphlets, proclamations, and books set apart block quotations by beginning each line with quotation marks, sometimes single and other times double. Here is an example:

> WE may, in the next place, view the farmer
> of Mount Vernon in his private life. " He was a
> " man of the ſtricteſt honor and honeſty, fair and
> " honorable in his dealings, and punctual to his
> " engagements. His diſpoſition was mild, kind
> " and generous. Candor, ſincerity, moderation
> " and ſimplicity were prominent features in his
> " character. He was an affectionate huſband, a
> " faithful friend, a humane maſter and a father to
> " the poor. He lived in the unvarying habits of
> " regularity, temperance and induſtry."

In addition to the above typographical anomalies, "Eighteenth-century writings tend to be rife with commas, by today's standards.... Dashes were often used in combination with other marks,—commas, semicolons, even periods (as this sentence demonstrates)."[1] This old-style typography is part of the charm of a book with so much history behind it.

1. Ellis Sandoz, ed., *Political Sermons of the American Founding Era: 1730–1805* (Indianapolis: Liberty Press, 1991), xxx-xxxi.

Mr. STRONG's

ELECTION SERMON,

MAY 13, 1802.

SERMON,

PREACHED ON THE

GENERAL ELECTION

AT

HARTFORD IN CONNECTICUT,

MAY 13, 1802.

BY JOSEPH STRONG, A. M.
PASTOR OF A CHURCH IN NORWICH.

HARTFORD:

PRINTED BY HUDSON & GOODWIN.

1802.

*At a GENERAL ASSEMBLY of the State of CONNECTICUT, holden
at Hartford, on the second Thursday of May, A. D. 1802— ·*

ORDERED, That the Honorable WILLIAM HILLHOUSE and
ELISHA TRACY, Esquires, present the thanks of this Assembly
to the Reverend JOSEPH STRONG, for his Sermon, delivered on the General Election, on the thirteenth instant, and
request a copy thereof for the press.

A true copy of Record,

Examined by

SAMUEL WYLLYS, SECRETARY.

ELECTION SERMON.

JEREMIAH, vi. 16.

Thus saith the Lord, stand ye in the ways and see, and ask for the old paths, where is the good way and walk therein, and ye shall find rest for your souls.

THE Jews were at no period in a more prosperous state on worldly accounts, than when Jeremiah commenced his prophetic labors. During the reign of Josiah, a prince highly accomplished both by nature and grace, the continuance of peace for a number of years had introduced plenty and ease ; though not without being accompanied with more than an equal proportion of vice and dissipation. Added to the complete prostration of private virtue, each social tie, whether it respected God or man, was violently broken asunder. Thus situated, it was the dictate neither of God's covenant love nor of that regard which he owed to the honor of his own character, to allow the existing state of things to continue uncorrected. The experiment of mercy having proved but too unsuccessful, every principle dictated that judicial infliction should be made its unwelcome substitute. Nothing remained to be done previous to such judicial infliction taking place, but to make solemn proclamation of the fact, accompanied with one more overture in favor of national amendment and safety. This delicate and arduous task was assigned to Jeremiah, a man exactly formed for the purpose in every view which can be taken of his character. Possessed of a mind constitutionally firm, his address was plain and forcible. He felt for all the interests of his country with ardor, though in subserviency to a far higher principle—disinterested regard to the prerogatives of Jehovah's character and law. As might be expected from such a messenger, acting under the immediate direction of heaven, each branch of his address was, to an unusual degree, pointed and solemn. " O daughter of my people gird thee with sackcloth and wallow thyself in ashes ; make thee mourning as for a son, most bitter lamentation. The bellows are burnt, the lead is consumed in the fire, the founder melteth in vain, for the wicked are not plucked away. Be thou instructed, O Jerusalem, lest my soul depart from thee ; lest I make thee desolate, a land not inhabited. Thus saith the Lord, stand ye in the ways and see ; and ask for the old paths, where is the good way, and walk therein, and ye shall find rest for your souls."

THE circumstances which dictated the text, being those now sketched, its more particular application to the present occasion, will naturally direct our thoughts to two enquiries :—

WHAT are those paths pursued by our fathers, which in a more distinguishable sense constitute the good way :—And

THE nature of that rest to be secured by walking in them.

IN view of the proposed outlines to the present attempt, it is far from my design to amplify in indiscriminate praise of ancient times, at the expense of those which are modern. Forward to concede the fact, that the age of the fathers was marked with numerous foibles or even faults, at the same time it will be contended, that in view of all circumstances it was an age to a superior degree exemplary and respectable ; it is therefore the joint demand of gratitude and interest, that we carefully select its virtues and copy them into our own practice.

WHILE standing in the way to see, there is no old path which more clearly and forcibly strikes the mind than the confirmed belief of our fathers in the

Christian scriptures. The fact is not to be question-
ed, that short of fifty years past, scarcely a single
avowed infidel either disgraced or endangered this
privileged part of God's American heritage. Every
voice was rather in union with that of the apostle,
" Lord to whom shall we go, for thou hast the
" words of eternal life." Good sense, accompanied with reverence for Jehovah, formed the prevailing character ; and the bible was seen to command
universal and unwavering esteem. The wide departure from such an happy state of sentiment and
feeling which has since taken place, is but too per-
ceptible and ominous. Numerous causes have conspired to produce the wide spread of infidelity among
us ; causes which continue to operate, and that not
without being much strengthened by the solicitude
which ever marks party spirit, to support its own
favorite cause whether right or wrong. The motives which excite the infidel to exertion, are injudi-
cious and malevolent in the extreme. The great effort of his life is to prostrate a system which can injure no one, and if true, promises essential advantage
to all. To leave out of view the solemn article of
death, with all that may ensue, the Christian scheme
of religion merits the highest esteem and most industrious encouragement. Both its doctrines and
moral precepts are adapted to promote personal enjoyment, strengthen the bands of social intercourse,
and reduce to consistency and order the discordant,
deranged interests of the world.

ELECTION SERMON.

ANOTHER of those good old paths, the subject of present enquiry, was an especial reference to the religion of the heart. Our fathers did not stop short with advocating a mere speculative religion, however rational and sublime; but superadded their confirmed belief of its inward, transforming influence. Morality was their frequent theme, though not to prevent its being a morality the fruit of pre-existing grace. Although such a trait in ancient character, may probably sink it in the esteem of some and even subject him who mentions it to the disgust and obloquy of those who take pride in their liberal modes of thinking, it ought and will be contended that experimental religion is a great and glorious reality. None ought to blush in mentioning its name or in urging it home to the heart. While in the case of the private citizen it forms an invaluable possession; to the Christian magistrate, it is in superior degrees necessary and advantageous. In exact proportion as the duties devolved upon him are weighty and arduous, he ought to cultivate an holy temper—place his supreme dependence upon God—and encourage the vigorous exercise of faith with respect to those rewards, which await the faithful servant. Are these remarks just, we certainly owe no thanks to those who are so forward at the present day to *rationalize* our holy and good religion. Too rational already for them to love it, their efforts are no better than disguised infidelity. While their professed object is to display its harmony and extend its popularity, they in fact do more

B

than the avowed infidel to disorganize its parts and enfeeble its energies.

IT may be proper, in this part of the discourse, also to remind you, how industrious our fathers were, to give existence and energy to moral senti-ment. Wherever the sphere of their influence ex-tended, they were forward to impress ideas of the di-vine existence and government—the ties of social re-lation—creature accountableness—and the solemn remunerations of eternity. They were under no ap-prehension of practising undue influence upon the untaught mind.' They did not conceive it an encroach-ment upon the rights of natural liberty, to prepos-sess the heart in favor of what is virtuous and useful. Foreign to the impressions of moral sentiment, the whole is put to hazard which constitutes well regula-ted community. Proper veneration for civil rulers is done with—good neighborhood ceases—the natural and powerful cement of families is destroyed—and the nearest connection in life treated with baseness and infidelity. As all must be sensible, the efforts of the present day that tend to such an unwelcome issue, are by no means small. In total disregard of the good example of the fathers, how many among us have the effrontery to circulate writings, and ad-vocate them in private conversation, the avowed design of which is to prostrate all distinctions in life —reduce man to a state of nature—vacate the so-lemn rights of marriage—and surrender the dearest interests of human nature to the guidance of appetite and passion. Such is the boasted philosophy which closed the eighteenth, and is with too much success, ushering in the nineteenth century. A commendable regard to the future respectability of the age in which we live, would almost prompt a desire that the powers for history were extinct—that no heart possessed the inclination or hand the ability to inform posterity, how base were the ideas and degenerate the practices of their fathers.

In this connection you will permit me to mention also, that spirit of social deference and subordination which strongly marked the age of the fathers. As for the fact, no person to a considerable degree advanced in life, will undertake to call it in question. Not to pain your feelings by a recital of what is now fact,—the time has been when children did not conduct as though they were compeers with their parents—when those covered with grey hairs were treated with reverence—when talents and literary improvement excited feelings of veneration— and when both legislative and executive office, were looked up to and obeyed as the institution of God. Let a selfish, equalizing spirit say what it may, society will never rise with regularity and firmness unless the feelings of rational subordination constitute its basis ;—feelings rarely operative, provided they do not commence with childhood, gradually forming into settled habit with the increase of years. With mankind, more the creatures of habit than of sentiment, when the latter principle does not operate to the extent which might be wished, the good influence of the former is by no means to be rejected. The parent and schoolmaster do more to make the child a good or bad citizen, than the whole which can be done through the remainder of life. It must be a great force indeed, which bends the full grown tree into a new direction. Bent aright at first, very little after labor is required to mould it to that particular situation in the great political machine, where it is most needed. Those who do not early commence the habit of commendable subordination and respect for superiors, almost without exception, prove themselves restless, troublesome members of community. A turbulent, incendiary temper, being the character of the child, will not fail to operate when arrived to years of manhood. The ring-leader of quarrel and faction among his play-mates, is certain of being an high toned demagogue, to whatever department of life providence afterwards assigns him. These remarks are jointly supported by theory and observation. Beyond most others, the spirit in question is one which society ought seriously to deprecate. The evidence of history is explicit to the point, that numerous well regulated governments have lost their liberties with every thing which mankind hold dear, by means of a single unprincipled, ambitious individual. Through the agency of intrigue or direct usurpation, they have thus in a day exchanged the brightest national prospects for the chains of unqualified slavery. There is no kind of government which more loudly reprobates this spirit, than what ours does. For though a republican government gives opportunity for the exercise of the fiery, uncontrollable spirit, yet the genuine principles of such a government are opposed to its existence.

ANOTHER noticeable fact, with respect to our fathers, was their strict adherence to the principle, that none ought to be elevated to public office except those whose opinions and behavior were strictly Christian. Brilliancy of talents was a secondary consideration in their view, when accompanied with an unprincipled heart. What confidence can the public mind reasonably place in men who spurn our holy religion and sanguinely calculate upon death as the termination of existence? Except that feeble principle the fashionable world stiles honor, what stimulus have they to the regular and useful performance of those duties made incumbent by office? With respect to such persons, in what consists the obligatory strength of oaths? The idea of future accountableness laid aside, an oath instantly dwindles to a mere cypher.—A not less weighty class of objections are adduceable against the scandalously immoral than against the avowed infidel. Elevated to office, the influence of example never fails to be doubly impressive. To emulate and copy high life is inseparable from human nature. Beauty and deformity of character in the peasant or beggar, strike the mind in a very feeble manner, compared with what they do when attach-

ELECTION SERMON.

ed to the rich and powerful. Cloathed with the
purple, vices the most base and odious, by a kind
of magic influence, become completely fascinating ;
—there being nothing more certain than that the
libertine magistrate, from whom the whole evil has
originated, will not do any thing to correct it either
by the enacting of laws or their after execution. It
is hard to conceive how the friends of society, and
especially those who profess themselves Christians,
can give their suffrage for men of the above description. Conscience must have had administered to it
some soporific draught, or it could not be the case.
Though it be a conduct which nothing can justi-
fy, two causes may assist to its explanation;—the
rage of party spirit, and the base arts of electioneering. Nearly without fail do these two great
scourges of community act in conjunction. Beyond
most other circumstances, political controversy has
a powerful operation to call into exercise the irasci-
ble, violent feelings of human nature. Rational,
calm thought laid aside, a wide opening is made to
misrepresentation and seduction. Those are never
wanting whose highest gratification consists in poi-
soning the public mind, and warping it aside from
the advancement of its great and permanent interests.
The advancement of some pecuniary interest, though
more commonly a wish to rise into office, is the
stimulus to such an insidious, contemptible line of
conduct. A people must have lost their native
good sense, when they cease most heartily to despise
the electioneering candidate. Persons who will adopt

and persevere in such a line of conduct, ought to be unfailingly viewed with disapprobation and disgust. They affront the discernment and impartiality of their fellow citizens, and in the place of a rightful claim to promotion they only deserve contempt and frowns. The honorable name *freeman* is most improperly applied to the one, who ceases to follow the dictates of his own unbiassed judgment and surrenders himself the tool of unprincipled intrigue. When we consider who are the individuals upon whom such intrigue is commonly practised, it is matter of surprise that its effect is not more extensive and ruinous. However good the intentions of the middle and lower classes of society, their habits of life and want of correct information upon numerous political subjects, greatly expose them to deception. The address made to their passions finds no corrective influence from the quarter of judgment. Although till of late, this state has exemplified nothing of the evil which is the subject of present remark ; it now fast gains ground, and is an omen dark to our future weal, and of course makes loud demand for vigorous opposition, from argument, example and law. The growing venality which marks elections is a circumstance which beyond most others, strongly indicates a premature old age to these American states. A most desirable matter would it be for this state, might it reassume its former dignified ground with respect to free, unbiassed suffrage, before such reassumption is rendered additionally impracticable.

ELECTION SERMON.

IT merits to be further remarked with respect to the good way which our fathers pursued ;—that they did not manifest an inclination constantly to innovate upon the established government. Both men and measures commanded their approbation and support, so long as nothing was discoverable unprincipled in the one, or essentially defective in the other. The correct political maxim no doubt had full possession of their judgment, that a less perfect form of government is preferable to one more studied and nicely balanced, that fails in the important article of execution. The fallacy of theory is in no instance more glaring, than with respect to plans of national government. The statesman often exhibits what appears consistent and beautiful upon paper which in course of carrying it into effect does not fail to produce the speedy and complete ruin of empire. A greater chimera was never imagined, than that a single form of government admits of universal application. It is the unquestionable right of every nation to adopt what kind of government it pleases ; but the great point is that its principles be adhered to with firmness and its duties fulfilled with punctuality. How fortunate would it have been, for the fairest portion of Europe, which in course of a few years past, has exhibited a strange and most forbidding spectacle to the world, had its citizens felt the unquestionable justice of these remarks and conformed to them in practice ? Mad with theory—infatuated by a spirit of overturn, they exchanged evils which required

redress for those still more pressing and to be depre-
cated. Has the daring enterprize of an individual,
given a successful check to such a state of things,
and from a chaos of confusion and tyranny produced a degree of national order and energy in government, the example, notwithstanding, is worthy of
universal notice and improvement. It teaches nations to appreciate a settled order of things, to
dread innovation, and to cling to their constitutional chart with increased gratitude and strengh of attachment. None but essential and glaring defects,
ever authorize experiment upon the forms, and much
less upon the principles of established government.
A pillar removed is never easily replaced, and how
often is it fact that the removal of a single pillar
exposes the building to certain and speedy destruction. The hazard thus incurred is often immense,
yet there is no circumstance of national exposure
to which the feelings of our nature more directly
and forcibly impel. Passing by all adventitious
circumstances, it is a radical propensity of the
human mind to dislike government. It implies
the relinquishment of certain rights, for the more
perfect security of others. It calls for partial sacrifice to a common interest, that the vigilance
and energies of that interest may give freedom of
exercise and permanency to those private rights which
are retained. To comply with the social compact
which is a dictate of the judgment, involves no small
share of self-denial. Owing to the restless temper of
man, his constant effort is to independence and self-

C

18   **ELECTION SERMON.**

direction. Hence the frequent efforts made, to counteract the constitutions of well regulated society.
Notwithstanding the numerous advantages derived
from governmental association, those restraints and
burdens it is under necessity to impose, have a direct tendency to excite the calumny or more daring
opposition of licentious and ignorant men. And
how perfectly do these remarks, inferable from
the structure of human nature, coincide with
our own observation ? The person who has noticed the progress of things in these states for a
number of years past, cannot fail to approve their
correctness. Under various disguises, the effort has
been constant to undermine our excellent constitution;—a constitution of government equally the work
of necessity and wisdom ; and no other evidence is
requisite in its favor, but the unexampled prosperity
of the country during the whole period since it began to operate. Inauspicious to the success of any
constitution however good, as the past convulsed
period has been, ours has succeeded to a wonder.
There is no class of citizens but what has been remarkably smiled upon, under its auspices. The
three great component parts of American society, the
farmer, merchant and mechanic, must fight against
their own interests, provided they calumniate its principles or endeavor to enfeeble its energies. Are certain burdens necessarily attached to all governments,
for the various purposes of their own support, and
the furtherance of justice upon the great scale, ours
has much the fewest of such burdens of any govern-

ment throughout the civilized world. It deserves
serious thought, which is preferable, such comparatively small burdens, or the complete prostration of all constitutional authority. Where there
is no form of government in operation, and of consequence no law, the state of things cannot be otherwise than unfortunate in the extreme. A country
which has experienced so much of divine benefi-
cence, in baffling the plots of foreign enemies, ought
to be very cautious not to lay violent hands on itself.
Such is clearly the joint dictate of commendable gratitude to the Father of all mercies and of a principle
of self-preservation. Smiled upon as our national
affairs have been for many years, they are not at
present beyond the reach of essential and permanent
detriment. Continuing to be divided among ourselves, the whole which mankind hold dear is put
to hazard. The order of society will of course be
deranged,—our liberties may be wrested from us—
our morals are certain to depreciate even below
what they now are—while triumphant infidelity is
but too likely to assume the place of godliness.

IT will only be further remarked of the fathers,
that they were powerfully actuated by a love of their
country. Many circumstances conspired to awaken
and give energy to such a principle. The persecutions which prompted their removal to this land—
the multiform hardships and dangers which marked
distant establishments in a savage country—and the
constant effort made to abridge, or wholly vacate

their charter rights, gave increased strength to feelings constitutional in the human mind. Attached to the parent state by strong ties, they still at no period shewed themselves forgetful that they had a country of their own. Benevolent and just to all, their views and exertions were at the same time, to a degree, local. They felt and conformed to those high obligations which they were immediately under to themselves and to their posterity. How fortunate would it have been for us as a nation, had the same love of country operated with equal force at a more recent date? Foreign attachments have been one principal source of the numerous embarrassments under which we have and do continue to labor. Hence in particular those violent party animosities, which cannot be either denied or excused. For the citizens of an independent nation to attach themselves with warmth to the views of this or the other country, is equally servile and impolitic. The real point both of dignity and interest lies here, to remember that we are Americans, and prove ourselves equally independent in conduct, as in name. May it not be hoped that the late pacification among the contending nations of Europe, will operate to extinguish party spirit and consolidate our union upon the broad basis of harmonized views, feelings and exertions?

A FEW remarks upon the closing paragraph of the text will complete the present attempt. " And ye shall find rest to your souls." The nature of this rest admits no question. Intimately related as the good behavior of the present life may be to the rewards of eternity, this is not the principal object of the passage now under review. Its primary reference is to those worldly advantages which are national. The whole extent of life often fails to realise the rewards of private virtue; but those of public, national virtue are never thus distant. The natural course of things, seconded by the promise of Jehovah, insures the event "that righteousness exalteth a nation." Nations are often exalted, as the result of divine sovereignty, foreign to their own good behavior, yet such exaltation is most commonly judicial and greatly insecure as to its permanency. How far our national exaltation is of such a character demands careful enquiry. Upon whatever principle we account for the fact, the allotments of providence to us as a nation have been without example. The ground we now occupy, in some points of view, is elevated and commanding, though not to supercede a laudable wish to advance still higher. However eligible our present situation, it leaves room for much improvement. Did we pursue the good ways which our fathers trode, with that industry which their example recommends; each interest of our country whether natural or moral, literary or political, would be essentially advanced.

AGRICULTURE connected with a growing population—mercantile enterprize—the arts and sciences —industry and economy through all the various classes of society—energetic government, and the wide diffusion of united views and exertions with respect to national interests, could not fail to form the result. With fervent piety and good morals added to these circumstances, it is hard to conceive what further internal improvements a people could wish. The principles of happiness and prosperity among themselves being thus firmly established, they may safely calculate upon " sitting under their own vine and their own fig-tree, with none to make them afraid." And in view of this sketch of " rest to the soul"—of national emolument, aggrandizement and security, who of us but must feel grateful that it has been already so far realized, and who will refuse solemnly to pledge all his future exertions for its completion? In a superior degree indebted to a sovereign all-gracious providence for public blessings, yet we cannot insure to ourselves their future continuance ulness through the instrumentality of personal exertion. Means and the end are as closely connected in the civil, as in the natural world. Not an individual who assists to compose community, fails to have numerous and weighty duties devolved upon him for the promotion of the general weal. While moral and religious principles should never be out of view, as a stimulus to action through the different grades of society ; each grade ought to study and carefully adhere to its own particular department of action. The private citizen ought to be in the habit of industry, punctuality in dealing, and submission to constituted authority. Those who minister at the altar must study uncorruptness of manners, purity of doctrine and the whole fervor of zeal in the best of causes. Those in executive office, should be equally careful never to overleap the boundary of law, or see its requirements trampled under foot with impunity. In the judicial department, an high regard to law and justice must never be subordinated to party interest or a fear of rejection from office. With respect to the legislator, his ideas upon every subject which comes before him ought to be correct, his views superior to the influence of local attachment, his firmness too great to be shaken by the strong collision of party, and his integrity bottomed upon a good heart. With the body politic thus classed, each one confining himself to his own proper province, order and perpetuity are certain to constitute its great prominent features. Peculiarly privileged in this state from the proper combination of these various social powers, we are probably not more indebted to either of them, than to a wise and upright legislative magistracy. From the first establishment of Connecticut to this day, a large proportion of those annually chosen to legislate, have no doubt, to an happy extent, exemplified the character of the good ruler drawn by the pen of inspiration, " The God of Israel said ; the rock of Israel spake unto me, he that ruleth over men must be just, ruling in the fear of God. And he shall be as the light of the morning when the sun riseth, even a morning without clouds ; as the tender grass

ELECTION SERMON.

springing out of the earth, by clear shining after rain."

Under an impression that the public suffrage, the current year, has fallen upon characters not less meritorious than those who have possessed the same honorable designation ;—may I be permitted to recommend and urge, that they recollect with care and adhere with firmness to that general system of policy, which has rendered this state, for nearly two centuries, united and secure, prosperous and respectable. With the past thus a model for future procedure, the demand is direct and forcible, that science and religion should continue to command the liberal patronage of the civil arm. Fostered by legislative aid, they are certain to make large remuneration for all the pains and expense. A treasonable wish to enfeeble and ultimately prostrate the varied interests of community, can in no way be so easily corrected, as by the diffusion of knowledge and the sentiments of piety. Good principles and an immoral behavior sometimes incorporate, yet as a general rule the corrective power of the former over the latter is great. There is no so eligible mode of discouraging vice, as by a marked preference in the laws in favor of virtue. While wise and upright legislators duly appreciate these foundation principles, and encourage a spirit of reliance upon Jehovah for his special direction, it may be calculated with confidence, that they will legislate well, and should on no account fail to live in the hearts of a grateful people.

WITHOUT confidence in government, it cannot fail to sink into contempt and all the unhappiness of enfeebled operation. Few greater blessings are there than good rulers and good laws;—though let it not be forgotten that they form a blessing which subjects may realize or reject as they please. I have no doubt as a general fact, it is more the fault of the people than of the ruler, that their expectations from government are not answered. With that mutual confidence between those who govern and those who are governed, which ought to prevail, no essential interest would be put to hazard; tyranny and anarchy would be kept at an equal remove; and by a close combination of views and exertions, each interest whether private or public, individual or social, would rapidly progress to its greatest possible extent.

UNDER the special direction of a sovereign, holy providence, may such prove the future lot of this particular state and of those connected states, which assist to compose our growing and respectable empire. ! Wise for ourselves, as it could be wished we were, the prophet's flattering anticipation in view of his beloved country, would not be either too sanguine or flattering in view of our own, " Thine eyes shall see Jerusalem a quiet habita-

D

tion, a tabernacle that shall not be taken down. Not one of the stakes thereof shall be removed, neither shall any of the cords thereof be broken.   But there the glorious God will be unto us a place of broad rivers and streams ; wherein shall go no galley with oars, neither shall gallant ship pass thereby.   For the Lord is our judge, the Lord is our lawgiver, the lord is our king, he will save us."

A
DISCOURSE,

DELIVERED AT

HEBRON,

AT THE CELEBRATION OF THE

ANNIVERSARY OF

AMERICAN INDEPENDENCE,

JULY 4th, 1799.

By CYPRIAN STRONG, A. M.
PASTOR OF THE FIRST CHURCH IN CHATHAM.

HARTFORD:
PRINTED BY HUDSON AND GOODWIN,
1799.

27

A DISCOURSE, &c.

DEUTERONOMY iv. 34.

Or hath God assayed to go and take him a nation from the midst of another nation, *by* temptations, *by* signs, *and by* wonders, *and by* war, *and by a* mighty hand, *and by* a stretched out arm, *and by* great terrors, *according to all that the Lord your God did for you in Egypt, before your eyes?*

GREAT and interesting events have ever been considered, as meriting a particular memorial. It has not been uncommon, to perpetuate such a memorial, by the institution and observation of annual rites and festivals.——The messengers which God sent to the Hebrews, his ancient covenant people, very frequently called their attention, to great and signal national events ; as appears from the sacred writings. How frequently did they recapitulate, the various deliverances which that people had experienced ? A recollection of such events was considered, as being eminently calculated to solemnize the minds of the people, and to render them sensible of their obligations to Jehovah. This is without doubt, the use which is to be made of the signal interpositions of Divine Providence, in favor of a people.

4

ALTHOUGH the propriety of joy and feſtivity, at the remembrance of great and intereſting events, cannot be queſtioned ; yet, it is a truth ever to be infiſted on, that, on ſuch occaſions, our hearts ſhould be above all, impreſſed with a ſenſe of the agency of God, and our indebtedneſs to his bounty and liberality.

THE Independence of the United States of A-merica, or their tranſition from being a diſtant and dependant branch of the Britiſh Empire, to a ſtate of abſolute independence, and being admitted to rank with the nations of the earth, is an epoch of ſuch importance, as has obtained an annual celebra-tion in the various capitals, and in a multitude of leſs conſpicuous towns, throughout the United States.

IN a commemoration of this great event, we ſeem to be more than countenanced by the inſpired wri-tings. Though it may be and probably is true, that the ſeaſons which have been conſecrated to that de-ſign, have been too much abſorbed in ſuch mirth and gaiety as have not been ſufficiently regulated by religious views and conſiderations.

IN the paſſage of ſcripture which has been read, you obſerve, that Moſes calls up the attention of the Hebrews, to the important period and event of their being formed into a diſtinct nation—taken out of the midſt of another nation, by great temptations, (or trials) by ſigns, by wonders, by war, by a mighty hand, and by an out-ſtretched arm. There is, in this, an undoubted reference to the deliverance of the Iſraelites, from Egyptian bondage, under which they had groaned for a long time ; and their being made a diſtinct and independent people, no lon-ger ſubject to the control and mandates of an Egyp-tian king. Moſes lays a particular emphaſis on this, as being a very ſingular event, which claimed a par-ticular remembrance, and demanded the higheſt ad-miration. Hath God aſſayed to go and take him a nation, from the midſt of another nation, according to all that the Lord thy God did for you in E-gypt! &c. As if he had faid, this is a ftrange and memorable event ;—an event which ought fo to im-prefs you minds, as never to be forgotten by you.

In the American revolution, we have a repetition of the fame wonderful interpofition of Divine Prov-idence. Although the colonies, which now compofe the United States, were at a diftance from the feat of the Britifh government, yet I need not inform this audience, that we were confidered as being under its control; and the Britifh parliament claimed a right to make laws for the colonies, which were binding, in *all cafes* whatfoever. And it is well known, that they extended their authority fo far, as to tax us at pleafure, for the purpofe of raifing a revenue. It is very true, that we were not reduced into a ftate of fuch complete bondage as the Ifraelites were in E-gypt; yet, it is equally true, that a principle was advanced, by the Britifh parliament, which, if pur-fued to its full length, muft have terminated, in the fame fervitude and ignominious bondage.—It was that *principle* which alarmed the fears and aroufed the apprehenfions of the people. It was a view of its confequences, and a determination never to fubmit to them, that called forth the patriots of America to arms, and fupported them in the arduous con-flicts which enfued. It was at this time, and under circumftances fo fimilar in kind, to thofe of the If-raelites in Egypt, when they were taken to be a na-tion, that the Supreme Being took the United States, and raifed them up to a ftate of independ-ence. And, as the Egyptian nation, from out of which God took the Hebrews was great and power-ful, fo it was as to the nation from which the United States were taken.—The refources of Great-Britain were aftonifhingly great—her navy rendered her mif-trefs of the feas, and the moft powerful nations on earth, trembled at her military prowefs.

Our deliverance and national independence took place, like that of the Hebrews, by *temptations*, by *figns*, by *wonders*, by *war*, by *a mighty hand* and an *out-ftretched arm*. The conflicts which were endured were unfpeakably great—the wonderful interpofitions of providence were numerous and fingular. The event is of fo late a date, that the various occurrences which took place are now frefh in your memories, and need not an enumeration.

In the cafe of the Hebrews, God qualified and raifed up Mofes, as the leader of his people ; whofe wifdom and integrity, under the direction of Jehovah, conducted the Hebrews, through the ftormy period of their national birth. In like manner, God raifed up a WASHINGTON, whofe memory will always be precious to the friends of the revolution ; and qualified him, as a leader and commander of the American armies, through the bloody and arduous conteft for national independence.

THE birth of nations is an event, which Mofes the leader of God's ancient covenant people confidered, as being worthy of a commemoration. We at once fee it to be fuch, as the Hebrews are refpected. Their deliverance from the hand of Pharaoh, and being put into the enjoyment of liberty and national independence, was confidered as an event of fuch a magnitude, as to be commemorated from generation to generation. The defign of the inftitution of the paffover was, to commemorate this great and interefting event. Hence, this direction was given, at the time of its inftitution. " And thou fhalt fhew thy fon, in that day, faying, this is done becaufe of that which the Lord did unto me, *when I came forth out of Egypt*. And it fhall be for a *fign* unto thee upon thine hand, and for a *memorial* between thine eyes, that the law may be in thy mouth ; for, *with a ftrong hand, hath the Lord brought thee out of Egypt. Thou fhalt, therefore, keep this ordinance from year to year.*" Whoever takes a view of the revolution which has terminated in the independence of the United States, will fee the fame

32

7

reafon, in kind, why its citizens fhould perpetuate the memory of that important event.

As to American Independence, it became an ob-object of confequence, at the very time in which it took place. It is very probable, indeed, that in any future period, it would not have been brought about. America, at the time of the commence-ment of the revolution, had become an object of fuch confequence, that it provoked the jealoufy and tempted the rapacity of the mother country. It was then that Great-Britain thought it fafe, to affert thofe claims, which fhe meant ever after, to make the rule of her adminiftrations. It was then, that the weaknefs, pufillanimity, and dependant feelings of the Americans were thought to be fuch, as would induce them to admit the extraordinary claims of the Britifh parliament, and to give a convenient oppor-tunity for eftablifhing a precedent, which would for-ever rivet the chains of flavery and fecure the fubjec-tion of the feveral colonies.—But that time, which was confidered as fo favorable to Great-Britain, was the very time in which thofe claims ought to have been made, had our particular intereft been alone confidered.

IT is true, indeed, that the numbers, ftrength, and experience of the Americans were fuch, as in human view, were inadequate to a fuccefsful refift-ance, when compared with the numbers, ftrength, and experience of Great-Britain; yet, perhaps, no time could have been more favorable. At that time, the minds of Americans were in full vigor. They were not depreffed by habitual flavery. It is proba-ble, they would never have had the fame fenfibility, and been fired with the fame zeal and intrepidity, in defence of their natural rights in any future period. They would, in all probability, have been lefs united, and confequently more feeble in refifting fuch claims, had they been more gradually introduced, or de-layed but for a few years.—'I he attack was made, when the Americans had juft arrived to a ftate of such maturity, as most sensibly to feel for independence.

THERE are a few, who, at this time in the day, affect to believe, that it would have been as well, if not better, if America had still continued in a state of dependence on Great-Britain. But must not the minds of such be greatly misinformed, relative to the state of the two countries; and the policy which would certainly dictate the measures of Great-Britain?—Had she not claimed such powers, as if exercised, must forever drain America, of all the profits which arise from commerce and industry? Had she a right to tax us at pleasure, without our consent; and would she have been wanting in putting the plenitude of her power into exercise? Was she not loaded with a most enormous debt—a debt which would be uniformly increasing, and would ever afford a pretext for the most wanton and extravagant exercise of such power? And would it not be always found, extremely convenient, to alleviate her own burthens by increasing the burthens of Americans?

INDEPENDENCE was not only important in its nature, but the time when it was declared was of all periods the most advantageous; as it was a time, when we were better united for such a struggle, and were disposed to make a more manly and obstinate resistance to external acts of oppression, than, perhaps, at any other period.

THE advantages arising to us, from a state of independence appear, not merely in our having escaped the miseries and calamities arising from being subjected to a foreign administration, which must ever have made it an object to drain us of our wealth and to keep us in a state of servility; but, also, in our having it in our power to regulate our own concerns—to take the advantages arising from our own industry and commerce—to nourish and cherish internal peace, without being necessitated to embroil ourfelves in the quarrels, and to fuffer from the enemies of other nations.

Our independence merits a moft grateful memorial on account of the many great and diftinguifhing interpofitions of Divine Providence in the eftablifhment of it. I barely mention this, as time will not permit me, fo much as to name the many fingular interpofitions of providence of this nature. Befides, it is prefumed they muft occur to many of your minds on the flighteft recollection.

I proceed, therefore, to obferve further, that our national independence deferves to be had in remembrance, on account of the excellent civil conftitution which has been beftowed on us. Of all the civil conftitutions which have been formed by the wifdom of man, perhaps, no one has ever been adopted, which is fo well calculated to render a people profperous and happy, as that of the United States.—A conftitution, which, on the one hand, fecures fo much liberty to the fubject, and at the fame time contains fuch energy, and provides fuch powerful checks againft abufes of every kind. The conftitution of Great-Britain has been much admired and loaded with encomiums, as the conftituted powers contained in it, are fo equally balanced and guarded. But, after admitting every thing which can be fairly faid of the Englifh conftitution, it is prefumed, the wifdom which dictated that of the United States muft be far fuperior. The checks which it provides againft abufes and ufurpations, are much more extenfive and effectual, than can be pretended in the former cafe. There is, indeed, in the conftituent parts of them, a great fimilarity. By the Britifh conftitution, there are three diftinct branches in the national legiflature; as King, Lords, and Commons. In the national legiflature of the United States, there are the fame diftinct branches, the Prefident, Senate, and Reprefentatives. But in the former, the King and the Lords are *hereditary* and en-

B

tirely *independent.* By the conftitution of the United States, on the contrary, every branch of our national legiflature is *eletive.* The men who compofe them can be in office, but for a fhort time, without being re-eleted. Each branch of the legiflature is under the influence of the ftrongeft checks, and holden by the moft forcible ties to faithfulnefs. Their reign is fo temporary, as that the opportunity to form and execute fchemes of corruption is very limited. The natural propenfity of the human mind, to diftinition and eminence, will form a powerful check againft fuch meafures as are injurious to the people ; and will impel to fuch as are calculated to fecure and promote their real interefts. As long as the people of the United States are well informed and virtuous, fo long they will be free, and their government uncorrupted. It is in their power, to remedy the evils, arifing from having wicked and defigning men at the head of government—they can lift up and pull down at pleafure. If government be not wifely adminiftered, the fault muft be in the people ; for the frequent eletion of every branch of the national legiflature, if wifely executed, is a fufficient remedy to all the mifchiefs arifing from a corrupt adminiftration. In this refpet, our national conftitution ftands glorioufly diftinguifhed from that of Great-Britain ; and, American liberty is more extenfive, and much better fecured than that of the Englifh. Befides, fhould experience point out any neceffary alterations, they may be made, with as much facility as the fafety of the community will admit. This is one confideration which renders our independence eminently worthy of a moft joyful commemoration.

THE peace and happinefs, which the people of the United States have enjoyed, further fhows, why we fhould joyfully commemorate the era of our national independence.

REPUBLICAN governments have generally, if not univerfally, been ftormy and tempeftuous. This ob-

'fervation is juftified, by the hiftory of former republics. And there is a fufficient caufe for it. Where
a government is free and elections frequent, there
is abundant opportunity for demagogues to practife their arts on electors—to raife cabals—fow the
feeds of diffentions, and to keep the public mind in
a ftate of fermentation. But, the United States,
fince the eftablifhment of their independence, have
been, on the whole, the moft happy people—have
enjoyed the greateft fhare of national happinefs,
which has ever been experienced by the nations of
the earth. Some little convulfions have formerly
rifen, but our government, although fo favorable
to liberty, has, ftill, fufficient energy to put a period
to them.

From the time of the eftablifhment of our national government, till the commencement of hoftil-
ities, between rival nations in Europe, union and
harmony, peace and friendfhip have extended thro'
the nation ; and every tide has brought in our fhips,
laden with the riches of foreign climes.

Since that period, our internal peace has been,
to a confiderable degree interrupted. This, however, has not originated from any defect in our national government. Foreign politics and intrigues—
the diffemination of principles, which are unfriendly
to morality and every kind of government that has
force and energy, have been the origin of our national divifions. It is not indeed, unnatural to fuppofe, that the attachments and antipathies, which
exifted in the minds of the citizens of the United
States, fhould have produced a temporary divifion.
The minds of the people having been irritated, at
the violent meafures which had been taken by Great-
Britain, and having, in a time of diftrefs, experienced the aid of France her competitor ; and, befides, confidering the avowed pretenfions of France
in favor of human liberty, it is not very furprifing,
that fome, in the ardor of enthufiafm, fhould have
nourifhed a partiality in her favor. But, fince, in

the progrefs of events, it has become fo obvious, that her governing maxim has been, to " *divide and conquer*"—to feparate people from their government; and have laid the ax at the root of religion and morality, as well as to all kinds of government, republican and monarchical, it is high time to beware—to turn our attention to the fupport of our own government, and to combine our whole force in its defence. There is now fo much light, concerning the principles and objeдt of the French adminiftration, that an advocate for it, can hardly be confidered, in a more favorable point of light, than as being an enemy to all government and order, both civil and religious.

THE evils we have experienced, as has been obferved, have arifen from external circumftances and meafures; not from the nature and conftitution of our own government. While the attention of the citizens of the United States was confined, to their own affairs and internal concerns, they were eminently profperous and happy. And it is prefumed, their happinefs would have been continued to this day, had they not liftened to foreign intrigues; and could have been pleafed, with a government which had energy, as well as a regard to equal and rational liberty.

ANOTHER confideration, which further illuftrates the propriety of commemorating our national independence is, the advantages we are now under to be a happy and profperous people. It is true, there is no government however wifely conftituted and adminiftered, but what may be inadequate to the purpofe of rendering a people happy. Such may be the jealoufies and biaffes, lufts and paffions of men, that nothing can render them happy;—the beft meafures and moft direдt means may be baffled, by the unreafonable prejudices and paffions of men. Neverthelefs, in the United States, we have the faireft chance for happinefs, arifing from our fituation, natural advantages and civil conftitution, of all people in the world; if we are only faithful to cultivate and improve them.

THE enlargement of territory, can never be an object of pursuit, if our desires are kept within the limits of moderation. The extent of the United States is sufficient, to render them one of the greatest nations on earth. Their natural advantages and resources, taking into consideration, all those articles which are necessary for support and defence are equalled, perhaps, by no nation in the world. The necessaries of life are produced in great plenty. The articles which are necessary for defence—such as for naval equipments—all the implements of war, including arms and ammunition, are within our reach, without having recourse to distant countries.

SUCH is our civil constitution, that the security of liberty, property and every natural right, is left at the election of the people; so far as will consist with a proper degree of energy in government. Our rulers, or those who stand at the head of our national government, will be just such men as we are pleased to elect.—That we have and ever shall have, men of talents and abilities to legislate and govern, we have no reason to doubt. And it will be our own fault, if we have not such men at helm. Our danger arises from sloth and inattention on one hand, and from prejudices and lusts on the other. It is in the power of the people, to have just such men and just such an administration as they please. If electors are without information, and will give in their suffrages at random—if they will suffer themselves to be wheedled by designing men and artful demagogues, they may forge their own chains and rivet them. But, it is in their power, with proper care, to secure to themselves a government and administration, which will render them prosperous and happy. And, what further can we expect or desire?

FINALLY; I would just observe, as another reason for the annual commemoration of our national independence, that it exhibits to the world, a public evidence and teftimony, that the people do approve of their own government, and will unite in the fupport and defence of it.———The eftablifhment of fuch an idea, is of great importance at all times, and efpecially at the prefent time. It is a fact, which cannot be reafonably doubted, that the hoftile meafures which the French Directory have been purfuing, relative to the United States, have been grounded on a prefumption, that we are a divided people—that there is a prevailing oppofition to our own government. Indeed, we can hardly be furprifed, that fuch conclufions fhould be formed ; for it has certainly been the principal bufinefs, of fome diftinguifhed characters, to foment and increafe divifions—to difaffect the minds of people and to blow the trumpet of fedition.—As the hoftile meafures of France, have proceeded from fuch an apprehenfion, it becomes important, that we manifeft, in every proper way, our attachment to our own government, and purfue every meafure, which will evidence our union, and exhibit a determination to fupport it. And, the annual commemoration of our independence, is one way, in which our attachment to our own government may be properly manifefted. It is true, that men, who are difaffected and are under the influence of Jacobinic principles, may unite in fuch a celebration, merely as a cloak, to fecure themfelves from the refentments of the true friends of government. But, fuch hypocritical conduct, is founded on the idea, that fuch a commemoration of our independence, carries the appearance of union and friendfhip to government.—As all the hopes of France, which is the only nation that, at prefent, is difpofed to make war upon us, are grounded on a fuppofed exiftence of a prevailing diffatisfaction to our government, fo it is important, that we unite in giving every teftimony of our approbation of it and determination to fupport it. .

I SHALL now clofe, with a remark or two, arifing from the foregoing obfervations.

FIRST. It becomes us, on this anniverſary, to offer to the Supreme Being, our moſt fervent and devout acknowledgments.

I PRESUME, I am ſpeaking to an audience, which conſiſts of ſuch perſons, as believe in a univerſal próvidence; or, that God has the diſpoſal of all events. The ſacred ſcriptures teach us, with great explicitneſs, that the agency of God is concerned, in the riſe and fall of nations. Moſes, when ſpeaking of the deliverance of the Iſraelites from Egyptian bondage, and their being made an independent nation, aſcribes it to the agency of God.—The diſpoſing hand of God is as viſible, in taking the United States, " from the midſt of another nation," and raiſing them to a ſtate of independence, as it was in the caſe of the Iſraelites! It is true, that nothing of a miraculous nature occurred; yet the hand of God was as viſible in the American revolution, as in the other caſe. No human calculations could have aſcertained, the reſult of the conflict, between Great-Britain and the colonies, which now compoſe the United States. Theſe obſervations might be illuſtrated, by having recourſe to many facts, which are now freſh in the memories of the elder part of this audience.—But omitting them, we are taught, from the ſacred ſcriptures, to view ſuch events, as the effect of God's providential government. We ought, therefore, in a ſolemn and religious manner, to acknowledge God, and aſcribe the glory of all our deliverances to him.

As to the great revolution, which took place relative to the Iſraelites, in raiſing them from a ſtate of ſervitude to independence, Moſes obſerves, in the words after our text, " Unto thee it was ſhewed, that thou mighteſt know, that the Lord he is God; there is none elſe beſides him. Out of heaven he made thee to hear his voice, that he might inſtruct thee."—Let us then, on this occaſion, make our devout and religious acknowledgments to God. Let us acknowledge his agency and diſpoſing hand,

While we rejoice, let it be ultimately in God. May our joy be of a religious nature.

GOD has some great and important designs in the event, which has made such a revolution in American affairs, besides raising us to consideration among earthly kingdoms. He is constantly prosecuting, his great and glorious purposes. Let us give glory to him, and ascribe to him all power. Let us ever feel our dependence upon him ; and esteem his favor to be life and his loving kindness to be better than life.

FINALLY ; Let us unite in the defence of our national independence and government.

OUR independence is a rich and inestimable inheritance, which the Supreme Governor of the world has bequeathed to us ; and it has been secured, not only at the expense of great treasure, but of much blood. Our national constitution and government, are eminently calculated, to render us singularly happy. They are founded on the wisdom and experience of ages ; and may still be amended, if, on trial, they are found to be deficient. It is true, the government of the United States has energy ; and it is one of the most idle dreams, which ever entered the head of the most extravagant enthusiast, that a government, without energy, would ever answer the purposes of society.

THE professed respect, which is paid to our national independence, by the annual celebration of the day, on which, the Congress of the United States had the fortitude and heroism to make the declaration, is an implicit acknowledgment of its importance and of our determination to defend it.

THAT attempts have been made, to alienate the minds of the citizens of the United States, from the general government—That the demoralizing and disorganizing sentiments, which have spread over so great a part of Europe, and proved so destructive to the human race, have been disseminated in these States, and the most assiduous attempts made to foment divisions and raise cabals, against the general

government, will not admit of a rational doubt.
Divide and conquer, has been the object, which has
been invariably purfued, by the French government.
Whoever attends to their profeffions and arrets, refpecting the United States, and compares them with
the meafures which were purfued with *Switzerland*,
and terminated in the deftruction of the *Helvetic Union*, will fee their perfect fimilarity ; till their progrefs was arrefted, by the manly meafures which
have been taken by our general government, for the
defence and fecurity of our independence. Take a
critical view of the meafures, which were adopted
and invariably purfued, by the French Directory,
and which iffued in the ruin of *Switzerland*, as reprefented in the hiftory of *Mallet Du Pan*, and you
will fee, we have a loud call to fet up a double
watch, and to fummon up the moft invincible refolution, in fupport of our independence. Our great
object ought to be, to ftrengthen and fupport our own
government, and it is our wifdom, to have nothing
to do with the politics of other nations, further than
is neceffary, to prepare and qualify us, to defend and
fupport our national interefts.

To fay that there are no errors of any kind, difcov-
erable in our national adminiftration, would imply that
we have fomething more than men at the head of it.
Efpecially, if men of *anti-federal* and *jacobinical* principles could not trump up fomething of that nature,
which might appear plaufible, and would be fwallowed both by ignorant and defigning men, it would
be marvellous indeed !

BUT, my fellow-citizens, fince fo fair an inheritance is given us, by the beneficent Ruler of the U-
niverfe, after making due acknowledgments to him,
let us refolve to defend it—to be good fubjects and
good citizens. Let us refolutely fupport the government and conftitution of our own choice. Let us
guard againft the principles of modern philofophy,
difcountenance the intrigues and defigns which come

C

from abroad; and the efforts of defigning men within our own bofom.—Let that *patriotiſm*, which manifefts itſelf in ſupporting the meaſures of our own government, be cultivated and ſtrengthened. But, let that *mock patriotiſm*, which advocates foreign meaſures, concerted to divide and weaken us, and which, under a ſpecious zeal for liberty, is forever carping for faults in our own government, be repro-bated as the greateſt fiend to peace and order.

IN every poſſible way, let the bands of order and good government be ſtrengthened.—Let the princi-ples of our conſtitution be preſerved inviolate.—Let men of integrity and firmneſs, the friends of our independence, be the men on whom your eyes are fixed, as candidates for office.—May the hearts of the citizens, in the various branches and diſtriƈts of the United States, be united and cemented; and may the intrigues of defigning men be totally diſ-concerted. May our independence be maintained, and our children and children's children, as they ſhall come upon the ſtage, have occaſion to com-memorate it, till time ſhall be no more. AMEN.

A

DISCOURSE,

DELIVERED AT

NORTH-COVENTRY,

JULY 4th, 1799,

BEING THE

TWENTY-THIRD ANNIVERSARY

OF

AMERICAN INDEPENDENCE,

BY ABIEL ABBOT.

HARTFORD:

PRINTED BY HUDSON AND GOODWIN,

1799.

A DISCOURSE, &c.

I will make of thee a great nation.

THIS joyful anniverfary and the afpect of this affembly promife me a candid attention, while I endeavor to fhow what is neceffary to conftitute a great nation, point out fome alarming figns of danger to our national greatnefs and glory, and call upon you to avert thefe impending evils.

A country favorably fituated and fufficiently extenfive is neceffary to make a great nation. An equinoctial and polar fituation is nearly equally unfavorable to vigor of mind and body, and yields its puny inhabitants but a fcanty fupport. The vertical rays of the fun and an almoft entire abfence of his influence have nearly the fame effect upon its inhabitants. They turn the one into a barren heath, and diminifh and enfeeble the other. Hence, probably, we find no nations in fuch a fituation diftinguifhed for numbers, power, wealth, or civil and moral improvements. If we would find nations refpectable for greatnefs, refinement and happinefs, we muft turn our eyes to or near the temperate zone. Here the mind is vigorous, man feels his ftrength and dignity, arts and fciences flourifh, and moral obligation is known and revered. Here are found thofe nations, which have made the greateft figure and enjoyed the moft happinefs. This is the foil moft favorable to civil and religious advantages, and in which the root of defpotifm cannot long flourifh. Wherever it has pleafed God to plant a great, free and happy nation, we fhall find univerfally temperature of climate and a confiderable degree of fruitfulnefs of foil.

47

4

To thefe advantages muft be added a competent extent of territory. A commonwealth very contracted muft be ftraitened in the number of citizens, and in the means of defence. Where the people depend chiefly on agriculture, the moft fure and happy means of living and enjoyment, a fmall tract will not afford fufficient numbers nor wealth to give them commanding influence in the fcale of nations. The ambitious may make their attacks with fuccefs, or the nation will be dependent on allies and pay tribute. A commercial fituation of lefs extent may employ and fupport more people, produce more wealth, and be more eafily defended; but does not commonly nourifh thofe fons of valor who ficken the countenance of ambition, and palfy the arm of tyranny. A temperate and fruitful foil has always produced heroes, and where this has been fufficiently extenfive, national greatnefs and glory.

Our country, my hearers, yields to none in temperature of climate, fruitfulnefs of foil, and variety of productions. It is moft conveniently fituated for raifing and enjoying all the neceffaries and comforts of life. Wafhed by the Atlantic feveral hundred miles, an eafy exchange of the fuperfluous articles of our own country may be effected for the neceffaries and luxuries of foreign growth, and commerce flourifh to the profit of our citizens. Our territory is fufficiently extenfive to fupport numbers, which will make a great and powerful nation, and furnifh fufficient ftrength for defence againft the moft powerful foe, without depending on the brittle reed of foreign alliances. For temperature of climate, variety and fruitfulnefs of foil, and extent of territory, no fpot on the globe could be found, for which we fhould exchange without lofs. The lines are fallen to us in pleafant places, we have a goodly heritage.

Another important requifite for forming a great, refpectable and happy nation is a good form of government. This will give complexion to national character. The form of government muft eftablifh liberty with order. For what is man enslaved ? A mere machine subservient to the pleasure and use of another. His mind is stupified, the noblest energies of his soul are palsied, and he sinks beneath those designs and actions, which stamp human nature with dignity. The countenance and deportment of the unhappy African, born in slavery, forcibly express this melancholy truth. The more enlightened and generous European or American, chained to the gallies without hopes of redemption, presents the same horrible picture. Extend the idea to a community ; and what is a nation enslaved? A mere servile herd, void of literary, social and moral improvement, and more unfeeling than the beasts of the forest. This humiliating truth may be seen in the degraded character of the present barbarous inhabitants of those celebrated countries, where Thebes, Corinth, Sparta and Athens once stood; where learning, liberty and refinement were united ; where the free and confederated states of Greece withstood the arms, and rose superior to the gold of tyrants ; and where was seen the powerful influence of freedom on national character and happiness. But a free people need not be told the value of liberty ; ye know its worth. It was purchased with millions, and sealed with the blood of thousands. Nor was it purchased in vain. The acquisition of freedom has raised us to national independence, greatness and glory, and blessed us with constitutions of government, which with the blessing of heaven, will preserve our rights inviolate.

The opportunity, providentially given us, of constituting a government on the most liberal, rational and equal principles, has been wholly unparalleled. " I confess," observed a patriotic writer in the early stage of our revolution; " I have always looked upon this with a kind of enthusiastic satisfaction. The case never happened before since the world began. All governments we have read of in former ages, were settled by caprice or accident, by the influence of prevailing parties or particular persons, or prescribed by a conqueror. Im-

portant improvements have indeed been forced upon fome conftitutions by the fpirit of daring men,
fupported by. fuccefsful infurrections.   But to fee a
government, in large and populous countries, fettled from its foundation by deliberate counfel, and
directed immediately to the public good of the
prefent and future generations, while the people are
waiting for the decifion, with full confidence in the
wifdom and impartiality of thofe to whom they
have committed the important truft, is certainly
altogether new.   We learn indeed from hiftory
that fmall tribes, and feeble new fettlements, did
fometimes employ one man of eminent wifdom to
prepare a fyftem of laws for them.   Even this was
a wife meafure, and attended with happy effects.
But how vaft the difference! when we have the
experience of all ages, the hiftory of human focieties, and the well known caufes of profperity and
mifery of other governments to affift us in the
choice."   Of this propitious and unprecedented
opportunity the enlightened people of this country
appear to have reaped the higheft advantage.   The
individual ftates have conftitutions on the moft liberal principles, which fecure the moft precious
rights and privileges of every citizen, without any
unreafonable reftraint.   Elections are frequent,
which gives the people opportunity to difplace thofe
who are either unqualified or unfaithful, and to
promote to office the wife and honeft.   If the
people are faithful to themfelves in the exercife of
their privileges, their rights and liberties will remain on an unfhaken foundation.

Our rights and liberties derive a greater and
higher fupport and fecurity from the conftitution
of the United States.   By the union which is formed between the feveral ftates, each ftate participates the power and privileges of all the others;
and thus an energy is given to the feparate parts,
as well as to the combined whole of this great republic.   The federal government is as truly the
government of our own formation, as that of this
or any other ftate in the union.   It was framed

and adopted by " the people of the United States in order to form a more perfect union, eftablifh juftice, enfure domeftic tranquillity, provide for the common defence, promote the general welfare, and fecure the bleffings of liberty to themfelves and their pofterity." Thefe patriotic and glorious de-figns have been effected in a degree beyond the calculation of its moft fanguine admirers. This government effectually preferves the rights, while it fecures the order and profperity of the citizens, Where any right is given up, the individual re-ceives an hundred fold in the protection of his per-fon, property, and other privileges.

Nothing then is wanted in the forms of our gov-ernment to make us a great and happy nation, " If we," fays our worthy Prefident, " compare the conftitutions of other nations with thofe of the United States of America, we fhall have no rea-fon to blufh for our country; on the contrary, we fhall feel the ftrongeft motives to fall upon our knees, in gratitude to heaven, for having been gracioufly pleafed to give us birth and education in that country, and for having deftined us to live under her laws."

But unavailable will prove a temperate climate, extenfive and productive territory, and good forms of civil government to national greatnefs and hap-pinefs, unlefs accompanied with a fenfe of moral and religious obligation. By the greatnefs of a na-tion we may underftand its ftrength, its order, and the refult of thefe, its happinefs. All this is ex-preffed in one word, *religion*. Religion promotes union and confidence, and thus gives ftrength to a nation. It attaches the people to the govern-ment, and the government to the people. This union and mutual confidence of public and private characters is the moft formidable pofition, which a nation can take to face her enemies. A fenfe of moral obligation is highly conducive to fuccefs in all the operations of a good government. Men thus influenced will be faithful to their truft and dif-charge with punctuality and energy the duties of their office. Religion will make good rulers and good citizens. Such rulers and fuch citizens ftrike terror into their enemies. There is no accefs to them, but through the path of honor. Religion is the ftrength of a people more fure than this ; it fecures the protection of the God of armies. That people is invulnerable, which is fo protected ; the fortrefs is impregnable, which is fo defended.

An effential requifite to national greatnefs and glory is good order. And good order is but the political name for religion. Wherever religion fpreads an univerfal influence through fociety, there is nothing out of place ; there is no crowding for the higheft feats. It teaches each one to think others better than himfelf, and to wait unambitious, till he is bidden to go up higher. Religion lays fuch falutary reftraints, as, if refpected, there is no encroachment upon property, nor upon liberty. One neighbor feeks the good of another, and there is a lively circulation of love and kindnefs through the community. Religion muft therefore be the happinefs of a people ; it cannot fail of this confequence ; for when there is fecurity againft enemies abroad, and order, love and harmony at home, crowned with the gracious fmile of heaven, nothing is wanted to complete the picture of national felicity. Righteoufnefs exalteth a nation. That religion facredly regarded is effential to the profperous exiftence of a nation is witneffed from the experience of all ages. The ftates of Greece flourifhed, till a fenfe of moral obligation was weakened, and the way opened for the corrupting and fuccefsful influence of the gold of Philip. Rome was powerful and profperous till the poifon of Epicurean fentiments pervaded the nation ; and then fhe became a nurfery of corruption and crimes, and an eafy prey to her enemies. Thus religion will prove the ftrength, order and happinefs of a people. And no religion has been fo favorably calculated for the rectitude, fupport and comfort of the individual, or for the order, improvement and honor of fociety, as the

9

Chriftian. This maintained in its purity will effec‑
tually promote the profperity of a nation.

We, my friends, enjoy the privileges of this re‑
ligion, and may derive unfpeakable advantages
from complying with its duties. The pure ftreams
of truth may flow to us from this fountain, and
purify our hearts and refrefh us in the journey of
life. No religious privileges for the promotion of
individual or national rectitude, improvement,
glory and happinefs, can be found on the globe fu‑
perior to what we enjoy.

Thus we are favored by God with a healthful
climate, a various and fruitful foil, and an exten‑
five and well fituated territory ; the moft liberal
and beft conftitutions of government ; and the
moft valuable means of the beft religion ; all
which advantages wifely improved will, by the pro‑
pitious fmiles of heaven, effectually fecure and pro‑
mote our national greatnefs, glory and happinefs.

But all thefe advantages will prove infufficient to
fecure our national greatnefs and happinefs unim‑
proved. The fabric of our glory may be under‑
mined, and every thing valuable rifled from us.
Though this be a gloomy part of our fubject, I
cannot but mention fome alarming figns of danger
to our happy republic. Do not efteem them words
of courfe, if I mention topics often urged ; I wifh
there may not be increafed neceffity of urging them.

Here I may mention growing impiety ; I fay
growing impiety ; though it does not become me
to compare the prefent with former times. It is
certain that impiety has become very bold ; it
vaunts itfelf in fafhionable oaths and curfes, and
fometimes in a profane ridicule of things moft fa‑
cred. While this is the cafe, religion muft be at a
low ebb. For even granting that comparatively
few are thus openly profane, the reft by their fi‑
lence feem to lend them their countenance. But
were there a vital fpirit of piety prevailing among
us, every fpecies of profanenefs would be the re‑
proach of a man.

B

There is fcarcely a ftronger proof of impiety, than a profanation of the ·fabbath. This is the principal fence about religion. Break down but this, and the ark will be taken. There is too much reafon to apprehend that this fpecies of impiety is growing upon us. A few years fince there were feen few travellers, except fuch as were going to the houfe of God; and little bufinefs but that of neceffity and mercy. There is confeffedly a great change for the worfe in this refpect.

Neglect of the inftitutions of religion evidently indicates that its obligations are not duly felt, nor its duties performed. It fhows a coldnefs to the gofpel and its glorious Author, and leads to a general neglect of moral obligations. It is too manifeft that neglect of religious inftitutions is too prevalent, and is truly alarming.

Growing laxnefs of fentiments and morals may be mentioned as a fubject of alarm. Innovation and *reform*, a proftituted word, are the order of the day; and people are as defirous of licentioufnefs in religion, as in government. They will have a religion all reward and no punifhment, as well as a government all protection, and no energy or expenfe. Indeed the religion of the prefent day is made to appear much like its politics. A party uncandid fpirit is mixed with both of them; and thus is waxen cold brotherly love, that cement which binds in a fweet and fafe union both citizens and Chriftians. This laxnefs of fentiments, this breach of love, and fpirit of party and intrigue carry a threatning afpect to the greatnefs and glory of our country.

I have mentioned caufes enough for the decline and fall of our country, if they be not checked; but I have yet to mention what fills many thoughtful and judicious people with the deepeft apprehenfion. Thefe vices of profanenefs, this breach of the fabbath, this neglect of religious inftitutions, this defect of love and charity, are apt enough to thrive in any fociety, and at any time. But to what height will they grow, when foftered by the hand·

of revolutionary and atheiftical men ? This I firmly
believe is the danger, is the fate of our country at
this moment. I would fpare party and politics, till
I fee the ark of God, and my country in danger ;
then to be filent would be infidelity to my truft,
efpecially on this occafion. The moment is come,
when in our country, and in every Chriftian one,
politics and religion are blended. The dagger is
aimed at our government through our religion. I
make no apology then, while with an honeft heart
I fpeak my apprehenfions, and endeavor to raife
yours. It is as plain as the noonday fun from a
thoufand pioofs, above all from the corruption and
favage facrifice of the freeft and happieft governments of Europe, that the French Republic, fhall I
call it ! have fixed as their objeét, the thraldom of the
world, and as their means, univerfal corruption and
force. The firft of thefe means, corruption, has hitherto been at work amongft us ; and force, unlefs
where it has fallen on our defencelefs commerce,
has been only brandifhing its fword at a diftance.
Corruption in her very nature comes mafked ; fhe
ftalks not in public view ; fhe fifhes out in darknefs
her firft objeéts and her proper inftruments ; and
you fee her publicly only by the effeéts fhe has produced. But that this fiend has been amongft us,
we have had demonftrative proof. One public officer, it was afcertained to public fatisfaétion, was
corrupted with French livres. And Fauchet, the
grand almoner of the Direétory, lamented in his
intercepted difpatches the deficiency of *roleaus*,
which prevented his extending his charity to other
hopeful friends of his government.

But it is not the fingle virtue of political integrity, which has been affailed. This were too narrow
a field for corruption to traverfe, and, with our
prefent adminiftration, too difficult to effeét the defign. A bolder and more fatal blow has been aimed
at the religious principles of the nation. Corrupt
the mafs of people, and the corruption of the government follows of courfe. There is not a furer
policy to ruin a nation, than this. The French

have abolifhed the Bible with every mark of infult that could be invented. But there are a few choice political examples in it, which they referve for imitation. Such are the counfel of Balaam and the policy of Balak. The unwilling prophet could utter nothing but bleffing upon the Ifraelites before corruption had fpread her poifon, and then they became weak and vulnerable like other nations. This is the counfel and policy of the French. The developement of Robifon and Barruel is book proof of this. They have unfolded a " fcheme the moft extenfive, flagitious, and diabolical, that human art and malice have ever invented. Its object is the total deftruction of religion and civil order. If accomplifhed, the earth can be nothing better than a fink of impurities, a theatre of violence and murder, and a hell of miferies." It was originated by Voltaire, matured by Weifhaupt; its hot bed now is Paris; its nurfing fathers are the French government; its miffionaries are their generals and armies. Its firft fruits have been feen in France; Chriftianity expelled; its priefthood feized and murdered; its temples plundered; and its government a military defpotifm.

" The principles of the French are the pioneers of their arms; wherever thofe have corrupted, thefe have conquered and enflaved. This may be feen in all the countries they have overrun." But living at a diftance have we not efcaped the poifon of thefe teachers of atheifm? No; they flock in the ftreets of principal towns, and, as they find opportunity, infufe the venom. Every convert becomes a teacher. From the town the fentiments creep into the country; from being whifpered in a corner, they begin to be proclaimed upon the houfe top.

The immoralizing plan of the French is as fyftematic as their politics; it is a department of their politics. Thefe French atheifts in the country are not a few chance renegadoes, whom adventure or curiofity has brought to our fhores. That many of them are commiffioned from the five apoftles of

atheifm at Paris, who can doubt, if you confider
their abilities and indefatigable induftry and zeal?
They have not fent men alone, but books to corrupt us. Books infinuate themfelves, where men
could find no accefs. By his book a bad man mul-
tiplies himfelf into a million of evil counfellors;
he lights down upon a fociety like a fwarm of lo-
cufts, and neither the market nor the farm, the
town nor the country, can efcape him. In this
manner has the faith of the United States been op-
pugned by that infamous production entitled "the
age of reafon." From what country did this iffue?
From France. Who wrote it? A jacobin American. Under whofe aufpices? Thofe of the Executive Directory. Thoufands of copies were in-
ftantly exported to this country, and hawked about
from Georgia to Maine at half the fterling coft of
the impreffion. Was its author an Eaftern Nabob,
that he had wealth to defray the expenfe of this
abominable affault upon the religion of the country
which had the misfortune to give him birth? No;
he was a poor retainer to the men in power at Paris.
Judge then whence the "roleaus" came to defray
the expenfe of a publication, which was to " un-
hinge the faith of thoufands" in England and the
United States.

I have mentioned the influence and intrigue of
the French as employed chiefly againft our religion; to mention them as employed againft our
government more directly, would make a volume.
But which way foever employed, if fuccefsful, they
are alike fatal to our government and our religion.
It is time to tremble when we hear a word in defence of their principles, or in gratulation of their
fuccefs. We once gloried in their profperity, becaufe we foolifhly thought theirs the caufe of liberty; we fhould now glory in their defeat; for
theirs is now the caufe of univerfal fubjugation and
ruin. Can fuch a caufe have advocates among the
lovers of our country and religion? I fear it has
even among thefe. It is not the political demagogue alone, who, in pleading the caufe of France,

has his views of interest; there are doubtless some who are friends to piety and their country, who imagine the cause of France the cause of humanity. But let them read the history of Holland, Geneva, Venice, and Switzerland of recent date; it is written in letters of blood; the tears of the reader fall on every page. Let us all read. And when we come to Switzerland; when we have followed the historian through the mazes of French influence; when we have seen those States, once combined like our own in one powerful union; those states, long esteemed the happiest community in the habitable world; those states, free, enlightened, contented, loving their government to enthusiasm, preserved from change for centuries; those states, always inoffensive to other nations, and therefore seldom at war; when, I say, we have seen those states, till now firm as the Alps on which they lived, at length tottering with French influence, and then plunged headlong into remediless ruin by French perfidy and power; let us pause a moment and listen to the admonition issuing from the tomb of Swiss liberty and happiness. Do you not hear the expostulation in language like this;— " Art thou enlightened, America? So were these cantons. Are your states united? So were these. Is your government beloved? So was ours. Have you heroes and statesmen revered through the world? So had we. Are your altars of religion standing? So were ours. Do you court peace? So did we with sincerity, with sacrifice. Happy America, learn wisdom from wretched Switzerland. We trusted France; we listened to her protestations of friendship; we suffered her influence; we learned to endure her insults through hope they would not be repeated. Steady to her purpose, she corrupted our knowledge, dissolved our union, weakened our attachment to our government, calumniated our heroes and statesmen and destroyed their influence, cast contempt upon our religion; and when all was ready, in violation of a sacred treaty, let loose her savage army to finish the work of nine years intrigue." To this admonition may our country liften in feafon. The fame arts one by one are practifing upon thefe too unfufpicious ftates. The plan progreffes. Virginia and Kentucky have founded the horn of fedition. And it is unquef-tionable that emiffaries are with aftonifhing addrefs fpread through the ftates. If our principles are corrupted and delufion is effected, fome other na-tion may liften to the admonition, which fhall fhortly iffue from the tomb of American ruins. But may Almighty God turn the counfel of Ahith-ophel into foolifhnefs.

Thefe are fome of the figns of danger to the greatnefs and glory of our nation. Then permit me to call upon you to exert yourfelves against thefe illboding figns of the times. You fee the feveral fources of our danger ; guard against them all. But be moft watchful, where danger is moft fatal, on the fide of religion. Here we are vital, if the dagger reach us. And let us not think the ark is fafe, becaufe our meeting-houfes are ftand-ing, if they are thinly reforted to. Let us not think that the fabbath, that facred fence round our religion, is reverenced, merely becaufe, unlike the French, we have not yet difplaced it from our ca-lendar. We muft in truth reverence it, not doing our own pleafure on that day ; but call it a delight, the holy of the Lord, honorable. Let us not think that the name of atheifm will ftartle Ameri-can ears with horror, while profanenefs, that prac-tical atheifm prevails among us. Let us not ex-pect that the fpirit of religion will dwell among us, if we caft off the forms of it; or that we fhall long feel the influence of the moral precepts of the gofpel, if we neglect its pofitive inftitutions. In fhort, let us profefs and practife religion from per-fonal, national and evangelical confiderations. It is the happinefs of the individual ; it is the fafe-guard and glory of the community. Nothing but this can fave us from the ftorms of impending dan-gers. Religion will fhut the door against an evil influence, which is ufurping fuch power in the country. It will teach us to fay—O my foul, come not thou into their fecret; unto their affembly mine honor be not thou united.

The Prefident of the United States, whofe duty it is to watch for our fafety, hath recently told us, " that we are in circumftances of great urgency ; —that this is a feafon of imminent danger ;—that the moft precious interefts of the people of the United States are ftill held in jeopardy by the hoftile defigns and infidious arts of a foreign nation, as well as by the diffemination among them of thofe principles fubverfive of the foundations of all religious, moral and focial obligations, that have produced incalculable mifchief and mifery in other countries." When we thus hear the alarm from authority, it becomes us to be watchful, and with united zeal endeavor to avert the impending evils. Let us exert ourfelves in feafon. The foe is more eafily prevented, than expelled. There is ftill hope for us, if we are faithful to ourfelves. Our altars, though threatened and affaulted, are yet in their place. Our armies are yet vigorous with youth and numbers ; our generals are experienced; our navy, though fmall, is increafing, valiant and fuccefsful. The pillars of our government, tho' affailed with every engine of intrigue and malice, are ftill firm in their fockets. For thefe bleffings let us be thankful and praife God ; and in obedience to his laws truft in him that he will ftill be our fhield and falvation.

Let the celebration of this anniverfary remind us of the worth of our independence and national privileges, and imprefs our minds with the importance of ufing all means and of grudging no expenfe to preferve them. Though we love peace, let us be prepared for war, and at the call of our country gird on the harnefs, and manfully defend our altars and our government. May God difperfe the clouds, which now obfcure our political horizon, and caufe our national greatnefs, glory and happinefs to become as clear and refplendent as the noonday.

THE TREE OF KNOWLEDGE OF POLITICAL
GOOD AND EVIL.

A

DISCOURSE,

DELIVERED AT

COLEBROOK,

ON THE

TWENTY-FOURTH ANNIVERSARY

OF

AMERICAN INDEPENDENCE.

JULY 4th, 1800.

BY CHAUNCEY LEE, A. M.
PASTOR OF A CHURCH IN COLEBROOK.

If thou hadst known, even thou, in this thy day, the
things which belong unto thy peace !

JESUS CHRIST.

HARTFORD:

PRINTED BY HUDSON AND GOODWIN.

1800.

A

DISCOURSE, &c.

GENESIS iii. 2, 3.

*And the woman said unto the serpent, We may eat of
the fruit of the trees of the garden ; but of the fruit
of the tree which is in the midst of the garden, GOD
hath said, ye shall not eat of it, neither shall ye
touch it, lest ye die.*

DEUTERONOMY xxxii. 17.

*They sacrificed unto devils, not to GOD ; to gods whom
they knew not, to new gods, that came newly up,
whom your fathers feared not.*

THIS day, fellow-citizens, completes twenty-
four years since our country emerged from a
state of dependence upon a foreign power, and af-
sumed a rank among the nations of the earth, as
a free, and independent republic. The heroic
declaration, by which it was proclaimed to the
world, detailing the many cogent reasons of necef-
sity and national justice upon which it was founded ; together with the sacred pledge plighted for
its support ; and the solemn appeal made to heaven
for the vindication of our injured rights, has now
again been publicly exhibited to you, and received,
I doubt not, with mingled emotions of wonder,
gratitude and joy.

4

Supported by the arm of the Lord JEHOVAH, our venerable fathers in council, at a time when our country was in the loweſt ſtate of depreſſion and impotence—when ruin was near, and help afar off, or at beſt, but awfully doubtful—as with ropes about their necks, and for themſelves no other alternative, but the gibbet, or a triumphal arch ; blew the trumpet of American jubilee, and in the face of incenſed deſpotiſm declared, that we were, and of right ought to be, free, ſovereign, and independent ſtates.

The ſame ſpirit inſpired our citizens, in the cabinet and in the field. With the ſame firmneſs with which the declaration was made, it was ſupported by the ſword ; and an eight years bloody war in the purchaſe of independence eſteemed but a cheap price.

To recount in hiſtorical detail, the awful and animating viciſſitudes of this arduous conflict—the cauſes which induced—the means which ſupported, and the effects which have flowed from the declaration of American Independence, is foreign from my preſent purpoſe. Theſe have long ſince furniſhed the moſt engaging themes of the ſtateſman, the orator, and the poet. In this field all the flowers of rhetoric have already bloomed, and the fruits of genius been ripened and plucked. Happy were it for us, had the forbidden fruit remained untouched—had not the ſeeds of that noxious foreign plant, the Tree of *Liberty* and *Equality*, been ſown and cultured in the midſt of our political Eden, and had no tempter emerged from *Gallic Pandemonium* to ſeduce the virtue of our countrymen, by the poiſonous fruit of that *Bohon Upas* of human happineſs, that tree of knowledge of political good and evil (of good loſt, and evil gained) which corrupts the fountain of national felicity, diffuſes its poiſon through all the ſtreams of ſocial life and threatens the forfeiture and loſs of all the bleſſings of Independence.

CHAPTER 4

Yet fuch, alas! feems the unvaried lot of miferable man. Such the fhades which have ever dark-
ened and whelmed the brighteft fcenes of human
profperity. Difcontentment with every allotment
of Providence—murmurs and complaints in the
very furfeit of divine bounty and afpiring to be
Gods knowing good and evil, fill up the pages of
the hiftory of Man. Reftlefs ambition, indulgence
unreftrained, infatiable defire, and repining jealoufy, have marked the footfteps of human folly,
and led our untoward fpecies blindfold to deftruction. " God made man upright, but they have
fought out many inventions." In the Garden of
God, they invented a fepulchre. In the fruitful
field of America, the death of Religion and Government is projected, and the grave of Independence already dug. In the midft of every Eden
ftands the tree of knowledge, and rears its tower-
ing branches, heavy laden with its deadly fruit ;
and even the walls of Paradife itfelf, were infufficient to exclude the artful wiles of the hellifh
tempter. From the feed of the firft wicked invention, a ten thoufand fold crop has enfued, and
fpread itfelf, co-extenfive with the population of
man. The foil of human depravity has been moft
induftrioufly tilled. The field of human mifery is
nearly ripe. Yea, lift up your eyes, and behold
it already *black* for the harveft, and calling aloud
for the fickle.

But why, fome perhaps may fay, why this fingular and inaufpicious text ? Why thefe fevere and
uncharitable remarks ? What motives can actuate
the fpeaker, in his very exordium, to mingle gall
with the fweets of conviviality, and by drawing
fuch a dark cloud over our political horizon, attempt to damp the luftre of focial delights and
fhroud the day, devoted to feftivity and joy, in the
gloomy fadnefs of melancholy and remorfe ? Patience, fellow-citizens. In this fevere exercife of
felf-denial, be kind enough, for a little while to

6

help me bear the crofs ; and if the fubject do not
fufficienlv explain itfelf, let deferved cenfure upon
it.—For this you are referred to the fequel of my
difcourfe, with only this general obfervation at
prefent—that, if we are, what we profefs to be, a
Chriftian people, we fhall not difrelifh bible-in-
ftruction as ill timed or unprofitable upon any occafion ; and while we read this in our bibles, " Serve
the Lord with fear, and rejoice with trembling,"
we muft believe folemnity to be effential to true joy,
and godly forrow compatible with the pleafures of
feftivity.—If we are truly difpofed to rejoice in the
paft fignal mercies of God, towards us, as a people ; we fhall be equally prompt, to confider the
operation of his hands, and mark the afpects of divine providence in relation to the *prefent* fituation,
and *prefent* profpects of our country. If animated
with the love of virtue, we admire and celebrate
the worthy deeds and noble achievments of our
venerable fathers, now fleeping in the duft ; will
it not be natural and pertinent to inquire, how far
the character and conduct of their fons, are formed
and directed by the force of parental example ? And
who, or what are thofe new gods, that have newly
come up, whom our fathers feared not ? And in a
word, if in the fpirit of patriotifm, our fenfibilities
are feelingly excited, by a review of the paft dangers and perils of our country—if we exult in the
original attainment of our national independence,
and celebrate the means which conducted us to it ;
furely we fhall not feel indifferent to the prefent dangers, by which it is threatened, nor inattentive to
the only means by which this national bleffing, the
purchafe of our father's blood, may be preferved
and tranfmitted to their children's children.

For thefe reafons, and impreffed with thefe views,
while from the very occafion of the day your minds
are readily employed in retrofpect of the paft, I beg
leave to call your ferious attention to the *prefent*
ftate of things. I feel this my duty, both as a fel-

low-citizen, inviolably attached to the interefts of our common country ; and as a fpiritual watchman, folemnly bound to faithfulnefs in my facred truft. Difclaiming the talents of the ftatefman, the orator, or the hiftorian, mine only be the humble part of a gofpel minifter, to hold up to your view, the dangers which threaten our country, from prefent exifting evils, and point to the means of deliverance and fafety. In doing this, the cenfure of *political preaching*, will ever be as unheeded, as, in the prefent inftance, it is unexpected.

In recurring to the facred oracles, I have felected, as fources of inftruction, pertinent to the prefent anniverfary, the two diftinct paffages recited. They are confidered, in effect, as parallel texts, tho' the one hath refpect to man in his *primitive*, and the other to man in his *fallen* ftate. For this reafon they are chofen, and defigned to be improved in concert, to imprefs with their united ftrength, this great and important truth refpecting mankind in every character and ftate. That,

A reftlefs, factious fpirit conftantly impelling to innovation and change, is both unreafonable in its nature, and fatally pernicious in its effects. Or in other words,

That, *when mankind, either as individuals or nations, abandon thofe principles, and depart from that line of conduct, which* GOD *hath prefcribed, and by his word or providence, clearly pointed out, as the path of duty and happinefs—they do it at their utmoft peril—evil inevitably enfues, and certain deftruction is the end.*

Thefe doctrines, it is believed, equally flow from each of the forementioned paffages of fcripture refpectively, confidering them in their relations, connections, and confequences.

The better to receive their united weight of inftruction, let us now beftow a few thoughts in a particular and feparate examination of each.

The text in Genefis, refers to the original conftitution under which man was placed, and points directly to the fruitful fource of all the evils and miferies, which have ever embittered and poifoned the cup of humanity. Our firft parents then compofed the whole family of man. They were individuals—they were a family—they were a nation, and they were a world. As fuch they were confidered and treated by their benevolent Creator, in his covenant tranfaction with them. As fuch by nature, and by divine conftitution they ftood—as fuch they acted—as fuch they finned and fell, and as fuch they fuffered and died. God their Creator, was their Governor and King. He had made the moft ample provifion for the fupply of all their wants, and the gratification of every reafonable defire. They were under a moft free and happy government. They were bleffed with an excellent conftitution, by which all their rights and privileges were fecured; and fubjected to no other reftrictions, but thofe of the moft equal, wholefome, and falutary laws. And their government was calculated to have tranfmitted thefe ineftimable bleffings, inviolate to all the unborn millions of their pofterity, thro' the whole progreffion of the human race : For as a nation and a world they ftood, and in their conduct, all their pofterity were implicated and concerned.

And why, citizens, fhould this be thought ftrange? Our pofterity are as really implicated, concerned, and interefted in our prefent national conduct, and will as certainly enjoy, or fuffer the effects of it.

Our firft parents were mankind, and their national happinefs, like that of all other nations, was fufpended upon their obedience to the divine law— their continued conformity to the rules of righteoufnefs and juftice—abftaining from the tafte, or touch of the forbidden fruit, and chearfully according in that wife and beautiful order, which the God of nature had eftablifhed in the fyftem of his intelligent creatures. Thefe were all made known to them. Their path of national duty was clearly pointed out, and they were commanded to walk in it, and be happy.

9

How unaccountable is it then, how paffing ftrange, that, under thefe happy circumftances, they fhould apoftatize, and facrifice their national honor, independence and happinefs ! That the bright luftre of the world's fair morning, fhould fo foon be overfhadowed and darkened by the clouds of atheifm, infurrection and anarchy ! Can any fubfequent event of the like nature be brought as a parallel ? Truly, I know of none, unlefs it be the prefent, prevailing unreafonable diffatisfaction and implacable oppofition of Americans towards the adminiftration of conftituted authority, and the operation of the government of their choice :—one of all human governments the moft mild, benign and equal, upon which the fun ever fhone ; and the repeated infurrections which have actually arifen againft it in the very bofom of our country. Surely a more unreafonable and wicked oppofition againft civil government never blackened the pages of hiftory.

Let us further inquire, what were the immediate caufe, or caufes, which actually led to this firft grand apoftacy of mankind, and effected this awful revolution in the nation of Eden. This is an inquiry of moment, and productive of the moft pointed, practical, and important inftruction. It will afford the moft fure ground of argument, in reafoning by analogy, and applying the fubftantial evidence of paft events, and their confequences, in illuftration of the nature of *prefent* facts and *prefent* profpects—bottomed upon thefe fure *data*, that, like caufes under like circumftances, ever produce like effects. What then were the caufe, or caufes, the fubject of inquiry ? The anfwer is as obvious, as the queftion is interefting. It ftares us in the face at the firft glance. The moment we look at it, we fee that the effectual, immediately influential, and proximate caufe, which led to the very firft act of national degradation and mifery, and

B

revolutionized the garden of God, was—INFIDEL-
ITY—*Ye shall* not *surely die*. This was the new
god which then newly came up, which impelled
and supported the hand of mother Eve, while she
plucked the fruit of that forbidden tree, " whose
mortal taste, brought death into the world, and all
our woe." In this she literally sacrificed unto devils,
and not to God—to gods whom she knew not.

To this awful cataftrophe, other circumstances
conspired, in predifpofing, preparing, ripening,
and effecting the plan of the tempter. It feems that
a reftlefs fpirit of innovation, difcontentment with
prefent fituation and an afpiring ambition to be more
wife and happy was then, either for the firft excited,
or had previoufly taken root in the minds of the
young nation. But all this, for aught that appears,
might have been difpelled by the ftrong light of reafon and confcience, and entirely fubdued by the
force of innate virtue, never have led to the fatal
iffue ; had it not been for the officious aid of *foreign* influence. A wicked, artful alien, a banifhed
emigrant from the regions of blifs, foiled in a late
attempt to fubvert the government of Heaven, now
wings his way to this new world, ftill bent on mifchief, and finds means to introduce himfelf into the
garden of innocence and peace. The young nation, unfufpicious of danger, and not dreaming of
an enemy, were unprovided for a fudden attack,
and indeed lay open to his wiles. The better to infure the fuccefs of his wicked enterprize, the villain
chofe not to appear in his true character, but affumed the form of a *ferpent*, and taking advantage
of the weaker part of the community, the *woman*,
who, by analogy, may be called the *populace*,—in
this concealed and infidious manner, with all the
fawning arts of deceitful intrigue, commences his
attack. With much fhew of difinterefted friendfhip and generofity, mixt with an air of wonder
and furprize, he afks, " Yea hath God faid, ye
fhall not eat of every tree of the garden ?" Is it pof-

fible that you fhould be thus unreafonably reftric-
ted? thus deprived of the effential rights of men
and citizens? Eve anfwers in an honeft ftatement of
facts, as expreffed in the text—" We may eat of
the fruit of the trees of the garden; but of the fruit
of the tree which is in the midft of the garden,
God hath faid, ye fhall not eat of it, neither fhall
ye touch it, left ye die." Her mind was not yet
prepared for a compliance with the purpofe of the
tempter, until fired by the ideas of *Liberty* and
Equality.—He then throws off the mafk, and comes
out open and bold in the principles of infidelity,
and his blafphemous affertions of the divine tyranny. " And the ferpent faid unto the woman, ye
fhall not furely die : For God doth know that in
the day ye eat thereof, then your eyes fhall be opened (or *illuminated)* and ye fhall be as gods knowing good and evil."

Here is the origin, and the very quinteffence of
Jacobinifm. Never was a truer copy of an original
drawn, than that which is marked out by the
tongues, the pens, and the fwords of the modern
illuminators of mankind—the champions of *Liberty*
and *Equality, Health* and *Fraternity.* Their whole
fyftem is a perfect paraphrafe upon this text. They
have even refined upon the cunning of Satan, and
outdone him in his own arts. He contented himfelf with denying God's truth, and calling in queftion his goodnefs—while his followers have the fuperior effrontery of coming to the fame thing in a
fhorter way—by denying his *exiftence.*

With refpect to our firft parents, as the Moft
High, was both their God, and their King or civil
Ruler, it is evident, the object of Satan in tempt-
ing them to difobedience and rebellion, was nothing more nor lefs, than the abfolute deftruction of
all religion, and of all civil government. And
this too is the real object, the fervent wifh, and
grand defign of that reftlefs, indefatigable, diforganizing faction that have for years infefted our

country, and now begin their fong of triumph, in the fafcinating profpect of fuccefsful views. But let them remember, (and blufh, for their own, fince they cannot for their country's fhame) that they have not the honor of originality, but are only copiers, plagiaries and fervile imitators. This new god of their's, which has newly come up, made his appearance in our world almoft fix thoufand years ago ; and though he hath never before appeared in the fame form, yet it is the fame being, who in the fhape of a ferpent, then drove Adam out of Paradife.—Let them, therefore reflect, whether, it is not to him, rather than to GOD that they are facrificing. The very fyftem and creed of Jacobinifm, was preached and enforced upon mankind, by the grand adverfary of GOD and man, in the infancy of the world.

For the conviction of every one, we will recur a moment to the fermon of this hellifh preacher, and by expreffing it a little more at large, and in modern language, endeavor more thoroughly to inveftigate its latent principles. Then let candor fay, whether the paraphrafe be not juft.

Text.	*Tranflation.*
" And the ferpent faid unto the woman, ' Ye fhall not furely die."	'The Bible is a forgery. The pretended prohibitions, warnings and threatenings of Heaven, are the mere whimfies of imagination——idle bug-bears impofed upon the fuperftitious credulity of mankind, the better to awe them into fubjection to their mafters. The natural right of man is to enjoy liberty uncontrolled—to eat of every tree in the garden without exception, and indulge his appetites and paffions, with unlimited freedom. And as to the ghoftly diftinction of virtue and

Text.   *Tranſlation.*

vice, ſaints and ſinners, rewards and puniſhments, it is
equally arbitrary—wholly unfounded in reaſon or nature.
It is all a farce. Too long already have you been gulled of
your rightful liberty, by the
pompous rant of Heaven and
Hell. *Death is an eternal ſleep,*
where hope and fear are buried
together, and neither ſorrow,
nor joy exiſt beyond it. The
Sun of Liberty now ſhines.
Awake from your long delu-
ſion and be free.

"For GOD doth
know that in the
day ye eat thereof,
then your eyes ſhall
be opened and ye
ſhall be as gods
knowing good and
evil."

You are held in ignorance
of your rights by men in power, whoſe intereſt it is to keep
you in ignorance, the better to
ſupport their own pre-eminence
and domination, and inſure
your ſubjection and ſervitude.
For they *know that in the* very
day theſe ſhackles are taken off,
the blinding films of prejudice,
fear, and ſuperſtition removed,
and the arts of *prieſtcraft* and
ariſtocracy ceaſe to operate, *your
eyes will be opened* to the knowledge of your juſt rights, the
rights of *Liberty* and *Equality*
—You will know that you are
gods as well as they, as great,
as wiſe and as good—that all
men are equal—equally deſerv-
ing to rule—that all ſubordination is tyranny, and all authority, however veſted, exerciſed
by one man over another is un-

Text.   *Tranflation.*

fufferable oppreffion ; and that therefore their ufurped domin-ion, muft immediately tumble. —Would you then deferve well of your country, Eden muft be revolutionized—no longer be a monarchy, but a republic, *one and indivifible.*— Affert your rights.—Expunge the tyranny of fubordination. Rife fuperior to the reftraints of law. Eat freely of the tree of knowledge in the midft of the garden. Say what you will, Do what you will. Write, print and publifh what you will, true or falfe, provided your end be the deftruction of all conftituted authority. Shake off thefe impofing fhackles of *religion* & *government,* by which the human mind is enflaved, genius crampt, the freedom of inquiry fettered, the liberty of the prefs reftrained, and the fource of human enjoyment and perfectibility, muddied and choaked up. Do this and re-ceive the *fraternal embrace.*

The other paffage of facred writ comes next un-der confideration. In it we find the fame fentiment expreffed equally clear and pointed ; and the theory of the tempter actually carried into practice. " They facrificed unto devils, not to God ; to gods whom they knew not, to new gods that came new-ly up, whom your fathers feared not." This is a part of that memorable fong, which the great lead-er of God's ancient people, wrote and left on re-cord for the inftruction and warning of his people :

particularly to guard them againft all future inno-
vations upon their religion and government. It is
to be viewed as the dying advice, and farewel addrefs of that Ifraelitifh Wafhington, of fimilar import and inftruction with that of our American
Mofes.

In the paffage we find the guilt of political apoftacy, and the danger of an unreafonable fpirit of
innovation upon the ancient and approved ufages,
and inftitutions, religion, and government of their
fathers, painted in the moft glaring colours ; efpecially when taken in connexion with the preceding
and following context.

Original.	*Comment.*
Verfe 15. But Jefhu-run waxed fat and kicked : thou art waxen fat, thou art grown thick, thou art covered with fatnefs : then he forfook God which made him and lightly efteemed the rock of his falvation.	Here is defcribed the infolent pride and arrogance of profperity—luxury and diffipation—immorality and profanenefs, ingratitude and contempt of God.
16. They provoked him to jealoufy with ftrange gods, with abominations provoked they him to anger.	Profanation of divine inftitutions-—fubverfion of the true religion—utter corruption of morality.
17. They facrificed unto devils not to God, to gods whom they knew not, to new gods, that came newly up, whom your fathers feared not.	Jacobinifm complete.
18. Of the rock that begat thee thou art unmindful and haft forgotten God that formed thee.	Pride and Ingratitude.

Original.	*Comment.*
19. And when the Lord faw it he *abhorred* them, becaufe of the provoking of his fons and daughters.	The divine example held up for our imitation.
20. And he faid, I will hide my face from them, I will fee what their *end* fhall be—	Accordingly it is fully proved by experiment ; we all fee what their end is—*Confufion and anarchy, revolution and uproar, rapine and murder.*
—for they are a froward generation, children in whom is no *faith*.	Difciples of Voltaire ; obftinate, incorrigible infidels.
21. They have moved me to jealoufy with that which is not God ; they have provoked me to anger with their vanities ; and I will move them to jealoufy with thofe which are not a people : I will provoke them to anger with a *foolifh nation*.	*America*, rejoicing in their fucceffes—imbibing their principles—following their footfteps—refigning her national Independence, and haftening to the fame fate.— This fate is pointed out in what follows—
23 and 25. I will heap mifchiefs upon them, I will fpend mine arrows upon them. The *fword* without, and *terror* within fhall deftroy both the young man and the virgin, the fuckling alfo with the man of grey hairs.	*Foreign* and *civil* wars —the rage of faction— private and public affaffinations. The fyftem of *terrorifm*—the indifcriminate flaughter of the *guillotine*, and all the horrors of the reign of *Robefpierre*.

Such, citizens, is the cloud which now broods over our political horizon. Thefe are the horrible profpects of democratic revolution. Here we behold in clear light, thofe new gods that have newly come up, whom our fathers feared not, and the facrifices they require of their votaries. Here is the Tree of *Gallic Liberty,* and the fruit which it bears —that tree of knowledge of political good and evil, planted in the midft of our garden, around which fo many of our infatuated countrymen are rallying, eager to comply with the advice of the tempter— hungering for the tafte of its deadlv fruit.

Let us now combine the inftruction of both texts, under the following twofold arrangement.

1. As they primarily refpect, the one our firft parents in the garden, and the other, the Ifraelites in the land of promife; fo in applying them to our own country, we may confider America as the *Canaan* of the nations, and the *Eden* of the world.

2. In the midft of our national garden ftands the tree of knowledge of political good and evil. Under this head I fhall endeavour more particularly to expofe the nature and properties of this tree, by pointing out, without tafting or touching, a variety of its fruits, and the national confequences of eating them.

As each of thefe divifions contains fufficient fubject for a volume, no more can be attempted in the limits of the prefent difcourfe, than the compilation of a kind of index to the fyftem, hinting here and there at fome of the more prominent parts ; referring the reft to the information and good fenfe of my audience ; and committing the improvement wholly to your patronage and care.

The knowledge, fellow-citizens, you all poffefs of the history and geography of our country—of its fertility and extent—its firft fettlement, rife and progrefs—its rapid population and improvement in all the beneficial arts of civilized life—its advantages, wealth and refources natural and acquired— its dangers and deliverances—its privileges, immunities and bleffings civil and religious, and in a word, its copious fund of all the means of human enjoyment, and of every thing tending to make a

C

nation great, powerful and independent, refpected abroad, and happy at home ; joined with a predilection for our native foil, the country which gave us birth, the religion of our fathers, and the government of our choice, under whofe benign influence and protection, we have fo long feafted on all the delights of focial life, and the infinitely variegated bleffings of freedom, as men, as citizens, and as Chriftians ; this knowledge, I fay, which enlightens your minds, and this patriotifm which glows in your breafts, muft fuperfede the neceffity of any arguments or proofs upon the firft head, fimply for the purpofe of *information ;* a more fenfible and thorough conviction only is wanting. Of the rich and diftinguifhing bleffings which the great and beneficent Parent hath poured with fuch profufion into the lap of our country, none of us can be ignorant ; and yet perhaps but few fufficiently prize them. My only object and wifh, therefore, with refpect to the bleffings we hold under the Author of nature purchafed by the blood and treafure of our country, is to infpire you with that ftrength of efteem and attachment for them, which the dangerous exigency of prefent circumftances require—fufficient to unite and impel our exertions to fnatch them from the yawning vortex of atheifm and anarchy.

We live in a land that may juftly be ftyled the Eden of the world ; and of all the trees of the garden we may freely and fafely eat—one only excepted, the tree of licentioufnefs and fedition, which alas is growing in the midft of the garden.

We live in a land flowing with milk and honey. And what article of enjoyment is contraband ? Nothing but wormwood and gall. We are forbidden only to mingle bitter with our fweets. Our means of every national and political bleffing are abundantly liberal, and nothing forbidden, but the mad privilege of *felf deftruction,* for which however, many are contending, with a zeal equalled only by their malice and intrigue.

In the bleffings of religion and government and all their happy fruits, our country appears to fymbolize with the nation of Eden, and with the chofen defcendants of Abraham, the favored inhabitants of the promifed land. But like the former we are faft yielding to the artful fuggeftions of the tempter, afpiring to be gods knowing good and evil, and reaching forth after the forbidden fruit. Like Jefhurun too, we have waxen fat and kicked; lightly efteemed the rock of our falvation, and are facrificing to new gods, that have come newly up, whom our fathers feared not.

Would time permit, it would be eafy, and might be inftructive and profitable, to fketch out a parallel, between ancient and American Ifrael. This general reflection, however, muft not efcape us, that, like them diftinguifhed by the mercies of Heaven, and like them too apoftatizing from the GOD of our fathers, we have reafon to fear the like awful feverity of divine judgments. For,

2. In the midft of our national garden, ftands the tree of knowledge of political good and evil. This we are now more particularly to examine by the fruits it bears, and the effects of thofe fruits.

This tree, to the difgrace of our country, is in the midft of our political garden. It grows and flourifhes only in the foil of human depravity. Its trunk is *Infidelity.* As it extends upward, it foon divides into two large main branches, and thefe are *Atheifm* and *Anarchy.* Thefe branches, however, the worfhippers of the tree diftinguifh by different, and more fpecious names—the former they call the *Age of Reafon,* and the latter, the *Rights of Man ;* while with a very impofing air, they fondly call the body of the tree *Liberty* and *Equality.*

From thefe main branches aforementioned fhoot out innumerable other fmaller limbs and twigs. A few of which are fuch as the following—

Political regeneration—popular infurrections—private affaffinations—Public maffacres—Revolutions—

Revolutionary tribunals—Jacobin clubs—National Conventions—Directories—Consuls—Health and *fraternity—Bulletins* and *Guillotines—Requisitions—Douceurs—Forced loans—Foreign robbery—Egyptian crusades—Self adjuration—Public debauchery—Private* and *national perfidy—Terrorism—Patriotism* (Parisian civism) *Republican Sabbath* (a drunken *decade)*— Republican feasts *(Sans Cullotides)—Republican baptism* (water-murder)—*Goddess of Reason* (a naked strumpet)——*Republican Psalms* (Marsellois, Carmagnole, Ca Ira) *Law of nations* (the art of plunder)—*National faith* (diplomatic skill)—*National honor* (Revenge)—*National friendship* (L'argent)—*Morality* (contempt of shame)—*Public virtue* (civic oaths)—*private virtue* (a child's rattle)— *Death, an eternal sleep—Religion (priestcraft)— Government (tyranny)—Destruction to the enemies of* Liberty *and* Equality—*Universal domination.*

It will be objected, perhaps, that this *role d'equipage* is the description of a *foreign* tree. True. But let us not flatter ourselves too far with the goodness of our own soil. The nature and properties of this tree are not altered or improved by soil or climate. If this evil actually exist in our country, similar causes will produce similar effects. If it be the same species of tree that is now growing in our political garden, we may fairly conclude, that its branches and fruit will be, for substance, the same in both hemispheres.

Before we particularize these fruits, I cannot but notice a striking similarity between their effects upon their votaries, and the effects of the fruit of the original tree of knowledge upon the inhabitants of Eden. When our first parents had yielded to the arts of the tempter, impelled by conscious guilt, " they hid themselves among the trees of the garden." Just so the disciples of Jacobinism, as soon as they have eaten of the forbidden fruit, immediately skulk, and mingling themselves with the mass of good citizens, endeavor to *hide* themselves, and

carry on all their nefarious operations in the darknefs and fecrecy of intrigue.

Nearly allied to this is another circumftance.
" Adam and Eve knew that they were *naked* and
fewed fig-leaves together, and made themfelves
aprons." And what are the aprons of Jacobins by
which they ftrive to conceal the nakednefs and deformity of their *real* views and intentions? The fig-
leaf profeffions of *pure republicanifm*—flimfy, but
fpecious pretexts of zeal for the public good—high
founding attachment to the principles of the conftitution—a patriotic concern for the *liberties* of
their country, and ranting declamation againft *un-
conftitutional* meafures.

One circumftance further, in which the copy
fymbolizes with the original, and the character is
complete. *An inflexible obftinacy in wrong.* Like
the ruins of the original apoftacy, all human means
appear ineffectual to reclaim them. They are wilfully blind to all the true beauties of government—
dead in every principle and practice of political error and mifchief. The means of perfuafion addreffed to them are thrown away. The moft powerful arguments are vain ; and the knowledge of
facts before their eyes makes not the leaft impreffion.
I much doubt, whether among all that clafs of citizens, a fingle inftance of political converfion can
be produced.

A few of the principal fruits of the Jacobinic
tree, I fhall now briefly mention ; for endlefs
would be the tafk to recount them all.

1. One of the practical principles which appears
as a fruit upon this tree, in tendency deftructive of
the focial compact, is, that the reftraints of government, however conftitutional, are infringements
upon the natural rights of man. Hence, no diftinction between liberty and licentioufnefs—between
the rights of the governing and the governed :
hence, the ground of fubordination is exploded,
and liberty and government fet at irreconcileable

variance : and hence too, originates that miftaken maxim or motto, *Liberty* and *Equality*, taken in the moft unlimited fenfe; from which, as the firft prin-ciple and foundation ftone of the whole fyftem, flow all its abfurd and diforganizing principles and practices, in the moft abundant profufion. The

2d *Fruit*, growing upon the fame clufter, is an ungenerous, unreafonable diftruft of conftituted authority, a total want of confidence in civil ru-lers. The functionaries of civil government, muft have no power to do good, fo certain it is, they will abufe it and do mifchief. A man chofen to civil office, however fair and unimpeachable his character for moral and political integrity, before his election, yet commences the downright villain, and the faithlefs tyrant as foon as ever he begins to act in his public character : And though he legif-lates for himfelf, as well as his conftituents, and lays no burden upon them, but what he equally lays upon himfelf, his meafures are all ariftocratic and oppreffive. And hence the idea adopted as a *practical*, if not an *avowed* principle, that the con-ftituted authorities are not the organs of the public will; and that the acts of government are not, *in the firft inftance*, of any binding force, but only as the people at large are pleafed to approve of them and fubmit to them.

Upon this very ground, pretending themfelves to be the people, fprang up the *Democratic Societies*, for a check upon government—or in other words, as a third houfe of legiflation, paramount to both houfes of Congrefs—affuming the right of can-vaffing and cenfuring all their proceedings, and neg-ativing a bill that has paffed both houfes, and re-ceived the executive fanction and fignature.

3d *Fruit*. That religion and government have no connection. Government is not to be influenced or guided by the principles of religion; nor is re-ligion, nor religious inftitutions intitled to the fof-tering care of government. Hence, to be divefted

of all religious fentiment is an excellent qualification in a civil ruler. No matter what his creed—
if he be an infidel or *Atheiſt*, ſo much the better,
provided he be thoroughly imbued with the principles of Jacobiniſm, and ſupremely devoted to the
cauſe of France. And hence too, the cry of *prieſtcraft* is already ſet up. Miniſters of the goſpel,
cannot teach their people how to conduct themſelves
as peaceable good ſubjects of a free and happy government, and warn them to ſhun the rocks which
threaten the deſtruction of their country, but lo !
they are the hirelings of men in place—preaching
politics inſtead of religion, and graſping, forſooth,
after authority and power. The

4th Fruit of this tree, is a blind, ſtupid, ſottiſh
admiration of the government of France, in all its
vertiginous motions, windings, revolutions, and
abominations. A ſpirit of *championiſm* to juſtify,
or to the utmoſt to palliate all their follies and ex-
ceſſes, and their acts of national injuſtice and vil-
lainy ; particularly towards our own country.

5th Fruit. The abſurd acknowledgement of an
infinite debt of *gratitude* to France—under the
maſk of which they would fain involve us in all
the horrors of the European war ; by precipitating
our country to take arms in the cauſe of France ;
and by yielding to all the ſolicitations and intrigues
of the tempter, to ſurrender our national peace,
freedom, wealth and independence, after the example of Holland, as the ſmalleſt token of obligation.

6th Fruit. An inveterate hatred againſt conſtituted authorities, and all the principal and moſt worthy officers in adminiſtration of the federal government In the proſecution of this, all the arts of
inſinuation, ſecret intrigue, perſonal invective, and
the ſhameleſs abuſe of open lying defamation,
through the medium of tongues, pens, books and
newſpapers are the worthieſt means employed.

7th Fruit. A conſtant oppoſition, and noiſy ſe-

ditious clamor againſt all the meaſures of government without diſtinction ;—imputing them to the
worſt of motives, and as deſigned to effect the worſt
of ends—to *Britiſh* inflùence—to oppreſſive views,
and ultimate aims to ſubvert the liberties of our
country. Their oppoſition ſeems more particularly
levelled againſt thoſe meaſures of government which
are ſpecially calculated to ſecure our peace abroad,
and tranquility at home—to guard againſt foreign
aggreſſion, and internal ſedition and rebellion.
Witneſs the mad uproars of democratic fury againſt
the *Britiſh ireaty*—the clamors againſt the *alien*
and *ſedition* laws ; and the means of providing for
the national defence by equipping a naval force, and
raiſing a land army.

But ſtrange and unaccountable as it is, this Jacobinic faction is now prevailing in our country, and
even aſſuming the air of triumph. Both in con-
verſation and newſpapers, marks of exultation are
diſcoverable ; and the certainty of a Jacobinic adminiſtration, as the fruit of the next election, is
avowed by every mouth, and ſcattered through every ſtate.—What the conſequences of ſuch an event
will be, does not require the ſpirit of prophecy to
foretel, but the extent of the evil baffles the powers
of human numbers to calculate. In the train may
be counted the deſtruction of the government, under
which we are now free, proſperous and happy—
the deſolation and pillage of our country, and our
very ſoil ſoaked with the blood of its inhabitants.

I cannot do better juſtice to the ſubject, nor to
my own feelings, than by reciting a pretty lengthy
extract from that excellent public addreſs lately
made by a very reſpectable character, high in the
councils of America ; whoſe means of information
none can doubt, and whoſe tried integrity, and
long and faithful public ſervices, juſtly entitle him
to the eſteem and confidence of his country : I
mean the honorable Speaker of the Houſe of Rep-
reſentatives.

25

" It is now eleven years fince the prefent gov-
‘ ernment has commenced its operations. During
‘ this time, I will not fay that all its meafures have
‘ been perfeſt, for it has been conduſted by human
‘ agents. I will however declare it has not erred
‘ from intention—it has committed no aſts from in-
‘ juſtice and oppreſſion—it has never wantonly im-
‘ pofed any public burden. On the contrary in
‘ the impofition of thofe it deemed indifpenfible,
‘ it has fought every alleviation, in its power. It
‘ received the charge of our public affairs at a time
‘ when by the imbecility of our former fyſtem, the
‘ reputation which our nation had acquired by its
‘ glorious and fuccefsful ſtruggle for freedom and
‘ independence was almoſt annihilated ; when con-
‘ fidence, public and private was almoſt deſtroyed;
‘ when ſtates had become the rivals of each other ;
‘ and legiſlative hoſtility was not only declared, but
‘ vigoroufly profecuted by them ; when our fede-
‘ rative importance was derided and infulted, and
‘ we were faſt becoming, not indeed in *name*, but in
‘ *faſt*, the colonies of the maritime nations of Europe;
‘ and when loaded, as the people were, with taxes,
‘ and univerfally complaining of their weight and
‘ burden, inſtead of a diminution of the debt, the
‘ intereſt accumulated, and unpaid, was nearly the
‘ amount of one half the principal.

‘ Receiving the charge of our national intereſts,
‘ under thefe circumſtances—having a new and un-
‘ tried fyſtem to put into motion—having provifion
‘ to make for a large debt, the price of our free-
‘ dom and independence ; for which the former
‘ government had been found inadequate—and hav-
‘ ing by its own wifdom, without the aid of pre-
‘ cedent by which to regulate its courfe, to devife
‘ the means of executing a conſtitution, which was
‘ intended *to form a more perfeſt union, eſtabliſh juſ-*
‘ *tice, enfure domeſtic tranquility, provide for the com-*
‘ *mon defence, promote the general welfare, and fe-*

D

' *cure the blessings of liberty to ourselves and posterity* ;
' surely the men on whom this mighty task was
' devolved, had a right to expect from a generous
' people, a candid construction of their honest in-
' tentions.   A just review of the effects which have
' been produced by the progress of their labors,
' will determine, how far they are intitled to in-
' dulgence or approbation.

   ' The government has had to contend with dif-
' ficulties which were neither foreseen nor expected;
' for who could have believed that in less than ten
' years, we should have to defray the expence of
' suppressing two insurrections, raised by the artful
' misrepresentations of wicked men ? Yet this, to
' the disgrace of our country has been the case. We
' have been obliged to sacrifice treasure to purchase
' peace with the powers of Barbary, and to redeem
' our citizens there from slavery. We have been
' at great charge in sustaining a long and expensive
' Indian war, and in the protection of our frontiers
' —we have suffered immensely by the plunder of
' our commerce ; we have fortified our ports and
' harbors ; we have replenished our magazines, and
' we have created a very considerable navy. Cred-
' it, public and private is restored. Our naviga-
' tion is infinitely extended ; our tonnage now ex-
' ceeding that of Great Britain, at the commence-
' ment of the present reign. Yet our debt at the
' beginning of the present year, was four millions
' less, than at that of 1791, when we first began
' the payment of the interest. But what is infinitely
' more dear to humanity, under circumstances of
' extreme irritation, such has been the temper, the
' moderation, and magnanimity of the government,
' that peace has been preserved, and we have kept
' ourselves separated from the scenes of horror
' which are desolating Europe. It is too, soothing
' to the honest pride of an American, that all men,
' our own degenerate citizens, and jacobin renega-
' does from other countries among us, excepted,

' speak in terms of refpect and honor of the con-
' duct of our government. Is not this, my fellow-
' citizens, when it can with truth be added, that
' it all has been effected without one act of tyranny
' or oppreffion, a glorious reverfe of our fituation
' in 1789 ? Yet have not all thefe things fecured
' to the government the affections of the people,
' or *itfelf* againft the malignant enterprifes of its en-
' emies. I fpeak not now of New-England ; that
' is, I truft, effentially found. But at this moment
' it is a doubt, whether, throughout the nation,
' the friends or the enemies of the government are
' the moft numerous. How has this been effec-
' ted ? To give a full anfwer to this queftion, would
' requiie a hiftory in detail of the oppofition with
' all its windings and turnings, from the meeting
' of the federal Convention, to the prefent day.
' Suffice it to fay, that the party, unfteady in all
' things elfe, in their attention to two objects, have
' been undeviatingly pertinacious—in their malig-
' nant flander of the character of thofe, whom they
' believed poffeffed the public confidence, and in
' their mifreprefentation of the meafures of gov-
' ernment. As an inflance of the firft, we cannot
' but remember, the great, the good, the glorious
' Wafhington, the pride of our country, the orna-
' ment of human nature. Him they reprefented as
' ambitious, altho he never fought, but always
' fhunned public office—as the tool of Great
' Britain, altho he had fevered America from her
' empire—as a man of no religion, although no
' one was more refpectfully obfervant of religious
' duties. In fhort for his moft eminent virtues, they
' charged againft him the oppofite vices. At the fame
' time they have directed the moft grofs and flande-
' rous abufe againft all his friends, and thofe whom
' they deemed the moft influential fupporters of his
' adminiftration.
    ' With regard to the meafures of government,
' if its enemies may be credited, it has performed

' no one meritorious act, but its whole conduct
' has been mifchievous. Endlefs would be the
' tafk, to expofe and correct all the vile flanders
' which have been wantonly lavifhed upon it ; nor
'' is the attempt neceffary—inftances enough will
' occur to the recollection of every man who feels
' for the honor of his country, or perceives his
' own intereft to be connected with the prefervation
' of the conftitution. It will be fufficient to fay
' that the government has been charged with con-
' duct, faithlefs as it refpected our foreign connex-
' ions—iufidious and traiterous as it related to the
' domeftic adminiftration. By thefe means, alarms
' and fufpicions have been created, a government,
' I will not fay *perfect*, but honeft and patriotic, has
' been flandered, and the effects (for why fhould
' not the truth be declared?) have become exten-
' five and alarming. Your danger which is great,
' though not defperate, I have thought it my duty,
' among the laft acts of my public life, to proclaim
' to you. GOD grant, that I may be miftaken in
' the magnitude of this danger ; but I do moft fol-
' emnly declare that my conviction is perfect, that
' it cannot be averted, but by being more exten-
' fively, than at prefent known, in this part of the
' United States."

Such, fellow-citizens, are the nature, properties and fruits of the tree of Jacobinifm. Such the
fatal confequences of fheltering under its branches,
and of liftening to the fyren voice of the tempter
in plucking, and tafting its deadly fruit ! Thefe
are the new gods, that have come newly up, which
our fathers feared not, and to which they were
perfect ftrangers. They, thro' the tempeft of the
revolutionary war, under a national government,
which, in itfelf, was little more than an advifory
council of fafety, united by their common intereft, and their common danger, ftood firm and immoveable. The voice of Congrefs was heard with
affection and reverence. Their recommendations

had all the force of law. While wifdom and dignity attended their fteps, public confidence gave energy to all their meafures.—And why, in the name of wonder, why, under a government which unites *energy* with freedom, built upon a Conftitution, defigned among other important ends " to form a more perfect union, and infure domeftic tranquility," when threatened with the moft tremendous mifchiefs of the oppofite evils, why does not the common danger again unite us in the common caufe, and infpire us with the fame refolutions, as with one heart, and one foul, to maintain our excellent government, preferve our national happinefs, and pour confufion upon its foes ? For believe me, Citizens, our dangers are not vifionary and trifling, but real and formidable. Never was a period in the whole courfe of the revolutionary war, in which our danger was more imminent and awful ; and in which the happinefs and the very exiftence of our country was in a more alarming and critical fituation. It is high time therefore, for us to awake from our lethargy, and attend to the means of our fafety—left, while we are dreaming of our nation's glory, celebrating her Independence, and affecting to defpife the intriguing vigilance of our internal enemies, fudden deftruction fall upon us, and that without remedy. It becomes us not to fink down into the torpor of inaction and fupinenefs, and defpair of the Commonwealth, becaufe evils are at the door, and dangers ftare us in the face. Such was not the conduct of our fathers, whofe virtues we admire and celebrate—this was not the way in which they fought the battles of freedom, and fecured and tranfmitted to their children, the glorious legacy of independence. No. Their zeal increafed as dangers and difficulties increafed ; and their fortitude rofe paramount to every difcouragement.

Our government, citizens, is peculiarly founded on *public virtue.* It lives, it exifts in the public *sentiment*, and public integrity.—The world is now looking on, and the dubious experiment is now trying, *whether there be virtue enough in human nature to support a free Republican government.* The fate of our government will forever decide the question. And evident it is, if we do not secure the foundation ; if we tamely suffer that to be sapped and undermined, the fair superstructure, must and will tumble, and all the hopes of our country, and of mankind, be buried in its ruins !—The consequences too, as to ourselves, are equally obvious—if we cannot live under a *free* government, we must, and shall have a *despotic* government.

Let it ever be remembered, citizens, as a principle of the first magnitude and importance ; let it be engraven on your hearts, as with a pen of iron, and with the point of a diamond, that, ALL OUR DANGER ORIGINATES FROM OURSELVES. Not all the *foreign* powers on earth combined against us, can effect our ruin, without our *own* aid. If America fall, and add another example to the long melancholy list of departed Republics, she will owe her destruction to her *own* hands.

The present day, therefore, is a day for action and alarm, and not for security and sloth. It is a day which tries men's souls. It is a cause in which there are not, there *cannot* be any *neuters*. " He that is not with us, is against us, and he that gathereth not with us, scattereth abroad." Mark the temporizing, lukewarm patriot for a *decided* foe. His professions of patriotism, are as hollow and as blasting as the east wind. To temporize with the enemies of government by any conciliatory midway concessions is dastardly—it is to kick about in sport our father's ashes. To discover a lukewarm stoical apathy when the happiness of our country, and every thing dear and valuable on this side Heaven is at stake, is *worse* than treason.—If we would shew ourselves worthy of our ancestors—if we would escape the execrations and curses of poster-

ity, we muſt attend to the means of our political
ſalvation, and be up and doing without delay. We
muſt cleave to the GOD of our fathers, and not ſacrifice to thoſe new gods, that have come newly up,
whom our fathers feared not. We muſt venerate
the inſtitutions and uſages of our anceſtors, both
religious and civil. We muſt faithfully inſtruct
our children in the principles of *true* religion, and
true liberty. We muſt obſerve GOD's Sabbaths, and
reverence his ſanctuary. We muſt preſerve the
fountains of public honors and offices, pure and
unſullied, and with conſcientious patriotiſm exerciſe the high privilege of freemen, in the choice of
our civil rulers. We muſt rally around the ſtan-
dard of our government, pledging in its ſupport,
after the example of our revolutionary fathers,
" our lives, our fortunes, and our ſacred honor."
And to every inſinuation of the tempter, let us
make this determined reply " we may eat of the
fruit of the trees of the garden ; but of the fruit of
the tree which is in the midſt of the garden, GOD
hath ſaid, ye ſhall *not eat* of it, neither ſhall ye
touch it, leſt ye die."

and that in a third, total ruin was prevented; is plainly and manifestly to be attributed to the skill and firmness of a youth between nineteen and twenty-three, acting in the last said only in a voluntary office.

After acquiring, both in public and private life, the universal esteem, through the following season of peace, he was chosen, in the year 1774, one of the Representatives in the first Congress. Here his former reputation, and the proofs which he daily gave of superior wisdom and worth, induced that body to appoint him, in 1775, commander in chief of the American armies, employed to resist the hostilities of Great Britain. This hazardous office he accepted with that diffidence, which always accompanies and announces merit, and with a firmness of decision, which no future embarrassment could move. Under a government just formed, and marked with infinite weakness; in a country composed of separate and detached sovereignties; a simple a people, not yet seriously connected; at the head of armies formed of mere militia, a band of recruits yet to be made soldiers, and of officers ignorant of the discipline which they were to teach, and of the movements which they were to guide; strangers, rivals, and sometimes enemies; without ammunition, arms, clothes, or money; enlisted for a summer; and plunged by inexperience into all the exposures, disappointments, disease, and miseries, of unprovided military life; he became the body of union to the people, and to the soldiery, guided the one to wisdom, and led the other to victory. In his own letters,† not less illustrious commentaries than those of Cæsar, and on a more glorious war, he is seen, through the veil of his modesty, to have been the pillar, on which the country suspended itself; the

Mr. FLINT's DISCOURSE

ON THE DEATH OF

GENERAL WASHINGTON.

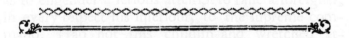

A country, an army, hosted in person's service, experience—their harassed to command; but skill, no activity—the people entirely tempered... naked or great and many sorrows...

... Hey were now called to suffer. ... the army was formed of militia and party militia... of villains, and private offences... were...

... when ... he ... had acquired with the ... appearances ... but ... experience ... the lessons ... attended ... his time with disasters, ... his encampment from ... in ... General Howe through Pennsylvania, his defeat near Trenton, his elusion of Lord Cornwallis at Trenton, his consequent march through New-Jersey, in which he defeated the British corps at Princeton, and the address, with which he preserved the appearance of a considerable force at Morristown, where, through the winter, he had only eleven or twelve hundred men, and these under a successive inoculation, to resist the whole British army.

But his military life had also its seasons of prosperity. His successes were, however, almost always obtained at the head of a force, inferior to that of his enemy, and of consequence were, in an eminent degree, the result of his own efforts. Like the illustrious men, to whom I have compared him, he had the happiness of ending the great controversy, in which he had engaged, and in which his country was... with a final and complete triumph. All that, for which he fought, and that the greatest prize, which excites human contention, he gained; and lived long enough to reap a glorious reward of

* See Note D.   † See Note E.

158

A

DISCOURSE,

DELIVERED AT HARTFORD

FEB. 22, 1800,

THE DAY SET APART BY RECOMMENDATION OF
CONGRESS, TO PAY A TRIBUTE OF RE-
SPECT TO THE MEMORY OF

GENERAL

GEORGE WASHINGTON,

WHO DIED, DECEMBER 14th, 1799.

By ABEL FLINT,
PASTOR OF THE SOUTH CHURCH IN HARTFORD.

HARTFORD:

PRINTED BY HUDSON AND GOODWIN.

1800.

THROUGH his plantation, on which he retired, ran a stream, stored with fish. This fishery, two days in the week he made, together with his own boats and nets, the property of the surrounding poor; and frequently directed his servants to aid them in taking and curing their booty.

In the course of the war, he wrote, as I have been well informed, to his friends in Virginia, a proposal to free his servants, should the Legislature think it consistent with the general welfare. This plan he has realized in his will; and the public are already informed, that it will be speedily executed by his most respectable Executrix.

AFTER the surrender of Yorktown, he returned, at the end of eight years absence, to visit his family. His servants had voluntarily arranged themselves in two lines, from his mansion house to the creek which runs below the door. At length the time in sight, their humble and affectionate domestics, sent up a shout of joy, and uttered an extravagance of transport; the women by shrieking, beating their breasts, and tearing their hair, and the men by cries and tears, and all the gesticulations, with which nature

A

DISCOURSE, &c.

MY HEARERS,

THIS day completes fixty-eight years fince the birth of the illuftrious *George Washington*, formerly leader of the American people, in their ftruggle for independence ; twice fucceffively Prefident of the United States of America ; and late Lieutenant-General and Commander in Chief of their armies. For many years the anniverfary of his birth has been obfeived as a day of feftivity. Its return was wont to infufe into the people of America peculiarly pleafing emotions. They welcomed it as the natal day of one whom they highly efteemed for his talents and virtues ; to whom they felt grateful for his beneficial labors on their behalf ; and to whom they ftill looked as a counfellor for advice, and as an experienced leader to guide their armies if difturbed by domeftic, or invaded by foreign enemies. But alas ! the fcene is changed ; their hopes are blafted. The FRIEND, the FATHER, the political DELIVERER of his country no longer lives ! Having accomplifhed the purpofes for which he was defigned in the counfels of Heaven, the fovereign difpofer of all events has called him from life ; he now fleeps with his fathers in the peaceful tomb. And thofe feftive fongs with which this day has been accuftomed to be celebrated muft give place to mournful ftrains. " The joy of our heart is ceafed ; our dance is turned into mourning. For this our heart is faint ; for this our eyes are dim."

IN compliance with the recommendation of our national Legiflature, communicated in a proclamation from

97

6

our refpeincluded Chief Magiftrate, we have now affembled in
the fanctuary of the Lord, not to hail the birth day of the
Man we loved, with fongs of joy, but in accents of woe
to lament his death, and to pay a tribute of refpect to his
memory. Called upon by my fellow-citizens, I am now
to addrefs you on the mournful occafion. I fhould fhrink
from the tafk were it not for the known candor of my audience. I feel myfelf incompetent to do juftice to fo great
a character, and unable to fuggeft any new ideas on a fubject
on which my hearers have already heard and read fo much.
Any thing new concerning the life or character of GENE-
RAL WASHINGTON cannot be expected from me. With the
various particulars of his life many of you are better acquainted than myfelf ; and his character has been already
delineated to you in a manner which I cannot expect to
equal. But the portrait of a friend is not the lefs pleafing
for being often viewed. I flatter myfelf therefore, that you
will favor me with your attention, and that your candor
will excufe a repetition of ideas which you may have heard
before. What I propofe is to notice fome of the leading
traits in the character of that great man for whom our nation this day mourns ; to recommend his virtues to your
imitation ; and to make fome religious and moral reflections
on his death. My remarks will be grounded on the following paffage of infpiration :

ISAIAH iii. 1, 2, 3.

*BEHOLD the LORD, the LORD of Hofts, doth take
away—the mighty man, and the man of war—the
prudent—the honorable man, and the counfellor.*

WHEN, my brethren, has there appeared a character to whom the epithets here ufed by the Prophet
might be applied with fo much propriety as to the

7

great *WASHINGTON*? He was truly a *mighty man*, as
he was endowed with an affemblage of talents very
rarely found combined in one man;—talents which
qualified him for diftinguifhed ufefulnefs to the
country that gave him birth, and which fecured to
him the applaufes of an admiring world. He was
mighty in war and *mighty* in peace; fingularly eminent in public and equally amiable in private life.
Uniformly guided by a fenfe of duty, he feems to
have been free from the influence of every fordid,
of every mean paffion, and to have been exempt
from thofe foibles which are often found to attend
men worthy in other refpects.

HE was a *man of war*. At a very early period
of life, he became diftinguifhed for his fkill as a
military commander, and often led the forces of his
native ftate in dangerous enterprifes. On all occafions he acquitted himfelf with honor and gained
the applaufes of his country, " difplaying uniform-
" ly uncommon fortitude under perfonal hardfhips,
" perfevering induftry, cool and undaunted brave-
" ry, and the moft brilliant military talents."
When the late war, which happily terminated in
the eftablifhment of the United States as a free and
independent nation, commenced, all eyes were
turned to the man, who had already fo highly fignalized himfelf, as the moft fuitable perfon in the
nation, to take the command of their armies. With
that felf-diffidence which ever accompanies true
merit he accepted the command. At the call of his
countrymen, indignant at their wrongs, and defir-

ous to free them from an oppreffive yoke, he re-
linquifhed the pleafing charms of a happy retirement and expofed himfelf to fcenes where every
thing dear to man was at ftake. Of the manner in
which he executed this important and dangerous
commiffion, I need not fpeak. The various events
of the war, which are frefh in the recollection of
many of my hearers, from their having either borne
an active part in them or intimately known them at
the time, and which thofe of us in earlier life have
heared from our fathers, bear an ample teftimony
to his intrepid bravery, fingular prudence, great
prefence of mind, uncommon knowledge of mankind, and great fruitfulnefs in the invention of refources to extricate himfelf, the army, and the
country from dangerous fcenes. When the war
terminated he difplayed the fame magnanimity which
he had before manifefted. In a dignified manner
he refigned his commiffion, and retired to the peaceful walks of private life.

COMPARE him with ALEXANDER, JULIUS
CÆSAR, CHARLES of Sweden, or FREDERIC of
Pruffia, to whofe names hiftory has attached the
epithet of great. As military commanders they
were great, but they were guided either by a mad
ambition to extend their conquefts, by a wifh to en-
flave their country, by a precipitate rafhnefs, or a
thirft for military glory. They unreluctantly facrificed the lives of thoufands to gratify their own
ambition ; and though we may be dazzled with the
rapidity and extent of their conquefts, we muft

ſhudder at the recital of the carnage, deſtruction
and miſery with which thoſe conqueſts were attended ; we muſt deſpiſe the men for the meanneſs of
the views by which they were actuated. Compared with theſe how truly, how uniformly great does
the HERO of America appear ! Entirely free from
thoſe ſordid principles which have fixed an indelible
ſtain upon their reputations, he was guided ſolely
by a regard to the public weal. He unſheathed his
ſword not to enſlave his country, but to redreſs its
wrongs; and when this object was accompliſhed, he
returned it to its ſcabbard, and retired to ſhare with
others the happy fruits of his toil.

THE *prudent, the honorable man, and the coun-*
ſellor. Equally appropriate to the character of General *WASHINGTON* are theſe epithets with thoſe already noticed. Prudence was a very ſtriking trait
in his character. He exhibited many marks of uncommon diſcretion, through the whole courſe of
his life, both in the field and in the cabinet. When
commanding the armies of his country, and when
at the head of its civil government, he was many
times placed in trying ſituations ; he was called to
paſs through ſcenes which not only would have diſ-
couraged a mind leſs firm and reſolute than his,
but which required a diſpaſſionate coolneſs, a ſaga-
cious prudence to prevent their iſſuing in the greateſt evil. The manner in which he conducted in
ſuch ſituations evinced the ſuperiority of his underſtanding and his profound prudence. In this virtue

B

he shone unrivalled, and it was owing to this that he never committed an action which, in the view of impartial posterity, will tarnish a reputation more splendid than that of any of the sons of men.

A CHARACTER more uniformly *honorable* than his history does not record. He was loaded with every honor which his country had to bestow, and continually received marks of esteem and respect from all parts of the civilized world. Of these honors he proved himself worthy by a conduct uniformly noble, great and honorable. Free from those blemishes which are often found to stain the characters of men great in many respects, our beloved chieftain never was known, in public or in private life, to be guilty of an action irreconcileable with honor, dignity or propriety. In discharging the duties of those high stations which he was called to fill, he was connected with men of every character, the base as well as the worthy. Tho often disgusted with the meanness and littleness of the former, from a becoming dignity of deportment he never departed : tho attempts were often made to injuire him, by ambitious and designing men who were envious of his talents and virtues, and who wished to deprefs him that they might exalt themselves, we find him ever conducting towards them so as to give them no just occasion to impeach his honor or to reproach him of treating them unworthily. To those who know the embarrassments he met with from officers under his command, during the revolutionary war, to those who are acquainted with the continual obftacles thrown in his way, by the enemies of his administration, during his prefidency, I appeal for the truth of thefe remarks.

His having been twice chofen Prefident of the United States by the unanimous fuffrages of the electors of every ftate, evinces the high opinion which his fellow-citizens entertained of him as a *Counfellor*, as a political ruler.—His conduct through the whole courfe of his adminiftration fhows that the opinion of his countrymen was not ill-founded, that their confidence was not mif-placed. When firft called to the chief magiftracy, his fituation was peculiar. The form of government at the head of whofe adminiftration he was placed was new. He had to tread in an unbeaten path, and in many refpects to eftablifh regulations not only for himfelf but for his fucceffors in office. The friends of the conftitution, defirous of its permanent eftablifhment, looked to him with an anxious eye, knowing that much depended on the meafures which he fhould adopt ; and equally attentive were its enemies to watch his actions hoping to find fomething which they might make ufe of as an inftrument for the fubverfion of the government. The great wifdom with which he difcharged the duties of his high office, and the happy fruits of his adminiftration, aftonifhed the world no lefs than the fplendid talents which he had exhibited as a military commander. He difplayed the fame dignified conduct, the fame fagacious prudence, and the fame elevation of mind which had marked his character in other fcenes. And when

he declined a re-election and once more retired to
private life, he gave occafion to his country and to
the world at large again to admire his moderation,
his freedom from an unworthy ambition, his patriotifm, his magnanimity.

HE was not permitted to enjoy, for any length
of time, the retirement he had fo ardently wifhed.
He faw his country threatened by an infidious foe ;
and tho arrived at a time of life when he might
have juftly plead an exemption from any further
public fervice, he confented again to put himfelf at
the head of the American army, fhould that army
be led to action ; at the fame time declining, as
he had ever before done, any pecuniary reward for
his fervices.

To this view of his character I beg leave to add
another trait which tended ftill more highly to exalt and enoble him. I allude to his reverence for
the GOD of his fathers. The fuperintending Providence of the Moft High he ever acknowledged.
To this he afcribed his fucceffes, not to his own
fkill and prowefs ; to this he afcribed the profperity
of the United States, not to the wifdom and labors
of their rulers. On all fuitable occafions he expreffed a becoming gratitude to GOD for his kind
interpofitions in behalf of the army or the nation ;
and when defeated in any of his expectations, he
devoutly acknowledged the fame Providence and
fubmiffively bowed to the rod.

13

THUS was he ever both great and good ; great as a warrior ;—great as a politician ;—great as a private citizen ; and good as a humble worfhipper of GOD.

SOON after he received and accepted the appointment of Commander in Chief of the armies of the United States, it pleafed the great arbiter of life and death fuddenly to terminate his earthly courfe. Mature in years, loaded with honors, loved by his country, applauded by the world, he fell a victim to a fhort difeafe. He beheld the approach of death with calmnefs, and expired without a groan ; appearing great in death as he had been in life.

THE memory of a man poffeffed of fuch ufeful and uncommon talents, and who devoted thofe talents to the fervice of the nation, will, I truft, ever be held dear by the people of America. His great virtues and his fplendid actions we fhall recount to our children and they to theirs ; and millions yet unborn will " rife and call him bleffed." Every future return of this day will bring to mind *the mighty man and the man of war; the prudent, the honorable man and the counfellor ;* and fo long as a regard for true merit, fo long as gratitude fhall exift in the human mind, the memory of *WASHINGTON* will be dear to the country which, under the bleffing of Heaven, he raifed to empire by his fword, and eftablifhed in peaceful profperity by his counfel.

BUT, my hearers, fimply to pronounce an eulogy upon a departed friend is not the only way in which we ought to fhow refpect to his memory. In addition to this we fhould imitate his virtues and obferve his wife counfels. Suffer me therefore again to prefent to your view the friend whofe death we now lament, and to propofe his example for imitation.

FEW of us indeed fhall ever be called to command armies or to adminifter civil government. Many of his great and fplendid actions it will not therefore be in our power to imitate. Still we muft endeavor to be actuated by principles fimilar to thofe which governed him, if like him we wifh to leave a good name behind us.

WE find him ever ready to obey the calls of duty, not fuffering any confiderations of private eafe and convenience to reftrain him. His courage was not that rafhnefs which fometimes impels men to rufh upon danger wholly regardlefs of confequences : It was combined with coolnefs—with difcretion which led him to weigh well the probable iffue of his conduct. Here we have an example worthy our imitation. Let a fenfe of duty be the leading principle of our actions, and animate us ever to do what, upon due deliberation, we believe to be right. Let us learn to " think on our ways," to " ponder the paths of our feet," and with intrepidity encounter every danger to which we may be expofed in the difcharge of our duty. Let not

a thirſt for popularity, let not a fear of incurring
the cenſure of the weak or the wicked ever deter
us from performing the duties attached to our reſpective ſtations in life. Deſpiſing " that popular-
" ity which is raiſed without merit and loſt without
" a crime," let us aim to ſecure " that applauſe
" which will ever be beſtowed on great and virtu-
" ous actions."

THE patriotiſm and public ſpiritedneſs of our
deceaſed political father were ſhining traits in his
character, which alſo we ſhould ſtrive to imitate.
Free from that narrowneſs of mind which leads
many people to confine all their regards to themſelves, he felt for others, he loved his country, and
devoted his whole time and energetic talents to objects which might benefit the nation and the world.
His love to the country was real ; it was not that
noiſy ſhow of patriotiſm which leads many to de-
claim much concerning the public good who are
actuated only by a baſe ambition ; and who are liberal of their cenſures of thoſe in office, merely from
a wiſh to exalt themſelves upon the ruin of others.
Often did the great patriot whoſe death we now lament ſacrifice his private eaſe and intereſt to advance the public good ; and he manifeſted that he
was entirely free from a ſelfiſh ambition to elevate
himſelf and from an avaricious deſire to amaſs
wealth at the expenſe of the public. Let thoſe
who boaſt ſo much of their patriotiſm evince themſelves equally free from ſelfiſh views, and we will
allow the juſtice of their claims. My hearers, let

us all cultivate that love to our country which will ever lead us to be fubmiffive to its laws, to refpect its rulers, and to aid them in the adminiftration of government, inftead of continually throwing obftacles in their way. And let us ever remember that good citizens will never feek redrefs for any fuppofed injuries except in. a legal and conftitutional manner.

WE may, in the next place, view the farmer of Mount Vernon in his private life. " He was a " man of the ftricteft honor and honefty, fair and " honorable in his dealings, and punctual to his " engagements. His difpofition was mild, kind " and generous. Candor, fincerity, moderation " and fimplicity were prominent features in his " character. He was an affectionate hufband, a " faithful friend, a humane mafter and a father to " the poor. He lived in the unvarying habits of " regularity, temperance and induftry."

IT is too commonly the cafe that men who dazzle the world by the fplendor of their public actions, who are diftinguifhed for martial courage or political wifdom, are deficient in private virtues. Tho great in public, in private they manifeft a want of true magnanimity, by indulging pride, oppreffion, injuftice, anger, ill-nature and exceffive gratifications. When the world at large is looking upon them they will try to appear great and honorable; but when viewed only by the domeftic circle they appear even mean and contemptible.

Not fo the truly dignified *WASHINGTON*. In the peaceful walks of private life he appeared amiable, as he did great when at the head of armies, or when prefiding over the government of a nation.

It is in thefe private virtues more particularly that we fhould view him as an example, and endeavor to imitate him. Thefe virtues have more real influence on human happinefs than thofe fplendid actions which aftonifh the world. They may not give a man fo high a degree of celebrity, but they yield an internal peace more truly grateful than the applaufes of a misjudging world. Let us then feduloufly cultivate and practife that honefty and generofity, that candor and fincerity, that moderation and felf-government, that temperance and attention to the domeftic virtues which were exemplified in the life of the American CINCINNATUS.

While thus attentive to all the focial virtues, he was not unmindful of the duties of religion. Tho his avocations were numerous, yet " in his al-
" lotments for the revolving hours of the day reli-
" gion was not forgotten. Feeling, what he fo of-
" ten publicly acknowledged, his entire depend-
" ence on GOD, he daily, at ftated feafons, retired
" to his clofet, to worfhip at his footftool, and to
" afk his divine bleffing. He was remarkable for his
" ftrict obfervation of the fabbath, and exemplary
" in his attendance on public worfhip."

C

WHATEVER other endowments a man may poſſeſs, if deſtitute of all regard for religion,—if entirely inattentive to what he owes to GOD, he is deficient in that which gives real worth and dignity to man. Without goodneſs there can be no true greatneſs; and without religion there can be no true goodneſs. A becoming veneration for the character of JEHOVAH, a reverence for his word and inſtitutions, and a ſincere obedience to his precepts, in addition to the practice of thoſe duties which reſult from our reſpective ſtations in life, are neceſſary to complete a perfect character.—Theſe are alſo neceſſary to render us acceptable to that GOD without whoſe approbation we muſt be miſerable however applauded by the world. To the duties of religion, as preſcribed in the volume of divine revelation, let us carefully attend. Let us cheriſh that " fear of the LORD which is the beginning of wiſdom," and reject with abhorrence thoſe falſe principles which teach that an individual or a nation may be great without religion. I will cloſe this branch of my ſubject with an extract from the addreſs of our late illuſtrious Chief to his fellowcountrymen, when he declined a re-election to the chief magiſtracy.

" OF all the diſpoſitions and habits which lead " to political proſperity, religion and morality are " indiſpenſible ſupports. In vain would that man " claim the tribute of patriotiſm who would labor " to ſubvert theſe great pillars of human happineſs, " theſe firmeſt props of the duties of men and cit-

·" izens. The merely politician, equally with the
" pious man ought to refpect and to cherifh them.
" A volume could not trace all their connections
" with private and public felicity. And let us with
" caution indulge the fuppofition, that morality
" can be maintained without religion. Whatever
" may be conceded of the influence of a refined
" education on minds of a peculiar ftructure, rea-
" fon and experience both forbid us to expect that
" national morality can prevail in exclufion of re-
" ligious principle."

THESE ideas, juft in themfelves, acquire additional importance by coming from one whofe extenfive knowledge of men and things qualified him
to judge of the influence of religious and moral
principles.

THUS, my hearers, have I endeavored to prefent to your view fome outlines of a character de-
fervedly dear to the people of America ; and to recommend his example to your imitation, as the
moft proper way of paying refpect to his memory.
I have not aimed to pleafe the imagination by the
charms of novelty, or to intereft the feelings by the
flights of fancy. I have, in a plain manner, exhibited to you a character which you have long efteemed ; and if what I have faid fhall induce any
to feek to imitate him in his virtues, my higheft ambition will be gratified. A few reflections, by
way of improvement, will clofe this difcourfe.

In the firſt place, We are led from our text to acknowledge and adore the hand of GOD in the life and death of men who are diſtinguiſhed for their talents, and who are made bleſſings to a nation. " The LORD reigneth, let the earth rejoice." Whenever in the courſe of his Providence, he hath any great deſign to accompliſh he qualifies men for the purpoſe. And when his deſigns are anſwered *he taketh way the mighty man and the man of war, the prudent, the honorable man, and the Counſellor.* Sometimes ſuch men are removed at periods when their continuance in life ſeems neceſſary for the happineſs of millions. Thus does GOD teach us that vain is the help of man, and that our help ſtandeth alone in him in whom is everlaſting ſtrength. Let us ſubmiſſively bow to his will, and devoutly commend ourſelves and our country to his merciful protection.

SECONDLY, While we humble ourſelves under the late frown of divine Providence, let us be truly grateful to GOD for ſo long continuing to us the important life and beneficial labors of the great and good man who has been lately taken from us. There were many periods when, to human appearance, his removal would have been a greater calamity to this nation ; nay when our very exiſtence as a nation ſeemed to depend upon the preſervation of his life. He lived to conduct his country to independence and empire ; he lived to aſſiſt in the formation of its excellent conſtitution, to preſide over its government for ſeveral years, and to give an example to his ſucceſſors in office of the manner in which the duties of that·high ſtation ſhould be filled, to inſure peace, proſperity and happineſs to the nation. That he was thus long preſerved to us merits our gratitude to him ·" by whom kings reign ·and princes decree juſtice."

LASTLY, The mournful occaſion of our preſent meeting leads us to reflect upon the vanity of human grandeur, the vanity of all earthly things. GOD alone is truly great, becauſe he changeth not. Man is continually changing : " At his beſt eſtate he is altogether vanity. His breath goeth forth, he returneth to his earth : in that very day his thoughts periſh ; and wherein is he to be accounted of ?" However dignified in character, however uſeful to others, he muſt yield to the ſceptre of death. " No man hath power over the ſpirit to retain the ſpirit ; ﹐neither hath he power in the day of death; and there is no diſcharge in that war." The rich and the poor, the high and the low muſt all crumble to the ſame undiſtinguiſhed duſt. When the hour of death ſhall come, all earthly grandeur will be found to be vain. It will be of no avail to have acquired the greateſt riches, if deſtitute of a treaſure in the heavenly world : It will be of no avail to have the honor which cometh from man if deſtitute of that which cometh from GOD. Therefore, my brethren, let us be ſolicitous above all things to ſeek an intereſt in him who is " the reſurrection and the life," who died to redeem from ſin and miſery all who ſhall believe in him. Let us aim to ſerve GOD and our generation faithfully, and " do with all our might whatever our hands fhall find to do," remembering that " there is no work, nor device, nor knowledge, nor wifdom in the grave whither we are haften-ing." AMEN.

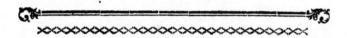

Mr. ELLIOTT's DISCOURSE,

ON THE DEATH OF

GENERAL WASHINGTON.

A

DISCOURSE,

DELIVERED ON

SATURDAY, FEBRUARY 22, 1800,

THE DAY RECOMMENDED BY THE CONGRESS OF THE
UNITED STATES TO LAMENT THE DEATH AND
PRONOUNCE EULOGIES ON THE
MEMORY OF

GENERAL

GEORGE WASHINGTON.

By JOHN ELLIOTT,
PASTOR OF A CHURCH IN GUILFORD.

PUBLISHED BY REQUEST.

HARTFORD:

PRINTED BY HUDSON AND GOODWIN.

1800.

A DISCOURSE, &c.

JOSHUA xxiv. 29.

And it came to pass, after these things, that Joshua, the son of Nun, the servant of the Lord, died.

THE birth of an empire to independence and sovereignty is, to the whole world, an interesting event; interesting in proportion to the probable extent of its future connexions, and the effects this event and these connexions will produce, in distant climates and remote periods of time.—— Few nations, if any, justly appreciating the unalienable rights of human nature, or even their self-interest, can sit unconcerned spectators of the mighty struggle for liberty, in which her votaries and children are called, from time to time, to engage. Ever since the discovery of America, its affairs have deeply claimed the attention and been the subjects of the policy of the kingdoms of Europe. It needed no more than human wisdom to foresee that the vast increase of population, and access to the hidden stores of nature, in a new world, would excite an universal spirit of enterprize, enlarge the boundaries of science, and expand, to a much broader extent, the wings of active and enriching commerce.——Actuated by these views, various nations early made colonial establishments in the newly-discovered country, which, tho not immediately lucrative, promifed, at a future period, permanent and extenfive advantages. Mutual jealoufy between the fovereigns who claimed the right of foil, from difcovery or conqueft, and from whofe dominions fettlers emigrated to thefe diftant regions, foon arole, and a defire to protect and advance the welfare of their infant colonies proved the fource of rancorous and bloody wars.

The Britifh fettlements in North-America were extenfive, and fo happily fituated that they flourifhed to a degree far furpaffing thofe of any other nation. They prefented a wide and inviting profpect for emigration and commerce, and ftreams of opulence, which would naturally increafe with the progrefs made in the cultivation of the wildernefs, flowed back and enriched the native country. That they would, at fome period, arrive to manhood, affert their rights and break by violence, the fhackles of foreign oppreffion, was perfectly confiftent with the natural courfe of human affairs, and early predicted.

A fundamental error in the principle of parliamentary legiflation and a fyftem perfeveringly maintained by the Britifh government evidently calculated to cramp the genius, reprefs the enterprize, and drain the wealth of the colonifts, prepared the American mind for the aufpicious event. Every perfon of difcernment contemplated the conteft as violent, requiring an immenfe facrifice of blood and treafure; but the object was of fuch vaft magnitude, that no facrifice was thought too great, no price too dear, to obtain and fecure heaven-born liberty.

ardor and natural energy of his countrymen, and who, by his addrefs, fhould mould their opinions and conciliate their efteem.—Then was it that the Divine Director turned the eyes of the guardians of the public welfare to the great, the immortal WASHINGTON.

That we may improve this folemn occafion to the glory of the living God, and realize the propriety of a national mourning, let us attend to the following confiderations.

FIRST. God is the all-wife Sovereign of the univerfe and fupreme arbiter of nations.

He is the great Lord over all, the Almighty Ruler of the fkies ; fits enthroned in glory unfading, and crowned with honors everlafting. His kingdom extends to all worlds and all periods, and his dominion will have no end. With fway uncontroled and power irrefiftible, He overrules all 'events on earth. He hath been and will be conftantly and unalterably, carrying on a grand fcheme, in the whole circle of fublunary affairs, for his own glory and the good of his church, from the beginning to the end of time. In the rife and fall of empires and kingdoms, in the mighty revolutions which occur among nations, in the alternate beams of profperity and clouds of adverfity which they experience, the ALMIGHTY difplays his glorious perfections and high fupremacy. Doth a nation rife to eminence and greatnefs, fhine in the arts of peace, or prove fuccefsful in thofe of war ; or is it caft down from the zenith of opulence and glory, overtaken with fad reverfes, and plunged into infamy and ruin, the Lord hath done it. When according to the counfels of heaven, great and highly interefting events and revolutions, in the condition and government of a country, are about to be accomplifhed, divine wifdom ever introduces upon the theatre of life, fuch talents, characters and concurrence of circumftances, as are neceffary for the completion of the work. Such inftruments are prepared for the management of public concerns, that the end defigned will not fail. When the Hebrew tribes were to come up from the land of cruel bondage, MOSES, the fervant of the Lord, was fent, with a divine commiffion, to lead them forth with figns and wonders.—When the vaft continent of America, which for ages, had been embofomed in the pathlefs ocean, and lain hidden from the view of the civilized world, was to be difcovered, COLUMBUS was infpired with an unconquerable fpirit of forefight and enterprize, with dauntlefs fortitude to execute his projected fchemes, and explore unknown feas and diftant regions of the earth.—When the period had arrived that the banners of independence fhould be unfurled in thefe oppreffed colonies, a new empire be erected on the broad bafis of rational liberty, and the United States, fpurning the galling yoke of foreign tyranny, fhould affume a name and rank among fovereign nations, the ALMIGHTY prepared the illuftrious WASHINGTON to organize the untutored band and lead the marfhalled battalions to the bloody combat. Extraordinary and fingularly eminent characters, who foar far above the brighteft of their contemporaries, are not often needed to accomplifh the defigns of Providence. For this end divine power, wifdom and goodnefs will ever provide fit and adequate inftruments ; but characters with uncommon talents and extent of capacities are not raifed up, unlefs fome field is opened for their difplay. A fecond dignified perfonage, tho qualified by the gifts of nature to fhine with unrivalled luftre, like him whofe exit from time, we this day, as a nation, bemoan, will not obtain equal celebrity, until a fcene is unfolded for the ufeful exhibition of the fame fupereminent talents, which rendered him, fo juftly, the glory of his country and the admiration of the world.

9

Among all nations, whether more barbarous or more polifhed, men of military genius have obtained a vaft afcendency in the minds, and received high-founding applaufe from the bulk of mankind. The heroic exploits of fignalized commanders have employed the pen of the hiftorian, the eloquence of the orator, and the fancy of the poet. Undiftinguifhed praife however, is by no means, juft. Unlefs directed by moral principle and improved for the good of mankind, eminent talents are awfully deftructive of human happinefs : Thofe who poflefs them become the curfe of heaven and the fcourge of the human race.

The fame of ALEXANDER hath been borne on every wind. Monarchs graced his triumph and extenfive regions owned his fovereignty. But what were the benefits refulting to mankind from his mighty victories, his extenfive conquefts ? He wept that there was not another world to conquer : With much propriety might the world weep at the appearance of another fuch conqueror !——CÆSAR, at the head of the Roman legions, vanquifhed and fubdued the numerous and valiant tribes, which fpread over the wide extent of territory between Rome and Britain. What advantage has been derived from thefe martial achievements ?—Great warriors have too often been the butchers of their fellowmen ; and the eclat which attended them, has been in proportion to the defolating havoc which marked their progrefs.

But when a man endowed by nature with an exalted genius and evidently formed for great undertakings, applies it uniformly and with its utmoft energy, to the fole benefit of mankind, to the utter exclufion of the idea of private emolument ; when he ftands forth the undaunted champion of liberty, inflexibly determined, at the hazard of every thing dear, to redrefs the grievances of his coun-

B

try, raife her from the duft of foreign proftration, boldly affert her rights and maintain her dignity ; and, having accomplifhed the great object for which his fword was drawn, nobly refufing the reward which his toils and facrifices richly deferved, retiring from public fcenes and employments, to the peaceful fhades of private life ; he exhibits a finifhed pattern of the Man, the Hero, and the Lover of his country. To him, as an agent in the work of the Lord, ought a tribute of gratitude and praife to be returned and beftowed.

II. God fometimes exercifeth a peculiar providence toward an oppreffed people, and by fignal interpofitions faves them from overthrow and ruin.

The two moft remarkable inftances, in the annals of the world, to verify this obfervation, are the Jewifh and American nations.—To refcue the former from under the defpotim of Pharaoh, MOSES was efpecially raifed up, by a peculiar train of circumftances educated at the Egyptian court, where a favorable opportunity for the improvement of his natural talents was enjoyed ; and honored with a commiffion from heaven, in the terrible difplay of divine power, to bring them forth from the houfe of bondage. At the red fea JEHOVAH proclaimed, by his wonderful acts, his determination to fave his chofen people from the hand and cruelty of the proud oppreffor.—The hiftory of events, from the cataftrophe of the red fea to their entrance upon the promifed poffeffion, is replete with wonders.

The fupport of between two and three millions of fouls, in a barren defert, for the fpace of forty years, fo that their food did not fail, nor their cloaths wax old, is one of the moft furprizing and wonder-working providences of which we can poffibly conceive. The flinty rock muft gufh with refrefhing ftreams, the manna muft defcend from heaven, and the quails cover the camp, to nourifh and preferve the Ifrael of the Lord.

11

When their heaven-guided march was compleated and the fair inheritance brightened before their
eyes, as Moses, that eminent instrument of divine
goodnefs to the chofen tribes, was not allowed to
go over Jordan, Joshua was ordained the organ of
divine communication, to lead them to the peaceable poffeffion.—In providing, according to the pe-
culiarity of circumftances, fuch illuftrious characters as Moses and Joshua, furnifhing them with
fuch extraordinary qualifications, and enabling
them to perform fuch wonderful deeds, we fee fpecial tokens of the divine prefence and care.

Clearly manifeft and little lefs fignal, was the
hand of heaven in the American revolution.—In
the conteft which decided the fate of this empire,
on the one hand is feen entering the field, a nation
poffeffed of immenfe wealth ; an eftablifhed fyftem
of drawing into effectual energy its ample refources ; a fleet which rode in triumph on the ocean,
commanded by officers thoroughly fkilled in naval
affairs and infpired with the higheft fentiments of
honor, and manned with feamen, who were inured
to the havoc of death, and whofe pulfe beat high
for the glory of their king and country ; an army,
trained in all the terrible difcipline of war, formidable from its numbers, bold from its fuccefs, e-
quipt with every neceffary for the camp and the
field, and led by Chiefs adorned with laurels gathered on the bloody plains of Europe :—On the
other, a nation is beheld, fpread over a wide extent
of territory, expofed on either fide to hoftile invafion or favage incurfion, without an organized army, or navy, without military ftores or military
knowledge ; without officers to command or foldiers accuftomed to the rigor of fevere difcipline and
fubordination ; deftitute of every requifite for carrying on a war, and having no general government,
to fyftematize public affairs and wifely improve the
great advantages which the God of Nature had be-

ftowed upon the country.—How ftriking the contraft! Calculating on common principles, how vaft
was the fuperiority on the fide of our foes! How
awfully portentous the cloud which then gathered
over America!—But thefe renowned commanders
were captured and the laurels were plucked from
their brows, or their prowefs was unavailing; hardy veterans, by thoufands, invaded our fhores, and
either enriched our fields with their blood, or
yielded to fuperior force. Never was Britifh valor
more completely foiled! Never was Britifh pride fo
deeply humbled as in the lofs of two whole armies
in fo fhort a term!—When the fabric of independence tottered to its bafe, when the fanctuary of liberty was ready to be demolifhed, when the name of
the United States was ready to be blotted out forever, and the illuftrious characters who adorned the
revolution to be branded with eternal infamy, the
Supreme Sovereign faid, Let America be free, and
America was free. " *If it had not been the Lord
who was on our fide, when men rofe up againft us,
then they had fwallowed us up quick, when their wrath
was kindled againft us. Bleffed be the Lord, who hath
not given us a prey to their teeth.*"

There was a particular providence in unfolding
the fcene gradually, in uniting the feelings of a
great people in the abhorrence of tyranny, in rendering the patriots of America willing to run the
moft imminent hazard of property, of fame and
of life, and in having ready a chofen inftrument,
with fome experience and a profound judgment, to
execute the divine purpofe of our political falvation.—The winds, the waves, the ice, and the
floods were made to confpire to attain the fame
end. In the foreign connexions which we were enabled to form; in the lively fympathy of a great
and magnanimous monarch, fince doomed by popular phrenzy to an untimely fate; in the refpect
and obedience paid through the land to a mere

shadow of government, at a time highly favorable
for the uncontrollable paffions of man; in the
events of battles; in the almoft miraculous prefervation of the invaluable life of our heaven-honored
Hero, and in numerous confpicuous inftances, we
trace the fpecial interference of the ALMIGHTY in
the eftablifhment of our independence and empire.

III. The moft eminent and extenfive fervices to
mankind will not fave from death.

This relentlefs and infatiable foe hath triumphed,
and will continue to triumph, over the moft elevated mortals. His dominion is eftablifhed over all
the race of Adam. The great and the fmall, the
high and the low, the honorable and the defpifed,
muft lie down in the grave. MOSES had his tafk
affigned him in life, his fphere of ufefulnefs allotted. The defigns of heaven in preparing him to
act in an extraordinary capacity being accomplifhed,
he was removed from time. JOSHUA, his fucceffor,
acted his part on the theatre of life, in leading the
children of Ifrael to the quiet poffeffion of the
conquered country, and then yielded to the mighty
deftroyer of human kind. The fame may be faid
of the moft affluent, the moft beloved, the moft
honoured among the fons of men. Name CRÆ-
SUS, SOLOMON, or any even the moft renowned
princes, " the brighteft ornaments of thrones and
of humanity," and it will be found that their
earthly career was clofed by the fame melancholy
event. The grim tyrant affaults the fplendid pal-
ace with equal boldnefs and with equal fuccefs, as
the humble cottage. He is not difmayed by the en-
figns of office, the regalia of courts, the elevation
of ranks. Thefe, at a fingle blow, he levels with
the duft and buries in undiftinguifhed ruin. Death
afcends the throne and plunges headlong its high
poffeffor.—Nay, more than monarchs bow to the
fatal ftroke, for WASHINGTON is fallen !—Let not
the greateft of generals, the moft eminent of ftatef-

men, the moſt highly eſteemed and moſt dearly beloved of men, expect to eſcape death, for WASH-
INGTON is fallen ! Let not the man " firſt in war,
firſt in peace, and firſt in the hearts of his countrymen" hope to avoid the deadly arrow, for
WASHINGTON is fallen !—Since the peerleſs trophy
obtained on Calvary's mount, have few ſo ſplendid,
graced the triumph of the king of terrors ! O
Death ! How numerous, how ſignal are thy victories ! In every age, in every country, in every climate, doſt thou diſplay thy ſable enſigns in ſolemn
pomp ! Palaces are in thy dominion and kings are
thy ſubjects. Thou reigneſt in more complete empire than the crowned worms of the duſt ; to-day,
they wield a ſceptre over thouſands and millions of
the human race ; to-morrow, they bow to thine
all-devouring ſword !——Haughty conqueror !
Why could not thy fury be appeaſed by the numerous victims which are conſtantly ſacrificed at thy
ſhrine ? Why didſt thou enforce thy claim upon the
beloved Father of his country ? Why ſpread the
mantle of mourning over a nation, over millions,
at a ſingle blow ?—Never again ſhall ſuch an opportunity be offered, ſuch an object be preſented to
thy dart : And he ſhall riſe and live, when thou
art forever deſtroyed by the almighty power of the
Prince of Peace.

IV. Men of ſuperior excellence ought, while living, to be reſpected, and, when dead, remembered with gratitude.

Good rulers are a diſtinguiſhed bleſſing. They
are the gift of God to any people. The Giver is
not to be forgotten becauſe of the greatneſs of the
gift.—Talents and virtue, in an high degree, are
the great requiſites for thoſe who fill exalted ſtations.
Talents, to be uſeful and efficient, muſt be adapted to the peculiar genius, ſituation and circumſtances of a country. Thoſe which, in their diſplay, would entitle to an high ſeat in the temple of

fame, under fome circumftances, and in fome ftages of fociety, would little conduce, in others, to
the fplendor of high renown. Opportunities for
the exhibition of fuch as claim high and unrivalled
pre-eminence do not often occur. Revolutions in
politics and government ufually open the wideft
field, and prefent the broadeft theatre for the exertion and application of all that is rare, great and
magnanimous. In trying and dark periods in the
ftate of nations, the world hath been aftonifhed, at
times, with the view of a refplendent fun, burfting
from the clouds of obfcurity and beaming with ra-
dient brightnefs in the political horizon. His
fplendors, while they dazzled the eye, have diffufed light over the face of community and fpread
joy to thoufands of trembling hearts.—In feafons
when tempefts fhake the pillars of ancient eftablifh-
ments, and the diforganization incident to material
changes at home clouds the afpect, talents more
original in their nature, and different in their kind,
are required, than in fcenes of public tranquillity,
when the fky is unclouded and the fun fhines with
luftre.

The mariner who, without difficulty or difhonor,
could fteer the fhip, when the furface of the ocean
was fmooth, the breeze of wind gentle and the
noon-day fun lighting the heavens and the earth,
would be driven from the helm, when the face of
the great deep was violently convulfed, the elements, in fierce contention, howled, and the horrors of midnight enveloped the waves and the firmament in impenetrable gloom.

It is to be obferved that a univerfal genius, or a
man endowed with abilities to conduct, with wifdom, energy and fuccefs, civil and military arrangements, is a rare phenomenon. To be crowned with laurels won by valor and fkill in the field of
battle, and to fhine, like the light of heaven, a-
mong the celebrated and diftinguifhed fenators of a

nation is rarely the lot of any mortal.—Virtue is the guide for the profitable and useful improvement of great and splendid talents. Misapplied they resemble the sweeping deluge, the destructive tornado or ungovernable flames. They spread devastation in an hour, which years cannot repair.—How important is it, that great men should also be good men!

When a MOSES, a JOSHUA, a DAVID, a SOLOMON are exalted to be rulers and legislators, they should be honored as chosen of the Lord.—Real merit, without envy or detraction, should receive, from a grateful people, an ample reward. A *worthy* patriot is a glorious title; add to this *disinterested*, and you rise higher in the scale of worth and admiration. When God removes from earthly scenes those who have filled high stations with dignity, usefulness and applause, such dispensations ought not to pass unnoticed. They are deeply interesting to the future welfare of a country. Shall singular worth, shall the unremitted efforts of the most shining talents for public good, shall the most noble achievments, the most heroic enterprizes be forgotten, the moment the mortal remains of the possessors and actors are deposited in the silent vault? Such praise-worthy deeds ought to be recorded on the hearts of their countrymen, more lastingly than on tables of brass. and the blessings enjoyed should ever remind us of the toils, the dangers, and the virtues of those, by whom they were obtained.

The children of Israel testified their solemn and affectionate remembrance of MOSES by mourning, at his death, thirty days.

Let us improve the subject by the following reflections.

1st. God hath designed this land for many important purposes of his glory and the good of mankind.

17

Earthly affairs are controlled by divine wifdom, power and goodnefs. Great were the preparations made, in the ftate of the nations, for the glorious appearance of the Meffiah in the flefh; and the mighty revolutions of the prefent æra are doubtlefs defigned as preparatory fteps to the happy, milennial ftate of the Chriftian church. The whole hiftory of events fince the firft fettlement of this empire, the great things which God hath done for us as a nation, and in fpecial his kind providence in bleffing us with " the Hero of the age," are ftanding teftimonies and evident prefages that aufpicious and extenfive defigns are yet in the womb of time. " The kingdom is the Lord's, and He is governor " among the nations." Our natural and political fituation opens high and animating profpects. Our internal refources are immenfe, and our ftrength increafing with fuch rapidity, that every external preffure may foon be fet at defiance.

The fyftem of the federal government is new in the annals of the world, combining, beyond any example in ancient or modern times, liberty, order and energy. The freedom of religious enquiry, belief and worfhip, fully enjoyed, removes the caufes of heavy grievances among fome nations, and weakens the temptations to infidelity in others. Science diffufes her benign influence among all claffes of citizens. The enterprizing fpirit of America explores every region and corner of the earth for the acquifition of wealth, and the bravery of her martial fons affords the ftrongeft hope, that when refiftance to foreign foes is neceffary, by the bleffing of heaven, it will not be without fuccefs.

This land feems deftined by heaven to be an afylum for the perfecuted and oppreffed among the nations of Europe. From the corruption, tyranny and butcheries which deftroy the greateft portion

c

of human felicity on the eaftern continent, may they
fly to thefe hofpitable fhores and fhare in the ineſtimable bleſſings of liberty. The foundation feems
evidently laid for vaſt improvement in politics, fcience and morals ; for an happy, flourifhing and powerful empire ; an empire, refpected for its government, its laws, its purity of religion, its commerce
and its numbers ; a theatre on which the glories of
the Redeemer's kingdom will, in the latter day, be
illuſtrioufly difplayed.

2d. We learn the mutability of fublunary things.
Statues of brafs are corroded by the gnawing tooth
of time ; the moſt durable monuments of art
crumble to the duſt ; crowns fall from the head.
Cities loofe their magnificence ; empires are buried in the gulph of oblivion ; and all earthly glory
fades. Can it then be furprizing that the moſt beloved, the moſt renowned mortal, fhould, to day,
fhine in the higheſt fplendors of the earth, and to-
morrow lie low at the feet of death ? That this may
be the cafe our affembling in the divine courts this
day is a folemn proof.

The Almighty difpofer of human events hath
commiſſioned death to triumph over WASHINGTON,
the father and the faviour of his country ! A complete delineation of the character, the virtues, the
exploits of this highly diſtinguifhed man, I fhall
not attempt. Even eulogy blufhes when employed
on fo fublime a theme and confeſſes that to do perfect juſtice is beyond her power. His life and his
deeds are the higheſt encom'ums which can poffibly
be beſtowed, and the fame of thefe will blazon, till
time and earth fhall be no more. Future Xeno-
phons fhall record his ever-memorable heroifm ;
future Homers defcribe his glowing ardor amidſt
embattled hoſts—future Miltons invoke the mufe's
aid to tune his praife, and future Robertfons detail the battles he fought, the victories he won, the
heroes he conquered. Greece ſtands abafhed, and

Rome hangs her head ; and in future ages, when the poet, the hiftorian, and the orator have celebrated the fages, the conquerers, the patriots of antiquity, and lavifhed upon them a profufion of praife, the trumpet fhall found ftill louder the name of WASHINGTON and conclude the lift.

The defcription given above will fhew the feeble and deftitute fituation of the colonies when WASHINGTON was appointed commander in chief of their forces. It was foon found that the public confidence was not mifplaced.

During the revolutionary war he difplayed fuch talents as faved his country and aftonifhed the world. With great means, great effects may be produced ; but to produce great effects, with fmall means, requires much higher wifdom. Here the American Hero fhone, like the fun in the firmament. In retreating where a ftand would have been ruin to the caufe, even when greatly cenfured ; in concealing the real ftate of his force from his enemies and from his own army ; and in various ways, annoying, diftreffing and efcaping the foe, he exhibited confummate prudence and forefight. Had it not been for the peculiar difafters and embarraffments with which he was neceffitated to contend, one half of the excellencies of his character, the unfhaken fortitude of his mind, and the wonderful extent of his mental refources, would not have been known. Trenton and Princeton will ftand, to the end of time, monuments of his readinefs to feize a favorable opportunity to attack, of his foundnefs of judgment and military addrefs.—His fame foon fpread beyond the Atlantic and one of the firft potentates in Europe did not difdain to place a gallant army under his command.—The independence of his country being eftablifhed, like Cincinnatus, he refigned his eminent ftation, and, accompanied by the plaudits and fervent prayers of millions, retired to the cultivation of his eftate. Had CÆSAR, or had CROMWELL commanded the army, a military despotifm would have been eftablifhed ; but WASHINGTON's magnanimity was equal to his fuccefs !

By the unanimous fuffrages of his fellow-citizens was he repeatedly called to the prefidency of the United States. At length he retired from public life, fondly hoping to fpend the evening of his days in that retreat for which he had long and ardently fighed. A gathering cloud involves the nation in darknefs and threatens the demolition of the noble fabric cemented by the blood of thoufands; his country again calls ; the eye of age brightens into youth, the fword is drawn ; when, lo, the fummons of death arrives !—He loved his country, he adored the fupreme Ruler, afcribing to Him the glory of all fuccefs ; he beheld the great objects for which he embarked upon the tempeftuous ocean of public life obtained, and, magnanimous and ferene in death, hath bid the earth adieu.

WASHINGTON, the pride of America, the glory of the age, now fleeps in the land of filence and of death. The brighteft fun in our national horizon is gone down to rife no more. While to the high mandate of heaven's fovereign, with humble fubmiffion, Americans bow, well may they weep ! The Hero, the patriot, the fage ; their friend, their benefactor is laid in the duft. Does a family gather around the bed of a fond, a dying parent, and pour out a flood of tears, when the folemn hour of parting arrives ; and fhall not the children of Columbia weep, when the father of his country lies low ? Yes. Let the tear of fenfibility gliften in every eye. Another fuch occafion will never call. Ye war-worn foldiers, know that your beloved commander is configned to the tomb. Ye aged fires, know that he, under whom your fons have fought, and bled, and died, is now no more ! Ye virgins, teftify your grief that your friend, your father, your guardian has fled. Let the whole mafs of people feel and realize, that the great defender of their rights, himfelf " a fenate" and " an hoft," hath finifhed his earthly career.

> " From Vernon's facred hill dark forrows flow,
> Spread o'er the land, and fhroud the world in woe.
> Afk hoary age from whence his forrows come,
> His voice is filent, and his forrow dumb ;
> Enquire of infancy, why droops his head,
> The pratler lifps—Great WASHINGTON is dead."
> In fad refponfes founds from fhore to fhore,
> " Our Friend, our Guide, our Father is no more."

But let not the hearts of Americans defpond. A noble and majeftic pillar in the national fabric is broken, but the corner ftone is not removed. He who rendered our deplored chief fo rich a bleffing, lives forever ; and tho' he hath now fpread darknefs about our paths, can eafily difpel the cloud and caufe the fun to fhine.—Characters, wifely felected and worthy of public honors, adorn our fenates, dignify our tribunals of juftice, and fill the executive departments of government.

Trained under the aufpices of the beft of inftructors, military leaders are ready to draw the fword, and, under the fanction of the Almighty, lead the fons of liberty to fame, to glory and triumph.

American youth ! Let the hallowed flame continue to burn in your bofoms. On you devolves the arduous, but the glorious tafk to fave your country from anarchy, from infamy, from fubjugation. By the blood which hath fertilized the plains, by the bones which have whitened in the fun, by the memory of the valiant heroes who have fallen ; by the numberlefs bleeding hearts, the bitter offspring of the revolution; by the hopes and profpects of pofterity—by the afhes of WASHINGTON, be adjured to prove yourfelves worthy of an inheritance, refcued from the fangs of tyranny at a price fo dear !

Let the meritorious fervices of our departed Hero and his patriotic brethren in the field, whether
they nobly fell or furvived the furious ftorm, fecure
to them their juft reward, a " deathlefs fame."
Let his " fpotlefs example" be followed, his wife
moral and political maxims inculcated and remembered, his virtues, many and eminent, public and
private, be admired, be imitated; his invaluable
legacy be engraven upon every heart. Let us praife
the Lord that he hath lived in an high degree of
ufefulnefs, enjoyed the love and the admiration of
his countrymen to the concluding fcene, far beyond HANNIBAL, COLUMBUS, and a long train of
the moft worthy patriots; and come at laft to the
grave in a good old age, with untarnifhed glory and
unfullied honor.

As the conclufion of the whole ; remember that
death will fooner or later cut down every individual.—Earthly honors are fading, worldly glory tranfitory. Thofe of heaven are immortal ; that of
the upper world perpetual. The approbation of
our judge will be infinitely more important than the
wailing and lamentation of millions. This alone
is our paffport to the kingdom of glory. Let me
then point you to an example compared with which
that of WASHINGTON is obf ured with clouds, and
to the death of a fuperlatively dignified perfonage,
which caufed nature to agonize with groans, that
of the glorious and exalted Redeemer. Calvary's
mount hath witneffed the folemn and tremendous
fcene of a divine perfon yielding up the Ghoft.—
Our beloved Hero lies in the folitary tomb, but the
celeftial conqueror burft the bands of death, the
bars of the grave, and afcended to the realms of
eternal light and day. High in the heavens, manfions are prepared for the recepti n of all who fin-
cerely believe. To that world of peace, and joy,
and glory fhall all his faithful followers, in God's

23

own time be exalted.   The valley of death is firſt to
be traverſed, but the light will ſoon burſt forth and
bright proſpects open to view.—To thoſe bliſsful
regions may we all aſcend through the infinite merit of the great Redeemer !

A

DISCOURSE,

DELIVERED AT

NEW-HAVEN,

FEB. 22, 1800;

ON THE CHARACTER

OF

GEORGE WASHINGTON, Efq.

AT THE

REQUEST OF THE CITIZENS;

▼▼▼▼▼▼▼▼▼▼▼▼▼▼▼▼▼▼▼▼▼▼▼▼▼▼

By TIMOTHY DWIGHT, D.D.
PRESIDENT OF YALE-COLLEGE.

▲▲▲▲▲▲▲▲▲▲▲▲▲▲▲▲▲▲▲▲▲▲▲▲

PRINTED BY THOMAS GREEN AND SON,

NEW-HAVEN:

1800.

A PROCLAMATION,

BY THE PRESIDENT *of the United States of America.*

WHEREAS the Congrefs of the United States have this day refolved, " That it be recommended to the People of the United States to affemble on the 22d day of February next, in fuch numbers and manners as may be convenient, publicly to teftify their grief for the death of general George Wafhington, by fuitable eulogies, orations and difcourfes, or by public prayers:" and " That the Prefident of the United States be requefted to iffue a Proclamation for the purpofe of carrying the foregoing refolution into effect." Now THEREFORE, I John Adams, Prefident of the United States of America, do hereby proclaim the fame accordingly.

Given under my hand and the feal of the United States, at Philadelphia, the fixth day of Junuary, in the year of our Lord, one thoufand eight hundred, and of the Independence of the United States the twenty-fourth.

JOHN ADAMS.

By the Prefident,

TIMOTHY PICKERING, *Secretary of State.*

IN purfuance of the foregoing proclamation, the citizens of New-Haven convened and appointed a committee, with full powers, to make fuitable arrangements for a public teftimony of the refpect of the citizens for the memory of General George Wafhington. Purfuant to this appointment the committee agreed on the following exercifes and marks of grief, which were exhibited on the 22d inftant.

AT fix o'clock in the morning, the folemnities of the day were introduced by the tolling of all the bells for half an hour. The tolling was repeated at nine and twelve o'clock. The flag of the United States was displayed, on the public fquare, at half ftaff, and the fhipping in the harbour difplayed colours, through the day, at half maft.

4

AT two o'clock P.M. the citizens affembled, in unufual concourfe, at the brick Meeting-houfe, where were performed the following exerciſes :

1. A Funeral Anthem.
2. An appropriate Prayer, by the Rev. James Dana, D. D.
3. Muſic.
4. A Sermon, by the Rev. Preſident Dwight.
5. The reading of Gen. Waſhington's farewell Addrefs, to the Citizens of the United States, on declining public Life, by the Rev. Bela Hubbard.
6. A pertinent Prayer, by the Rev. John Gemmil.
7. A Funeral Dirge.

THE citizens of both ſexes wore, on the left arm, black crape, or ribbons, as badges of mourning ; the pulpit was dreffed in black ; fecular bufinefs was fufpended ; the exercifes were folemn and impreffive ; and the attention and conduct of the citizens evidenced their gratitude for the eminent fervices, and their veneration for the diftinguifhed virtues, of the illuftrious man, whofe death they deplored.

AT a Meeting of the Committee of Arrangements, February 24, 1800, RESOLVED, That the thanks of the citizens of New-Haven be prefented to the Rev. Timothy Dwight, D.D. for his pertinent and eloquent Difcourfe, delivered on the 22d inftant, and that a copy be requefted for publication.

RESOLVED, That the proceedings of the town, the difcourfe, and General Waſhington's farewell addrefs, be publifhed for the benefit of the citizens of New-Haven, and to perpetuate the remembrance of the melancholy occafion.

By order of the Committee,

HENRY DAGGETT, *Chairman.*

———▼▼▼▼▼▼▼▼▼▼▼▼▼▼▼▼▼▼▼▼▼▼▼———

DEUTERONOMY, XXXIV. 10, 11, 12.

*And there arose not a prophet, since in Israel, like un-
to Moses, whom the Lord knew face to face;
In all the signs and wonders, which the Lord sent
him to do in the land of · Egypt, to Pharaoh, and
to all his servants, and to all his land;
And in all that mighty hand, and in all that great
terror, which Moses shewed in the sight of all Israel.*

TO praise such as have lately died, is the in-
stinctive conduct of sorrow. From those who sur-
round the bed of a departed friend, the first accents,
which succeed the involuntary burst of anguish, are
enumerations of his real or supposed virtues. Even
in the mouths of the intelligent, and in the chambers
of the refined and delicate, the praise is warm and
unqualified, and nature overleaps every bound, raised by artificial decorum. Among nations less enlightened, open and strong commendations of the
dead are inwoven in the established manners, and
demanded by common decency; while, among savages, funeral songs, replete with passionate sentiments, glowing imagery, and excessive panegyric,
are prominent features of national character, and
splendid parts of public celebration.

To this general voice of nature Revelation has
added its supreme sanction. The text, which I have
just now read, is an eulogy of the highest kind.

When we remember the numbers, and the character, of the prophets who followed Mofes ; when we confider that of this number were Samuel, David, Ifaiah, and Daniel ; we cannot but feel,, that it would have been difficult to afcribe to him a more honorable character.

WHAT then has been the caufe, that no efforts of the mind have been lefs approved, than funeral eulogies ; and that an infipid panegyric is become proverbial phrafeology ? Has it not been, on the one hand, that grief, and not reafon, has given birth to the praife, and that grief alone can admit its truth, or feel its propriety ? Has it not been, on the other hand, that the Eulogift has come, in form, to make the moft of his theme ; to create a character which has not exifted, and to fupply worth which' he does not find ; to difplay his ingenuity, rather than the features of the deceafed ; and to gain applaufe for his own talents, rather than refpect for the fubject of his panegyric. For thefe, or fome other reafons, few attempts of this nature have fucceeded ; and the effort to gain efteem for the dead has terminated in producing contempt for the living.

BESIDE the difficulties, always attendant on attempts of this nature, the prefent occafion involves fome, which are peculiar. The fubject of eulogy at this time is fo fplendid, as to induce, and authorize, every man to demand all that can be faid by the human genius, and to ftipulate for its nobleft efforts only ; fo near to the heart of an American, as to warrant an unqualified rejection of whatfoever falls beneath its expectations, and its wifhes ; fo often and fo illuftrioufly panegyrized, both at home and abroad, as to leave little chance for novelty, or fuccefs. The very name of Wafhington has become an equivalent to the higheft human dignity and worth, and all additions to it have long paffed rather for the mere unburdening of an American heart, than for the means of honouring his chara&er. Where fo much is demanded, and fo little will be accepted, temerity only can furnifh confidence to the fpeaker, and perfuade him, that he fhall fatisfy the wifhes of his fellow citizens.

To fome perfon, however, the tafk, affigned to me, muft have fallen ; and to none could it have fallen without anxiety. I have ventured upon it, with an intention to perform a duty, not with a hope to fulfil expe&ation. Funeral panegyric I have always fhunned ; and would more willingly have avoided it on this occafion, than on any other.

THIS apology, which may probably feem long, and ufelefs, will, it is hoped, neverthelefs prove of fome ufe to the fpeaker. It is hoped, that it will, in fome degree, juftify the undertaking, and explain and vindicate the manner in which it will be executed ; that it will lead my audience to expe&, and fhew the reafons why I fhall exhibit, a plain and chaftized account of my fubje& ; and that it will induce them to confider what I fhall affert, however it may differ from their opinions and feelings, as believed and felt by me.

HUMAN greatnefs is of many kinds, and appears under many forms ; but the diverfities of perfonal greatnefs have their foundation in the intelle&, and in the heart. How far this is, in either cafe, the refult of the original ftru&ure of the mind, and how far of effort and acquifition, it is probably impoffible for man to determine. We fee fome a&ually great ; but the caufe, and the means, have in a degree been, hitherto, in a ftate of uncertainty.

IN all cafes, in which this diftin&ion has been atchieved, whether intelle&ual, or moral, there muft

to fuperior endowments and attainments, be fuper-
added, by Providence, a happy field, in which they
may be advantageoufly difplayed.   Some object
feen, and felt, by the mind, to be of fufficient importance to juftify high and ardent efforts, and to
repay the labours, and the fufferings, which attend
them, muft be prefented to the underftanding, and
lay hold on the heart.   In this fituation, if ever,
the man rifes above himfelf, feels his powers in a
new manner, exerts talents of which he was before
unconfcious, and virtues which had hitherto been
dormant.   Himfelf, as well as the world, is aftonifhed at what he is, and at what he does ; the fifh-
erman is changed into an Apoftle ; the* trader of
Mecca becomes the founder of a religion, and an
empire, embracing a fourth of mankind ; and the
‡leader of a gang of thieves afcends the throne of
Perfia, and places beneath his feet the fcepter of
Hindoftan.

AMONG thofe occafions, which have lifted man
above his ordinary fphere, none have difplayed with
more fplendor, either talents, or virtues, than the
revolutions of religion and empire.   The conqueft
of nations, and the fubverfion of governments, formed, as well as exhibited, Nebuchadnezzar, Cyrus,
Alexander, Hannibal, Cæfar, Ghengis, Timur-bec,
Kouli Khan, Frederic, 2d. Hyder Ali, and various
others of a fimilar character.   To all thefe the pride
of victory, the extenfion of conqueft, and the increafe
of dominion, rofe in full view ; and, with a fafci-
nation wholly irrefiftible, prompted them to con-
trive, to dare, and to attempt, beyond the limits of
ordinary belief.   When we contemplate thefe men,
however, our admiration is always mingled with
difguft ; and the few things in their characters, which
claim efteem, are loft in the multitude of thofe,

---

* Mahommed.   ‡ Nadir Kouli Khan.

9

which force abhorrence. The luftre fhed around them is gloomy and difmal ; a glare of Avernus ; a " darknefs vifible ;" at which the eye gazes with a mixture of aftonifhment and horror. We ficken, while we read their exploits ; and blufh, that fuch fcourges of the world fhould have claimed a common nature with ourfelves.

But there have been happier occafions for calling into action, and into light, the fuperiour faculties of man. Empire. and religion have, at times, changed for the better. Men have arifen, whom the world has not only admired, but revered, and loved ; to whom applaufe was not the mere outcry of aftonifhment, but the filent and fteady teftimony of the underftanding, the cheerful and inftinctive tribute of the heart. When oppreffion was to be refifted, government to be reformed, or the moral ftate of mankind to be renewed, the Ruler of the Univerfe has always fupplied the means, and the agents. Where to the human eye the whole face of things has worn an uniform level ; where every family was loft in infignificance, and every citizen was a peafant, and a flave ; energy, afleep under the preffure of weary circumftances, and talents, veiled by humble and hopelefs obfcurity, have been roufed into action, and pufhed forward to diftinction and glory.

Among the men, who, at fuch periods, have rifen to eminence, the Prophet, who is the fubject of my text, is unqueftionably the firft. In all the talents which enlarge the human mind and all the virtues which ennoble the human heart, in the amiablenefs of private life and the dignity of a ruler, in dangers hazarded and difficulties overcome, in fplendor of deftination and the enjoyment, and proofs, of divine complacency, he is clearly without a rival. Companions, perhaps fuperiors, he

B

may find in some single walk of greatnefs ; but in the whole progrefs he is hitherto alone.

FOR this preeminence he was plainly fitted by nature, and education, by the manner of his life, and the field of his employment. Born with a foul fuperior to his kind, educated in the firft fchool of wifdom, trained to arms, and to policy, in the moft improved and powerful court in the world, and nurtured in wifdom ftill more fublime in the quiet retreats of Midian, he came forth to his great fcene of public action, with the moft happy preparation both for fuccefs and glory. God was about to accomplifh a more important revolution than had ever taken place, and had formed and finifhed the inftrument, which fo illuftrious a defign required.

IN whatever courfe of life, in whatever branch of character, we trace this great man, we find almoft every thing to approve, and love, and fcarcely any thing to lament, or cenfure. When we fee him at the burning bufh, facrificing his diffidence to his duty, and refolving finally to attempt the firft great liberation of mankind; when we accompany him to the prefence of Pharaoh, and hear him demand the releafe of the miferable victims of his tyranny; when we behold him laying Egypt wafte, and fummoning all the great engines of terror and deftruction to overcome the obftinacy and wickednefs of her monarch ; when we follow him to the Red Sea, and behold the waters divide at his command, to open a paffage for the millions of Ifrael; and at the fame command return, to deluge the Egyptian hoft; when we trace him through the wonders of Sinai, and of the wildernefs ; when we mark his fteady faith in God, his undoubting obedience to every divine command, his unexampled patriotifm, immovable by ingratitude, rebellion, and infult, his cheerful communication of every office of power and

profit to others, and his equally cheerful exclufion
of his own defcendants from all places of diftinction ;
when we confider his glorious integrity in adhering
always to the duties of his office, unfeduced by
power and fplendour, unmoved by national and fingular homage, unawed by faction and oppofition,
undaunted by danger and difficulty, and unaltered
by provocation, obloquy, and diftrefs ; when we
fee him meek beyond example, and patient and perfevering, through forty years of declining life, in
toil, hazard, and trial ; when we read in his writings
the frank records of his own failings, and thofe of
his family, friends, and nation, and the firft efforts
of the hiftorian, the poet, the orator, and the lawgiver; when we fee all the duties of felf government,
benevolence, and piety, which he taught, exactly
difplayed in a life approximating to angelic virtue ;
when we behold him the deliverer of his nation,
the reftorer of truth, the pillar of righteoufnefs, and
the reformer of mankind ; his whole character fhines
with a radiance, like the fplendour, which his face
derived from the Sun of Righteoufnefs, and on
which the human eye could not endure to look.
He is every where the fame glorious perfon ; the
Man of God; felected from the race of Adam ;
called up into the mountain, that burned with fire ;
afcending to meet his Creator ; embofoming himfelf in the clouds of Sinai ; walking calmly onward
through the thunders and lightnings ; and ferenely
advancing to the immediate prefence, and converfe,
of Jehovah. He is the greateft of all prophets ;
the firft type of the Saviour ; conducted to Pifgah,
unclothed of mortal flefh, and entombed in the duft,
by the immediate hand of the Moft High.

In a fphere, in fome refpects lefs fplendid, but
in the eye of wifdom and virtue fcarcely lefs honourable, Paul, alfo, rofe to finifhed glory and greatnefs, as the enlightener, and reformer of mankind.

He was not, like Mofes, the emancipator of a nation, the head of a new church, or the founder of an empire; but he was the moft illuftrious follower of the Son of God, in eftablifhing Chriftianity, and in accomplifhing the falvation of men. No labours of man claim a higher moral diftinction, than his; no mind was ever fo expanded, or elevated, with the nobleft knowledge; no heart was probably ever warmed with more various, or more exalted virtue. No man ever ftruggled more firmly with dangers; or rofe more glorioufly above difficulties; regarded friends with more affection, or enemies with more compaffion; felt for himfelf lefs, or his fellow men more; or attained a more fublime and unmingled piety, than Paul. To his labours mankind are, directly, more indebted, than to thofe of any other man, for the moral wifdom, the virtue, the peace, and the happinefs, which they now enjoy.

Such excellence we are not to look for among thofe, who have received no fupernatural affiftance; yet, in fimilar revolutions of empire, fimilar emancipations of mankind, and fimilar renovations of the human character, both talents and virtues have appeared with high luftre and dignity. As proofs of this affertion, many names of no fmall celebrity might be recited here, were it neceffary; but it will be fufficient for the prefent occafion, to mention three only, as diftinguifhed, in my view at leaft, above others. Thefe are the firft, and fecond Guftavus, of Sweden, and Alfred the Great, of England. Were not his character clouded by fome ferious defects, I fhould add to this lift Henry the fourth, of France.

The firft Guftavus accomplifhed for Sweden what the great man, whofe character and death we are affembled to commemorate, accomplifhed for us; a deliverance from political thraldom, and the

eftablifhment of political freedom and fafety. Illuftrioufly defcended, diftinguifhed in early youth for
a feries of honourable actions, and already the object of governmental confidence and public hope,
he was trepanned by the treachery of Chriftiern the
third, of Denmark, one of the moft faithlefs, proud,
and bloody tyrants, that ever difgraced the name
of man; was thrown into prifon, and fecretly ordered to be put to death; folely becaufe his claims of
power in Sweden were great, and his worth gave
the faireft promife of feeing them fubftantiated.
Releafed from his dungeon by the good offices of a
generous Danifh Nobleman, he efcaped through
many dangers to his native country. There friend-
lefs, forfaken, feen only to be fhunned, and known
only to excite the dread of death for not betraying
him to Chriftiern, he at length betook himfelf to the
mountains of Dalecarlia; a province yet but half
fubdued, and inhabited by a generous band of peafants, glowing with the unconquerable love of liberty. Here unknown but by diftant rumour, without
authority, without a friend, without a fhilling, and
hunted by the Ufurper and his creatures through
every folitude and cell, he wrought in the mines,
to procure his daily bread. But fuch a man cannot
be long obfcured. The peafants of Dalecarlia he
found ftill brave and fincere, and boldly invited them
to victory and freedom. Charmed by his dignity
and gracefulnefs of perfon and demeanour, fafcina-
ted by his eloquence, and fecure under his conduct
and bravery, thefe plain men followed him eagerly
into the field of conflict; to any other a field of defpair; to him, of hope and triumph. At their head,
he met the veterans of Denmark, only to defeat
them; and fat down before their caftles, only to
take them. Within a fhort period, he overran, and
redeemed the whole of his native country; every
where prefent; the animating, informing, directing

principle of the army, and of the nation ; and by the unanimous voice of the Estates was advanced to the throne. In this high station, enjoying every testimony of public respect short of adoration, for his distinguished wisdom, gallantry, patriotism, and piety, he revived the agriculture, renewed the wasted cities and villages, restored the commerce, re-established and improved the justice, secured the liberty, reformed the religion, and engrossed the hearts, of his grateful nation. " In all other respects," says the Catholic* writer of his life, " except the introduction of Lutheranism into his kingdom, he deserves the praise and admiration of posterity."

THE second Gustavus, having, from the age of 18, reigned in Sweden, with singular wisdom, equity, and glory, for twenty years, appeared in Germany, 1631, in the illustrious character of Defender of the Protestant religion, against the last great efforts of the Catholics, in that country, for its destruction; and gloriously lost his life in establishing the cause, for which he died. He is thus described by a respectable modern historian.§

" No prince, ancient or modern, seems to have possessed in so eminent a degree, as Gustavus Adolphus, the qualities of the hero, the statesman, and the commander ; that intuitive genius which conceives, that wisdom which plans, and that happy combination of courage and conduct which gives success to an enterprise. Nor was the military progress of any leader equally rapid, under circumstances equally difficult; with an inferiour force, against warlike nations, and disciplined troops, commanded by able and experienced generals."

" BUT Gustavus had other qualities beside those

* Vertot.　　　　§ Russell.

of a military and political kind. He was a pious Chriftian, a warm friend, a tender hufband, a dutiful fon, an affectionate father. The fentiments fuited to all thefe fofter characters are admirably difplayed in a letter from him to *Oxenftiern, written a few days before the battle of Lutzen, in which he loft his life." In this letter is the following memorable paffage.

"Confider me as a man, the guardian of a kingdom, who has ftruggled with difficulties, and paffed thro' them with reputation, by the protection and mercy of heaven; as a man, who loved and honoured his relations, and who neglected life, riches, and happy days, for the prefervation and glory of his country, and faithful fubjects ; expecting no other recompenfe, than to be declared the prince, who fulfilled the duties of that ftation, which Providence had affigned him in the world."

" THE merit of Alfred (fays Hume) both in public and private life, may with advantage be fet in oppofition to that of any monarch or citizen, which the annals of any age or nation can prefent to us. He feems indeed to be the model of that perfect character, which, under the denomination of a fage or wife man, philofophers have been fond of delineating, rather as a fiction of their imagination, than in hopes of ever feeing it really exifting: fo happily were all his virtues tempered together ; fo juftly were they blended ; and fo powerfully did each prevent the other from exceeding its proper boundaries ! He knew how to reconcile the moft enterprifing fpirit with the cooleft moderation ; the moft obftinate perfeverance with the eafieft flexibility; the moft fevere juftice with the gentleft lenity ; the greateft vigour in command with the moft perfect

* His Minifter.

affability of deportment ; the higheſt capacity and inclination for ſcience with the moſt ſhining talents for action ;" * and, let me add, the warmeſt devotion and piety with the utmoſt candour and liberality. " His civil and military virtues are almoſt equally the objects of our admiration ; excepting only, that the former, being more rare among princes, as well as more uſeful, ſeem chiefly to challenge our applauſe."

As a fourth in this dignified groupe, may, with the fulleſt confidence, be placed the hero, ſtateſman, and father, of our own country. I have introduced a ſummary account of theſe great men into this diſcourſe, that by comparing his character with theirs, and ſeeing them ſtand ſide by ſide, my audience may be enabled to form a more accurate eſtimate of his worth. Greatneſs is a term wholly comparative ; its true import is, therefore, to be ſeen by compariſon only. On the one hand, ſuperiority to the common maſs, and on the other approximation, equality, or eminence, with reſpect to ſuch as have been thus ſuperior, is all that is intended by the word. As Moſes and Paul were the greateſt human characters among ſuch as have been ſupernaturally aſſiſted ; and the three princes, whom I have here characterized, were, if I miſtake not, the firſt among thoſe, who have become great by means merely natural ; to ſuſtain a fair reſemblance to theſe men muſt be highly honourable ; to be near them, an enviable diſtinction ; to equal them, the crown of the moſt exalted ambition.

As the ſphere of Paul's exertions was peculiar, he muſt of courſe be paſſed by in ſuch a deſign. As Moſes was inſpired, and ſuſtained by a peculiar agency of the Moſt High, the compariſon with him

* See Note A.

muſt in many reſpeƈts be unfairly inſtituted. Yet a ſtrong reſemblance between him and the hero of our own country is ſo evident, that the recital of it is become almoſt proverbial. The occaſions, the talents, the virtues, the divine interpoſitions, and the iſſue, were ſo ſimilar, as to ſtrike the moſt undiſcriminating eye, and to find an eaſy acknowledgment from every tongue. Particularly, the preeminence of Moſes to all the great men in Iſrael, marked ſo ſtrongly in the text, and the like diſtinƈtion juſtly claimed by the American leader, not only over his countrymen, but over all men of the preſent age, form a moſt honourable ground of compariſon.

THAT General Waſhington is, with propriety, introduced as a proper companion to the three illuſtrious princes, whom I have mentioned above, as a companion, whom, on equal terms, they may be fairly ſuppoſed cheerfully to welcome to their number and rank, will, I truſt, appear from a juſt account of his charaƈter.

THERE are two methods, in which ſuch an account may be advantageouſly given; a recital of what he has done, and an exhibition of the attributes which he manifeſted.

IN very early life, he began to be, in a ſenſe prophetically, diſtinguiſhed for wiſdom and conduƈt ſuperior to his years ; and executed ſo ably ſeveral important commiſſions, which he received from the legiſlature of Virginia, as to ſecure their confidence, and command the applauſe of the whole country. Such truſts have been rarely committed to ſo young a man, and have probably been never better lodged in the hands of any man. That in the exiſting circumſtances ſucceſs was, in one of the caſes, completely atchieved; that, in a ſecond, ſo little diſaſter enſu-

C

18

ed ; and that, in a third, total ruin was prevented ; is plainly and chiefly to be attributed to the skill and firmness of a youth between nineteen and twenty-three, acting in the last case only in a voluntary office.

AFTER acquiring, both in public and private life, the universal esteem, through the following season of peace, he was chosen, in the year 1774, one of the Representatives in the first Congress. Here his former reputation, and the proofs which he daily gave of superiour wisdom and worth, induced that body to choose him, in 1775, commander in chief of the American armies, employed to resist the hostilities of Great-Britain. This hazardous office he accepted with a *modesty, which always accompanies and announces merit, and with a firmness of decision, which no future embarrassment could move. Under a government just formed, and marked with infantine weakness ; in a country composed of separate and deranged sovereignties ; amidst a people now first seriously connected ; at the head of armies formed of mere militia, a band of scouts and yet to be made soldiers, and of officers ignorant of the discipline which they were to teach, and of the movements which they were to guide ; strangers, rivals, and sometimes enemies ; without ammunition, arms, clothes, or money ; enlisted for a summer ; and plunged by inexperience into all the exposures, discouragements, diseases, and miseries, of unprovided military life ; he became the body of union to the people, and to the soldiery, guided the one to wisdom, and led the other to victory. In his own letters,‡ not less illustrious commentaries than those of Cæsar, and on a more glorious war, he is seen, through the veil of his modesty, to have been the pillar, on which the country suspended itself; the

---

* See Note B.   ‡ See Note C.

foul, by which the army was formed, quickened, and actuated. In the midst of the immense and momentous concerns, lying alway on his mind, no want, nor its supply ; no suffering, nor its relief ; no evil, nor its remedy; no improvement in the affairs of the army, or the country, nor the means by which it might be best accomplished ; eluded his attention. He is there proved, and without intending it, to have been the source of almost every important measure, the origin of the great mass of meliorations, in our system.

In this war, for which we were so unfurnished, as to render it, in the eye of sober judgment, more like Quixotism than justifiable enterprise, his cautious wisdom, more necessary, more varied, and more extraordinary, than that of the celebrated Roman, justly gained him, abroad, as well as at home, the title of the American Fabius. To the minds of unskilful, ardent, and partial judges, however, this wisdom, without which we now clearly see our country must have been lost, appeared to result from imbecility and fear. So far did this opinion, together with some concurring circumstances, operate, as to engender a serious attempt to raise a foreigner, in every respect his inferiour, to the supreme command. Had not this childish and wretched attempt been ably and strenuously opposed, had not the great body of officers of distinction solemnly pledged themselves to each other never to serve, while he lived, under any other commander, there is reason to fear, that it would have succeeded. Of this glaring attempt against him his mind, superior alike to favour and to frowns, took no other notice, than what has been buried in silence. Satisfied with himself, and strong in the attachment of those whom he commanded, he rose above every attack, danger, and enemy.

A country, an army, fituated as were ours, carried misfortune in their face. The country was unfkilled and unfurnifhed; and its councils, compofed indeed of great and good men, were yet in no degree verfed in the bufinefs, which they were now called to direct. The army was formed of brave and hardy foldiers, and of gallant and fenfible officers; but it was gathered, and difperfed, in a day; and, when moft neceffary, and prefented with the faireft opportunities of fuccefsful enterprife, had difappeared. Never did he appear greater, than in thefe feafons of trial and depreffion. No enterprifes of his fhine with more luftre, than his decampment from *Long-Ifland, his retreat from General Howe through New-Jerfey, his defcent upon Trenton, † his elufion of Lord Cornwallis at Trenton, his confequent march through New-Jerfey, in which he defeated the Britifh corps at Princeton, and the addrefs, with which he preferved the appearance of a confiderable force at Morriftown, where, through the winter, he had only eleven or twelve hundred men, and thefe under a fucceffive inoculation, to refift the whole Britifh army.

But his military life had alfo its feafons of profperity. His fucceffes were, however, almoft always obtained at the head of a force, inferior to that of his enemy, and of confequence were, in an eminent degree, the refult of his own efforts. Like the illuftrious men, to whom I have compared him, he had the happinefs of ending the great controverfy, in which he had engaged, and in which his country was the ftake, with a final and complete triumph. All that, for which he fought, and that the greateft prize, which excites human contention, he gained; and lived long enough to reap a glorious reward of

* See Note D.   † See Note E.

his labours in the peace and safety, the veneration and blessings, of his countrymen.

His political, was not less honorable than his military, career. When, under the weakness and inefficiency of the Confederation, these States were falling asunder, and tumbling into anarchy and ruin, he contributed, at the head of the General Convention, more, by his wisdom, virtue and influence, than any other man, to the final adoption of the Federal Constitution ; and thus saved his country a second time. Twice summoned by the unanimous voice of the nation to the Presidency of the General Government, he there, in a series of wise, firm, and generous measures, stepped often between the State and destruction. His Proclamation of Neutrality, particularly, was the hinge, on which, at that time, the whole well being of our country turned. No public measure was ever more necessary, more happily timed, or more prudently conducted. To that measure is it probably owing, that we are allowed thus peaceably to assemble, this day, in honour to his memory.

The lustre of all his military and political actions, and the glory of his whole character, apparently incapable of addition, he has nevertheless enhanced by two singular traits of distinction; his refusal to accept of a compensation for his services ; and his repeated, voluntary resignation of his high offices, whilst in the entire possession of universal veneration, and perfectly assured of the unanimous public suffrage. I do not here intend, that great men ought of course to decline pecuniary rewards; or to retire, in all circumstances, from public to private life. It could not have been the duty of either of the princes, whose character I have given. But no duty forbade him to do both ; and in doing both he has secured a glory, which is singular. Nothing could have so discovered his selfpossession, evinced his superiority to ambition, or proved his mind to be the residence of patriotism and principle.

In private life he was the same dignified character. All his affairs were superintended by himself, and were of course always in exact order and prosperous thrift. To his neighbours, to the public, to all men, he was just, generous, and humane; to the * poor a steady, and conspicuous benefactor; and to his family whatever is found in the fullest and most amiable discharge of the domestic duties.

Through the plantation, on which he resided, ran a stream, stored with fish. This fishery two days in the week he made, together with his own boats and nets, the property of the surrounding poor; and frequently directed his servants to aid them in taking and curing their booty.

In the course of the war, he wrote, as I have been well informed, to his friends in Virginia, a proposal to free his servants, should the Legislature think it consistent with the general welfare. This plan he has realized in his will; and the public are already informed, that it will be speedily executed by his most respectable Executrix.

‡

After the surrender of Yorktown, he returned, at the end of eight years absence, to visit his family. His servants had voluntarily arranged themselves in two lines, from his mansion house to the creek which runs before the door. When he came in sight, these humble and affectionate domestics sent up a shout of joy, and uttered an extravagance of transport; the women by shrieking, beating their breasts, and rending their hair; and the men by cries and tears, and all the gesticulations, with which nature,

See Note F.

23

in uninformed and unpolifhed fociety, gives vent to
exceffive paffion. When he had croffed the creek,
he delayed his progrefs to his beloved abode, to
fhake all the adults by the hand, and to fpeak ten-
derly and affectionately to the children. " Never,"
faid the gentleman, from whom I received this information, " was I fo delightfully affected, except
at the furrender of Yorktown ; and then, only becaufe I confidered the independence of my country
as fecured."

On the attributes, manifefted by this great man
in his conduct, I beg leave to make the following
obfervations.

General Washington was great, not by means
of that brilliancy of mind, often appropriately term-
ed genius, and ufually coveted for ourfelves, and
our children ; and almoft as ufually attended with
qualities, which preclude wifdom, and depreciate
or forbid worth; but by a conftitutional character
more happily formed. His mind was indeed inven-
tive, and full of refources ; but its energy appears
to have been originally directed to that which is
practical and ufeful, and not to that which is fhewy
and fpecious. His judgment was clear and intuitive beyond that of moft who have lived, and feemed inftinctively to difcern the proper anfwer to the
celebrated Roman queftion ; * Cui bono erit ? To
this his inceffant attention, and unwearied obfervation, which nothing, whether great or minute, efcaped, doubtlefs contributed in a high degree. What
he obferved he treafured up, and thus added daily
to his ftock of ufeful knowledge. Hence, although
his early education was in a degree confined, his
mind became poffeffed of extenfive, various, and exact information. Perhaps there never was a mind,

* What good purpofe will it anfwer ?

on which theoretical speculations had less influence, and the decisions of common sense more.

At the same time, no man ever more earnestly or uniformly sought advice, or regarded it, when given, with more critical attention. The opinions of friends and enemies, of those who abetted, and of those who opposed, his own system, he explored and secured alike. His own opinions, also, he submitted to his proper counsellours, and often to others; with a demand, that they should be sifted, and exposed, without any tenderness to them because they were his; insisting, that they should be considered as opinions merely, and, as such, should be subjected to the freest and most severe investigation.

When any measure of importance was to be acted on, he delayed the formation of his judgment until the last moment; that he might secure to himself, alway, the benefit of every hint, opinion, and circumstance, which might contribute either to confirm, or change, his decision. Hence, probably, it in a great measure arose, that he was so rarely committed; and that his decisions have so rarely produced regret, and have been so clearly justified both by their consequences and the judgment of mankind.

With this preparation, he formed a judgment finally and wholly his own; and although no man was ever more anxious before a measure was adopted, probably no man was ever less anxious afterward. He had done his duty, and left the issue to Providence.

To all this conduct his high independence of mind greatly contributed. By this I intend a spirit, which dares to do its duty, against friends and

25

enemies, and in profperous and adverfe circumftances, alike ; and which, when it has done its duty,
is regardlefs of opinions and confequences.

Nor was he lefs indebted to his peculiar * firmnefs. He not only dared to act in this manner,
but uniformly fuftained the fame tone of thought
and feeling, fuch, as he was at the decifion, he ever
after continued to be ; and all men defpaired of operating on him unlefs through the medium of conviction. The fame unchanging fpirit fupported
him through every part of his aftonifhing trials, during the war ; and exhibited him as exactly the
fame man after a defeat, as after a victory; neither
elated nor depreffed, but always grave, ferene, and
prepared for the event.

From other great men he was diftinguifhed by an
exemption from favouritifm. No man ever fo en-
groffed his attachment, as to be fafe, for a moment,
from deferved reproof, or cenfure ; nor was any
man ever fo difrelifhed by him, as, on that account,
to fail of receiving from him whatever applaufe, or
fervices, his merit could claim. Hence his friends
feared, and his enemies refpected him.

His moderation and felf government were fuch
that he was always in his own power, and never in
the power of any other perfon. Whatever paffions
he felt, they rarely appeared. His conduct, opinions, and life, wore unufually the character of mere
intellect. Hence he was never found unguarded,
or embarraffed ; but was always at full liberty to do
that, and that only, which expediency and duty demanded. A ftriking inftance of this trait in his
character is feen in the well known fact ; that he ne-

D

* See Note G.

ver exculpated himfelf from any charge, nor replied
to any calumny. His accufers, for fuch he had,
had opportunity to make the moft of their accufa-
tions; his calumniators, if their confciences permitted, to fleep in peace.

His juftice was exact, but tempered with the utmoft humanity, * which the occafion would fuffer.
His truth no fober man, who knew him, probably
ever doubted. Watchful againft his own expofures
to error, he was rarely found erring ; jealous of doing injuftice, if he has done injuftice, it is yet, I believe, unrecorded.

His refervednefs has been at times cenfured. To
me it appears to have been an important and neceffary characteriftic of a perfon fituated as he was.
In familiar life a communicative difpofition is generally pleafing, and often ufeful ; in his high ftations
it would have been dangerous. One unguarded or
ambiguous expreffion might have produced evils, the
remedy of which would have been beyond even his
own power. No fuch expreffion is recorded of him.

His punctuality was extreme. He rofe always
with the dawn ; he dined at a given minute ; he
attended every appointment at the moment. Hence
his bufinefs public and private was always done at
the proper time, and always beforehand.

No perfon appears to have had a higher fenfe of
decorum, and univerfal propriety. The eye, following his public and private life, traces an unex-
ceptionable propriety, an exact decorum, in every
action ; in every word ; in his demeanour to men of
every clafs ; in his public communications ; in his
convivial entertainments; in his letters; and in his

* See Note H.

164

familiar converfation ; from which bluntnefs, flattery, witticifm, indelicacy, negligence, paffion, and
overaction, were alike excluded.

FROM thefe things happily combined, always
feen, and feen always in their native light, without
art, or affectation, it arofe, that, wherever he appeared, an inftinctive awe and veneration attended
him on the part of all men. Every man, however
great in his own opinion, or in reality, fhrunk in his
prefence, and became confcious of an inferiority,
which he never felt before. Whilft he encouraged
every man, particularly every ftranger, and peculiarly every diffident man, and raifed him to felf-pof-
feffion, no fober perfon, however fecure he might
think himfelf of his efteem, ever prefumed to draw
too near him.

WITH refpect to his religious character there have
been different opinions. No one will be furprifed at
this, who reflects, that this is a fubject, about which,
in all circumftances not involving infpired teftimony,
doubts may and will exift. The evidence concerning it muft of courfe arife from an induction of particulars. Some will induce more of thefe particulars, and others fewer; fome will reft on one clafs,
or collection, others on another; and fome will give
more, and others lefs, weight to thofe which are induced; according to their feveral modes, and ftand-
ards, of judging. The queftion in this, and all o-
ther cafes, muft be finally determined before another
tribunal, than that of human judgment; and to that
tribunal it muft ultimately be left. For my own
part, I have confidered his numerous and uniform
public and moft folemn declarations of his high veneration for religion, his exemplary and edifying attention to public worfhip, and his conftancy in fecret devotion, as proofs, fufficient to fatisfy every

perſon, willing to be ſatisfied. I ſhall only add, that if he was not a Chriſtian, he was more like one, than any man of the ſame deſcription, whoſe life has been hitherto recorded.

As a warrior, his merit has, I believe, been fully and readily acknowledged ; yet I have doubted whether it has always been juſtly eſtimated. His military greatneſs lay not principally in deſperate ſallies of courage ; in the daring and brilliant exploits of a partiſan : Theſe would have ill ſuited his ſtation, and moſt probably have ruined his cauſe and country. It conſiſted in the formation of extenſive and maſterly * plans ; effectual preparations, the cautious prevention of great evils, and the watchful ſeizure of every advantage ; in combining heterogeneous materials into one military body, producing a ſyſtem of military and political meaſures, concentering univerſal confidence, and diffuſing an ‖ influence next to magical ; in comprehending a great ſcheme of war, purſuing a regular ſyſtem of acquiring ſtrength for his country, and wearing out the ſtrength of his enemies. To his conduct, both military and political, may, with exact propriety, be applied the obſervation, which has been often made concerning his courage ; that in the moſt hazardous ſituations no man ever ſaw his countenance change.

PERHAPS, I ſhall be thought to have dwelt too long, and too minutely, on his character. I hope I ſhall be juſtified, partially at leaſt, when it is remembered, that I have been ſeizing the beſt opportunity, which I ſhall ever enjoy, of teaching, in the moſt affecting manner in my power, the youths committed to my inſtruction, and forming a part of

* See Note I.　　　　　‖ See Note J.

this audience, the way to become great, refpeﬆable, and ufeful.

SucH, my friends and fellow citizens, was the man, whofe death we are aﬄembled to lament, and whofe worth we commemorate. Like the illuﬆrious fubjeﬆ of my text he ﬆands alone in his nation. Like him he was great in the fplendor of defignation, in wifdom, in effort, in fuccefs, in the importance of his talents, virtues and labours, to the nation over whom he prefided in war and peace; in the eﬆimation, the love, and the tears, of his country. On this refemblance I have dwelt lefs, becaufe I fuppofe others have dwelt more; yet I cannot forbear to add, that in the death of thefe diﬆinguiﬁhed men there is a fimilarity not a little ﬆriking. Both died in advanced years, but without any previous decay of faculties, or glory; both left their refpeﬆive nations, not indeed eﬆabliﬁhed, but fo far advanced, as not abfolutely to demand a continuance of their fuperintendency; and both were honored by a national and fpontaneous mourning, as the laﬆ tribute of public veneration. Miraculous fupport our nation could not hope for under any leader; but the fignal interpofitions of Heaven in our behalf, while under his guidance, ought never to be forgotten.

To Americans his name will be ever dear; a favour of fweet incenfe, defcending to every fucceeding generation. The things, which he has done, are too great, too intereﬆing, ever to be forgotten. Every objeﬆ which we fee, every employment in which we are engaged, every comfort which we enjoy, reminds us daily of his charaﬆer. The general peace, liberty, religion, fafety, and profperity, ﬆrongly imprefs, in every place, what he has done, fuffered, and atchieved. When a Legiﬂature aﬄembles

.to enact laws ; when Courts meet to distribute justice ; when Congregations gather to worship God; they naturally, and almost neceffarily, fay "To Wafhington it is owing, under God, that we are here." The farmer purfuing his plough in peace, the mechanic following the bufinefs of his fhop in fafety, afcribes the privilege to Wafhington. The houfe which, uninvaded, fhelters us from the ftorm, the cheerful firefide furrounded by our little ones, the table fpread in quiet with the bounties of Providence, the bed on which we repofe, in undifturbed fecurity, utters, in filent but expreffive language, the memory, and the praife, of Wafhington. Every fhip bears the fruits of his labours on its wings, and exultingly fpreads its ftreamers to his honour. The ftudent meets him in the ftill and peaceful walk ; the traveller fees him in all the profperous and fmiling fcenes of his journey; and our whole country in her thrift, order, fafety, and morals, bears, infcribed in funbeams, throughout her hills and her plains, the name and the glory of Wafhington.

From a fubject fo fingular, and fo edifying, it is not eafy to fail of gaining ufeful practical inftruction. Particularly, the ineftimable benefits which we have derived from the efforts of this great man, cannot but prompt every ingenuous mind to remember, with unceafing gratitude, the goodnefs of God in beftowing upon us fuch a bleffing; God, who formed and furnifhed him for labours fo ufeful, and for a life fo glorious. In what a manner muft the late war have clofed, had the fupreme command of our armies fallen to a weak or unprincipled man ? What would have been its iffue, had the powerful attempt to difplace him, and to fubftitute a foreigner, fucceeded ? Think, I befeech you, of the uniform condition of a conquered nation ; a nation too, confidered as rebels by their conquerors. Think what

it would have been to have had your armies betray-
ed, your lands ravaged, your houses burnt, your
beft citizens brought to the halter, your wives and
daughters difhonoured, and your children houfelefs,
naked, and famifhed. · Think of the long and hopelefs period, through which the broken fpirit, the ruined morals, the wide-fpread ignorance, and the loft
energy, of your country would have perpetuated
your miferies, and prevented your pofterity from e-
merging again to the character of men, and the
bleffings of freemen.

To thefe wretched fcenes contraft your prefent
freedom, peace, fafety, glory, and felicity. To
whom are they owing? The heart fpontaneoufly anfwer, " Firft to God, and next to Wafhington." I
mean not to detract from the wifdom, bravery, or
worth, of his generous companions in the council,
and in the field. Cheerfully do I render to them
the illuftrious honours, which they have merited,
and won ; and heartily do I rejoice to fee thofe, who
ftill live, fuftaining and increafing, in fo many inftances, the high eftimation, which they had fo amply deferved of their country. But in all that I have
faid of their illuftrious Chief they will be the firft to
unite, becaufe they have known him more intimately than others. With them will all their countrymen inftinctively accord ; for his labours have been fo
great, fo good, fo endearing, that they cannot but be
feated in every American heart. May our gratitude to the Author always accompany, and totally
tranfcend, our admiration of the inftrument ; let it
infpirit every reflection, and mingle with every joy.

By him, alfo, are our rulers, at the prefent and
at every future period, taught how to rule. The
fame conduct will ever produce fubftantially the
fame effects ; the fame public well being, the fame

glory, the fame veneration. To be wife and good; to forget, or reftrain, the dictates of paffion, and o-bey thofe of duty; to feek fingly the public welfare, and lofe in it perfonal gratification; to refift calmly and firmly the paffions, and purfue only the interefts, of a nation, is the great fecret of ruling well. When thefe things are exhibited in the ftrong light of example, and crowned with fuccefs and honor, they are taught in a manner beyond meafure more impreffive, than can be found in rules and arguments. Here they are already tried, and proved. Here they are feen furrounded by all their delightful attendants, and followed by all their happy confequences. The conviction produced is complete, the impreffion fupreme. From this great example all rulers may learn wifdom, and our rulers more than any other. They are rulers of the very people, who loved and reverenced him, and who will, of courfe, love and reverence them, fo far as they tread in his footfteps. They, alfo, know and feel his character, and fuccefs, more than is poffible for others. Wifdom, therefore, and duty demand of them, and in a peculiar degree, ftudioufly to copy fo glorious a pattern.

THE youths, alfo, of our country, who wifh to become great, ufeful and honourable, will here find the beft directions, and the moft powerful incitements. To be great, ufeful, and honourable, they muft refemble him. The very actions, which he performed, they may indeed not be called to perform; the fufferings, which he underwent, they may not be obliged to undergo; but the attributes, which he poffeffed and difplayed, muft, in a good degree, be poffeffed and difplayed by them alfo.

LET them particularly remember, that greatnefs is not the refult of mere chance, or genius; that it is not the flafh of brilliancy, nor the defperate fally of ambition; that it is, on the contrary, the combined refult of ftrong mental endowments, - vigorous cultivation, honourable defign, and wife direction. It is not the glare of a meteor; glittering, dazzling, confuming, and vanifhing; but the fteady and exalted fplendour of the fun; a fplendour which, while it fhines with preeminent brightnefs, warms alfo, enlivens, adorns, improves, and perfects, the objects, on which it fhines: glorious indeed by its luftre; but ftill more glorious in the ufeful effects produced by its power. Of this great truth the tranfcendant example before us is a moft dignified exhibition. Let them imitate, therefore, the inceffant attention, the exact obfervation, the unwearied induftry, the fcrupulous regard to advice, the flownefs of decifion, the cautious prudence, the nice punctuality, the ftrict propriety, the independence of thought and feeling, the unwavering firmnefs, the unbiaffed impartiality, the fteady moderation. the exact juftice, the unveering truth, the univerfal humanity, and the high veneration for religion, and for God, always manifefted by this great man. Thus will future Wafhingtons arife to blefs our happy country.

As a nation we may derive from him many kinds of inftruction and profit. This occafion will, however, allow me to infift on one only : The fteady purfuit of that policy, which he fo uniformly and fuccefsfully purfued, and has fo forcibly recommended. In his farewell to the country which he fo loved and defended, we have his laft, and to us his dying words; a moft impreffive recommendation of the beft means of our national welfare; the fum of all the political wifdom, which he had imbibed from his vaft experience; the fubftance of that policy, by which alone our fafety and happinefs can be enfured. In it we are moft affectingly taught to preferve

E

our union ; to defpife trifling difcriminations ; to
reverence our conftitution ; to reject watchfully all
affociations and factions, formed to oppofe it ; to
preferve a well balanced adminiftration ; to encourage literary inftitutions ; to promote, as of primary
importance, morality and religion ; to cherifh public
credit ; to obferve juftice and good faith towards
all nations ; to cultivate harmony and peace with
all ; to indulge antipathies and favouritifm towards
none ; to refift, as dangerous and deadly, all foreign
influence ; to connect ourfelves, politically, as little
as poffible ; and to hold, as much as maybe, a ftrict
and perpetual neutrality towards powers at war.
Here all the national interefts of America are con-
fulted ; here all its political wifdom is fummed up
in a fingle fheet. Nothing can be added, nothing
without injury taken away. How greatly are thefe
precepts recommended by the character of their
author, and by the fuccefs with which they have
been followed in practice. How ftrongly are they
enforced by his labours for our country, by the glory which he attained while fteadily purfuing them,
and by the manner, and the time, in which they
were delivered. Happy, beyond meafure, is it for
thefe States, that he purfued them fo long ; that
they have been fo clofely followed by his able and
virtuous fucceffor ; that they are now the only policy of our government, and the efficient policy of our
country. Happy, beyond meafure, will it be, if
our nation fhould henceforth make them its great
political creed, and the only rule of its political
meafures, at home, and abroad. Faction, party,
diffention, will then ceafe ; murmurs be loft in peace
and profperity ; intrigues be rendered infamous and
hopelefs ; foreign influence no more lift up its fnaky
head ; the danger of invafion vanifh ; the government our country totter no more ; the great political problem, Whether a free and happy Republic
can be durable, be finally and propitioufly folved ;

35

and Americans find lefs reafon to lament, that Wafhington is dead; becaufe they will ftill fee him live in the policy and glory, the fafety and peace, the virtue and felicity, of his beloved country.

N O T E S.

A.

It is a curious fact, that Hume, although he is obliged to recite the extraordinary piety of Alfred, yet totally omits the mention of it in his panegyric on his character.

B.

For fpecimens of the peculiar modefty of General Wafhington fee his written acceptance of the chief command of the army, and his acceptance of the Prefidency. Obferve, alfo, the fact; that he never made his great actions any part of the fubject of his converfation.

C.

There have been many doubts concerning the character of General Wafhington, as a writer. Various perfons have denied, that he was at all, or in any refpectable degree, the author of the feveral compofitions, which are prefented to the public, as his. It may be a fatisfaction to my readers to be informed, that the addrefs to the officers of the army in reply to the letters of Major Armftrong, was penned by his own hand, and never feen by any perfon, until after it was publicly delivered. The originals of his anfwers, alfo, to the addreffes prefented to him, in his laft tour through the Eaftern States, are now on file (as I am informed from high authority) in his own hand.

When he began to read the abovementioned addrefs to the officers, he found himfelf in fome degree embarraffed by the imperfection of his fight. Taking out his fpectacles, he faid, " thefe eyes," my friends, " have grown dim, and thefe locks white, in the fervice of my country, yet I have never doubted her juftice."

The ftyle of General Wafhington, it is obferved by the authors of the Britifh critic, is ftrongly marked with that dignified fimplicity, which is the proof of a great mind.

36

D.

Upwards of 9000 men, together with the great body of artillery, ammunition, horfes, carriages, cattle, provifions, &c. were conveyed from Long-Ifland to New-York, while the Britifh army was fo near, that their men were diftinctly heard at work with their pick-axes and fhovels. The river is near a mile wide, and the decampment lafted thirteen hours; yet the enemy were perfectly ignorant of the meafure, until it was completed. It ought here to be obferved, that, about 2 o'clock in the morning, a thick fog providentially favoured the retreating army.

E.

The firft knowledge, which Lord Cornwallis had of the retreat of General Wafhington, was in the morning; a few minutes before the noife of the cannon at Princeton was heard at Trenton. Sir William Erfkine, it is afferted, urged Lord Cornwallis to place a ftrong body of troops at the bridge over Sanpink Creek; apprehending, that General Wafhington would retreat into the heart of New-Jerfey rather than attempt to crofs the Delaware. This, however, was refufed. Very early in the morning, Lord Cornwallis, while in bed, was informed, that General Wafhington had decamped. Sir William at that moment came in. His Lordfhip afked him, whither he believed the American General to be gone. At that inftant, the artillery was heard from the neighbourhood of Princeton. "My Lord," faid Sir William, "General Wafhington tells you where he is. Do you not hear him calling to you to come after him?"

So filently was this retreat conducted, that the American centinels at the bridge knew nothing of it, until themfelves were ordered to quit their poft.

F.

To the fuperintendant of his eftate he wrote from the army in the following terms.

"Let the holpitality of the houfe be kept up with refpect to the poor. Let no one go hungry away. If any of this fort of people fhould be in want of corn, fupply their neceffities, provided it does not encourage them in idlenefs. I have no objection to your giving my money in charity when you think it will be well beftowed; I mean that it is my defire, that it fhould be done. You are to confider, that neither myfelf nor my wife are in the way to do thefe good offices." See Doctor Trumbull's Sermon. Note.

G.

In a letter from a gentleman in Alexandria to his friend in Hartford, publifhed in the Connecticut Courant, it is declared, that General Wafhington clofed his own eyes. Thus, it appears, his firmnefs forfook him not even in the article of death.

H.

[The humanity of General Wafhington has been impeached, and his character virulently attacked, with refpect to the execution of Major Andre ; but he was moft unjuftly impeached. I am warranted to declare, that he felt and exhibited the tendereft compaffion for that unfortunate young man, and that Major Andre often expreffed to an American officer, of high refpectability, the very polite and humane treatment, which he received from General Wafhington.]

I.

Among the plans devifed by General Wafhington for military operations, and expreffive of his greatnefs of mind, I beg leave to mention the plan for attacking the Britifh on the Delaware, in three points at once, of which only the attack on Col. Rahl at Trenton fucceeded, the others being prevented by the ice; the plan of attacking the troops at Princeton ; the plan of croffing the Brandywine to attack Lord Cornwallis ; the plan of attack at Germantown ; the plan of the bold and fuccefsful attack on Stoney Point ; and the great plan of capturing the Britifh force at Yorktown, involving the complete illufion of Sir Henry Clinton.

To thefe ought to be added a bold and mafterly defign of attacking the whole Britifh force on New-York Ifland, near the clofe of the campaign in 1782. In this defign Col. Talmadge was to have attacked the enemy on Long-Ifland, the preceeding night, with a body of 750 choice troops, and thence to have marched on horfeback to Hell-Gate, where boats, ready to receive him, were to have tranfported the corps to the oppofite fhore. Another body under the command of a General Officer was to have marched to kingfbridge, to attack the enemy in front, and to keep them in full expectation of being affaulted there only : while the main body of the army was to have gone

in boats down Hudfon's River, and, landing below the enemy in the night, was to have made the principal attack on
their rear. The American army was at this time in gieat
force, and perfectly dilciplined and fupplied. Had this defign been attempted, there is every reafon to believe, that,
attacked at one moment, in front, flank and rear, at day-
break, and with total furprife, the triumph over them muft
in all probability have been complete. It was prevented
by a circumftance wholly providential. Two Britifh frigates
moved up the North River the preceeding day, anchored
directly oppofite to the American army, and thus prevented
the intended embarkation. There is not a reafon to imagine, that the Britifh commander had a fufpicion of the defign formed againft him. It is however happy, that it mif-
carried ; for the provifional articles of peace had been already figned in Europe. Of the above defign I have the beft
information.

J.

[In no period of General Wafhington's military life did his
talents and conmanding influence appear more confpicuous
than at the battle of Monmouth. The flower of the army
under General Lee were retreating before the enemy, and
almoft without having made any refiftance. When they
were thus thrown back upon General Wafhington, at the
head of his fatigued and illfupplied army, it is furprifing,
that the panic did not become general. General Wafhington brought his own troops forward, checked the Britifh,
and foon convinced Lee's flying troops, not only, that there
was no occafion for their retreat, but that they could defeat
the enemy. General Wafhington never had full credit for
this heroic exploit ; and it has been thought, that if full
juftice had been done by the Courtmartial, General Lee
would have been cafhiered.]

[His aftonifhing power of commanding the minds of men
was often exemplified in quieting mutinies, of which he had
too many during his military courfe. But no writer has
done him juftice for his Fabian conduct when the army was
on the borders of difbanding. Some well written inflammatory pieces were addreffed to the army, after the prelimi-
nary articles of peace had been figned, inviting them not to
lay down their arms, until the country fhould do them juftice. Their toils and fufferings had ripened them for any

39
---

defperate undertaking. In the glorious office of Mediator between his country and the army he appeared with a dignity fupreme. He convened and addreffed the officers ; the hurricane of paffion fubfided, and reafon, duty, and peace refumed their dominion. The addrefs, and the public orders which followed it, are perpetual monuments of his greatnefs and patriotifm.

N. B. For the Notes included in brackets I am indebted to Col. Talmadge.

THE

PRESIDENT's ADDRESS.

TO THE PEOPLE OF THE UNITED STATES.

FRIENDS AND FELLOW-CITIZENS,

THE period for a new election of a Citizen, to adminifter the executive government of the United States, being
not far diftant, and the time actually arrived, when your
thoughts muft be employed in defignating the perfon, who
is to be cloathed with that important truft, it appears to me
proper, efpecially as it may conduce to a more diftinct expreffion of the public voice, that I fhould now apprife you
of the refolution I have formed, to decline being confidered
among the number of thofe, out of whom a choice is to be
made.

I beg you, at the fame time, to do me the juftice to be
affured, that this refolution has not been taken, without a
ftrict regard to all the confiderations appertaining to the relation, which binds a dutiful citizen to his country ; and
that, in withdrawing the tender of fervice which filence in
my fituation might imply, I am influenced by no diminution
of zeal for your future intereft ; no deficiency of grateful
refpect for your paft kindnefs : But am fupported by a
full conviction that the ftep is compatable with both.

The acceptance of, and continuance hitherto in the office
to which your fuffrages have twice called me, have been
a uniform facrifice of inclination to the opinion of duty, and
to a deference for what appeared to be your defire. I conftantly hoped, that it would have been much earlier in my
power confiftently with motives, which I was not at liberty
to difregard, to return to that retirement, from which I
had been reluctantly drawn. The ftrength of my inclination to do this, previous to the laft election, had even led
to the preparation of an addrefs to declare it to you ; but
mature reflection on the then perplexed and critical pofture
of affairs with foreign nations, and the unanimous advice of

perfons entitled to my confidence, impelled me to abandon the idea.

I rejoice, that the ftate of your concerns external as well as internal, no longer renders the purfuit of inclination incompatible with the fentiment of duty, or propriety : And am perfuaded whatever partiality may be retained for my fervice, that in the prefent circumftances of our country, you will not difapprove my determination to retire.

The impreffions with which I firft undertook the arduous truft, were explained on the proper occafion. In the difcharge of this truft, I will only fay, that I have with good intentions, contributed towards the organization and adminiftration of the government, the beft exertions of which a very fallible judgment was capable. Not unconfcious, in the out-fet, of the inferiority of my qualifications, experience in my own eyes, perhaps ftill more in the eyes of others, has ftrengthened the motives to diffidence of myfelf : And every day the increafing weight of years admonifhes me more and more, that the fhade of retirement is as neceffary to me as it will be welcome. Satisfied that if any circumftances have given peculiar value to my fervices, they were temporary, I have the confolation to believe, that while choice and prudence invite me to quit the political fcene, patriotifm does not forbid it.

In looking forward to the moment, which is intended to terminate the career of my public life, my feelings do not permit me to fufpend the deep acknowledgment of that debt of gratitude which I owe to my beloved country, for the many honors it has conferred upon me ; ftill more for the ftedfaft confidence with which it has fupported me ; and for the opportunities I have thence enjoyed of manifefting my inviolable attachment, by fervices faithful and perfevering, though in ufefulnefs unequal to my zeal.—If benefits have refulted to our country from thefe fervices, let it always be remembered to our praife, and as an inftructive example in our annals, that under circumftances in which the paffions, agitated in every direction, were liable to miflead, amidft appearances fometimes dubious—viciffitudes of fortune, often difcouraging in fituations, in which not unfrequently want of fuccefs has countenanced the fpirit of criticifm—the conftancy of your fupport was the effential prop of the efforts, and a gurantee of the plans by which they were ef-

F

fected.' Profoundly penetrated with this idea, I shall carry it with me to my grave, as a strong incitement to unceasing vows, that Heaven may continue to you the choicest tokens of its benificence—that your union and brotherly affection may be perpetual—that the free Constitution, which is the work of your hands, may be sacredly maintained—that its adminiftration in ever department may be stamped with wifdom and virtue—that, in fine, the happiness of the people of thefe States, under the auspices of liberty, may be made complete, by so careful a preservation and so prudent a ufe of this blessing, as will acquire to them the glory of recommending it to the applause, the affection, and adoption of every nation which is yet a stranger to it.

Here perhaps, I ought to ftop. But folicitude for your welfare, which cannot end but with my life, and the apprehension, of danger natural to that folicitude, urge me on an occasion like the present, to offer to your solemn contemplation, and to recommend to your frequent review, fome fentiments ; which are the refult of much reflectio n of no inconfiderable obfervation, and which appear to me all-important to the permanency of your felicity as a people. These will be offered to you with the more freedom, as you can only feel in them the difinterefted warnings of a parting friend, who can poffibly have no perfonal motive to bias his counfel. Nor can I forget, as an encouragement to it, your indulgent reception of my fentiments on a former and not diffimilar occafion.

Interwoven as is the love of liberty with every ligament of your hearts, no recommendation of mine is neceffary to fortify or confirm the attachment.

The unity of Government which conftitutes you one people, is alfo now dear to you. It is juftly fo ; for it is a main pillar in the edifice of your real Independence, the fupport of your tranquility at home, your peace abroad ; of your fafety ; of your profperity ; of that very liberty which you fo highly prize. But, as it is eafy to forefee, that from different caufes and from different quarters, much pains will be taken, many artifices employed, to weaken in your minds the conviction of this truth ; as this is the point in your political fortrefs, againft which the batteries of internal and external enemies will be moft conftantly and actively, (though often covertly and infiduoufly) directed, it is of infinite moment that you fhould properly eftimate the immenfe value of your National Union, to your collective and individual happinefs; that you fhould cherifh a cordial, habitual, and immoveable attachment to it; accuftoming yourfelves to think and fpeak of it as of the palladium of your political fafety and profperity, watching for its prefervation with jealous anxiety; difcountenancing whatever may fuggeft even a fufpicion that it can in any event be abandoned; and indignantly frowning upon the firft dawning of every attempt to alienate any portion of our country from the reft, or to enfeeble the facred ties which now link together the various parts.

For this you have every inducement of fympathy and intereft. Citizens, by birth or choice, of a common country, that country has a right to concentrate your affections. The name of AMERICAN, which belongs to you in your national capacity, muft always exalt the juft pride of patriotifm, more than any appellation derived from local difcriminations. With flight fhades of difference, you have the fame religion, manners, habits and political principles. You have in a common caufe, fought and triumphed together; the Independence and Liberty you poffefs are the work of joint councils, and joint efforts, of common dangers, fufferings and fucceffes.

But thefe confiderations however powerfully they addrefs themfelves to your fenfibility, are greatly outweighed by thofe which apply more immediately to your intereft. Here every portion of our country finds the moft commanding motives for carefully guarding and preferving the union of the whole.

The *North*, in an unreftrained intercourfe with the *South*, protected by the equal laws of a common government, finds in the productions of the latter, great additional refources of maritime and commercial enterprife, and precious materials of manufacturing induftry. The *South* in the fame intercourfe, benefiting by the agency of the *North*, fees its agriculture grow, and its commerce expand. Turning partly into its own channels the feamen of the *North*, it finds its particular navigation invigorated—and while it contributes, in different ways, to nourifh and increafe the general mafs of the national navigation, it looks forward to the protection of a maritime ftrength, to which itfelf is unequally adopted. The *Eaft* in a like intercourfe with the *Weft*, already finds,

and in the progreſſive improvement of interior communications, by land and water,—will more and more find a
valuable vent for the commodities which it brings from a-
broad, or manufactures at home. The *Weſt* derives from
the *Eaſt* ſupplies requiſite to its growth and comfort—and
what is perhaps of ſtill greater conſequence, it muſt of neceſſity owe the *ſecure* enjoyment of indiſpenſable *outlets* for
its own productions to the weight, influence, and the future
maritime ſtrength of the Atlantic ſide of the Union, directed by an indiſſoluble community of intereſt as *one nation.*
Any other tenure by which the *Weſt* can hold this eſſential
advantage, whether derived from its own ſeparate ſtrength,
or from an apoſtate and unnatural connection with any foreign power, muſt be intrinſically precarious.

While then every part of our country thus feels an immediate and particular intereſt in Union, all the parts combined cannot fail to find in the united maſs of means and efforts, greater ſtrength, greater reſource, proportionably
greater ſecurity, from external danger, a leſs frequent interruption of their peace by foreign nations; and what is of
ineſtimable value! they muſt derive from Union an exemption from thoſe broils and wars between themſelves, which
ſo frequently afflict neighbouring countries, not tied together by the ſame government; which their own rivalſhips
alone would be ſufficient to produce, but which oppoſite foreign alliances, attachments and intrigues would ſtimulate
and imbitter. Hence likewiſe they will avoid the neceſſity
of thoſe overgrown military eſtabliſhments, which under
any form of government are inauſpicious to liberty, and
which are to be regarded as particularly hoſtile to Republican Liberty: In this ſenſe it is, that your Union ought to
be conſidered as a main prop of your liberty, and that the
love of the one ought to endear to you the preſervation of
the other.

Theſe conſiderations ſpeak a perſuaſive language to every reflecting and virtuous mind, and exhibit the continuance of the Union as a primary object of a patriotic deſire.
Is there a doubt, whether a common government can embrace, ſo large a ſphere?—Let experience ſolve it. To
liſten to mere ſpeculation in ſuch a caſe were criminal.
We are authoriſed to hope that a proper organization, of
the whole, with the auxiliary agency, of governments for
the reſpective ſubdiviſions, will afford a happy iſſue to the

experiment. 'Tis well worth a fair and full experiment. With such powerful and obvious motives to Union, affecting all parts of our country, while experiment shall not have demonstrated its impracticability, there will always be reason to distrust the patriotism of those, who in any quarter may endeavour to weaken its bands.

In contemplating the causes which may disturb our Union, it occurs as matter of serious concern, that any ground should be furnished for characterising parties, by *Geographical* discriminations—*Nothern* and *Southern*—*Atlantic* and *Western*; whence designing men may endeavour to excite a belief, that there is a real difference of local interests and views. One of the expedients of party to acquire influence, within particular districts, is to misrepresent the opinions and aims of other districts. You cannot shield yourselves too much against the jealousies and heart burnings which spring from these misrepresentations : they tend to render alien to each other those who ought to be bound together by fraternal affection.—The inhabitants of our western country have lately had a useful lesson on this head : They have seen, in the negociation by the Executive, and in the unanimous ratification by the Senate, of the Treaty with Spain, and in the universal satisfaction at that event, throughout the United States, a decisive proof how unfounded were the suspicions propagated among them, of a policy in the general government and in the Atlantic states unfriendly to their interests in regard to the Missisippi ; they have been witnesses to the formation of two treaties, that with Great-Britain and that with Spain, which secure to them every thing they could desire, in respect to our foreign relations, towards confirming their prosperity. Will it not be their wisdom to rely for the preservation of these advantages on the UNION by which they were procured ? Will they not henceforth be deaf to those advisers, if such they are, who would sever them from their brethren, and connect them with aliens ?

To the efficacy and permanency of your Union, a government for the whole is indispensable. No alliances, however strict, between the parts can be an adequate substitute ; they will inevitably experience the infractions and interruptions which all alliances in all times have experienced—Sensible of this momentous truth, you have improved upon your first essay, by the adoption of a constitution of a government better calculated than your former for an intimate Union, and for the efficacious management of your common concerns. This government, the offspring of your own choice, uninfluenced and unawed, adopted upon full inveſtigation and mature deliberation, completely free in its principles, in the diſtribution of its powers, uniting ſecurity with energy, and containing within itſelf a proviſion for its own amendment, has a juſt claim to your confidence and your ſupport. Reſpect for its authority, compliance with its laws, acquieſcence in its meaſures, are duties enjoined by the fundamental maxims of true liberty. The baſis of our political ſyſtems is the right of the people to make and to alter their conſtitutions of government. But, the conſtitution which at any time exiſts, till changed by an explicit and authentic act of the whole people, is ſacredly obligatory upon all. The very idea of the power and the right of the people to eſtabliſh government, pre-ſuppoſes the duty of every individual to obey the eſtabliſhed government.

All obſtructions to the execution of the laws, all combinations and aſſociations, under whatever plauſible character, with the real deſign to direct, controul, counteract or awe the regular deliberation and action of the conſtituted authorities, are deſtructive of this fundamental principle, and of fatal tendency. They ſerve to organize faction, to give it an artificial and extraordinary force—to put in the place of the delegated will of the nation, the will of a party, often a ſmall but artful and enterpriſing minority of the community ; and, according to the alternate triumphs of different parties, to make the public adminiſtration the mirror of the ill concerted and incongruous projects of faction, rather than the organ of conſiſtent and wholeſome plans digeſted by common councils and modified by mutual intereſts.

However combinations or aſſociations of the above deſcription, may now and then anſwer popular ends, they are likely in the courſe of time and things, to become potent engines, by which cunning, ambitious and unprincipled men, will be enabled to ſubvert the power of the people, and to uſurp for themſelves the reins of government ; deſtroying afterwards the very engines which have lifed them to unjuſt dominion.

Towards the preſervation of your government, and the

permanency of your prefent happy ftate, it is requifite, not only that you fteadily difcountenance irregular oppofition to its acknowledged authority, but alfo that you refift with care, the fpirit of innovation upon its principles, however fpecious the pretexts. One method of affault may be to effect in the forms of the conftitution, alterations which will impair the energy of the fyftem, and thus to undermine what cannot be directly overthrown. In all the changes to which you may be invited, remember that time and habit are at leaft as neceffary to fix the true character of government, as of other human inftitutions that experience is the fureft ftandard, by which to teft the real tendency of the exifting conftitution of a country—that facility in changes upon the credit of mere hypothefis and opinion, expofes to perpetual change, from the endlefs variety of hypothefis and opinion ; and remember, efpecially, that for the efficient management of your common intereft, in a country fo extenfive as ours, a government of as much vigor as is confiftent with the perfect fecurity of liberty, is indifpenfible. Liberty itfelf will find in fuch a government, with powers properly diftributed and adjufted, its fureft guardian. It is, indeed, little elfe than a name, where the government is too feeble to withftand the enterprifes of faction, to confine each member of the fociety within the limits prefcribed by the laws, and to maintain all in the fecure and tranquil enjoyment of the rights of perfon and property.

I have already intimated to you, the danger of parties in the ftate, with particular reference to the founding of them on geographical difcriminations. Let me now take a more comprehenfive view and warn you in the moft folemn manner againft the baneful effects of the fpirit of party, generally.

This fpirit, unfortunately, is infeparable from our nature, having its root in the ftrongeft paffions of the human mind. It exifts under different fhapes in all governments —more or lefs ftifled, controled, or repreffed ; but in thofe of the popular form, it is feen in its greateft ranknefs and is truly their worft enemy.

The alternate dominion of one faction over another, fharpened by the fpirit of revenge, natural to party diffention, which in different ages and countries has perpetrated the moft horrid enormities, is itfelf a frightful defpotifm—But

48

this leads at length to a more formal and permanent defpotifm.—The diforders and miferies, which refult, gradually
incline the minds of men to feek fecurity, and repofe in the
abfolute power of an individual ; and fooner or later the
chief of fome prevailing faction more able or more fortunate
than his competitors, turns this difpofition to the purpofes
of his own elevation, on the ruins of Public Liberty.

Without looking forward to an extremity of this kind
(which neverthelefs ought not to be entirely out of fight)
the common and continual mifchiefs of the fpirit of party are
fufficient to make it the intereft and duty of a wife people to
difcourage and reftrain it.

It ferves always to diftract the Public Councils and enfeeble the Public Adminiftration. It agitates the community
with ill founded jealoufies and falfe alarms ; kindles the
animofity of one part againft another, foments occafionally
riot and infurrection. It opens the door to foreign influence
and corruption, which find a facilitated accefs to the government itfelf through the channels of party paffions. Thus
the policy and will of one country are fubjected to the policy and will of another.

There is an opinion that parties in free countries are ufeful checks upon the adminiftration of the government, and
ferve to keep alive the fpirit of Liberty. This within certain limits is probably true, and in governments of a monarchical caft, patriotifm may look with indulgence, if not
with favour upon the fpirit of party. But in thofe of the
popular character, in governments purely elective, it is a
fpirit not to be encouraged. From their natural tendency
it is certain there will always be enough of that fpirit for
every falutary purpofe. And there being conftant danger
of excefs, the effort ought to be by force of Public opinion,
to mitigate and affuage it. A fire not to be quenched ; it
demands uniform vigilance to prevent its burfting into a
flame, leaft inftead of warming, it fhould confume.

It is important likewife, that the habits of thinking in a
free country, fhould infpire caution, in thofe entrufted with
its adminiftration, to confine themfelves within their refpective conftitutional fpheres, avoiding in the exercife of the
powers of one department to encroach upon another. The
fpirit of encroachment tends to confolidate the powers of
all the departments in one, and thus to create, whatever

the form of Government, a real defpotifm. A juft eftimate of that love of power, and pronenefs to abufe it, which predominates in the human heart is fufficient to fatisfy us of the truth of this pofition. The neceffity of reciprocal checks in the exercife of the political power ; by dividing and diftributing it into different depofitories, and conftituting each the guardian of the public weal againft invafions by the others, has been evinced by experiments ancient and modern ; fome of them in our country and under our own eyes. To preferve them muft be as neceffary as to inftitute them. If, in the opinion of the people, the diftribution or modification of the conftitutional powers be in any particular wrong, let it be corrected by an amendment in the way, which the conftitution defignates—But let there be no change by ufurpation ; for though this, in one inftance, may be the inftrument of good, it is the cuftomary weapon by which free governments are deftroyed—The precedent muft always greatly overbalance in permanent evil any partial or tranfient benefit which the ufe can at any time yield.

Of all the difpofitions and habits which lead to political profperity, Religion and Morality are indifpenfable fupports. In vain would that Man claim the tribute of Patriotifm, who would labor to fubvert thefe great pillars of human happinefs, thefe firmeft props of the duties of men and Citizens. The mere Politician, equally with the pious man ought to refpect and to cherifh them.—A volume could not trace all their connections with private and public felicity. Let it fimply be afked where is the fecurity for property, for reputation, for life, if the fenfe of religious obligation defert the oaths which are the inftruments of inveftigation in Courts of Juftice?—And let us with caution indulge the fuppofition, that morality can be maintained without Religion. Whatever may be conceded of the influence of refined education on minds of peculiar ftructure ; reafon and experience both forbid us to expect that national morality can prevail in exclufion of religious principle.

Tis fubftantially true, that virtue or morality is a neceffary fpring of popular government. The rule indeed extends with more or lefs force to every fpecies of free government. Who that is a fincere Friend to it can look

G

with indifference upon attempts to fhake the foundation
of the Fabric?

Promote, then as an object of primary importance, inftitutions for the general diffufion of knowledge. In proportion as the ftructure of a government gives force to
public opinion, it is effential that public opinion fhould be
enlightened.

As a very important fource of ftrength and fecurity,
cherifh public credit. One method of preferving it is to
ufe it as fparingly as poffible ; avoiding occafions of expence by cultivating peace, but remembering alfo that
timely difburfements to prepare for dangers, frequently
prevent much greater difburfements to repel it : Avoiding
likewife the accumulation of debt, not only by fhunning
occafions of expence, but by vigorous exertions in time
of peace to difcharge the debts which unavoidable wars
may have occafioned, not ungeneroufly throwing upon
pofterity the burthen which we ourfelves ought to bear.
The execution of thefe maxims belongs to your reprefentatives, but it is neceffary that public opinion fhould
co-operate. To facilitate to them the performance of
their duty, it is effential that you fhould practically bear in
mind that towards the payment of debts there muft be revenue ;—that to have revenue there muft be taxes—and
none can be devifed which are not more or lefs inconveni-
ent and unpleafant—that the intrinfic embarraffment infeparable from the felection of the proper objects (which is
always a choice of difficulties)—ought to be a decifive motive for a candid conftruction of the conduct of the government in making it, and for a fpirit of acquiefcence in the
meafures for obtaining revenue which the public exigencies
may at any time dictate.

Obferve good faith and juftice towards all nations ; cultivate peace and harmony with all—Religion and Morality enjoin this conduct ; and can it be, that good policy does
not equally enjoin it ? It will be worthy of a free, enlightened, and (at no diftant period) a great nation, to give to
mankind the magnanimous and too novel example of a people always guided by an exalted juftice and benevolence.
Who can doubt that in the courfe of time and things, the
fruits of fuch a plan would richly repay any temporary advantages which might be loft by a fteady adherence to it ?
Can it be, that Providence has not connected the perma-

nent felicity of a Nation with Virtue? The experiment, at least, is recommended by every sentiment which ennobles human nature.—Alas! is it rendered impossible by its vices?

In the execution of such a plan, nothing is more essential than that permanent, inveterate antipathies against particular Nations, and passionate attachments for others should be excluded; and that in the place of them, just and amicable feelings towards all should be cultivated. The Nation which indulges towards another an habitual hatred, or an habitual fondness, is in some degree a slave.—It is a slave to its animosity or to its affection, either of which is sufficient to lead it astray from its duty and its interest. Antipathy in one nation against another disposes each more readily to offer insult and injury, to lay hold of slight causes of umbrage, and to be haughty and intractable, when accidental or trifling occasions of dispute occur.

Hence frequent collisions, obstinate, envenomed and bloody contests. The Nation, prompted by ill will and resentment, sometimes impels to war the government, contrary to the best calculations of policy. The government sometimes participates in the national propensity, and adopts through passion what reason would reject; at other times, it makes the animosity of the nation subservient to projects of hostility instigated by pride, ambition, and other sinister and pernicious motives. The peace often, sometimes perhaps the liberty of Nations has been the victim.

So likewise, a passionate attachment of one Nation for another produces a variety of evils. Sympathy for the favorite Nation, facilitating the illusion of an imaginary common interest, in cases where no real common interest exists, and infusing into one the enmities of the other, betrays the former into a participation in the quarrels and wars of the latter, without adequate inducement or justification. It leads also to concessions to the favorite nation of privileges denied to others, which is apt doubly to injure the Nation making the concessions; by unnecessarily parting with what ought to have been retained; and by exciting jealousy, ill will, and a disposition to retaliate, in the parties from whom equal privileges are withheld: —And it gives to ambitious, corrupted or deluded citizens (who devote themselves to the favorite Nation) facility to betray, or sacrifice the interests of their own country, with

190

put odium, fometimes even with popularity ; gilding with the appearances of a virtuous fenfe of obligation a commendable deference for public opinion, or a laudable zeal for public good, the bafe or foolifh compliances of ambition, corruption, or infatuation.

As avenues to foreign influence in innumerable ways, fuch attachments are particularly alarming to the truly enlightened and independent patriot. How many opportunities do they afford to tamper with domeftic factions, to practice the arts of feduction to miflead public opinion, to influence or awe the public councils ; fuch an attachment of a fmall or weak, towards a great and powerful nation, dooms the former to be the fatellite of the latter.

Againft the infiduous wiles of foreign influence (I conjure you to believe me, fellow citizens) the jealoufy of a free people ought to be *conftantly* awake ; fince hiftory and experience prove that foreign influence is one of the moft baneful foes of Republican Government. But that jealoufy to be ufeful muft be impartial ; elfe it becomes the inftrument of the very influence to be avoided, inftead of a defence againft it. Exceffive partiality for one foreign nation, and exceffive diflike of another, caufe thofe whom they actuate to fee danger only on one fide, and ferve to veil and even fecond the arts of influence on the other. Real patriots, who may refift the intrigues of the favorite, are liable to become fufpected and odious ; while its tools and dupes ufurp the applaufe and confidence of the people to furrender their interefts.

The great rule of conduct for us in regard to foreign nations, is in extending our commercial relations, to have with them as little *political* connection as poffible. So far as we have already formed engagements, let them be fulfilled with perfect good faith.—Here let us ftop.

Europe has a fet of primary interefts, which to us have none, or a very remote relation. Hence fhe muft be engaged in frequent controverfies, the caufes of which are effentially foreign to our concerns. Hence therefore, it muft be unwife in us to implicate ourfelves, by artificial ties, in the ordinary viciffitudes of her politics, or the ordinary combinations and collifions of her friendfhips, or enmities.

Our detached and diftant fituation, invites and enables us

to purſue a different courſe. If we remain one people, under an efficient government, the period is not far off, when we may defy material injury from external annoyance ; when we may take ſuch an attitude as will cauſe the neutrality, we may at any time reſolve upon, to be ſcrupulouſly reſpected ; when belligerent nations, under the impoſſibility of making acquiſitions upon us, will not lightly hazard the giving us provocation ; when we may chooſe peace or war, as our intereſt, guided by juſtice, ſhall counſel.

Why forego the advantages of ſo peculiar a ſituation? Why quit our own, to ſtand upon foreign ground ? Why, by interweaving our deſtiny with that of any part of Europe, entangle our peace and proſperity in the toils of European ambition, rivalſhip, intereſt, humour or caprice ?

'Tis our true policy to ſteer clear of permanent alliances, with any portion of the foreign world ; ſo far, I mean, as we are now at liberty to do it ; for let me not, be underſtood as capable of patronizing infidelity to exiſting engagements. I hold the maxim no leſs applicable to public than to private affairs, that honeſty is always the beſt policy. I repeat it, therefore, let thoſe engagements be obſerved in their genuine ſenſe. But in my opinion, it is unneceſſary, and would be unwiſe to extend them.

Taking care always to keep ourſelves, by ſuitable eſtabliſhments, on a reſpectable defenſive poſture, we may ſafely truſt to temporary alliances for extraordinary emergencies.

Harmony, liberal intercourſe with all nations, are recommended by policy, humanity and intereſt. But even our commercial policy, ſhould hold an equal and impartial hand ; neither ſending or granting excluſive favours or preferences—conſulting the natural courſe of things ; diffuſing and diverſifying by gentle means the ſtreams of commerce, but forcing nothing ; eſtabliſhing, with powers ſo diſpoſed, in order to give trade a ſtable courſe to define the rights of our merchants, and to enable the Government to ſupport them ; conventional rules of intercourſe, the beſt that preſent circumſtances and mutual opinion will permit, but temporary, and liable to be from time to time abandoned or varied as experience and circumſtances ſhall dictate ; conſtantly keeping in view, that 'tis folly in one nation to look for diſintereſted favours from another ; that it muſt

54

pay with a portion of its Independence for whatever it may accept under that character; that by such acceptance, it may place itself in the condition of having given equivalents for nominal favours, and yet of being reproached with ingratitude for not giving more.—There can be no greater error than to expect, or calculate, upon real favours from nation to nation. 'Tis an illusion which experience must cure, which a just pride ought to discard.

In offering to you, my countrymen, these counsels of an old affectionate friend, I dare not hope they will make the strong and lasting impression I could wish—that they will controul the usual current of the passions, or prevent our nation from running the course which has hitherto marked the destiny of nations : But if I may even flatter myself, that they may be productive of some partial benefit, some occasional good ; that they may now and then recur to moderate the fury of party spirit, to warn against the mischiefs of foreign intrigue, to guard against the impostures of pretended patriotism ; this hope will be a full recompence for the solicitude for your welfare, by which they have been dictated.

How far in the discharge of my official duties, I have been guided by the principles which have been delineated, the public records and other evidences of my conduct must witness to you and to the world. To myself, the assurance of my own conscience is, that I have at least believed myself to be guided by them.

In relation to the still subsisting war in Europe, my Proclamation of the 22d of April, 1795, is the index to my plan. Sanctioned by your approving voice, and by that of your Representatives in both Houses of Congress, the spirit of that measure has continually governed me ; uninfluenced by any attempts to deter or divert me from it.

After deliberate examination, with the aid of the best lights I could obtain, I was well satisfied that our country, under all the circumstances of the case, had a right to take and was bound in duty and interest to take a neutral position. Having taken it, I determined, as far as should depend on me, to maintain it, with moderation.

The considerations which respect the right to hold this conduct, it is not necessary on this occasion to detail. I will only observe, that according to my understanding of the matter, that right, fo far from being denied by any of the Belligerent Powers, has been virtually admitted by all.

The duty of holding a neutral conduct may be inferred, without any thing more, from the obligation which juftice and humanity impofe on every nation, in cafes in which it is free to act, to maintain inviolate the relations of peace and amity towards other nations.

The inducements of intereft for obferving that conduct will beft be referred to your own reflections and experience. With me, a predominant motive has been to endeavour to gain time to our country to fettle and mature its yet recent inftitutions, and to progrefs without interruption, to that degree of ftrength and confiftency, which is neceffary to give it, humanly fpeaking, the command of its own fortunes.

Though in reviewing the incidents of my adminiftration, I am unconfcious of intentional error : I am neverthelefs too fenfible of my defects not to think it probable that I may have committed many errors. Whatever they may be, I fervently befeech the Almighty to avert or mitigate the evils, to which they may tend. I fhall alfo carry with me the hope that my country will never ceafe to view them with indulgence ; and that after forty-five years of my life dedicated to its fervice, with an upright zeal, the faults of incompetent abilities will be configned to oblivion, as myfelf muft foon be the manfions of reft.

Relying on its kindnefs in this as in other things, and actuated by that fervent love towards it, which is fo natural to a man who views in it the native foil of himfelf and his progenitors for feveral generations ; I anticipate with pleafing expectation that retreat, in which I promife myfelf to realize, without alloy, the fweet enjoyment of partaking, in the midft of my fellow-citizens, the benign influence of good laws under a free government—the ever favorite object of my heart, and the happy reward as I truft, of our mutual cares, labours and dangers.

G. WASHINGTON.

United States, }
17th September, 1796. }

Mr. STRONG's DISCOURSE,

ON THE DEATH OF

GENERAL WASHINGTON.

A

DISCOURSE,

DELIVERED ON

FRIDAY, DECEMBER 27, 1799,

THE DAY SET APART BY THE CITIZENS OF
HARTFORD, TO LAMENT BEFORE GOD,

THE **DEATH** OF

Gen. George Washington ;

WHO DIED DEC. 14, 1799.

BY NATHAN STRONG,

PASTOR OF THE NORTH PRESBYTERIAN CHURCH IN HARTFORD.

HARTFORD:

PRINTED BY HUDSON AND GOODWIN,

1800.

FUNERAL SERMON.

MY BRETHREN,

SO general an appearance of affliction was never depicted here before. To ftand in this immenfe concourfe of fellow citizens, where every face is marked with forrow, almoft unmans the fpeaker. Verily there is a great mourning here to-day, like the mourning of Ifrael when MOSES died, and to improve the occafion let us turn to

EXODUS xi. 3.

—Moreover the man MOSES was very great in the land of Egypt, in the fight of Pharoah's fervants, and in the fight of the people.

IT muft be a folemn feafon, when a great people lament before the LORD, the death of thofe, whom his infinite goodnefs hath made the inftruments of their greateft benefits. On fuch occafions the mind muft be impreffed with the fovereignty of GOD, and frailty of man in his beft earthly eftate; and a tender and refpectful

6   FUNERAL SERMON.

remembrance of deceafed virtues will open all hearts to a mutual condolence. All bleffings are from GOD, who upholds the civil ftate, girds the civil and military rulers of men, and keeps his church in peace and quietnefs, thro the influence of his fervants who fear his name.

The LORD hath fet his king upon his holy hill of Zion, who is the CREATOR, REDEEMER, and JUDGE of men. He is GOD forever on the throne in heaven, and thro the earth, and to fulfil his counfels he works thro inftruments prepared by himfelf, and made worthy of acting in his name, and bearing the marks of a divine commiffion. There have been but few men in the world eminently great, and thofe have, in general, been on the fide of virtue. There have been many tyrants and deftroyers, for it requires only fmall talents to work ruin; but to build up, to blefs, to humanize fociety, to defend the oppreffed, to vindicate human liberty, and at the fame time reftrain licentioufnefs, is an arduous tafk; where none but good men will be inclined to expofe themfelves, and which none but great men are able to accomplifh.

That we may on this occafion, honor the fupreme Sovereign of the world, and duly eftimate the public lofs fuftained, let us,

1. Contemplate the providence of GOD in raifing up great and eminent men, and qualify-

FUNERAL SERMON.

ing them for the good which they are appointed to do to mankind.

In the formation of such persons, there must be a union of rare and great natural talents, with an eminent love of moral virtue. Whenever God hath a great work to do in the world, he forms instruments fitted for the trust to be reposed in them, who are possessed of talents, guided by his providential care, and inspired with a spirit of understanding from himself, whereby they are enabled, whatever difficulties and opposition may occur, to do the things determined for them.

We know that those, who despise a supreme providence, are prone to refer every remarkable thing, either to a certain blind necessity of nature which they cannot describe, or to the effects of accidental but uncommon genius ; indeed like other foolish men who think themselves to be wise, they have recourse to any means which will hide the being, the holy perfections, and the providence of God. Herein infidels show themselves to be at an equal remove from piety, wisdom and truth ; and that they are as far from discerning in what the true greatness of a creature consists, as they are from being good and pious.

The rise of eminent and good men is one of the highest displays of a supreme Providence, for they always appear at periods, when there is a work prepared for them to do, for the honor of GOD and the good of the world, and at no other times; fo that we may confider their formation and introduction to the fcenes of action, their good lives and their great actions, evidential of a SUPREME BEING, of the ftability of his counfels and the irrefiftible energy of his government.

Divine wifdom, in the provifion of means and inftruments, always hath regard to the magnitude of the work that is to be done by them in the world, under the direction of his providence. To accomplifh a great work in the earth he maketh his own inftruments great, either thro uncommon natural endowments, affifted by a feries of propitious providences; or by a fupernatural aid evidencing their commiffion and the prefence of GOD with them in difcharging fome important truft, or in both of thofe ways at the fame time. MOSES, the Father, Lawgiver, and Commander of Ifrael was great, in the fight of Ifrael his people, and in the fight of Pharaoh and his fervants their enemies, both by uncommon natural endowments and by fupernatural aid. The FATHER of his Country, for whofe deceafe we mourn before the LORD this day, was made great in the fight of his people, and of all their enemies, by his eminent natural endowments, which GOD was pleafed to aid by a fe-

FUNERAL SERMON.

ries of propitious providences, for the falvation and good government of his country.

When we fee remarkable inftruments of providence coming into action, it indicates an interefting period in that fcheme of divine counfel, which will be forever unfolding ; and when fuch inftruments of blefling to mankind are withdrawn by the power which raifed them up, it becomes caufe for public mourning and fear ; caufe for mourning, for every good man will regret the departure of virtue from the earth ; caufe of fear, for we are told that the righteous are taken from the evil to come, and that while they live, GOD will fpare an ungrateful people from judgments, for their fakes.

When a MOSES, a CYRUS, and a WASHINGTON were brought on the ftage of action, it was to effect changes in the ftate of mankind, favorable to religion and civil rights, which could not have been done, in the manner that divine counfel chofe to execute, under the aufpices of common characters, nor even of great men, as greatnefs is ufually eftimated in this imperfect world. Thefe actors in the fcenes of the world, were fpecially raifed up, and guided by an infinite GOD, to atchieve things which will ever make them celebrated in the hiftory of mankind and of the church.

B

FUNERAL SERMON.

Much honor is due to them as inftruments of Almighty goodnefs. Let their virtues—their love and friendſhip to human nature—their juſtice—their firmnefs in holding the fword of the LORD—and their political eminence as rulers and lawgivers; let thefe be admired and remain perpetual examples to fuch as wiſh to be on GOD's fide ; but let the glory of faſhioning them from the womb, of girding them to lead his armies, of inſpiring them to give laws to nations or creating new commonwealths, and of enabling them to die great as they had lived ; let the glory of thefe things be given to GOD.

It can be no glory to a man, either living or departed, to fay that the great things he hath done for his country, either by his fword or fceptre, were done without a divine aid ; for all confiderate perfons would know it to be a falfe eulogy. Even infidels, in the midſt of their vain pretenfions, know there is a divine providence ; and in the profane words they utter on this fubjeét, they fpeak the wiſnes of their hearts, and not the dictates of their confciences and of their better underſtandings. Such men are like actors in a farce, faying that which they know to be untrue, and it is a falfe complaifance to fuppofe they may be honeſt ; for it is very evident they dare not truſt their own honefty, when danger and death approach them.

FUNERAL SERMON.

The higheſt honor which we can give to mortals, is to ſay, that the infinite Author of life,
power and wiſdom, made them greater and more
virtuous than other men, inſpired them with
talents above their brethren, and filled them with
a rare underſtanding, to do things for the glory
of God and the good of mankind, which were
not permitted to others.—Many have made a
conſpicuous figure for a ſhort ſeaſon and within
national limits, who were neither great nor good ;
but death is written on the glory of ſuch, by the
pen of future hiſtorians, nor is it their privilege
to live in the affections of mankind, or to be
held up as examples for forming the morals of
the world. Their praiſe reſted in adventitious
circumſtances found in the corruption of courts,
and an era of falſe opinions, and was never
ſpoken by plain and good men, who were not
poiſoned by ſenſuality and the expectations of unprincipled ambition ; but the merits of great and
good men, are ſeen by perſons of every deſcription. The peaſant deſcries them as ſoon as the
man of letters.—They are more admired by the
virtuous yeomanry of a country, than by the
gay circle who bow and flatter to make themſelves noticed.

Such inſtruments of God's goodneſs to men,
have a divine impreſſion on their character, ſeen
by all virtuous people—all look to them as

12   FUNERAL SERMON.

being, under GOD, fathers, defenders in war, and rulers in peace. Such was MOSES to the Hebrews, and such was WASHINGTON to us. If any expect me this day to draw his character with precision, let me beg such to recollect that they are expecting an impossibility, and that it is as much beyond me to do this as it is to be such a man as he was. All will allow, that he was formed by the providence of GOD, to walk in a path where other men cannot guide their steps, and to be an eminent agent in the formation of a new empire, which is to be conspicuous in the future history of mankind ; but what it is to be such an instrument of the infinite Ruler, what divine energies meet in originally forming and providentially guiding, and how those energies were consciously felt and exerted by the recipient, certainly is not for me to tell and for but few of mankind to conceive.

MOSES was formed to rescue the ancient and eastern Israel from bondage, and after they were rescued to form their civil, military, and religious state, and be an instrument of delivering the moral law to mankind in a new manner ; and he was, in every respect, perfected for the office to which heaven designed him.

WASHINGTON was formed to rescue from bondage the modern and western Israel of the LORD, and after they were saved from foreign enemies by his fword, to fave them, a fecond time, from deftruction by themfelves ; from the miferies of anarchy ; and to bring them into a ftate of government, whereby they might be preferved from devouring one another, and being devoured by the whole earth. Thefe were great objects in the divine government, and worthy of that difplay of his fufficiency, which was made in the provifion of inftruments. The glory of furnifhing protectors muft belong to GOD, and if the people who have been faved are pious, they will praife him for the means of executing his moft gracious counfel. The formation of great characters, for the good of mankind, is really an exhibition of GOD's providential efficiency, and is obferved by the pious as a difplay of himfelf, thro the inftrumentality of means made for his own glory. Their progrefs and their works thro life are the unfolding of his gracious counfels, and their exit from time is to be marked as a temporary withdrawment of the remarkable energies of divine providence, in favor of thofe who have been his care. For this reafon, the whole congregation of Ifrael mourned thirty days when MOSES died ; and for the fame reafon the American Ifrael mourn when WASHINGTON dies.

We are not to think, that the LORD can give counfel and preferve, only by thofe who have been great inftruments of falvation ; nor are we to diftruft a future divine care ; or to fuppofe that he will not raife up inftruments according to the day and exigencies in which they have to act ; but ftill the withdrawment of fo great a benefactor, under exifting circumftances, is to be devoutly and penitentially noticed as a divine frown ; efpecially when we confider the evidence that he was remarkably formed to be the father and deliverer of his country. None who have confidered the American revolution with its fubfequent events and the ftate of our country, can deny this ; nor can they doubt the evidence of a moft wonderful interpofition of heaven, in the formation and continuance of one fo fitted to fupply our great national wants.

2. There are two kinds of evidence by which great and good men are clearly commiffioned from on high, to act a confpicuous part, under GOD, in his government of the world. The firft is, fupernatural works which evidence them to be immediate organs of divine power and truth fpeaking to men. The fecond, is uncommon natural talents and moral integrity, accompanied with fit opportunities for their exertion. In the cafe of MOSES, both thefe evidences were united to anfwer particular purpofes in the divine government of the world, at that period of time.

His natural abilities and moral attainments were great, and continued to the end of his life ;

FUNERAL SERMON.

for when he died an old man, his eye was not dim, nor his natural force abated. He was ſkilled in the learning of the world, and eſpecially in the wiſdom of that people, whom he was deſigned by the power of GOD to overcome. By a ſpecial providence, he was brought into a ſtate of power and riches, and reputedly the ſon of Pharaoh's daughter, that having had an experimental taſte of worldly wealth and pleaſure, and found its vanity compared with the delights of moral and pious integrity, he might not be bribed from his duty by any worldly overture, when he came to a ſtate of confidential truſt.

Whoever reads his hiſtory as a lawgiver and military leader, conſidering the condition of the world in thoſe ages when he acted, muſt be convinced that he was a great and good man, even apart from thoſe ſupernatural aids, which he received to evidence his appointment and authority from heaven, and that he had that uncommon genius and ſelf-command which all can ſee and admire, but only a rare few can imitate in the ſcience and practice of legiſlation and government.

Alſo, he was a good man, fearing the providence and adoring the holineſs of the GOD of Iſrael. If he had not been poſſeſſed of religious rectitude; neither great natural talents, nor acquired attainments, nor ſupernatural aid could have given him fo venerable an appearance in the eyes of his people, and fanctified their judgment in the opinion of all posterity. At the head of the LORD's Ifrael he was a meek man, and humble in the midft of greatnefs. He efteemed himfelf one among many brethren and citizens, and relying on a divine providence to lead him and the people to whom his life was confecrated, he was never forfaken, but witneffed a gracious prefence thro his whole adminiftration.

To the evidence that he was divinely commiffioned, which arofe from great natural talents and uncommon piety, we may add the fupernatural works he was enabled to perform, and the revelations which were made to him. To learn the reafon, why thefe additional and great evidences of the divine prefence were given to Mofes, we muft confider the extent of his commiffion. The flood had once cleanfed the world of idolatry, but at the time of this great prophet, the nations in their new difperfion had forgotten the LORD, and the worfhip of idols had become almoft univerfal. The people of Ifrael, who were defcendents of Abraham, were defigned to be depofitaries of a written law of religion, and the works of providence, which regarded them and their enemies, were intended to fhow that their LORD JEHOVAH, was the GOD of the whole earth.

FUNERAL SERMON.

Thefe intentions of heaven were foretold to their fathers, and to accomplifh the divine prom-ife it was neceffary a character like MOSES fhould' be raifed up. who, being mighty in word and deed, fhould confound the idolizing nations, fo that the world might look upon him and fee that his LORD was the true GOD. Alfo, that no other ruler of men had been like unto him, in all the figns and wonders which he was fent to do, and in all that mighty hand and all that terror which he fhewed in the fight of Ifrael and their enemies. This was the reafon for a fupernatural evidence of his divine commiffion being added to thofe rare talents and piety, which he poffeffed in com-mon with other great and good men, who were made by GOD, in their refpective times, to honor his name and blefs mankind.

3. At other times GOD hath raifed up his eminent fervants and fent them abroad into the world, without this fupernatural evidence of their commiffion from him ; and indeed this hath been his ufual manner in providential govern-ment. But in all fuch cafes, there hath been to the confiderate obferver, fufficient notices of GOD's fpecial providence, in forming his inftru-ments and guiding and making them fuccefsful in his hand, to execute the counfels of his will. The production of rare talents at a time when they are needed to execute the benevolent purpofes of

C

18   FUNERAL SERMON.

Providence, and preparing the way for their exertion, is a fufficient evidence that GOD is with
the actor. In this part of my difcourfe I fhall
pafs over many inftances of the truth of this
doctrine—many eventful epochs in the hiftory of
the world and the church—many great characters in the cabinet, in the temple of the LORD
and in the field, who were raifed by the almighty
providence of GOD, at fit times to execute his
pre-determined counfels for the benefit of men;
and I fhall come down to our own times and the
occafion which hath gathered us before the
LORD, the death of General WASHINGTON.
Among modern characters there hath been none
to whom the words of our text would more per-
tinently apply.   He was very great, both in the
fight of his own people, and in the fight of all
their enemies; nor at the time of his death, was
his eye dim, nor his natural force abated.   As
thro his life, fo at the time of his death, circumftances feem to have been fpecially ordered by divine providence to hide human weaknefs, and
make him an extraordinary example to men, in
fortitude and in all the moral virtues.   The common age of man had not in him, impaired a
great underftanding, nor any of thofe energies
which decide in the cabinet or execute in the
field.

THIS GREAT MAN WAS AN AMERICAN BY
BIRTH, and the country raifed by his fword into

212

FUNERAL SERMON.

independence, and which he afterwards governed as fupreme magiftrate, gave him the political
and moral fentiments, which made him illuftrious in fcenes of action.   He early commenced
the life of a foldier, and while a young officer,
Monongahela witneffed, and Britons owned the
talents of the young American, in faving from
flaughter the remains of an army fufficiently
humbled by favage fury and policy.   Even, at
that time, the talents of the youth caufed a prediction that he would be the faviour of his country, but little was it conjectured how the prediction would be fulfilled.*

It certainly cannot be expected of me, on this
occafion, particularly to recite the events which
have made him beloved by his country, and
owned as their preferver, under the providence
of God, who girded him for the field, and filled
him with the fpirit of underftanding in all national concerns.   To make fuch a recital requires
all the volumes, which have been, and the more

---

* In a note to a fermon preached by that eminent fervant of
CHRISr, Prefident DAVIES, before Capt. Overton's independent
company of volunteers, raifed in Hanover county, Virginia, Aug.
17, 1755, entitled, " *Religion and Patriotifm . the conftituents of a good
foldier,*" as an example of this character, the author fays, " As a
" remarkable inftance of this, I may point out to the public that
" heroic youth, Col. WASHINGTON, whom I cannot but hope prov-
" idence has hitherto preferved in fo fignal a manner, for fome im-
" portant fervice to his country."   Whoever reads this muft be
convinced that there were early prefages of that great and good
character, which General WASHINGTON hath fince difplayed, and
that his greatnefs did not arife from a feries of accidental events.
The man WASHINGTON was great in his youth, and prepared by
almighty Providence to protect the American ftate and church.

FUNERAL SERMON.

numerous ones which will be written on this great subject.—It muſt ſuffice for me to ſay, that General WASHINGTON was the point of ſtrength around whom the political fathers and the military defenders of this country have rallied, and where they repoſed their earthly confidence, from the moment a revolution was contemplated, as the only poſſible means of avoiding foreign oppreſſion, down to the preſent time. In a period of almoſt thirty years, we have ſeen many changes, many dangers from within and without, from foreign artifice and internal folly and caprice; and during the whole of this term, WASHINGTON has been the name, which would raiſe a martial ſpirit and point its energies by the waving of his ſword; or ſooth the multitude to peace, quietetneſs and ſubordination, as his voice and pen adviſed.—Theſe influential energies of the man, were not confined to the uninformed multitude only; for they had as much impreſſion on deliberating ſenates, as on armed ſquadrons;—he was as much the angel of peace as of war;—as much reſpected, as deeply reverenced in the political cabinet for a luminous coolneſs of diſpoſition, whereby party jealouſy became enlightened and aſhamed of itſelf, as he was for a coolneſs of command, in the dreadful moment, when empires hung ſuſpended on the fate of battle.—His opinions became the opinions of the public body, and every man was pleaſed with himſelf when he found he thought like WASHINGTON.

FUNERAL SERMON.

Our revolutionary war began fuddenly, when the country was wholly unorganized in every department, that was neceffary to maintain and enjoy an independent ftate among the nations. There was paffion enough, among all orders of men ; but paffion can endure only for a moment, and there is no fafety in its dictates.

It was General WASHINGTON who came coolly to the fcene of action, under a mighty impreffion of the greatnefs of the labor to which he had permitted himfelf to be proclaimed, and for which, thro the affiftance of GOD, he was found able both in word and in deed. He ordained fyftem—induced regularity—was found capable of reducing a half-armed multitude to military bravery and obedience, and for a long time had apparently to create the means, from day to day, by which he defended his country.

It fince appears, that while doing this in camp, his pen was the organ of wifdom and of a perfevering firmnefs to the councils of the union and of the feveral ftates ; and that the great men, who fhone like ftars of the firft magnitude, in the feveral parts of the American hemifphere where GOD had placed them, fhone brighter for their communication with him.— His name foon became reverenced by our enemies, and wherever they heard of him, they joined the apprehenfion of a fenate and hoft. His name and the fear of him, and of

a few tried men and foldiers, who were the heads
of military departments and in the line of actual fervice, often fhielded the country againft
mighty hofts, and finally faved the commonwealth and made it independent.

The fame even of hiftorians will be eternized,
in relating how he with the band of his brother
officers, and a patient, perfevering, gallant army
under them, vindicated the foundation of A-
merican empire, and then retired into the clafs of
peaceful citizens, to eat the hard-earned, and in
many inftances, fcanty bread of repofe.

General WASHINGTON was formed and placed, in every refpect, by the hand of Providence
to perform the duty determined for him by infinite wifdom.   He was fkilled, by an early education, in human fcience.   He expreffed on all
fit occafions, a reverence of GOD, and his governing providence in all the events of individual
life and of empire, and reforted to the throne
of grace and called on thofe around him to do
the fame when danger threatened, or when fuccefs claimed his praife.   He had a luminous underftanding—a mind above the ruffle of paffion
—was as far from the gafconade of mock heroifm as he was from a fervile fear of men and danger.   Nothing was too fmall to call his attention,
if it regarded the public good ; at the fame time
he was naturally formed to look on great objects,

FUNERAL SERMON.

and furvey in one comprehenfive view, an empire in all its civil and military interefts.—He feemed intuitively to look thro men, and know the extent of their capacities to underftand, and their abilities for exertion, and from this it came that the heads of departments thro his advice, were filled in general with fuch extraordinary integrity and talents for exertion; and this was one circumftance which effentially conduced. to American triumph.—If the created honors, which are given by crowns and royal nations could have bribed him, many a time he would have been ftolen from us; but he efteemed it the greateft honor, to be the defence of a free people. American freedom, and independence were written on his heart, and he importunately breathed out a defire for them in all his devotions to heaven. Under the aufpices of this great warrior, who was formed by the providence of GOD to defend his country, the war was ended, and America ranked among the nations. He who might have been a monarch, retired to his own Vernon, unclothed of all authority, to enjoy the blifs of being a free private citizen. This was a ftrange fight, and gave a new triumph to human virtue—a triumph that hath never been exceeded in the hiftory of the world, except it was by his fecond recefs, which was from the prefidency of the United States.

After the revolutionary war was ended, experience foon taught that freedom cannot fub-

FUNERAL SERMON.

fift without government. Anarchy became more dangerous than Britain with all her hofts had been before, and we were near defpair. The impreffive feelings of danger, again led the people to afk the aid of General WASHINGTON, and he greatly affifted in forming a conftitution which we hope will be perpetual. By the voice of the people, he became once and again the Prefident of the union, and continued thus until, in his opinion, the complete organization of the civil ftate, permitted him to retire a fecond time into private life, giving in all refpects a new example to men and the world, that a virtuous mind finds its higheft delights, in the enjoyments of folitude and in beholding others happy.

A third time danger menaced his country—a third time his country called—he heard his fellow-citizens and his children and took his fword, and bid them truft in GOD, and keep his laws, and the ordinances of a good government and they fhould be fafe. When lo! the experiment became too great for humanity to exhibit any longer, and he who rules the univerfe, and hath great men and nations in his hand hath removed him by death.

Do not all our civil rulers fay, Know ye not that a great man and a prince hath died in Ifrael to day.—Do not all the pious look after him heavenward, and fay, My father, my father, the chariots of Ifrael, and the horfemen thereof.

FUNERAL SERMON.

—Ye rulers of the civil ſtate, ye defenders of the land, know ye, that it will be no evidence againſt the firmneſs of your minds to weep this day. Ye young defenders of your country; ye virgins the offspring of thoſe who fought the American battles, weep with your parents.

Concerning the final exit of our great and de-, parted friend, private information thus ſays, That he died with one days illneſs, " that his " great and good mind, remained unhurt and " unclouded thro the cloſing ſcene, that he ex- " preſſed his ſenſe of its near approach, and " ſaid it had no terrors for him." Thus may all who have ſerved under him, and all the peo- ple of the LORD die.

I have only a word more to ſay to you my brethren, by way of improvement.

1ſt. Let us praiſe and adore the providence of GOD, for raiſing up ſuch an inſtrument to ſave this country from oppreſſion. It was the work of GOD's moſt gracious providence, and marvellous in our eyes; let us now with reverence adore the ſovereignty, which hath withdrawn the gift. Let us remember to adore that Providence which our departed FATHER adored, and taught us to truſt. Let us keep far away from thoſe princi- ples of infidelity and atheiſm which he abhorred, and which in the preſent æra of nations, is both the cauſe and the means, whereby a holy GOD is puniſhing an ungrateful world.

D

26   FUNERAL SERMON.

2ndly. Let us feek that public fpirit in our feelings and practice, which guided him, fo honorably thro life and brought him to fo peaceful an end. You my hearers, are the moft of you private men, but if you fear GOD ; if you honor his government, and keep his precepts ; if you love the ftate and continue to maintain a righteous government, you may die unclouded, and fay death has no terrors for you.

3dly. Under this bereaving event, there are but two grounds of confolation remain for us ; the LORD who hath been our GOD, and the defender of our country is ftill on the throne ; and he hath prepared an ADAMS to fucceed our WASHINGTON ; for we already fee the fpirit of ELIJAH refting on ELISHA.

4thly. Let us ever remember the political opinions of our deceafed father. He was an American both in principle and feeling, as well as by birth. While he loved all men, and refpected the rights of all nations, his moft ardent affection was for the houfehold of his country. And as his enlightened life drew towards a clofe, he had a moft deep fenfe, that the people whom he had faved by his fword, could be preferved in future profperity, only by a firm adherence to the principles of their own government, and the religion of their fathers.

May the LORD be with the American ftates to preferve them. AMEN.

CHAPTER 10

SKETCHES OF THE LIFE OF
GENERAL WASHINGTON.

GEORGE WASHINGTON was born on the 11th of February A. D. 1732 O. S. His perſon was conſiderably above the middle ſize, but of a dignified and graceful form. His countenance exhibited ſtrong marks of that fortitude and wiſdom which always ſhone in his character ; and at once ſpoke the hero and the man. At an early period of life, he was thought worthy of the confidence of his native ſtate, and while only twenty-one years of age was, at his own requeſt, ſent on a difficult and important miſſion. During the diſpute which originated the war which concluded in 1763, the French, pretending to claim the territory in the vicinity of the river Ohio, committed many acts of hoſtility and violence upon the Britiſh ſubjects by erecting forts in their dominions, and ſeizing their perſons and ſending them priſoners to Canada. Complaints being made to the governor of Virginia of theſe outrages, he determined to ſend ſome ſuitable perſon to the French commandant near the Ohio, to demand of him the reaſon of his conduct, and inſiſt upon his evacuating the fort lately built in that quarter. General WASHINGTON, then being a major, offered his ſervice, which was thankfully accepted. The diſtance to be travelled was more than 400 miles, and one half of the rout lay through a wilderneſs, inhabited only by ſavages. Taking proviſion on his back, he ſat out, attended by a ſingle companion. When he arrived and delivered his meſſage, the officer refuſed to comply with the demand, and claimed the whole country as belonging to the king his maſter.

The Ohio company could not brook this diſappointment of their hopes, and prevailed on the Britiſh government to inſtruct the colonies to oppoſe with arms theſe encroachments on their territory. In the year 1754 Virginia ſent Col. WASHINGTON with the command of 300 men towards the Ohio. An engagement between them and a party of the French took place, in which the latter were defeated. In conſequence of this event, the commandant of the French marched againſt Col. WASHINGTON with 900 men, partly Indians, and attacked him. He made a brave defence, behind a ſmall unfiniſhed entrenchment, which he called fort Neceſſity, and obliged the French officer to grant him honorable terms of capitulation.

The hoſtile conduct of the French produced, both in England and America, the reſolution of driving them out of the whole territory claimed by the Engliſh. General Braddock was accordingly ordered from Ireland to Virginia with two regiments, and was there joined by as many Americans as made in the whole 2200 men. General Braddock was a brave man, but with a ſupercilious contempt of the Americans, he greatly ſlighted the Virginia officers and men. Col. WASHINGTON who then com-

manded the Virginia troops, begged his permiſſion to march before him and with the Americans, who were acquainted with that
kind of ſervice, ſcour the woods ; but was refuſed. The General
puſhed on incautiouſly with 1400 men, and fell into an ambuſ-
cade of French and Indians, by whom he was defeated and mor-
tally wounded on the 9th day of June 1755. The Britiſh
were thrown into confuſion, but the Americans more accuſtomed
to ſavage warfare, were not much diſconcerted. They continued unbroken under Col. WASHINGTON, and by covering the
retreat of the Britiſh, prevented their being entirely cut off.
Ever ſince this battle was fought, General WASHINGTON has
had the credit of ſaving the remains of that unfortunate corps
by his maſterly addreſs and good conduct.

After the peace of Paris, in 1763, Gen. WASHINGTON retired to his eſtate, where with great induſtry and ſucceſs he pur-
ſued the arts of peace.   Since this time there ſeems to be no hiſtorical monument of his public life until he was returned a delegate from the ſtate of Virginia to the memorable congreſs of
1774.   This venerable band of patriots and ſtateſmen might glory
in reckoning among their number the ſage and hero of America.

On the 15th day of June 1775, he was unanimouſly choſen,
by the continental congreſs, to fill the important and dangerous
ſtation of commander in chief of the forces raiſed, or to be
raiſed for the defence of American Liberty. His election preſented the uncommon ſpectacle of a man raiſed to the higheſt
honors his country could beſtow, without exciting either compe-
tition or envy.   On the day following, the Preſident of Congreſs announced to General WASHINGTON his appointment ;
to which he, ſtanding in his place, replied—

" Mr. Preſident,

" Though I am truly ſenſible of the high honor done me in
this appointment, yet I feel great diſtreſs from a conſciouſneſs,
that my abilities and military experience may not be equal to the
extenſive and important truſt : however, as the Congreſs deſire
it, I will enter upon the momentous duty, and exert every power
I poſſeſs in their ſervice, and for ſupport of the glorious cauſe.
I beg they will accept my moſt cordial thanks for this diſtinguiſhed teſtimony of their approbation.

" But leſt ſome unlucky event ſhould happen unfavorable to
my reputation, I beg it may be remembered by every gentleman
in the room, that I this day declare with the utmoſt ſincerity, I
do not think myſelf equal to the command I am honored with.

" As to pay, ſir, I beg leave to aſſure the Congreſs, that as
no pecuniary conſideration could have tempted me to accept this
arduous employment, at the expenſe of my domeſtic eaſe and
happineſs, I do not wiſh to make any profit from it.   I will
keep an exact account of my expenſes.   Thoſe I doubt not they
will diſcharge, and that is all I deſire."

To do juſtice to that part of the life of General WASHINGTON which is included within the time of the American war, would require a detail of all the principal events which took place in that hard ftruggle for liberty, and would greatly exceed the limits of thefe fketches. The evacuation of Bofton, the maf- terly retreat from Long-Ifland and New-York, croffing the North river and the retreat through New-Jerfey, the brilliant coup-de-main at Trenton, the more fplendid affair at Prince- town, the battle of Germantown, the battle of Monmouth, the capture of Stoney-point, thefe are a few of the events which were directed by his wifdom, or effected by his arm; and are but refting places in his glorious career through this bloody con- flict. During the progrefs of the war the confidence of the Congrefs was, on many occafions, manifefted to him, by votes of thanks and applaufe, and by medals ordered to be prefented to him in commemoration of particular inftances of heroifm and generalfhip. So great indeed was their truft in his abilities and virtue, that from time to time they increafed his powers as com- mander in chief until he was little lefs than univerfal dictator.— In no inftance can he be accufed of abufing thofe powers; and the time arriving when they were no longer neceffary for the pub- lic good, he cheerfully refigned them.

The event which finifhed the American war and added the laft wreath to the brow of WASHINGTON, was the capture of Lord Cornwallis with 7000 Britifh troops, at Yorktown in the month of October 1781. This fuccefs was gained by the im- mediate valor of the combined troops of America and France; but the wifdom of the plan and energy of the execution muft be attributed to him. On this triumphant occafion his heart was filled with joy and gratitude to heaven for his wonderful fuccefs. A fhort extract from his orders on this great day, will evince- that amidft all his profperity, he was not unmindful of that GOD whofe directing hand had pointed out to him the path of glory. " Divine fervice fhall be performed to-morrow in all the brigades and divifions. The commander in chief, recommends that all the troops that are not upon duty, do affift at it with a ferious de- portment and that fenfibility of heart, which the recollection of the furprifing and particular interpofition of Divine Providence in our favor claims."

Every one knows that towards the clofe of the war our troops were unpaid and the credit of the United States at its loweft ebb. At this period an attempt was made to inflame the minds of the officers and foldiers, by a feditious and artful publication, inviting them while they had arms in their hands, to redrefs their own grievances. Perhaps in no period of the war was the con- duct of the commander in chief, fo politic, fo magnanimous, fo worthy of himfelf, as at this interefting and alarming crifis. No fooner were thefe mutinous and inflammatory papers fcattered through the camp; than the General convened the officers to- gether, and in a fpeech well calculated to calm their minds, he

pledged himfelf to ufe all his faculties and influence in their favour, and urged them to rely on the future juftice of their country.   He conjured them " as they valued their honor, as they
refpected the rights of humanity and as they regarded the military and national character of America, to exprefs their utmoft
deteftation of the man, who was attempting to open the flood-
gates of civil difcord, and deluge their rifing empire with blood."
His attempt was fuccefsful ; and the officers and foldiers returned to their duty and confented to wait for the tardy juftice of
their country.

At the return of peace, General WASHINGTON repaired to
Annapolis, where Congrefs was in feffion, for the purpofe of
refigning his command.   The 23d day of December 1783, was
fixed for the ceremony of his refignation.   He attended Congrefs on the day with many diftinguifhed perfons, where he addreffed the prefident in the following fpeech :

" Mr. Prefident,

" The great events on which my refignation depended, having
at length taken place, I have now the honor of offering my fincere congratulations to Congrefs, and of prefenting myfelf before
them to furrender into their hands, the truft committed to me, and
to claim the indulgence of retiring from the fervice of my country.

" Happy in the confirmation of our independence and fovereignty, and pleafed with the opportunity afforded the United
States of becoming a refpectable nation, I refign with fatisfaction the appointment I accepted with diffidence ; a diffidence in
my abilities to accomplifh fo arduous a tafk, which however was
fuperfeded by a confidence in the rectitude of our caufe, the fupport of the fupreme power of the Union, and the patronage of
Heaven.

" The fuccefsful termination of the war has verified the moft
fanguine expectations, and my gratitude for the interpofition of
Providence, and the affiftance I have received from my countrymen, increafes with every review of the momentous conteft.

" While I repeat my obligations to the army in general, I
fhould do injuftice to my own feelings not to acknowledge, in
this place, the peculiar fervices, and diftinguifhed merits of the
perfons who have been attached to my perfon during the war :
it was impoffible the choice of confidential officers to compofe
my family fhould have been more fortunate ; permit me, Sir, to
recommend in particular thofe who have continued in the fervice
to the prefent moment, as worthy of the favorable notice and
patronage of Congrefs.

" I confider it as an indifpenfable duty to clofe this laft folemn
act of my official life, by commending the interefts of our dear-
eft country to the protection of Almighty GOD, and thofe who
have the fuperintendence of them, to His holy keeping.

" Having now finifhed the work affigned me, I retire from
the great theatre of action ; and bidding an affectionate farewel

CHAPTER 10

to this auguſt body, under whoſe orders I have long aḉed, I here offer my commiſſion, and take my leave of all the employments of public life."

From this time General WASHINGTON reſided at his retreat at Mount Vernon, until the deranged ſtate of our public affairs, and the total inefficiency of our confederation, had convinced the leading characters of our nation that a new form of government was neceſſary. At this time a convention was called, which met in Philadelphia in the year 1787. To this convention General WASHINGTON was ſent as a delegate from the ſtate of Virginia, and was choſen their Preſident during the term of their ſeſſion.

In the year 1789, he was unanimouſly choſen Preſident of the United States. No ſooner was he informed that he was again called to exchange his happy retirement for the ſtormy ſcenes of public life, than he prepared to meet the wiſhes of his country; and in a few days arrived at New-York. Here he accepted his appointment of Preſident of the United States, and informed both houſes of Congreſs, that he ſhould decline any compenſation for his ſervices—in the following manner; " When I was firſt honored with a call into the ſervice of my country, then on the eve of an arduous ſtruggle for its liberties, the light in which I contemplated my duty required that I ſhould renounce every pecuniary compenſation. From this reſolution I have in no inſtance departed. And being ſtill under the impreſſions which produced it, I muſt decline as inapplicable to myſelf, any ſhare in the perſonal emoluments which may be indiſpenſably included in a permanent proviſion for the executive department; and muſt accordingly pray that pecuniary eſtimates for the ſtation in which I am placed, may, during my continuance in it, be limited to ſuch actual expenditures, as the public good may be thought to require."

In the year 1793 the time for which his firſt appointment was made being expired, he was again elected; and having a ſecond time offiriated in the character of Preſident of the United States, he choſe to retire from the public ſcene and ſpend the remainder of his days in rural quiet and domeſtic tranquillity. He publiſhed his intention in an addreſs to the people of the United States, which, while it breathes the pure ſpirit of benevolence and patriotiſm, recommends to them in the moſt winning and impreſſive language the cauſe of virtue and religion.

After his farewel for a ſecond time, to all public honors, he retired to his favorite ſeat at Mount Vernon, where he reſided in the character of a private citizen, until the proſpect of a rupture with France turned the eyes of the government towards him as their only refuge during the impending ſtorm. His cheerful acquieſcence in accepting the office of Lieutenant General of the American forces, at a time when his age and former ſervices might have juſtified a refuſal, will long be remembered with ſentiments of affection and gratitude, by a generous people.

Mr. Strong's

CENTURY SERMON.

ON THE UNIVERSAL SPREAD OF THE GOSPEL,

A

SERMON,

Delivered January 4th,

THE FIRST SABBATH IN THE NINETEENTH CENTURY

OF THE CHRISTIAN ÆRA.

BY NATHAN STRONG,

Paſtor of the North Preſbyterian Church in Hartford, Connecticut.

PRINTED BY DESIRE OF THE HEARERS.

[Publiſhed according to Act of Congreſs.]

HARTFORD:

PRINTED BY HUDSON AND GOODWIN.

1801.

ON THE UNIVERSAL SPREAD OF THE GOSPEL.

PSALM ii. 1—12.

*Why do the heathen rage, and the people imagine a vain thing ?—
The kings of the earth set themselves, and the rulers take counsel
together against the Lord, and against his anointed, saying,—Let
us break their bands asunder, and cast away their cords from
us.—He that sitteth in the heavens shall laugh : the Lord shall
have them in derision.—Then shall he speak unto them in his wrath,
and vex them in his sore displeasure.—Yet have I set my King
upon my holy hill of Zion.—I will declare the decree : the Lord
hath said unto me, Thou art my Son ; this day have I begotten
thee.—Ask of me, and I shall give thee the heathen for thine inheritance, and the uttermost parts of the earth for thy possession.—
Thou shalt break them with a rod of iron ; thou shalt dash them
in pieces like a potters vessel.—Be wise now, therefore, O ye kings ;
be instructed, ye judges of the earth.—Serve the Lord with fear,
and rejoice with trembling.—Kiss the Son, lest he be angry, and
ye perish from the way, when his wrath is kindled but a little.
Blessed are all they that put their trust in him.*

THE passing of ages continually brings into more
clear view truth which is interesting to divine glory
and to the Church of Christ. It unfolds many counsels of God, which were hid in his infinite and eternal wisdom, until declared by the event. It explains
many prophecies, which were but imperfectly under-

Note.—The extreme cold of the day, occasioned some parts
of the following discourse to be omitted in the delivery, which are
now committed to the press.

231

6   *On the universal spread of the Gospel.*

stood by those, who have given the most painful and prayerful attention to know the things, which were spoken by the ancient prophets, and placed on divine record, that their fulfilment might be a growing evidence for the truth of the scriptures ; and a standing consolation to the children of God, under the trials they must meet from the enemies of religion.—It is a great support to pious believers, to see the truth of God in the fulfilment of his own word ; and to observe how he is progressively enlarging his kingdom, displaying his character, and preparing the way for a glorious state of his Church on earth, as well as for its final consummation in glory.—The conclusion of the greater divisions, by which men have marked the succession of time, that they might be able to compute its lapse, naturally calls our attention to the things which have taken place ; and awakes up our curiosity to enquire into those which are soon to come.

THE commencement of a new century, is such an event as we never saw before and shall never see again. It is an event which not a fourth part of mankind, who are born into the world, do ever see ; and being such, it is calculated to excite many serious and interesting reflections on the departure of time ; on our gradual but steady approach to the consummation of all earthly things, when the whole that have lived, or shall live hereafter, will be embosomed in eternity ; on the progress of natural and moral science in the period of a century ; on the revolutions that have happened in nations, which are most wonderfully conformable to the predictions of the holy prophets ; and on the past, present and future state of the Christian Church. On each of these topics, much might be thought and said, that is interesting to the cause of morality and human happiness.—But I shall confine myself to the last thing which was mentioned, some remarks on the past, the present, and future state of the Christian Church. If the present state of things among the nations, and the changes that have happened in the paft century, are a train of events, that do, in a moft aftonifhing degree, prepare for the fulfilment of the divine prom- ife, that the kingdom of Chrift fhall fill the world ; and if viewed on a large fcale, they have a moft pro- pitious afpect for the gofpel, then furely pious minds will rejoice ; and as furely infidels ought to tremble for themfelves, and for the vain conteft in which they are engaged with the king in Zion.

I THE rather introduce fuch a fubject at this time, from knowing that many, who think lightly of the Chriftian religion and fcriptures, have been dif- pofed to exult in their own folly, from thinking the afpects of Chriftianity are altogether gloomy.—Some have gone fo far into this idea, as to reveal their per- fuafion, that after a few years more, a Chriftian profeffion, Chriftian Churches, and Chriftian teach- ers will be wholly difcarded in the world. In this they may fpeak as they deludedly think, nor fhall I difpute that the thoughts are pleafant to them ; but fuch an iffue of things is contrary to probability, judg- ing from the events of the paft century and the ex- ifting ftate of things in the world. Although there is a great want of piety and much corruption in the profeffing Church, and many infidels are intermin- gled with Chriftian believers, and alfo a great part of the world is ftill under the darknefs of heathenifm; yet thofe who believe the word of God, and are accuftomed to confider the operation of things in the divine government, fee much to confole them, and to raife their expectations of an approaching bleffed day in the Church and in the whole world. In thofe very events, which infidels fuppofe to be their ftrength, and which make them fo fanguine that the defire of their hearts is foon to be fatisfied ; the ob- ferving and humble Chriftian finds evidence that his Redeemer is on the throne; that he is giving up his enemies to be their own deftroyers ; and that the more calamities abound in the earth, at this pe-

8   *On the universal spread of the Gospel.*

riod, the nearer is the glorious coming of the peaceful kingdom of order, truth and righteoufnefs.—Thus, the faith of Chriftians is upheld in a period of great difficulties, which was one chief reafon, that a revelation of future events was given to the Church. Obferving a natural preparation for the fulfilment of the promifes promotes the fpirit of prayer; and animates them, in the ufe of means, to fpread the gofpel of Jefus to the uttermoft ends of the earth.

BUT while the friends of Chriftianity are enabled to difcover the prophetic figns of the times, there is every reafon to fuppofe, that the eyes of its enemies will be clofed.   Infidels, and thofe who reject piety, will not fee what God is doing in the earth.   While he is ufing them as inftruments in his hand, to fulfil his word and deftroy each other, intent on their own purpofes, they will think they are profpered. While in a feries of revolutions, in the old world, he is fcourging licentioufnefs by its own devices, and breaking down the ancient governments of oppref-fion, by thofe who hate all law and order, he is preparing the way for a ftate of things, in which licentious men will have no influence; government will be eftablifhed on the firm bafe of moral virtue and religion;   and law and righteoufnefs and fubordination will be more firmly eftablifhed in the earth, than ever before.—While he is purifying a corrupt Church by judgments;   he is fo far from forfaking the gofpel of his Son, that this is the direct means to give it the greateft influence in the world;   fo that his Church may become fair as the fun, clear as the moon, and terrible as an army with banners, to all licentious people.

ALL this is fealed from the knowledge of the enemies of God.   Their unholy minds cannot fee the beauty of holinefs and of moral order and fubordination;   fo that it doth not appear defirable to them, that the Governor of the univerfe fhould produce fuch a ftate of things.   They cannot bear the apprehenfion of a **God,** who will bear down their lufts and paffions.—As they reject his word, they have not the evidence of the prophecies and divine promifes to direct their opinions. They have no conception of the nature, reality and power of godlinefs in the heart. As their whole delight is in the indulgence of fenfuality and pride, if they have power in their hands, they are wholly abforbed in the purfuits of fenfual gratification, and never reflect on the infinite fountain of natural and moral perfection. If they are deftitute of power, they ftill conjecture how they fhould conduct if they poffeffed it ; and fuppofe that thofe, who fortunately attain it, will fee the fame defirablenefs in vice and impiety which is difcovered by themfelves.—Such is the blindnefs of thefe perfons, that they cannot fee their own faces in the glafs of defcription. With fuch a ftate of the heart as they poffefs, and denying the word of **God,** it is not poffible they fhould fee the moral figns of the times, and difcern the overruling influence of **God,** in executing his promifes and threatenings. They will not know themfelves to be both the inftruments and the fufferers of divine vengeance. It is an old remark " that God permits thofe to be infatuated and blinded, whom he wills to deftroy." This hath always been true of particular finners, finful nations, and finful Churches ; and the previous remarks fhow why it is the cafe. It hath been thus with all the great civil and religious fyftems of impiety and oppreffion, which the holy providence of **God** hath brought to ruin, in the paft ages of the world ; and it will continue fo, until the earth is purified according to the promife.

It is therefore, no evidence, againft the truth of what is predicted on the ground of divine teftimony, that it is ridiculed by difbelievers. Their blindnefs and ridicule muft.be expected ; but let not Chriftians be blind alfo ; let not thofe for whofe confolation **God** hath revealed the feafons be indifferent ; let not

B

10   *On the universal spread of the Gospel.*

thofe, who are daily praying that Chrift would come in the glory of his kingdom here on earth, ceafe to fearch the holy word, and to mark the figns in providence that their prayer is heard, and their Lord hath arifen from his place, and is going through the earth to overthrow and beat down, until he hath prepared a glorious place for his throne.

THE time of our Saviour's appearance on earth was moft eventful in the fulfilment of ancient prophecies; but it was not feen by his enemies, and on this fubject he thus reproved them, " O ye hypocrites, ye can difcern the face of the fky; but ye cannot difcern the figns of the times !" He confidered their ignorance of a plain fulfilment of ancient prophecies, as an evidence of great impiety. And we may obferve, that it was the Sadducees, who were the infidels of that age, whom he thus reproved, which fhows how blind they were to the great work which God was doing. Let not Chriftians be guilty of a fimilar impiety, at a time the moft eventful in the fulfilment of ancient prophecy, of any fince our Redeemer's appearance on earth.

WHILE it is faid, that there is an evident natural preparation, for a general fpread of the gofpel through the world, it is not meant, that Chriftianity hath not many evils and much oppofition to meet; nor that its profeffors will not be tried and punifhed for their lukewarmnefs, and perhaps in fome inftances, be perfecuted for the gofpel's fake. But true Chriftians will not by this be terrified and turned away from the faith, for they are the followers of a Saviour who fuffered; and it appears to have been the defign of infinite wifdom, that during the humiliated ftate of the Church, his followers fhould through much tribulation enter into the kingdom of heaven. As their Redeemer gives them grace to live; fo they humbly hope, that if called to fuch an event, he will furnifh ftrength to die triumphantly, in what-

ever manner, and at whatever time, his wifdom fees
will moft promote the caufe of truth.—The raifed
expectations of irreligious men, that Chriftianity is
on the wane, do not decide the point; neither do
they difprove what I have faid, that the general ftate
of things in the world exhibits a wonderful natural
preparation, for the fulfilment of holy prophecy, that
the gofpel of Chrift fhall become univerfal, and that
meafuring time on the large fcale of centuries, the
period is very near.

In bringing this fubject before you, I fhall,

I. Mention fundry divine promifes, that in due
time, the gofpel and the Chriftian Church fhall fill
the world, to the exclufion of Heathen ignorance
and of all falfe religion.

II. I shall endeavor to defcribe, as may be collected from the facred prophecies and the fulfilment
of them recorded in hiftory, what appears to have
been the fcheme of divine counfel in this matter ;
what progrefs the gofpel fhould make ; the hindrances which fhould arife ; and how and when the
promife fhould be glorioufly fulfilled.

III. I shall take a view of the prefent ftate of
the world and of the nations, with refpect to Chriftianity, by which we may fee an amazing preparation
for the fulfilment of the gracious and glorious
promife.

I. I am to mention fundry divine promifes, that
in due time, the gofpel and the Chriftian Church
fhall fill the world, to the exclufion of Heathen ignorance and of all falfe religion.

The explicit predictions of fuch an event, and
thofe in which it is plainly implied, are far more than
I can mention ; and they were expreffed in every
age of revelation ; by all the divine prophets under

12 *On the universal spread of the Gospel.*

the Mofaic difpenfation; by Chrift himfelf, and by the apoftolical writers who completed the facred canon. The early promife to Abraham, that in his feed all the nations of the earth fhould be bleffed, predicted this event, and it was abundantly repeated to the Hebrews, that in the days of the Meffiah, their expected prince, all the Gentiles fhould obey him ; and that the glory of all the kingdoms fhould be given to Zion and to Jerufalem, which were typical names for the true Church of God, which now fubfifts under the Chriftian form.

THE fuffering and the exalted ftate of the Redeemer ; alfo, the fuffering and glorious ftate of his Church in the world, were both matter of prediction in the ancient prophets. Not attending to thefe different ftates, and how exactly they are defcribed in the prophetic writings, hath produced many falfe opinions, both among Jews and Chriftians. Inattention to the clear prophecies, of the humiliation and the fuffering ftate of Chrift in the world, was one reafon that the Jews denied him to be the expected Meffiah. In the fame manner, by not attending to the prophetic defcription of the firft periods of the Chriftian Church ; how it fhould be agitated by errors, corrupted with immorality, and oppofed by infidelity, both in an Heathen and Antichriftian form ; how long and dreadful the ftruggle fhould be ; what an opportunity it would furnifh to develope the wickednefs of the human heart, and to difplay the juftice of God in the punifhment of apoftacy : fome Chriftians have been led to defpair of fo bleffed a ftate to come in the Church on earth, as is very explicitly promifed in the prophets. They have fpiritualized, in an application to the fanctification and comforts of particular Chriftians, many things that were written defcriptive of the general glory and peace and increafe of the Church. Thus to lofe fight of this future glory, of Zion hath many bad effects. It is departing from that general view of his counfels, which

On the universal spread of the Gospel.

God faw it beft to reveal; it difheartens the fincere, and makes them ready to yield before infidelity; it lowers their apprehenfions of that degree of perfonal holinefs and joy, which by faithfulnefs, good men may attain in this world ; it expofes them to affim- ilate with the fentiments and practices of the ungod- ly ; and it cools their defires and exertions for the converfion of the Heathen nations, and for purify- ing the Chriftian Church from the errors and impu- rities into which it hath fallen.

A LARGE part of the book of Pfalms is prophetic. The whole of the pfalm from which I am difcourfing is a prophecy, concerning the Saviour, and the Chrif- tian ftate of the Church ; and contains many prom- ifes and threatenings. It was written about 1040 years before the birth of Chrift ; and though pen- ned at that vaft diftance of time, it gives a general view of the ftate of things under the Chriftian dif- penfation. A confiderable part of it hath been already fulfilled, and a natural preparation for the completion is moft apparently haftening, as we fhall fee in the end of this difcourfe. The anointed of the Lord, of whom the prophet fpeaks hath been born. The kings of the earth, and the rulers of the Jews and of the Heathen Roman empire, took counfel againft him and his caufe, faying, " Let us break their bands afunder and caft away their cords from us." The event hath demonftrated, " that he who fitteth in the heavens laughed and had them in de- rifion. He fpake unto them in his wrath and vexed them in his fore difpleafure." Although they were permitted, for a fhort feafon, to profper, and cruci- fied the Lord's anointed according to his fore-deter- minate counfel, wrath was coming upon them to the utmoft. The Jewifh ftate and rulers, in about forty years from that event, were vexed and broken by the moft memorable judgments, which continue to this day. God hath preferved them a feparate peo- ple, in all their difperfions thro' the earth, to be, in

14 *On the universal spread of the Gospel.*

the firft inftance monuments of his vengeance, and fecondly, that in the end of defolations, he may fhow his great power, grace, and the truth of his prophetic word, by converting and bringing them into the land of their fathers.

THE Heathen Roman empire, for three hundred years, perfecuted the Church of Chrift. During all this period, Chriftianity increafed in the face of perfecution, the moft dreadful tortures, and all earthly difcouragements. Although he, who fitteth in the heavens, permitted this to try the faith and patience of his faints, and to fhow that he could fpread his truth and increafe his Church againft all human oppofition ; yet he was laughing at the folly of his enemies and holding them in derifion. The vital ftrength of the perfecuting power was failing. In proportion as Chriftianity was perfecuted, by a multitude of operating caufes, by judgments from abroad and by inteftine divifions, Heathen Rome was finking to an utter ruin. God had fet the afcended Redeemer as king in Zion and through the earth, and committed the times and the feafons, and his Church and the kingdoms of the nations to his control. He wrought out of the fight of his enemies, and beyond the expectation of his friends, and his victory was great.

THE laft general perfecution under Heathen Rome, which was principally directed by the emperor Dioclefian, was extenfive, bloody and cruel beyond all which had preceded. It commenced about the year 300, and continued for ten or twelve years. Innumerable martyrs were facrificed with all conceivable torments ; Churches and places of worfhip were demolifhed ; and the fcriptures and thofe who poffeffed or read them were profcribed, that a knowledge of the gofpel might be banifhed from the earth. The enemies of Chriftianity triumphed greatly, and openly declared, that the name and caufe of Chrift were banifhed from the world. It hath not

On the universal spread of the Gospel. 15

been uncommon for the ungodly to be thus deluded, in the moments immediately preceding their own downfall. It was thus, when the Egyptians purfued and inclofed the Ifraelites on the banks of the Red Sea ; when the Jews crucified Chrift ; and at the period of which I have been fpeaking ; and it is thus that difbelievers triumph at the prefent day. In this dark time, the king in Zion was preparing the means for an unexpected and glorious light. By a remarkable concurrence of circumftances, too many to be here mentioned, in twenty years from the beginning of that moft awful perfecution, Conftantine, having obtained the empire, declared himfelf a Chriftian ; and from that period, it has generally been faid, that the empire became Chriftian. This was a vifible triumph worthy of the Redeemer, and delivered the Church from perfecution ; ftill it is not probable that it added to the love, faith and purity of profeffors. Profperity often corrupts while afflictions purify.

NOTWITHSTANDING the government was now propitious to a Chriftian profeffion, the wrath of God refted upon it, the blood of martyrs cried againft it, and the divine curfe muft have its courfe. To fhow divine indignation againft a perfecuting power, and to chaftife Chriftians now growing formal and voluptuous, a train of moft defolating judgments followed. The feat of government in 330 was removed from Rome to Canftantinople, and the Northern barbarous nations defolated and broke the empire in pieces. The fame Almighty power, which fulfilled the firft part of prophecy in this pfalm, will accomplifh the whole ; will execute the remaining threatenings and glorify the promife " afk of me, and I fhall give thee the Heathen for thine inheritance, and the uttermoft parts of the earth for thy poffeffion." Every thing in Heathen nations that oppofes an accomplifhment of the promife, " he will break with a rod of iron and dafh in pieces like a potter's veffel."

16   *On the universal spread of the Gospel.*

To fuch a threatening as this, the exhortation that follows is admirably adapted, " Be wife, now, therefore, O ye kings, be inftructed ye judges of the earth. Serve the Lord with fear and rejoice with trembling. Kifs the Son, left he be angry, and ye perifh from the way when his wrath is kindled but a little."

To recite all the prophecies, of the fpread of the gofpel through the world in the latter days, would include a large portion of the facred volume ; and to enter into a detail of their fulfilment, fo far as it hath taken place, as I have done in the laft inftance, would be endlefs.   I fhall recite a fufficient number of thofe prophetic promifes with only a few remarks. From pfalm xliv. to l. is a general defcription of the ftate of the Church.   It begins with the poffeffion of Canaan by the Hebrews ; then reprefents the low ftate of God's people under the oppreffion of their enemies ; defcribes the majefty of the Redeemer ; the fpiritual beauty of the Church, and the confidence of his people in their king ; and ends with a defcription of awful judgments on the enemies of the Lord, and the fpread of peace and truth through the earth.—" God is our refuge and ftrength, a very prefent help in trouble.   Therefore will not we fear, though the earth be removed, and though the mountains be carried into the fea : Though the waters thereof roar and be troubled, though the mountains fhake with the fwelling thereof.   There is a river the ftreams whereof fhall make glad the city of God, the holy place of the tabernacles of the moft High.   God is in the midft of her ; fhe fhall not be moved : God fhall help her, and that right early. The Heathen raged, the kingdoms were moved : he uttered his voice, the earth melted.   The Lord of hofts is with us ; the God of Jacob is our refuge. Come behold the works of the Lord, what defolation he hath made in the earth."   This work of great defolation he is now beginning.   Then follows the glorious iffue of thefe commotions, by which the

kingdoms had been moved and the earth melted.
" He maketh wars to ceafe unto the end of the earth ;
he breaketh the bow and cutteth the fpear in funder;
he burneth the chariot in the fire. Be ftill and
know that I am God ; I will be exalted among the
Heathen, I will be exalted in the earth."* The time
in which war is to ceafe and God be exalted to the
ends of the earth is yet future.—" All the ends of
the world fhall remember and turn unto the Lord :
and all the kindreds of the nations fhall worfhip before thee. For the kingdom is the Lord's and he is
governor among the nations."† This is promifed in
confequence of the fufferings of Chrift which are
defcribed in the firft part of the pfalm.—Under the
type of Solomon's profperity, the kingdom of Chrift
is thus defcribed, " In his days fhall the righteous
flourifh ; and abundance of peace fo long as the
moon endureth. He fhall have dominion alfo from
fea to fea, and from the river unto the ends of the
earth. They that dwell in the wildernefs fhall bow
before him, and his enemies fhall lick the duft. Yea
all kings fhall bow down before him ; all nations
fhall ferve him."‡

GOD was pleafed to give to his fervant Daniel, in
prophetic vifion, a defcription of the ftate of the
Church and of the nations, from his own time to the
end of the world. His prophecies have aftonifhed
mankind, and given great trouble to difbelievers, in
every age. Porphyry and other infidels, who lived
in the third and fourth centuries, obferving his exactnefs in the defcription of events, and in the computation of times expreffed in prophetic language,
made a vain pretence, that the book of Daniel was
written after fuch events had happened ; but he was
then amply refuted, and the later fulfilment of his
predictions are a continued refutation.—Daniel lived,
and came to a great age, under the Babylonian mon-

* Pfalm xlvi.   † Pfalm xxii. 27, 28.   ‡ Pfalm lxxii.

C

18   *On the universal spread of the Gospel.*

archy, which was the firft of the four great dominions, of which his prophecy fpake ; and was an actor
in very interefting fcenes, from about fix-hundred to
five-hundred forty years before Chrift's birth.   He
not only prophecied of Chrift, but foretold, with
great exactnefs, the time of his incarnation and
death.   He announced the fpeedy deftruction of the
Babylonian empire, which was then in its glory ; the
rife of the Medo-perfian dominion, and its deftruction before the Grecian or Macedonian.   He foretold the divifion of the Macedonian, at the death of
Alexander, into four great kingdoms, and gave a
particular account of the bitter woes, by which they
punifhed themfelves and deftroyed mankind.   He
alfo foretold the Roman empire which was to rife, by
defcribing its character, both in its Heathen and
Antichriftian form ; its vaft extenfion and long continuance; its wonderful policy and ftrength; its
oppreffion of the rights and confciences of men ; its
bitternefs againft the uncorrupted truths of Chriftianity and its bloody perfecutions ; its Papal idolatry ; and its modern divifion into the principal ftates
of Europe.—He limits the time of its continuance in
the Antichriftian form, to a " time, times, and the
half or dividing of time."   Three years and an half
in prophetic ; and counting a day for a year, twelve
hundred and fixty in common computation.   After
this he fays, " the judgment fhall fit, and they fhall
take away his dominion, to confume and deftroy it
to the end."*   Then he adds the promife, that the
kingdom of Chrift fhall fill the earth.   " I faw in the
night vifions, and, behold, one like the Son of Man
came with the clouds of heaven, and came to the
Ancient of days, and they brought him near before
him.   And there was given him dominion, and glory,
and a kingdom, that all people, nations and languages, fhould ferve him ; his dominion is an everlafting dominion, which fhall not pafs away, and his

* Daniel vii. 26.

kingdom that which fhall not be deftroyed.—And the kingdom and dominion, and greatnefs of the kingdom under the whole heaven, fhall be given to the people of the faints of the Moft High, whofe kingdom is an everlafting kingdom, and all dominions fhall ferve and obey him."*

In the fecond chapter of the fame prophecy, the four great dominions, which have been mentioned, are in prophetic vifion reprefented by an image of various compofition, which ftood and profpered until " a ftone, which was cut out without hands, fmote the image upon its feet, which were of iron and clay, and broke it in pieces. And the ftone that fmote the image became a great mountain and filled the earth."—The explanation of the vifion given by the prophet is, that " in the days of thefe kings, fhall the God of heaven fet a kingdom that fhall never be deftroyed : and the kingdom fhall not be left to other people, but it fhall break in pieces and confume all thofe kingdoms, and it fhall ftand forever."—This univerfal dominion of Chriftianity, fhall take place immediately on the fubverfion of the Roman Antichrift.

Since the beginning, the world hath been filled in every part, with a fucceffion of worldly dominions, fome Heathen and fome Antichriftian. They have rifen in fucceffion and devoured each other.— Thefe, which reigned in parts of the earth, where God was pleafed to reveal himfelf and place his Church, have been noticed in fcripture hiftory and prophecy, and others, without thefe limits, were moftly unnoticed in the facred volume. The greateft part of thefe governments have been formed and executed on the principles of pride and violence, and without the fear of God the fovereign king. They have been filled with the " tears of fuch as were oppreffed, and they had no comforter ; and on the fide of their

* Daniel vii. 13, 14. 27.

20   *On the universal spread of the Gospel.*

oppreffors was power, but they had no comforter.''
Thefe prophecies of Daniel promife us a time to
come, when the kingdom, and the dominion and
the greatnefs of the kingdom, under the whole heav-
en, fhall be given to the people of the faints of the
Moft High.   By this we do not wifh to underftand,
that civil government, either in the legiflative or executive branches, fhall be committed to the Church in
its ecclefiaftical capacity, for Chrift's kingdom never
was and never will be of this world.   But the meaning of the prophecy is, that men fhall generally be
pious and fincere profeffors in the Church of Chrift,
and by the direftion of providence and the choice of
mankind, thofe will be raifed to the higheft places
in civil truft, who are eminent for their obedience to
the truth.—Difbelievers will lofe all their influence
in fociety.—Civil laws will be in confiftency with
Revelation.—The ftate will encourage religion ; and
the prevalence of religion will difpofe the people to
maintain government, order, fubordination and juftice.   This will be giving the kingdom and the greatnefs of the kingdom, to the people of the faints of
the Moft High.   Nothing like this hath been general
in the world.   Although it be the nature of Chriftianity to ameliorate the condition of mankind, and
fpread peace, its bleffed effefts have been, in a great
meafure, limited by the wicked paffions of Men ;
and the Chriftian name deftitute of the reality, by
Antichriftian perverfion, hath for ages, tormented
a large portion of the earth.

Of all the ancient prophets, Ifaiah writes in the
moft evangelical ftrain.   He gave the moft clear defcription of the humiliation of Chrift, and his glory which was to follow ; of the Chriftian doftrines,
temper and praftice ; and of the amplitude and bleffednefs of the Church. when all nations fhould become obedient to the gofpel.   In the fecond chapter
of his prophecies, we find the following remarkable
defcription, '' And it fhall come to pafs in the latter
days, that the mountain of the Lord's houfe fhall

246

be eſtabliſhed in the top of the mountains, and ſhall be exalted above the hills, and all nations ſhall flow unto it. *And many people ſhall go and ſay, come ye and let us go up to the mountain of the Lord, to the houſe of the God of Jacob ; and he will teach us of his ways, and we will walk in his paths ; for out of Zion ſhall go forth the law, and the word of the Lord from Jeruſalem. And he ſhall judge among the nations and ſhall rebuke many people : and they ſhall beat their ſwords into plow-ſhares and their ſpears into pruning-hooks ; nation ſhall not lift up ſword againſt nation, neither ſhall they learn war any more.'' This is a promiſe, that all nations ſhall flow to the houſe of the Lord, and the world be filled with Chriſtian knowledge and peace.—In the fourth chapter of the prophecy of Micah is a ſimilar prediction. In the eleventh chapter of Iſaiah, where there is a promiſe of the Redeemer, and a deſcription of his kingdom and its bleſſed effects on the ſtate and moral character and conduct of men, the promiſe ends in theſe wonderful words, `` For the earth ſhall be full of the knowledge of the Lord as the waters cover the ſeas.'' From the beginning of the twenty-fourth chapter to the end of the twenty-ſixth, is a prophecy of the awful deſtructions, which are to precede the peaceful ſtate of the Church, interſperſed with promiſes of glory and peace and univerſal knowledge, to ſucceed the execution of divine judgments, `` And in this mountain ſhall the Lord of Hoſts make unto all people a feaſt of fat things, a feaſt of wines on the lees, of fat things full of marrow, of wines on the lees well refined. And he will deſtroy in this mountain the face of the covering caſt over all people, and the vail that is ſpread over all nations.''—`` At that time they ſhall call Jeruſalem the throne of the Lord, and all the nations ſhall be gathered unto it, to the name of the Lord to Jeruſalem, neither ſhall they walk any more after the imagination of their evil heart.*

* Jeremiah iii. 17.

22   *On the universal spread of the Gospel.*

In all the prophets of the Old Teftament we find fimilar reprefentations, too numerous to be here repeated, defcribing the peace, the glory, the univerfal extent of the vifible Church and kingdom. The qualities of this kingdom are defcribed to be, an high degree of knowledge ; abounding in the fervices of worfhip and praife ; purity of obedience to the divine law ; delight in God, in his falvation, and in his glory ; univerfal peace, fo that war fhall be no more known ; a righteous government thro' the earth, under which licentious men and difbelievers fhall not again difturb mankind ; and a communion between all the tribes of men in a fpiritual and general happinefs. The extent of this kingdom is, alfo, defcribed by fuch univerfal expreffions as the following ; all nations ; all people ; to the ends of the earth ; all the ends of the earth ; all flefh together ; under the whole Heaven ; with many others moft fignificant of a general fpread of the gofpel through the world.

Jesus Christ reprefented the fame glorious trûth in a number of his parables, when defcribing the kingdom of God or the Chriftian Church. This was the fpecial defign of the parables of the muftard feed and of the leaven whereby the whole lump was leavened. He declared that his gofpel fhould be preached in all the world. His commiffion to his difciples, and through them to his minifters of the following ages, was that they fhould go and teach all nations through the world. The Apoftle Paul prophecies, that the blindnefs which hath happened to Ifrael muft continue, until the period appointed for the fulnefs of the Gentiles to come in.

The Apoftle and prophet John, with whofe Revelations the facred canon is compleated, after he had, in the language of prophecy, defcribed the preceding periods, in the beginning of the twentieth chapter, fays, " And I faw an angel come down from Heaven, having the key of the bottomlefs pit, and a great chain in his hand. And he laid hold on the dragon, that old ferpent, which is the devil and fatan, and bound him a thoufand years, and caft him into the bottomlefs pit, and fhut him up, and fet a feal upon him, that he fhould deceive the nations no more, till the thoufand years fhould be fulfilled."— After this binding of fatan he defcribes a peaceful and glorious ftate of the Church.—Although there have been great, extenfive and wonderful effects of the gofpel, for many ages ; yet thefe and a multitude of fimilar promifes have never been fulfilled. There hath been no period of univerfal peace ; of a world filled with divine knowledge and holinefs ; of freedom from the errors and temptations of fatan and wicked men ; and of praife and obedience to God through the earth. The accomplifhment is yet to come, and there is more in the holy fcriptures leading us to expect it, than Chriftians generally fuppofe, who have not given themfelves to examine the fubject. We therefore expect, on the ground of a divine promife, that the gofpel and the Chriftian Church fhall fill the earth, to the exclufion of Heathen ignorance and of all falfe religion. Although infidels may fuppofe, that a Chriftian profeffion and the means of inftruction will foon ceafe from among men, they have a defperate and hopelefs battle to fight ; they have all the glorious promifes to fubvert ; the mouth of the Lord hath fpoken it, and his power and grace fhall fulfil !

II. I shall endeavor to defcribe, as may be collected from the facred prophecies and the fulfilment of them recorded in hiftory, what appears to have been the fcheme of divine counfel in this matter ; what progrefs the gofpel fhould make ; the hindrances which fhould arife ; and how and when the promife fhould be glorioufly fulfilled.

The prophecies and the promifes of God concerning the future ftate of things in the world and

24 *On the universal spread of the Gospel.*

in his Church, were defignedly fo expreffed, that men fhould not underftand them minutely until they were fulfilled ; and in fome inftances, they are unable to form any right apprehenfion of them, before the accomplifhment begins. The general reprefent-ations given are fufficient to preferve the hope and patience of the Church under fore trials, and to warn the wicked, the atheiftical and the apoftate, of the dreadful judgments, with which, in due time, they fhall be vifited ; while a more minute defcription of events and times would, on many accounts, have been improper to be communicated to the world.

SOME have attempted to ridicule the figurative imagery, which is ufed in the prophetic diction ; but hereby they fhow their weaknefs as well as the difbelief of their hearts. By the ufe of this figurative imagery, the divine Spirit was enabled to give a general view of the ftate and periods of things, without difcovering the particular men and nations, who fhould be the actors under providence, and this, in moft inftances, was not defigned ; alfo to exprefs many minute circumftances, which ought not to be previoufly known, in fuch figures as might be exactly traced after the accomplifhment, thereby becoming a mighty evidence for the truth of the holy fcriptures. Whoever juftly confiders the principal defign of the prophecies, and the difficulty there was in defcribing the great events of futurity, without making a difcovery of many things that had better be fecreted from the knowledge of men, until after the fulfilment ; will fee the infinite wifdom of God in adopting the figurative imagery of prophetic diction, and find herein an argument for the truth of divine revelation.

IT was clear to the firft Chriftians, that a future ftate of great profperity to the Church was promifed : but a fufficient number of events had not happened, in the fulfilment of prophecy, to inftruct them in the

periods of times which were defcribed, in prophetic language. Some expected that the thoufand
years of profperity would commence foon; while
others placed them, in expectation, at a greater diftance. It was, alfo, clear to the ancient Chriftians,
that an Antichrift would arife, which fhould be a
perfecuting power, and that he fhould be awfully
deftroyed by the brightnefs of the Redeemer's
fpiritual coming ; but when and where he fhould
arife they formed no true apprehenfions. They
generally feemed to fuppofe Antichrift would be
fome external power, which rejected the Chriftian
name, and they were ready to give this title to every
perfecuting prince or nation, which raged againft the
truth for the fhort feafon of a fingle life of man.

LEAST of all was there any general idea among
ancient Chriftians, that Antichrift would arife in the
very bofom of the Church ; that the Catholic Church
itfelf would become Antichrift ; that the minifters
of a religion, which required humility, would put
themfelves in the place of God ; and that Chriftian
temples would be filled with rites and images and
the worfhip of departed faints, but little different
from the pomp and fuperftition and demon worfhip
of Heathenifm, which feemed to be dying before
Chriftianity. The rolling away of eighteen centuries,
and the events which have happened, ferve as a key
to unlock the myftic page of prophecy. A great
part of the myftery is fully unfolded by the events,
which have taken place in the earth. Other things
are happening by the moft aftonifhing means ; and
we fee a natural preparation for the accomplifhment
of things future, which are foretold ; and among
thefe, for the fpread of the gofpel through the earth.

THE plan of divine counfel refpecting the oppofition to Chriftianity, its fpread, and its final triumph
and filling of the earth, which was foretold in the

D

26   *On the universal spread of the Gospel.*

---

prophetic page, may be feen in the four following fcenes, or fucceffive ftates of things ;—the two firft of which have been fulfilled, according to the divine prediction ; the third is now fulfilling ; for the fourth a preparation is making, and it will foon take place.

1. THE early ftruggle which Chriftianity had with Jewifh and Heathen oppofition, and its fuccefs and final triumph by the deftruction of thofe oppofing powers.

I GAVE fome account of this under the laft branch of difcourfe. Chriftianity appeared to obtain a fair introduction, in every part of the old Roman empire; and in the borders of feveral other nations, its allies and tributaries, where the Roman laws were never introduced. The early oppofition of the Heathen empire ; the perfecutions it effected ; and the divine judgments by which it was finking, through the agency of him, who ruleth the rebelling nations with a rod of iron, and dafheth in pieces thofe who oppofe him like a potters veffel, are reprefented by the opening of the fix firft feals, in the fixth chapter of John's Revelation.—The opening of the fixth feal, by prophetic images, defcribes the mighty concuffion there was in the empire at the fall of Heathenifm. The quaking of the earth is an emblem of great commotion and war.—The fun, moon, ftars and vifible heavens, are emblematic of earthly powers and thofe who poffefs and execute them. Thus, the wars of Conftantine ; his victories and his fuppreffion of all the perfecuting authorities, are reprefented by an eclipfe of the whole firmament of Heathen power. The earth quaked ; the fun became black as fackcloth of hair; the moon became as blood ; the ftars of heaven fell ; the heavens departed as a fcroll ; every mountain and ifland were moved ; the kings, the great men and the rich men called on the mountains and rocks, to fall and hide them from the face of him who fitteth on the throne, and from the wrath of the Lamb.   Thus awful and fublime, is the prophetic defcription of God's judgments on the empire, when Heathenifm was ejected from power ; and the hiftory of that period compares well with the defcription.

THE judgments by which the ancient imperial Roman power was ftill further reduced, after it took the name of Chriftian and by which currupt Chriftians were punifhed, are prophetically fignified, by the founding of the fix firft trumpets, in the eighth and ninth chapters of St. John's Revelation.—In this period the empire was wholly dafhed in pieces ; and the Chriftian Church, into which many corruptions in doctrine and practice were introduced, was punifhed by awful judgments.

THE way was prepared for the

2d STATE of things, the rife of Antichrift.

A NEW fpecies of oppreffion arofe, in many refpects different from any thing which had preceded. Civil pride and power, and ecclefiaftical oppreffion, fuperftition, avarice, hypocrify and cruelty combined to fcourge mankind, to darken counfel and fill the world with mifery.   Thofe, who were expecting an Antichrift from without the Church, become an Antichrift themfelves.   They loft the faith in its purity. —They departed from the fimplicity, the humility, and the holinefs of Chriftian practice, as they were enjoined by Chrift and his apoftles.—The power of godlinefs was departed from the Church, which ftill gloried in the name of Chriftian and Catholic.—The clergy left their place of diligent and exemplary inftructors in the houfe of Chrift, and watchmen for the fouls of men, and comforters of the meek and lowly brethren.—A hierarchy of various grades was forming.—Power and wealth and luxurious indulgences were fought, inftead of piety and a good converfation.—At firft general councils, and afterwards a Papal head claimed infallibility.   The con-

fciences of men were oppreffed ; their right to believe for themfelves was denied ; and the blood of
confcientious martyrs began to flow.—The fcriptures were denied to the people.—The facred fathers
affumed the power of pardoning fins for money ;
and by this, with the difpenfations which they granted to commit the moft horrid crimes, collected enormous fums from the mifguided people.—Inftitutions were every where founded, for both fexes, under the vows of celibacy, which became nurferies of
impurity cloaked under the pretext of religion.—
Civil power was affimilated with pontifical holinefs.
—All liberty, civil and religious was abrogated, and
kings, nations and a world enflaved by the will of
wicked men, under the name of vicegerents of God
and of the meek and lowly Jefus !—All this arofe
within the bofom of the Church, and it was Antichrift indeed, with more fearful features, than divine
prophecy itfelf had painted !—This ftate of things
began gradually to draw on in the fixth century ;
and in the feventh and eighth centuries the limbs of
the Antichriftian beaft manifeftly difplayed their
fhape.   In the twelfth, thirteenth and fourteenth
centuries, this tyranny, idolatry and blafphemy were
at their heighth ; for truth was obfcured, and it was
the reign of crimes.   Hiftory gives fuch information
concerning this period !

SUNDRY of the prophets predicted this apoftacy
and its deftruction.   It is noticed in the ancient
prophecy of Daniel, chap. vii. under the image of
the little horn, in which were eyes like the eyes of a
man, and a mouth fpeaking great things, which he
defcribes, verfe 21, " the fame horn made war with
the faints, and prevailed againft them."—Verfe 25,
" He fhall fpeak great words againft the Moft High,
and fhall wear out the faints of the Moft High, and
think to change times and laws : and they fhall be
given into his hand until a time, and times and the
dividing of time."—This great fyftem of civil and

religious oppreffion is alfo noticed, in many other places of the fame prophecy, which it would be tedious to mention on this occafion.

THE apoftle Paul predicts the fame apoftacy.—In his firft epiftle to the Theffalonian Church, he had given a defcription of the final day of judgment. Some paffages in this defcription, they mifunder-ftood, as an intimation of that day being near at hand, and to correct that miftake, he tells them in the fecond chapter of his fecond epiftle, not to be troubled and fhaken in mind on that account, becaufe great events muft take place in the world before the confummation of time. "Let no man deceive you by any means : for that day fhall not come, except there come a falling away firft, and that man of fin be revealed, the fon of perdition : Who oppofeth and exalteth himfelf above all that is called God, or that is worfhipped ; fo that he as God fitteth in the temple of God, fhewing himfelf that he is God.——— Whofe coming is after the working of fatan, with all power and figns and lying wonders, and with all deceivablenefs of unrighteoufnefs in them that perifh, becaufe they received not the love of the truth that they might be faved. And for this caufe God fhall fend them ftrong delufion, that they fhould believe a lie : that they all might be damned who believed not the truth, but had pleafure in unrighteoufnefs." Of the nature of this apoftacy he fpeaketh further in his firft epiftle to Timothy the fourth chapter.——— "Now the Spirit fpeaketh exprefsly, that in the latter times fome fhall depart from the faith, giving heed to feducing fpirits, and doctrines of devils ; fpeaking lies in hypocrify ; having their confciences feared with a hot iron ; forbidding to marry and commanding to abftain from meats, which God created to be received with thankfgiving of them which believe and know the truth."—Thefe paffages are a very marked defcription of the Antichriftian character, and fome of its errors and crimes. The apoftle Peter, alſo, in the third chapter of his ſecond epiſtle, predicts that in the *laſt days*, ſcoffers ſhall ariſe, walking after their own luſts, and ſaying, where is the promiſe of his coming? Meaning men, who have no ſenſe of moral obligation, of a holy God and his juſt judg: ments on ſin. By the *laſt* and *latter* days, the pro- phets appear uniformly to mean the period of Anti- chriſtian apoſtacy, eſpecially its concluding ſcenes.

But the ſtate of things under the apoſtacy, is moſt particularly deſcribed by the prophet John, in his viſions, of the two witneſſes prophecying in ſack- cloth 1260 days ; of the dragon perſecuting the wo- man, and driving her into the wilderneſs for the ſame time ; of a beaſt with ſeven heads and ten horns ; of a ſecond beaſt with two horns like a lamb, but ſpeaking as a dragon ; and of an impure woman, ſetting upon a ſcarlet colored beaſt, full of names of blaſphemy, having ſeven heads and ten horns ; and upon the woman's forehead written, myſtery, Bab- ylon the great, the mother of harlots and abomina- tions of the earth.—This is the ſecond ſtate of things deſcribed by prophecy, and it hath been accompliſh- ed, under the name of Chriſtian, ſuch an idolatrous, blaſphemous and oppreſſive power over the proper- ties, bodies and ſouls of men hath ariſen and troub- led the earth.

The period of time aſſigned by the prophets Dan- iel and John, for the duration of this oppreſſive power, is expreſſed three ways ; by a time, times and the dividing of time, or three years and an half ; by forty-two months ; and by twelve hundred and ſixty days. All theſe amount to the ſame, and ta- king a day for a year, which is the moſt common prophetic meaſure, are twelve hundred and ſixty years. The great difficulty, in knowing when the twelve hundred and ſixty years will expire, is to find from what time we muſt begin to count. The op- preſſive ſyſtem grew by a gradual acquiſition of pow- er and exerciſe of tyranny. Paul tells us even in

his time, " For the myſtery of iniquity doth already
work, only he who now letteth, will let, until he be
taken out of the way, and then ſhall that wicked
one be revealed.*—What let or hindered, was the
Roman empire in its Heathen form, which prohib-
ited all power to Chriſtians. After the empire became Chriſtian, the myſtery of iniquity was rapidly
working, as a preparation for the man of ſin to be
revealed. In view of the prophecies, good men have
been divided in opinion ; ſome counting the 1260
years from the year of Chriſt, 606, when the Biſhop of Rome aſſumed the name and was permitted to
exerciſe the power of univerſal Biſhop over the
whole Chriſtian Church. Others have counted
them from the year of Chriſt 756, when the Biſhop
of Rome, by an inveſtiture of the Exarchate of Ra-
venna, became a civil prince, in all reſpeɛts independent of any foreign power.—Counting from 606, the
twelve hundred and ſixty years will end in 1866.
Counting from 756, they will terminate in the year
2016.—It is probable they ought not to be counted,
in all reſpeɛts, from either of theſe or any other period. It will appear by examination, there hath
been, in a great number of inſtances, 1260 years
between events propitious to the riſe of Antichriſt,
and which furniſhed to him great acceſſions of power ; and other events, which were humbling and
bringing him low.—His decay will be progreſſive as
his riſe. By uſurping the power of univerſal Biſhop
he became a complete tyrant over the Church, and
it is probable, that in twelve hundred and ſixty years
from that time, or by the year 1866, the whole ſyſtem of religious oppreſſion and hereſy in doɛtrine,
and idolatry in praɛtice, will be ſwept away by the
juſt and purifying judgments of God.

THE acceſſion of temporal dominion, to the Biſhop of Rome, opened a ſcene new and intereſting.
Thoſe who had before tyrannized over the Church,

* 2 Theſſalonians ii. 7.

were now enabled to become tyrants among the nations. This union, of civil and ecclefiaftical power, made them terrible to the furrounding kingdoms ; and what could not be effected by civil negociation was carried by pontifical anathemas.—So long as princes poured their riches into the ecclefiaftical treaf-ury, the earthly head of the church affifted them, to bind heavier chains on their fubjects ; and thus the civil oppreffion on mankind was tenfold increafed. It is probable, that all civil inftitutions of oppreffion will be removed by the providence of God, before the year 2016, which completes the 1260 years, counting from 756, when temporal dominion was annexed to the Roman Church.

THIS amelioration of the civil ftate of mankind, muft be effected by the prevalence of a pure Chrif-tianity, and a holy mórality, in the hearts and practice of men ; for no other means are adequate to fo great an effect. The latter day glory of the Church is neceffary for univerfal freedom in the nations.— As an Antichriftian Church hath been an inftrument of oppreffion ; fo a Church formed on the princi-ples of our Redeemer, and practifing on gofpel precepts, is the only poffible inftrument of giving and preferving freedom among men. This the Church will do, not by affuming any degree of civil power into its own hands ; but preparing men to act wifely and juftly, in the civil departments allotted to them. Religion will prepare men to rule, to ordain wife laws, and execute them faithfully when called to high office.—It will prepare them to obey, to be friends of order and government, and act right in the place allotted them by divine providence.—It will, at once, banifh oppreffion and licentioufnefs ; and in this way, the Church of Chrift is neceffary for the freedom of the nations, and to bring fociety into fuch a ftate that men can enjoy equal rights. Some beginning, of the millennial purity of the Church, in doctrine, difcipline, a holy practice, and a fervent

love of God and men, is neceffary to banifh all civil oppreffion and eftablifh order thro' the earth.

To hear men philofophifing on fyftems of freedom, and on the reign of natural and equal rights,
and at the fame time, difcarding the Chriftian religion, which contains all the moral principles and
duties, by which fociety can be united and made
orderly ; fhows, that they are either deceitful above
all things, or deeply ignorant of the fubjects they difcufs, and wholly unqualified to give an opinion.
Although the gofpel decides not the queftion of preference, among the many forms of government in
the world ; yet it forbids all oppreffion public and
private, in nations and in individuals ; and its principles tend to freedom, juftice, benificence and order. If Chriftianity were banifhed from the world
all hope of univerfal civil freedom would be loft forever ; but there will be fuch a day of freedom, and
Chriftianity will be the means of its production.

Perhaps it may be inquired, why did the wifdom
of God permit fuch a corruption of Chriftianity,
and fuch awful confequences, as have been defcribed
in this difcourfe, to arife in the world ?

To fuch an inquiry it is certainly a true anfwer,
that his counfels are above human wifdom, and he
can bring the greateft good, temporal and eternal,
from the greateft fins of men. But fome of the reafons we may doubtlefs fee. It hath been a high difplay of the total depravity of men by nature, and a
much higher, in many refpects, than was ever made
by their oppofition to the ancient Jewifh difpenfation. To fee the Heathen world, all departing
from God ; ferving their own lufts ; worfhiping the
hoft of Heaven, ftocks and ftones, fourfooted beafts
and creeping things ; and filling the earth with violence.—To fee the Jewifh people, for many ages under the Mofaic œconomy, falling into idolatry and
every kind of error and vice, and kept in any kind

E

34   *On the universal spread of the Gospel.*

of order, only by the rod.—To fee that nation oppofing, blafpheming and crucifying the meek and benevolent Jefus, who came in conformity to the defcriptions of their own prophets, and who did them nothing but good ; and after God had by fpecial revelations and miraculous powers imparted to his fervants, which continued for a century of years, caufed the gofpel to be planted in its purity, meeknefs and holinefs, and Churches had been formed and organized in many lands ; after myriads of martyrs had died by Heathen hands to preferve the purity of faith and practice ; after men had beheld thofe perfecuting powers brought to awful ruin to punifh their cruel impiety; after all thefe things, to fee the Chriftian Church falling into idolatry, blafphemy, and civil and religious oppreffion, and even its minifters affuming the powers and prerogatives of God, and placing crimes on fale, was certainly the higheft difplay of the nature of fin, that hath ever been made in the world. It fhows, that a finful heart is always difpofed to rebel and depart from God ; and that neither the terrors of the law, nor the compaffions of redeeming love will renew the foul in holinefs.—It fhows that a difpenfation of grace, which is moft glorious for God and beneficial to the world, is not too facred to be profaned by finful men—It proves the influences of the Spirit to be neceffary for renewing the heart, in a love of the Lord and his holy inftitutions ; and that the regal power of Jefus Chrift is as much needed, to preferve the Church from deftruction by its own corruptions ; as to reftrain the violence of its external enemies.

3. The next ftate of things, which is the fubject of prophecy, is the deftruction of that Antichriftian apoftacy, of which the rife and continuance have already been defcribed.

This is reprefented in the prophecies of John, by the pouring out on men, in this kingdom and feat of the beaft, feven vials or cups of the wrath of God, containing the feven laft plagues ; and by the fall of Babylon, with the awful circumftances of commotion, mifery, fpoil and ruin attending it. We find this defcribed from the fifteenth to the nineteenth chapter of his Revelation. Babylon is the fame Antichrift, and it hath been a long time falling. It is probable we are now at the conclufion of the fixth vial or cup, and beginning of the feventh. By inteftine commotion and bloody wars, arifing from their own pride and avarice ; and by divers other judgments, the Antichriftian nations had been forely fcourged before the year 1500. Soon after this, it indeed appeared that the king in Zion was arifing to punifh apoftacy, according to his folemn predictions, and to reftore to the Church fome degree of primitive truth, evangelical piety, and fimplicity and holy fervor in worfhip and practice.

In the beginning of the fixteenth century, the Proteftant reformation began. The patience of the oppreffed people was exhaufted, and God raifed up faithful minifters to expofe the corruptions of the times and of the Church, and cloathed them with fortitude to meet the thunders and the tortures of Roman and Papal tyranny. Several nations revolted from the yoke. Sundry kings and princes broke the fetters with which the pretended vicars of heaven had bound them. A new light feemed to break forth on men, teaching them how far they had been led, and how fervilely they had been held, by the felf-originated powers of a blafphemous apoftacy.— Dreadful wars and cruel perfecutions fucceeded ; but in the end, through a large and refpectable part of Europe, the tyranny over confcience and good morals was greatly broken, and the ftate of men ameliorated. The proteftant and reformed Churches obtained a large eftablifhment ; fome features of the genuine religion of Chrift began to appear ; and thofe, who ftill adhered to the kingdom of the beaft, gnawed their tongues for pain.—Thefe events were predicted, by the running of the fifth cup of divine wrath on the feat of the beaft, whereby his kingdom was filled with darknefs.   From that time down to the prefent, the general train of events in the political world, hath been drying up the myftical Euphrates, or diminifhing the power wealth and influence of the Antichriftian Babylon.   Rome has become an infignificant name, and fcarcely is a thunder left in her vatican.   The old inftitutions of error and oppreffion are vanifhing, faft as the nature of things permits ; and the prefent quaking of Europe, together with all places which have, either proximity or intimate relations with it, is a fignal that the battle of the great day of God Almighty is begun, which will not end, until the world is purged of whatever is offenfive to the pure, holy, humble and fervent religion of Jefus Chrift.

In this purgation infinite wifdom is making great ufe of infidelity ; but let not infidels glory in this, as any evidence of their own rectitude, or that their character is pleafing in the fight of the Lord.   Let them not hence think, that they are not themfelves a part, even of the moft diftorted limb of the beaft ; a horn, which fpeaketh againft God more ftoutly than any of its fellows, or any that have gone before it, prepared by an avenging providence to deftroy the beaft, which had two horns like a lamb but fpoke like a dragon.   Infidelity is the laft ftage of apoftacy, commiffioned to eat the flefh and burn the body of the idolatrous fyftem, which had gone before it.   Paul's defcription of the man of fin, evidently points out the modern atheiftical principles, " Who oppofeth and exalteth himfelf above all that is called God, or that is worfhipped ; fo that he as God fitteth in the temple of God, fhowing himfelf that he is God."—The laft part of this defcription, " fo that he as God, fitteth in the temple of God, fhowing hmfelf that he is God," may fairly apply to the Roman Church, in the adoration offered to the fove-

reign pontiff, and in the claim of power to pardon
fin, which is the prerogative of God only.   This is
as God fitting in the temple of God.   But the firft
part of the defcription, " Who oppofeth and exalteth himfelf above all that is called God or that is
worfhipped," is peculiarly applicable to the principles of atheifm, which deny all moral obligation,
the fpiritual exiftence and perfections of Deity, and
all worfhip whatever.   Let not infidels glory becaufe they are permitted to be deftroyers.   They
are raifed up by the wrath of God, and their office
is not to comfort, but to defolate and punifh a wicked world.   Let not men of loofe principles, who
are unfriendly to vital and experimental piety, and
to order and juftice, think that either God or wifdom
or nature are on their fide.   Let them not fuppofe
that the holy Bible is going into obfcurity ; for by
a fulfilment of the divine threatnings, it is now becoming more than ever confpicuous and venerable.
Let them not think that the king in Zion hath forfaken his Church, becaufe he is purifying it, and
punifhing an apoftate Antichrift.   Let them not
think, that in a few years, a gofpel profeffion, Chriftian Churches and teachers will ceafe ; for they
ought rather to know, that God is making preparation for more abundant inftruction, more frequent,
more pure and fpiritual feafons of worfhip, and for
the more general influence of that kind of religion,
which gives the greateft offence to all impenitent
hearts.

4th. The fourth period or ftate of things, of
which prophecy fpeaks, is the general fpread of the
gofpel to the exclufion of Heathen ignorance and
falfe religion from the earth ; when the world fhall
be filled with the knowledge of the Lord as the waters cover the feas.   The fcriptural proof of fuch a
day I have already adduced, and therefore proceed
to the next general branch of difcourfe.

38   *On the universal spread of the Gospel.*

III. To fhow by a view of the prefent ftate of mankind and of nations, that there is an amazing natural preparation, for a fulfilment of the glorious promife, and that it is near at hand.

WE are not to expect any miraculous preparation for this event. It will be made in the natural order and courfe of things, and by natural means of extenfive operation. The natural preparation for fuch an event muft, principally, confift in two things. Firft, unfettering the human mind from fuperftition, and from the power of religious oppreffion; and fecondly, the general fpread of doctrinal knowledge through the earth.

IT is very evident, that in moft lands, where there is any degree of civilization, the human mind is in a great meafure unfettered from the power of fuperftition.—This is done by an increafed communication between men, and the advance of human fcience. This appears to be the cafe, by the advance of a free and friendly toleration between the feveral denominations of Chriftians, which never takes place under the reign of fuperftition. It, alfo, appears from the abounding of infidelity, and the moft loofe, unreafonable and impious fentiments concerning the moft facred things. People of piety, when free from fuperftition, are governed by principle; they love order and juftice both public and private; are willing to allow to God and the Redeemer their juft rights; and to keep the divine word and inftitutions. But when men of evil hearts, great pride, and little found knowledge, are loofened from fuperftition, they have no moral principles to govern them; and they run into infidelity and ftrange notions concerning the juftice and mercy which govern a univerfe; concerning God himfelf; concerning, nature, reafon, and the creature's uncontrouled right to direct his own moral fentiments and practice; and concerning fin, or rather the impoffibility that their fhould be any fuch thing as fin in rational creatures, whom they fuppofe capable of infinite perfectability, without the direction of divine wifdom and folely by the fortuitous concourfe of material atoms. Such perfons, judging from their own licentious defires and feelings, imagine that Chriftianity, its holy laws, its organs of inftruction and government are about to ceafe from the world. The abounding of thefe things fhows that the reign of fuperftition, which is a great impediment to rational religion, is in a meafure ceafing ; and tho' infidelity may fpeak with triumph for a moment, proves that there is a natural preparation of the human mind, for the gofpel to fpread through the earth.

FARTHER, it is alfo evident, that thofe oppreffive powers, which tied up the faith and perfecuted the confciences of men, are expiring by the juft judgments of God and a growing acquaintance with human rights. Dreadful will be the battle, bitter the revolutions, tyrant will follow tyrant, for a feafon, under a pretext of friendfhip for human freedom ; but through the direction of infinite wifdom, the period will terminate in the expulfion of civil and religious oppreffion on the one hand ; and of Atheifm, infidelity and a difpofition to anarchize on the other.

SECONDLY, There is an amazing preparation to fpread a doctrinal knowledge of the gofpel through the world.

WE may learn this at once by looking on the character and ftate of the nations. The greateft difficulties in chriftianizing men, are to gain accefs to them, and to plant the beginnings of gofpel knowledge and doctrine. Let us furvey the feveral quarters of the world. Chriftianity is known through the whole of Europe ; and when the remains of Antichriftian apoftacy are confumed, which God is now doing, by inftruments prepared to go any lengths, that the moft awful vindictive juftice will permit, the religion of Chrift will be left in its doctrinal purity. Thro'

all the north of Afia, Ruffian conqueft and coloni-
zation is planting the principles of the Greek Church;
and through a large part of its fouthern fhores and
the great iflands on its coaft, are colonies from Chriftian nations. Through the vaft Ottoman Empire,
which is fituate in the heart of the old world, fpreading into Europe, Afia and Africa, are innumerable
Chriftians of the Greek communion. By oppreffion
and poverty, for feveral ages, thefe Chriftians have
been almoft wholly unnoticed. When that empire,
which is now benumbed with the lethargy of approaching death, comes to its end without being
helped by any man, as it directly will, a multitude
of little collections of Chriftians, will be found planted in every part of it, who will come into immediate union with their brethren in other lands. The
fcience which fled from them before the Ottoman
conqueft, to enlighten the weftern and northern
parts of Europe, and prepare the way for the proteftant reformation ; after the Turkifh power is diffolved, will return back to them with modern improvements, to wake them from the imbecility and
fuperftition, into which they have been funk by a
moft fevere defpotifm. Through the fhores of Africa are colonies from Chriftian nations, a natural
preparation of providence to communicate the gofpel,
among the numerous tribes, with which the interior
of that great quarter of the world is populated. In
all the eaftern fhores of America, from north to
fouth, Chriftianity is planted ; and that tide of
men, which is rolling weftward, with an unparralleled
velocity of population, long before the prefent century is finifhed, will carry the gofpel of Chrift acrofs
to the Pacific ocean and the eaftern fhores of Afia.
Enterprize, commerce and navigation are in the
hands of thofe, who, if they have any religion are
Chriftians. Science, which is favorable to Chriftianity, is diffufing every where. One prophetic defcription of this time is " many fhall run to and fro
and knowledge fhall be increafed." The pious, in

all the Chriſtian nations, in a manner unexampled
before, have recently awoke to a ſenſe of their obligation, to tranſmit the goſpel to their Heathen fellow-creatures. Even the conſiderate part of the
Jews are looking with wonder on the ſcene. Thus
the king of Zion is ſpreading a natural preparation
around the world to have his goſpel become univerſal ! Yet infidels, in their blindneſs, think that
Chriſtianity is near the moment of its extinction !
The Lord of all the earth is working unſeen by them.
Think not, my readers, that I ſuppoſe the whole
world of mankind is become Chriſtian at once, for
it is far different from this. The world is yet filled
principally with wicked men and with error ; but
Chriſt is preparing to have it otherwiſe. When we
view this natural preparation in connection with the
divine promiſes, we may, without an imaginary
faith, believe, that within two centuries from this
time, there will be a favorable change in the ſtate of
mankind and the Church, that in many reſpects will
ſurpaſs all preſent apprehenſion.—When he hath
puniſhed and purified an apoſtate Church by his judgments and prepared the ſtate of the nations ; according to his promiſe he will pour out his Spirit on them,
who have a doctrinal knowledge, exciting their moſt
zealous endeavors to make this knowledge univerſal ;
the events of providence will be propitious to the
ſpread of truth, and Chriſtianity will be ſpread over
the face of the whole earth, in a manner, ſudden
beyond the conjecture of men. It is the way of infinite wiſdom, to have a long continued, and previous preparation for great events which is unſeen by
men. Revolutions, which fill our minds with deep
ſurpriſe at the moment of execution, on being
coolly reviewed, are ſeen to be the conſequence of
a thouſand operating cauſes, which were wholly unnoticed, before the event broke from the womb of
providence upon an aſtoniſhed world. When the
general ſtate of things is prepared, and circumſtan-
F

ces are propitious, a few inftruments, formed and raifed by divine providence, are able to take hold of the public feelings, and impel men to exertions and to changes in the political and moral ftate of things, which would have been thought incredible. And when we confider the promife, that the fpirit of the Lord fhall defcend like floods of water on a dry and parched ground ; let us not think the fulfilment of the prediction improbable. By the breath of his noftrils, the Lord can confume the wicked ; or by the power of his grace he can make them his friends, cloath them with zeal to act and fortitude to endure, in the fervice and patience of his kingdom.

LET us hail the beginning of a century, which will do more to prepare for the glory of the latter days, than any which have preceded.

THE probable events of this century are, a complete population, and the eftablifhment of the Chriftian religion, in every part of America.—The continuance of the commotions, which are exhaufting Europe, until all the remains of Antichriftian apoftacy are confumed, and the inftitutions of civil and religious oppreffion deftroyed ; and we may hope, that before the conclufion of the century, the Church of Chrift will be renovated, in that part of the world, in the purity, fimplicity, humility and holy zeal of the gofpel.—The Ottoman Empire will be diffolved and the gofpel appear to be rifing in purity and influence, in all thofe lands, which were once the chief theatre of Chriftian action ; but for ages, have been held in the chains of Mahometan ignorance and ferocity.—The eyes of the Jews, will begin to open on the madnefs of their infidelity, in rejecting their own Jefus ; and providence will prepare the way, for their collection in the land once poffeffed by their fathers ; for fuch an event is plainly foretold in the prophets.—Accompanying thofe

events, the greater powers of Afia, which now im-
pede the gofpel progrefs, will through fome means
now unforefeen by us, be fo broken and changed,
that they will no longer ftop the progrefs of Chriftian knowledge.

" THE commotion and earthquake of the nations
will be great, fuch as was not fince men were on
the earth, fo mighty an earthquake and fo great !"—
From the cruelties of men, the faithlefs ambition of
nations, and the violent efforts of infidelity and heathenifm, there will be great diftrefs on the earth ;
and it will appear, that fatan hath great wrath, becaufe he knoweth that the time is fhort before his
binding ; but we may hope, that in thofe places
where the preparation is neareft compleated, a ftandard will be fet up by the Spirit of the Lord againft
the enemy, and that there will be joyful refrefhings
from his prefence. That his people will be waked
up to come to the help of Zion, and to pray for its
increafe ; that many finners will be awakened and
converted ; divine knowledge increafe ; the communion between different denominations of Chriftians be enlarged ; and a fpirit of humble Godlinefs
prevail more and more among profeffors of the truth.

BEFORE I conclude this fubject, I ought to advert
to one part of the pfalm, which contains national
inftruction to all people under Heaven. " Be wife
now, therefore, O ye kings, be inftructed ye judges
of the earth. Serve the Lord with fear and rejoice
with trembling. Kifs the Son, left he be angry and
ye perifh from the way, when his wrath is kindled
but a little." If there be any governments in the
earth, which defpife Chrift and his fcriptures ; let
them fear the rod of iron that is in his hand, for he
will furely remember and humble them. If there be
any nation or parts of nations, who wifh to throw
off his yoke and the fpirituality of religion ; let them

44   *On the universal spread of the Gospel.*

remember they muſt have a part in the cup of his anger. The preſent is not like other times ; for the king of Zion hath ariſen to make a full end of all the powers that oppoſe him ; to judge the nations of the earth ; and the nation that will not ſerve him, ſhall be daſhed in pieces, like a veſſel that is marred in the hands of the potter.

THE extent of Babylon, that is devoted to drink the cup of divine wrath, may be much greater than many ſuppoſe.—The ſeat of the beaſt is in many reſpects different from his kingdom. The influence and vices of his kingdom, are far ſpread from the place where he aroſe and hath exerciſed chief power. They have traverſed oceans and planted themſelves in remote regions ; but wherever they have gone, the jealouſy of the Lord will find them out and execute the woe. In the eighteenth chapter of St. John's Revelation, there is an enumeration of the merchandiſe of Babylon, which ends with theſe two remarkable articles, " and ſlaves and the ſouls of men."—Let men of all nations and places inquire, whether, if the merchandiſe of Babylon be found with them, they are not parts of that body, which is to be given to the burning flame of revolution ? Whether they do not ſee among themſelves, the growth of principles, which tend to anarchize the multitude, and to put daggers for ſpilling their own and their children's blood, into the hands of men fiercely awaking from the moſt oppreſſive bondage. Wherever the practice of ſlavery exiſts, there is a natural preparation to execute the threatenings of God on thoſe, who deal in " ſlaves and the ſouls of men." Eſpecially this appears to be the caſe, where that kind of infidelity is introducing itſelf, which juſtifies any means, however immoral, to obtain an end, which is ſuppoſed to be right. Theſe dealers in the merchandiſe of Babylon are doubtleſs guilty and worthy of divine puniſhment ; and it is ſurpriſing, how a holy God is permitting many of them, to fall into principles, which being diffeminated among thofe whom they have oppreffed, are fpeedily to wake up the vengeance of injured millions. Gracious heaven, if poffible avert the fcene ; neverthelefs thy will muft be done, and if the parents muft expiate their fin, let the babes and children be fpared of thy fovereign mercy ! He that hath an ear let him hear !——

LET infidels and the irreligious of every defcription remember, that a full warning is given in the word of God ; and that although they reject the warning, they muft meet the execution. They have entered into a vain conteft with the King of kings, and there cannot be a higher proof of their eventual deftruction than this, " the mouth of the Lord hath fpoken it." If fuch have no care for themfelves, ftill let them have compaffion on their offspring. " The Lord our God is a jealous God, vifiting the iniquities of the father upon the children unto the third and fourth generation of them that hate him." There is great reafon to believe, that the offspring of thofe, who reject Chrift and his word, however fair and blooming their prefent profpects may be, fhall all be cut off before the day of millennial glory, and when that bleffed time commences they will be written childlefs.

LET profeffing Chriftians, who are in a ftate of coldnefs and backfliding, remember there is the fame danger for their pofterity. If through their failure in duty, their own children grow up in impiety and fail of eternal life ; there is reafon to fear all their offspring will be cut off before the millennial peace of the Church on earth. The arrows in the quiver of the Lord are many, and he can execute his judgments !

LET all the humble and holy wait for the coming of the Lord in his earthly kingdom ; let them

46   *On the universal spread of the Gospel.*

ceaſe not to pray, that Zion may become a praiſe in the whole earth.   Bleſſed are all they that truſt in the Lord and keep his commandments.   THE SPIRIT AND THE BRIDE SAY COME.   HE WHOSE TESTIMONY IS THE SPIRIT OF PROPHECY, SAITH, SURELY I COME QUICKLY: AMEN.   EVEN ſo COME LORD JESUS: AMEN.

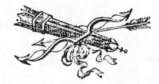

Mr. WELCH's

CENTURY SERMON.

A

CENTURY SERMON,

PREACHED AT

MANSFIELD,

JANUARY 1, 1801.

By MOSES C. WELCH,

PASTOR OF THE CHURCH IN MANSFIELD, NORTH SOCIETY.

HARTFORD :

PRINTED BY HUDSON AND GOODWIN.

1801.

A CENTURY SERMON.

.I SAMUEL vii. 12.

THEN Samuel took a ſtone, and ſet it between Miz-
peh and Shen, and called the name of it Ebenezer,
ſaying, Hitherto hath the Lord helped us.

THE children of Iſrael, though the covenant and
peculiar people of God, and favored with ſpecial and diſtinguiſhed privileges, were, yet, ſurroun-
ded with enemies, and paſſed through ſcenes of great
tribulation. And it is a truth, always to be remembered, that their afflictions were, generally, in conſequence of abuſing divine mercies. Their ſtory is
intereſting and full of inſtruction.

IN ſome of the preceding chapters we have an
account of an attack upon Iſrael by the Philiſtines,
their native enemies—of the ſlaughter and fall of
thirty thouſand of the people of God, and the capture of the ark by pagan hands. We are informed,
alſo, of the wonderful interpoſition of God, by his
providence, in favor of his people, and the reſtora-
tion of the ſacred cheſt.

6 A CENTURY SERMON

WHEN the ark was returned, and fixed in its proper place, upon the exhortation of Samuel, the Ifraelites put away their falfe gods, forfook their idolatry, which had provoked the Lord to forfake them, and repented and humbled themfelves for their fins. Samuel offered a facrifice on the folemn occafion, and, earneftly, cried to God in behalf of his repenting people. During the folemn fervice the Philiftines approached for another attack. But the Lord appeared the helper of his people, and, by a ftorm from heaven, accompanied with thunder and tempeft, defeated the Philiftines, and caufed them to fly, in great fear, before Ifrael.

ON this occafion, *Samuel took a ftone, and fet it between Mizpeh and Shen, and called the name of it Ebenezer, faying, Hitherto hath the Lord helped us.*

EBENEZER, as the learned explain the word, fignifies *a ftone of help*. This ftone, with fuch a fignificant name, was fet up as a ftanding memorial of the remarkable interpofitions of divine providence. It was the defign of the holy prophet that a view of it fhould call to remembrance the frowns of God upon that people, when the ark fell into pagan hands, and the Priefts were flain who miniftered at the facred altar, together with the wonderful manner in which it was reftored, and the very fignal deliverance in the defeat of their enemies.

THE words, in this view, may, naturally, fuggeft the idea that a wife people will, carefully, notice the providences of God, and keep them in remembrance.

REMARKABLE events, and fignal providences of God have, in former times, been kept in remembrance, by monuments, raifed, and fet up for that particular purpofe. We are told, in facred hiftory, the manner in which the paffing of Ifrael over Jordan was noticed, and the memory of it perpetuated.

Twelve men, one of each tribe, were ordered to take twelve ſtones out of the midſt of Jordan, and leave them, for a monument, in the place where they ſhould lodge the firſt night, after paſſing the river. Hereby God deſigned to affeƈt and impreſs the minds of after generations, with a view of the aſtoniſhing manner in which that people were con-duƈted over Jordan, and ſettled in the land of prom-iſe. For the ſame purpoſe a memorial was appoint-ed of the deliverance of Iſrael out of Egypt, when the firſt born of their oppreſſors were all ſlain. This exiſted, for ages, in the paſſover. Circumciſion perpetuated the memory of the Abrahamic covenant. Chriſtians, under the preſent diſpenſation, have a ſtanding memorial of the death of Chriſt. Yea, if we look back to the beginning of time, we ſhall find the ſeventh day · of the week conſecrated, and obſerved, as holy, in remembrance of the work of creation. And we find this, religiouſly, continued, by the people of God, until the change of the ſab-bath to commemorate a greater and more glorious work, that was completed by the reſurreƈtion of Jeſus.

WISE and virtuous people, on whom theſe things were enjoined, have, religiouſly, obſerved them ; and multitudes have derived, therefrom, great ben-efit and conſolation.

SINCE God has, in many inſtances, appointed monuments to keep in remembrance remarkable events ; and, ſince his people have, conſcientiouſly, obſerved his direƈtions, it is clear that a wiſe people will notice the providences of God, and lay them up in their minds.

VALUABLE conſequences may follow from per-petuating the memory of ſignal providences. For the inſtruƈtion and benefit of perſons in various ages of time, thoſe remarkable events relating to the church and people of God make a part of the

8   A CENTURY SERMON.

canon of fcripture, and have been, carefully, preferved in the facred volume. For the fame reafon
the hiftories of kingdoms and empires have been
written with great labor, and are handed down from
one generation to another. Through this channel
we are able to converfe with former generations, to
know the affairs of ancient times, and become
acquainted with interefting events, which, otherwife,
through the lapfe of ages, muft have been loft, and
buried in oblivion. For the fame reafon the hiftories of counties, towns, and focieties have been written and preferved. And for the fame reafon remarkable traits, in the characters of eminent and diftinguifhed men, have been publifhed to the world, and
handed down to thofe who come after them.

THE advantages of noticing the providences of
God, and perpetuating fignal events are numerous—
too numerous to be comprifed in one difcourfe.—
Barely to mention two or three of the moft plain and
obvious is as much as will be confiftent with the defign of this meeting. And,.

1. IT affords a fource of ufeful inftruction.—
When a people have before them a hiftory of paft
events, and are informed of fignal providences of
God, it opens to them an interefting fource of information. For this reafon Mofes, by divine direction, recorded the affairs of Ifrael, and the footfteps
of divine providence relating to that commonwealth,
through a number of fucceeding generations. For
the fame reafon did God command the Ifraelites to
teach their children the caufe and meaning of the
paffover, the occafion of the heap of ftones taken
out of Jordan, and other inftitutions in remembrance
of particular providences. It was the defign of God
that his people fhould know how he had conducted
towards their forefathers, that they might learn fomething of his true character, as well as the end and
defign of his moral government.

A CENTURY SERMON.

A HISTORY of former times is, moft admirably, calculated to produce this effect. How ignorant would be the prefent generation were it not for letters, and a hiftory of paft events ! This idea will ftrike us, forcibly, if we compare our prefent ftate with that of the untutored favage. Ignorant of letters, and without any hiftory of paft events, only what is derived from vague and uncertain tradition, his mind is barren as the heath. He knows but very little out of his own hut, or beyond the limits of his particular family, or tribe. He has a faint and imperfect idea of a great fpirit, while the character and perfections of the true God are, wholly, unknown. But we, by a hiftory of paft events—by a record of the providences of God have a fource of ufeful inftruction, from whence we may obtain ideas of great importance relating to natural and moral fubjects.

2. IN this way the idea of dependence on God is confirmed and eftablifhed.

WHAT will, more effectually, do this than a recollection and review of paft, and fignal providences ? What could, fo effectually, have done this, as it relates to Ifrael, as a view of what God had done for their fathers, even, from the time Abraham was called out from his father's houfe, until the fettlement of his pofterity, nearly five hundred years after, in the land of promife ? With the difficulties and ftraits into which God had brought his people ; with the deliverances granted them ; with the aftonifhing providences of God relating to their fathers ; with thefe things in full view, how was it poffible they fhould not be impreffed with a fenfe of dependence on God ? If any thing would effect this it muft be a recollection of paft and wonderful providences.— Such a view and recollection is fuited, in its own nature, to produce fuch an effect.

B

THE fame may be faid refpecting the prefent generation in our own country. Were we to recollect
fome of the wonders of divine providence relating
to this land, from the fettlement of the country to
the prefent period, we muft be ftupid, indeed, not
to feel our dependence. It is plain to all, but the
fool and the infidel, that creatures are, abfolutely,
dependent on the creator. Noticing the footfteps of
divine providence has a natural tendency to eftablifh
this idea.

3. IT ferves to give exalted conceptions of God.
There is nothing calculated, fo well, to give impreffive ideas of the greatnefs of God, and to exalt him
in our view as to regard the work of his hands, and
to notice his government of the world. Who can
view the great things God has done among the inhabitants of the earth, and not have exalted conceptions
of him ? He has *overturned, and overturned the nations* at his pleafure. When it was neceffary for the
accomplifhment of his purpofes, he has raifed up and
exalted a nation—fuffered them to continue in power, and bear down all before them, for a feafon,
and, by and by, has caufed them to fall in their turn,
and crumble to pieces. The Babylonian, Perfian,
and Grecian monarchies rofe in fucceffion, flourifhed
and conquered ; and in fucceffion were conquered,
and overcome. The laft of thefe gave way to the
greater power of the Romans. In thefe overturnings God was difplaying himfelf, and making way
for the introduction of chriftianity in the greateft
glory of the greateft pagan monarchy that ever exifted. The rife and fall of empires, and overturning
powerful monarchies, gives a ferious, contemplative mind exalted ideas of God.

As to Ifrael, the hand of God may be, clearly,
feen, in their fupport, beyond all human calculation. He difappointed the rage of their enemies,
and protected them from the evils defigned by thofe

who had, in human view, power to have deſtroyed
them.   That God who called them went before
them—guided them—protected and ſupported them.
When theſe things were noticed by their poſterity,
it muſt have given them exalted ideas of God.   And
ſo it does us, and all who, with attentive, believing
minds, read the ſacred ſtory.

THE providences of God relating to other nations
have, in proportion to their magnitude, the ſame
effect.   The hiſtory of our infant empire preſents
to us, and the world, an aſtoniſhing ſeries of wonders.   The hand of God is, wonderfully, viſible in
ſettling this country—in making an independent nation—in forming, and eſtabliſhing our conſtitution
of government, and in preſerving it, hitherto, from
being deſtroyed by the diſorganizing ſpirit of its bitter, and potent enemies.   In theſe and a multitude
of providences we may ſee the greatneſs, the power,
the wiſdom, and goodneſs of God.   A view of the
divine moral government is calculated in its own nature, to give us exalted ideas of the *Supreme Ruler.*

SINCE a view of ſignal events, and remarkable
providences is calculated to give uſeful inſtruction—
to eſtabliſh an idea of dependence, and to give exalted conceptions of God, theſe are ſufficient reaſons
why a wiſe people will, carefully, notice the providences of God, and keep them in remembrance.

HENCE, it may not be uninteresting to the feelings of this aſſembly to review, and call to mind
ſome paſt events.

IT is now more than a century and a half ſince the
firſt ſettlement of white people, through unparalleled
difficulties, was effected in New-England.   The firſt
adventurers were from Plymouth, in England, which
place they left, one hundred and one in number, on
the 20th of September 1620.   They arrived at Cape-

Cod.fome time in the month of November follow-ing, and fixed their abode at a place they calledNew-Plymouth on the 20th of December, which is 180 years from the prefent period. During that fpace of time new towns and counties have been, continually, forming.

The firft fettlements in what is now the county of Windham, began in 1686. A tract including Windham and Mansfield had, in 1675, been given by Jofhua, Sachem of Mohegan, to a certain num-ber of gentlemen named as legatees in his laft will. The next year this tract was furveyed and laid out in-to diftinct lots, and within about ten years the fet-tlements commenced. The fettlement of Windham and Mansfieldbegan about the fame time. The firft inhabitants were, principally, from Maffachufetts, feveral of them from the town of Barnftable, fome of whom were, originally, from England. Among the firft inhabitants was Mr. Robert Fenton, who came early to this town—married, and raifed up a family—lived here 'till the decline of life, and died, at an advanced age, at the houfe of one of his fons, in Willington. From him have defcended a nume-rous progeny, many of whom are ftill living in this, and the neighboring towns.

Mr. Samuel Storrs, Father of the late dea-con Storrs of this fociety was, originally, from Eng-land. He refided a number of years at Barnftable, from thence came here fomething more than a hun-dred years ago. From him have defcended the great number of that name, who, for many years, have made a large and refpectable part of the town ; and are, now, become numerous in feveral parts of New-England.

My information does not extend to all the fath-ers, and firft inhabitants. And, if it did, to men-tion them, individually, would exceed the propofed limits of this difcourfe. Among them, however, in addition to thofe already mentioned, I have heard the names of Dimmick, Hall, Dunham, Turner, Crofs, and Royce. Thefe, it is conceived, were the anceftors of thofe of the fame name among the prefent inhabitants.

ABOUT the fame time the fettlement of this town and Windham commenced, a fmall number of planters began at Pomfret. At a period, a little fubfequent to this, there were fettlements begun in Lebanon, Canterbury, and Plainfield. Windham, including Mansfield, was the firft incorporated town in the county. This took place in the month of May, A. D. 1692. On the 30th of January, A. D. 1700 the inhabitants of Windham agreed on a divifion of the town. This act was ratified, and Mansfield incorporated, by the Legiflature, the May following. A church was gathered, confifting of eight male members, on the 18th of October, A. D. 1710, and a Minifter ordained the fame day. The firft Minifter of the town was the Rev. Eleazer Williams, fon of the Rev. John Williams, of Deerfield, who witneffed the deftruction and burning of the town, by an army of Savages; and with feveral of his family, and a large number of his church and congregation, who furvived the cataftrophe, was carried into a wretched captivity, in the month of March, 1704. By the good providence of God that fon, who was, afterwards, the Minifter of this town, was abfent when the fore calamity fell upon Mr. Williams' family and people; and by the kind affiftance of fome benevolent gentlemen, was fupported, and fent to college during his father's captivity. Mr. Williams ferved the church and town as an able, pious, exemplary, fervent Minifter, about thirty-two years, until he was called from his labors by death, on the 21ft of Sept. A. D. 1742.

THE fucceffor of Mr. Williams was the Rev. Dr.

Salter, from Bofton.   He was ordained on the
27th day of June, A. D. 1744.   Dr. Salter commanded, to an uncommon degree, as well the refpect
of the aged, as the efteem and veneration of youth.
As a divine, a preacher, a friend to the cause and
honor of religion, he was exceeded by few of his
brethren.   He continued in his paftoral relation to
the church until his death, which was on the 14th
day of April, A. D. 1787.

In thefe two minifters Mansfield enjoyed a great
bleffing, and it pleafed the head of the church to hon-
or them as inftruments of good to many, by crown-
ing their labors with more than ordinary fuccefs.—
They, each of them, witneffed the travel of Chrift's
foul, to their great comfort.*

Dr. Salter was fucceeded by the Rev. Elijah
Gridley, who was ordained on the 8th day of April,
A. D. 1789, and dimiffed July A. D. 1796.

The fucceffor of Mr. Gridley is the prefent Paftor
of the church, the Rev. John Sherman, from New-
Haven ; who was ordained on the 15th day of November, A. D. 1797.

I am the more particular on thefe things becaufe
this fociety was, formerly, one with that ; and this
church grew out of that which was formed on the day
of Mr. Williams' ordination.   We are, alfo, now,
but one town—the people of the two focieties happily connected ; and in a fenfe, but one people.

The fettlements in this part of the town began
many years before the incorporation of the fociety.
For a number of the firft years there were only a
few fcattered inhabitants, and here and there a folitary dwelling.   From the beft information I am able

* During the miniftry of Mr. Williams and Dr. Salter, there
were added to the church feven hundred and fifty-fix perfons.

A CENTURY SERMON.

to collect, the settlement of this part of Mansfield commenced about the time the first Minister of the town was ordained, A. D. 1710. The first planters were from Norwich, in Connecticut—from Marlborough, Lynn, Medfield, and Barnstable in Massachusetts.

THE incorporation of this society was at the October session of Assembly, A. D. 1737 ; and the society held their first meeting, for the appointment of society officers, on the 1st day of December following. Joseph Strong, Esq. of Coventry, presided as Moderator. No regular church was formed in the society till after the ordination of Dr. Salter. The professors of religion continued their connexion with the church in the South Parish, and attended there, on special ordinances. After that period a church was formed here, which, it is presumed, took place, as had been the general practice, on the day the first Minister was ordained. This was on the 11th day of October, A. D. 1744. The first Pastor of this church was the Rev. William Throop, from Lebanon. He continued here, in the ministry, only from October 11th, 1744, to January 13th, 1746, when he was, regularly, dismissed by a consociation, convened at Scotland, in Windham. The cause of his dismission was the unhappy, divided state of the church and society. He was viewed by the council which dismissed him, as appears by their vote on the subject, " as a person well qualified with gifts and grace for the work of the gospel ministry." He was, accordingly, recommended to labor in the churches. Providence opened a door for his resettlement at Southhold on Long-Island, where he died of the dysentery, after having been, considerably, successful, and witnessed a revival of religion, and a reformation among his people, but a short time previous to his death.

THE society continued vacant, and in a broken

16   A CENTURY SERMON.

ftate, from the difmiffion of Mr. Throop 'till the year 1751, when the father† of him who now fpeaks to you was invited to preach here as a candidate.—— His labors were fo far acceptable to the people that they united in calling him for fettlement. He received the call of the church December 10th, A. D. 1751, and was ordained the 29th of January following. His life in the miniftry was thirty years and three months. How far he was faithful, or what his character as a Minifter, you will not expect me, particularly, to fay. Modefty will forbid my enlarging on the fubject. I may obferve, however, that he was allowed, by his acquaintance, to poffefs a good fhare of pulpit talents. He was beloved by the people of his charge, and refpected by a large circle of acquaintance abroad. He lived in great harmony with his people, for thirty years, and died, apparently, much lamented.

THE circumftances of his death many of you recollect. They are frefh in my mind, and you will not wonder at all, if my tender feelings are affected, at the prefent moment. He had been for a number of weeks previous to his death in a feeble, debilitated ftate ; but was able, generally, to attend the duties of the miniftry. He preached in the forenoon of April 28th, A. D. 1782, from John xvi. 33. *Thefe things I have fpoken unto you that in me ye might have peace. In the world ye fhall have tribulation. But be of good cheer ; I have overcome the world.* He returned to the houfe of God in the afternoon—at an early ftage of public fervice was taken extremely ill—left the pulpit—with difficulty was conveyed to his own houfe, and, before funrife the next morning, left the world.—The church, by

† The Rev. Daniel Welch, born at Windham, March, A. D. 1726. He married Mifs Martha Cook, who was born at Hartford, June A. D, 1734, and died December 11th, A. D. 1775. By her he had five fons and feven daughters, all of whom, except the fecond fon who died in infancy, furvived him.

this death, was again reduced to a widowed ftate; and the fociety continued vacant two years and two months.

Your prefent Paftor began his public labors here November 28th, A. D. 1782—received the call of the church October 1783, and was ordained June 2d, 1784. Hence it appears that this church, in 56 years, has witneffed the ordination of three Paftors —the difmiffion of one—the death of another, and the third is, now, in the 17th year of his minifte- rial life.

The firft meeting of the church for the appoint- ment of deacons was October 3d, A. D. 1745. At this meeting Mefs'rs. Cordial Storrs and Elna- than Brigham were elected. Thefe were the only deacons of the church 'till the death of deacon Brig- ham, April 10th, A. D. 1758. Deacon Storrs continued in office many years. He died October, 1782, aged 90. Soon after the death of deacon Brigham the church elected Mefs'rs Edmond Free- man, and Timothy Metcalf. The latter of thefe de- ceafed March 10th, A. D. 1773, aged 63; and the former February 13th, 1800, aged 89. Some time in the year 1773, the church elected Mr. Jona- than Gurley, who continued in office 'till he was cal- led from the world on Lord's day, November 1ft, A. D. 1778, aged 64. Thefe are all who have exercifed the office of deacon in this church until the prefent, one of whom was chofen in the year 1779,* and the other in December 1787.†

It would, undoubtedly, gratify the curiofity of many, as well as afford refrefhment and edification to fome, to have an account of the ftate of religion at various periods, and of particular feafons of gra-

---

* Deacon Oliver Dimmick.   † Deacon Jonathan Fuller.

C

cious vifits to the church.   But of this I am able to give you but an imperfeЄ account.   I have, it is true, been informed of fome faЄs relating to this fubjeЄ as far back as the early days of the fociety. The great reformation through the land, in the year 1741, which was powerful in many places, produced very fenfible effeЄs in this town.   That was about four years after the incorporation of the fociety, and about three before the formation of the church.   At that reviving feafon there were many in this town, and fome, I am not able to fay how many, in this fociety, hopefully, converted unto God.— There is one male yet living in the fociety, who fuppofes himfelf to have experienced a work of grace at that remarkable period.   But the moft of them are *gone*.   Thofe who appeared to embrace religion at that feafon united with the church in the South Parifh, where they remained until a door was opened for the ftated enjoyment of fpecial ordinances here.

THERE have been fome reviving feafons of a later date, like a refrefhing dew, but no great and plentiful fhower.   Enough, however, has appeared to fhow that God had not, wholly, forfaken an ungrateful people.   The plants have been kept alive, and fome have fprouted, and fprung up afrefh.   In the year 1781 there was fomething of this nature, and feveral united with the church.   The fpeaker was one of that number.   He had until that time (with fhame he ought to confefs it) lived without God in the world.   In that year he, for the firft time, formed a determinate refolution to ftand up for God, and be on the fide of the Saviour.

IN the year 1786 and '87 there was a fmall fpray of a fhower—feveral were brought in and profeffed Godlinefs.   In the year 1791 fome were awakened to the concerns of eternity.   Eight or nine were, that year, added to the church.

In the latter part of the summer of 1798 there appeared some hopeful beginnings of a religious awakening. This increased from week to week. Our assemblies on the sabbath, and other days, were full, and solemn. The minds of many were tender, and some greatly affected. *The fields* appeared *white unto the harvest.* It was refreshing to Christians to see a prevailing concern for the soul, and it was pleasure to speak to a serious, attentive, and affectionate assembly. About twenty-four were added to the church as the fruit of that season. And, Oh that they may witness a good profession ! There have made profession since my ordination sixty-six persons ; and ten have been received to our communion by recommendation from other churches. Two hundred and twenty-one children have been dedicated in baptism, and ten persons baptised on their own profession.

This number is but small when compared with the trophies of the Redeemer's victory in some other places. But we are not to despise *the day of small things.* When we consider it is all of God, and that we have no claim upon his mercy, we may well say, *This is the Lord's doing, and it is marvellous in our eyes.* We ought to extol and magnify the name of God that all have not been given up to utter ruin. Further,

It will, doubtless, be expected in a discourse of this nature that some notice will be taken of seasons of sickness and mortality, and the number of deaths. But for want of information from records I am not able, wholly, to gratify your curiosity on the subject. I am able to find no regular bills of mortality any further back than the year 1768 ; and from that time to June 1784, the best account I find is imperfect, as, during several of the first years, none but heads of families are noticed. Notwithstanding this deficiency, which must make a great difference in the aggregate number, the record contains one hundred and thirty-five. Thefe added to the number who have died fince that period, make three hundred and thirty-nine deaths in the fociety, in about thirty-two years.

THE feafons of the greateft mortality known among us were fome of the firft years of the revolutionary war. In one of thofe feafons the dyfentery prevailed, to an uncommon degree, and many fell victims to its rage. In another, there was a prevalent fever, the progrefs of which was marked with a degree of terror, and carried weeping, diftrefs, and death into a number of families. But we have had no general, and very fweeping mortality. The proportion of aged perfons in the bills of mortality will render this, at leaft, probable. Of the two hundred and four who have died within the laft fixteen years, thirty-eight, almoft one fifth, were feventy, and rifing of feventy years of age. One of the number had completed a full century.

THE prefent number of families in the fociety is one hundred and ninety-four, and the whole number of fouls, according to a late cenfus, amounts to eleven hundred and fifty-five. Notwithftanding the great number of deaths, and the ftill greater number who have moved into the new fettlements, at the northward and weftward, we are, at this time, no lefs than one thoufand, one hundred and fifty-five fouls.

THESE things may lead us, *my hearers*, to a number of ferious and very folemn thoughts.

OUR fathers where are they? They are not here. They are gone from the world. They have done with the revolutions of time. Days and months, years and centuries are, with them, no more. Thofe who laid the foundation of the church and fociety are gone, and have, the moſt of them, long ſince, bid farewell to the concerns of time. We are following after them, and treading a track never to be retrodden. Eternal, and moſt intereſting ſcenes will, ſhortly, open to our view ! But we are ſpared to ſee an important epoch in the annals of time. This day commences not only a new year, but a new century. Eighteen centuries have rolled away ſince the commencement of the Chriſtian era. The nineteenth is now begun. And who among us has ever ſeen ſuch a day as this ? Not one.—The aged man, with tottering ſteps, and leaning upon his ſtaff ; his cheek furrowed with age, and his temples covered with ſilvered locks, has not ſeen' ſuch a day. The oldeſt among us was born ſince the laſt century began.

Some of the founders of this church and ſociety were men of the ſeventeentn century. But theſe are gone. They have dropped away, and took leave of time. So it will be with us, and the preſent inhabitants before the century cloſes. Yes, though it is computed there are nearly, nine hundred millions of inhabitants on the globe, yet, before the century ends we may expect they will all go out of time.— Yea, we may expect more than double that number will be born and die within a hundred years. We ſhall not eſcape the general ruin. Shortly we ſhall be with the countleſs millions who are gone, and are going into the world of ſpirits. Solemn thought ! Weighty conſideration ! May it ſuitably impreſs our minds ! This day calls us to think, ſeriouſly—to look about us—to ponder the ways, and works of God.—

We have arrived, *my friends*, to a period from which it becomes us to extend our views each way. As a traveller from an eminence looks back upon the way he has paſſed over, and, alſo, beholds an extenſive proſpect before him ; ſo, from this riſing ground, we are to meaſure back the way, and

293

notice the events that are paffed, and, at the fame time, look forward, and anticipate what is before us. The eighteenth century has not only produced wonders here, a few of which we have mentioned ; but had we time we might notice an aftonifhing feries of events which have taken place in the earth. If we look back but a few years we may fee that it has difmembered the empire of Britain, and formed a new empire in this weftern world. It has produced furprizing revolutions in Europe, attended with a fhaking among the nations, and a moft violent ftruggle to revolutionize the world. It has produced a confpiracy againft religion, and a deep laid plot to overturn, and tear up chriftianity by the roots.— It has produced a miffionary fpirit in Europe, attended with ftrong defires, and great exertions to extend the borders of Chrift's kingdom, and fend the gofpel to perifhing fouls. This has reached America—fpread itfelf in the feveral ftates, and has great effect on the minds of many ferious Chriftians.— The clofe of the century has witneffed an outpouring of the divine fpirit, and revival of a glorious work of God, in various parts of New-England, and the United States. By this the Lord is counteracting the principles, and exertions of infidelity— confirming the truth of revealed religion—increafing the number of his friends, and ftrengthening the hands of Zion. By this God is giving ample proof that the exertions of earth and hell fhall never deftroy his church.

THE nineteenth century, no doubt, will produce as great, or greater events. '

WHAT will be the ftate of our nation through this eventful period, is known only to him who turns the wheel of providence. If, however, we avoid thofe evils which have deluged moft of the nations in blood, we may, undoubtedly, efcape their plagues. There is nothing, in human view, except it be our

A CENTURY SERMON.

own folly and wickednefs, to prevent our being the greateſt and moſt happy nation on the globe. But from a view of the depravity of man, and from ſome increaſing ſymptoms, we have reaſon to apprehend a *fever* has attacked us—that it will prey on the vitals of our conſtitution—corrode the ſeat of life—contaminate the whole ſyſtem, and iſſue in diſſolution.

HOWEVER this may be, yet the Lord has great things to effect in the earth. From the preſent ſtate of the world, as well as from the prophecies of God we have concluſive evidence that his judgments are not completed. The preſent century is, undoubtedly, pregnant with great and aſtoniſhing events.

As GOD was, for ages, preparing the way for Chriſt to come in the fleſh, and ſet up his ſpiritual kingdom among men ; ſo he is now preparing to eſtabliſh a kingdom of righteouſneſs, and peace in the earth. It is, evidently, now what the ſcriptures call, *the laſt days.* 2 Peter iii. 3. And it is emphatically, *The laſt time.* Jude 17, 18. *Mockers* appear *who walk after their own ungodly luſts,* and conſider the gratification of their animal paſſions as the great end of life. In this day, alſo, there are many who *ſcoff* at the religion and doctrines of the Saviour. This is true in the conſpiracy formed againſt chriſtianity, in the laſt century, and the open and ſhameleſs attacks of infidelity on the religion of the *bible.* A ſpirit of oppoſition to chriſtianity will, probably, continue to ſpread, increaſe, and ſhow itſelf, more powerfully, in time to come. Guided by the light of ſcripture prophecy we have reaſon to expect it. We are taught, indeed, that wickedneſs and infidelity will prevail, ſo greatly, in the world, that when Chriſt comes to vindicate his cauſe, and liberate his ſuffering friends he ſhall, ſcarcely *find faith on the earth.* Luke xviii. 8. Satan will be ſuffered to put forth violent exertions in ſupport of his own kingdom ; and for a ſeaſon he will appear to prevail, that his overthrow may be the more fignal, and his fall the greater. In prophetic language *fpirits of devils* fhall *go forth unto the kings of the earth, and of the whole world, to gather them together to the battle of the great day of God Almighty.* Rev. xvi. 14. The prevalence of infidelity, it may be expected, will occafion not only diforganizers of religion, but of fociety and government, as is now the cafe in fome parts of ancient chriftendom. This will produce war, and thofe dreadful attending evils defigned for the enemies of God. In this way have arifen thofe calamities which, now, convulfe the nations of Europe, and fhake, *terribly*, the earth. Thefe calamities will continue fo long as infidelity is fuffered to carry on open war with chriftianity.

But a period will come, and is, rapidly, approaching, when infidelity will hide its head. We are taught in the prophecies of God that Satan's kingdom fhall be overthrown, and a kingdom of righteoufnefs and peace be eftablifhed. When the fourth beaft mentioned in the 7th chap. of Daniel, and whofe violent ftruggles occafion the prefent diftrefs of nations, fhall be deftroyed, then *the kingdom, and the greatnefs of the kingdom under the whole heaven, fhall be given to the people of the faints of the Moft High.* Thus, although, *Thefe*, that is, infidels, *fhall make war with the LAMB*, yet *the LAMB fhall overcome them ; for he is LORD of lords, and KING of kings ; and they that are with him are called, and chofen, and faithful.* Rev. xvii. 14. Under the influence of a blaze of light from the fulfilment of prophecy, and a powerfully, preached gofpel, accompanied by a plentiful outpouring of the Spirit of God, infidelity will fink, deifm vanifh, and the caufe of Jefus triumph and prevail. Righteoufnefs and peace will then overfpread the earth.

There are reafons which incline us to believe thefe things will, in part, if not fully, be accom-

A CENTURY SERMON. 25

plifhed within the prefent century. This is to us, therefore, a joyful, and folemn period. Joyful in that we are fpared to fee it—folemn in view of the profpect before us and our children. You will, therefore, bear with me, a little longer, while I indulge my prefent feelings in fome ferious addreffes, fuggefted by the prefent period.

HEADS of families, and fuch as have children and youth under their care, will fuffer me to offer them a few thoughts.

MY FRIENDS AND NEIGHBORS,
WE are the creatures of God. He has brought us into exiftence, and given us, individually, the talents we are to improve. He does not defign this world fhall be our home. The fouls that animate thefe bodies are, by and by, to leave them, and appear before God. At that folemn period we are to give an account of our improvement, and receive our reward. At another period, ftill more diftant, thefe bodies will be raifed from the duft—be reanimated—appear with our fathers, mothers, and the affembled world, before the judgment feat of Chrift, and hear our final doom. Are thefe things fo ? They fpeak to us this day in language folemn as the grave, and weighty as eternity. And fome of the events we have noticed may fix them on our minds. Let me advife, therefore, and exhort that you give them fuch a ferious confideration as the nature of the fubject requires. Let fuch as, profeffedly, own the religion of Jefus live, agreeably, to their profeffion. Be exhorted to *ftand faft in the faith,* and let your light fhine before men. Make it evident to the world that you are the cordial friends of chriftianity, and will rifk every thing to fecure its honor. The difciple of Chrift muft forfake all and follow him.

THE period is advancing, and may not be far off,
D

when Chriſtians will be called to bear the reproaches, and contempt of a wicked world—when they will ſuffer greater perſecution than has been known in our day.   But theſe things need not move you.   Having *put on the harneſs* you are to follow your leader, relying on his Almighty arm for ſupport, and truſting his promiſe that you ſhall not be deſtroyed.   Another period is advancing when the *ſilver trumpet* will ſound among all nations, and *The ſtone cut out of the mountain without hands become a great mountain, and fill the earth.*   Real ſaints may take courage. They will not, though caſt down and afflicted, be finally overcome.   They ſhall enter into the *ſecret chambers*, and having the doors ſhut about them, be kept ſafe unto the end.

IF there be any who have no hope that they have choſen religion, and are, at preſent, thoughtleſs and unconcerned, let me adviſe you to make no delay in this important matter.   Be exhorted to determine whether there be any thing in religion, and make ſuch a choice as will render you ſafe for eternity.— Chooſe the fear of God as the firſt thing, and be on the ſide of the Saviour.   Further,

LET us, *my friends*, feel the weight of the charge that lies upon us reſpecting our children.   It is our duty to educate, and form their minds to uſefulneſs and activity.   It is our duty to bring them up to buſineſs, and to ſome uſeful employment.   Idleneſs is hurtful to perſons at any period of life.   It is the road to ignorance, vice, and ruin.   Habits of idleneſs in young life, eſpecially, prepare a perſon for poverty, diſgrace, and wretchedneſs.

WE ought, alſo, to take the moſt effectual meaſures to impreſs the young mind, with an idea of the reality, and importance of religion ; and teach it by precept, and example.   We ought, eſpecially, in this evil day, to guard their minds againſt the poiſon of

298

infidelity.   To this there are ftrong, and powerful
motives.   In this way, alone, can we honor God—
fecure our own good, and be in a way to fecure the
beft good and happinefs of our children and youth.

I now afk the patience of this affembly while
I offer a few words to the young people of the congregation.

MY DEAR YOUNG FRIENDS,
You are coming forward on the theatre of life at
a very important period.   It is the commencement
of a new century, and the morning of time with
a new empire.   It becomes you to fix thofe political fentiments which, in operation, will prove beneficial to the nation.   Within a fhort time you, and
thofe of your age, will be the principal actors on
the ftage.   Form your principles, therefore, on the
beft information you can obtain ; and, when formed, be firm and unwavering.   Read much in the
hiftorical part of the facred fcriptures, and from
thence learn the importance of government, and of
uniting virtue and abilities in thofe at the head of it.
You will there find the great influence of virtue, or
vice, in a civil ruler, on the ftate of a nation.   When
God's ancient covenant people were governed by
wife, and pious men, they profpered and were happy.   When rulers of a different character held the
reins, they mourned, and were afflicted.   And fo
it has, ufually, been with other nations.   But as you
will not, probably, many of you, be in a fituation
to be acquainted with the civil hiftory of the world
in general ; and as you will always, it is hoped, have
the bible in your hands ; fo I advife you to make
yourfelves well acquainted with the hiftorical part of
that *beft of all books.*   From thence you may obtain
the beft information on the fubject that will be within your reach.

ESTABLISH in your minds the importance of maintaining the government of your country, as the only means of fecuring its privileges. Never let that which has coft a fea of blood, as well as millions of money, be facrificed to the caprice of defigning and artful demagogues. Further,

LET me add, you are coming into life at a very critical period in another view. It is a day when the religion of the *bleffed SAVIOUR* is, boldly attacked. Europe affords affecting inftances of blafphemous attacks upon Chrift and his doctrines. There are many in this country who are imitating thofe pretended enlighteners of the world. A battery is opened, and the enemies of chriftianity are playing off their heavieft artillery againft our holy religion. In this boafted age of reafon you will often meet with men who will not fcruple to tell you the bible is a forgery, that religion is mere prieftcraft, and future punifhment a bugbear. Thefe, *my friends*, are the *doctrines of devils ;* and a belief of them is the *high road* to hell. But there is a natural aptitude in the human mind to embrace errors, and to throw off the reftraints of religion. If, therefore, you are not peculiarly, guarded you will fwallow the poifon and be undone forever. Be perfuaded to hear with prudence, examine with great caution, and fix your opinion wifely. Remember what the wife man fays, " The fimple believeth every word ; but the prudent man looketh well to his going." If you difcard the bible, and religion, you rifk the intereft of eternity, and will, too late, find your miftake. Be advifed never to throw away the bible 'till you are certain it is not a revelation from God. The matter is too interefting to be given up upon bold affertion, and mere declamation. You have a right to demand proof, and, if wife, you will take up fatisfied with nothing fhort of it. For in a firm belief of the doctrines of the bible, though it be not a revelation from heaven, you rifk nothing ; but in denying them, if it be a revelation, you rifk every thing.

A CENTURY SERMON.

Certainty, even, complete demonſtration on the ſide of infidelity, is the only ground on which you can venture, and be ſafe. Determine this and I am ſure you will retain the bible as a revelation from heaven, for a certainty on the other ſide is not poſſible.— There is not a deiſt in the world who pretends to it. I venture to challenge the united ſtrength of deiſm to prove that the Moſaic hiſtory, and the account of Jeſus Chriſt in the goſpels are not, literally, true. And if true the inſpiration of the bible is, indubitably, eſtabliſhed.

Be perſuaded to be on ſafe ground. Chooſe Chriſt as your Saviour and only hope, and receive his doctrines as a revelation from God. Adhere to the faith of the martyrs, and own the religion of your forefathers. Venture to die rather than abandon that which brought the firſt worthies to theſe American ſhores. In this way you will be prepared to rejoice though the world mourn, and drink, deeply, of the *vials* that are pouring out, and are, yet, to be poured out on the infidels of an enlightened age. In this way you will be prepared to meet death with a cheerful heart, and ſpring forward to join the bleſſed company on *Mount Zion*. Then, at the cloſe of the nineteenth century, when infidelity is ſunk forever—when the wilderneſs of America ſhall become a fruitful field—when the banner of the croſs ſhall be diſplayed from the Atlantic, through the vaſt tract, even, to the ſhores of the Pacific Ocean— when the Lord ſhall have planted flouriſhing churches all over this land, *And the ranſomed of the Lord ſhall return, and come to Zion with ſongs, and everlaſting joy upon their heads ;* then ſhall you look down from heaven and, with adoring Angels, admire the works of God. Then ſhall you join the ſong of Moſes and the Lamb, *Great and marvellous are thy works, Lord God Almighty, juſt and true are thy ways, thou King of ſaints !*

30   A CENTURY SERMON.

FINALLY.—May we all begin the new century with new refolutions in favor of Godlinefs. May we *gird* up our *loins*, and be *ftrong in the Lord.*— May we fet up our *Ebenezer*, ftrongly impreffed with this idea that *Hitherto hath the LORD helped, us.*

Mr. Backus's

CENTURY SERMON.

A

SERMON,

Delivered Jan. 1, 1801 ;

CONTAINING A BRIEF REVIEW OF SOME OF THE

DISTINGUISHING EVENTS OF THE

EIGHTEENTH CENTURY.

BY CHARLES BACKUS, A. M.

PASTOR OF A CHURCH IN SOMERS.

HARTFORD:

PRINTED BY HUDSON AND GOODWIN.

1801.

A Century Sermon.

JOB viii. 8, 9.

INQUIRE, I pray thee, of the former age, and prepare thyself to the search of their fathers : For we are but of yesterday, and know nothing, because our days upon earth are a shadow.

MAN continueth but a short time on the earth. The beginning of the individual who is permitted to see the greatest number of years, is *but of yesterday.* Since the age in which Job probably lived, human life has been shortened. Threescore years and ten, have, ever since the time of Moses, been considered as its extreme. *Our days upon earth are a shadow :* They are destitute of substantial happiness, they are constantly changing, they are soon at an end, and they leave no traces behind. "As the cloud is consumed and vanisheth away ; so he that goeth down to the grave shall come up no more. He shall return no more to his house, neither shall his place know him any more."

6   A CENTURY SERMON.

MAN's attainments in knowledge can be but
ſmall, in the preſent ſtate of his exiſtence. He
knoweth nothing in compariſon with what is to be
known. His knowledge would be circumſcribed
within much narrower limits than it is, if he could
not *inquire of the former age, and prepare himſelf to
the ſearch of their fathers.* By looking back to paſt
ages, we may greatly enlarge our minds, by means
of the attainments of our predeceſſors. By the help
of ſcripture hiſtory, we may, in ſome ſenſe, be contemporaries with the generations that lived thouſands of years before we were born, and can carry
back our reſearches to the beginning of the world.

As eighteen hundred years from the birth of Jeſus
Chriſt have paſſed, and as we, on this day, according to the common computation, begin the *Nineteenth Century,* it is propoſed to take a brief review
of ſome of the events which diſtinguiſhed the laſt
hundred years ; and to ſuggeſt a few hints relative
to the preſent ſtate of the world, and of the church
of God. In recurring to what we have ſeen, and in
looking back to the experience of our fathers, we
may find arguments to eſtabliſh and ſtrengthen our
faith in the divine government ; and motives to excite us to ſpend the momentary remnant of our days,
in the purſuit of that wiſdom which is the defence
and glory of man.

THE globe which we inhabit, has been ſailed
round oftener in the courſe of the laſt century, than
it had been in all the preceding ones. By the voyages
which have been made by circumnavigators, and
others, many iſlands have been diſcovered, and iſlands
heretofore known to the Europeans, as well as the
ſea-coaſts of the continents, have been more fully
explored. It has been in particular, diſcovered that
the American continent in its North-weſt part, is
divided from Aſia by a narrow ſtrait, that the
adjacent inhabitants on both ſides of the ſtrait are
alike, and that in their ſmall water craft they fre-

A CENTURY SERMON.

quently pafs and repafs. Late travellers have alfo
increafed the fum of geographical knowledge. By
voyages and travels, by the extenfion of commerce,
by the increafe of civilization, and by eftablifhing
regular and fwift means of communicating intelli-
gence between places remote from each other, the
inhabitants of the earth have had more mutual intercourfe within the laft century, than in any former
period fince they became very numerous. The republic of letters has received great acceffions, by late
writers of the natural as well as of the civil hiftory
of the world.

THE ftudy of antiquity, will be kept alive, and
will be increafed, by the conftant and rapid rife of
new fettlements made by civilized people in North-
America, and by late European fettlements fcattered
along the coafts of Africa and Afia, which border
on the Atlantic and Southern oceans. By exploring
the furface and bowels of the earth, in new countries, and in thofe little known by the moderns, frefh
materials will be furnifhed for natural hiftory ; and
in the fearch for thefe, as well as by other means, the
veftiges of the ancient inhabitants will come to light
and will be examined by the curious. The remains of
regular fortreffes of a very ancient date, found on
the weftern fide of the Alleghany mountains, afford
fome evidence that, many ages ago there lived a
people on this Continent, who had confiderable acquaintance with the arts of the civilized ftate ; and
muft therefore, have been in a higher grade of fociety than the Indians were, when Columbus vifited
thefe fhores. Afia continues to promife a large harveft to the antiquarian, for ages to come. This
appears, in particular, from the publications of the
learned fociety eftablifhed at Calcutta, by the late Sir
William Jones. Oriental literature, after a temporary decline, has revived, and is rifing into much
higher repute than it had a few years ago.

8   A CENTURY SERMON.

An acquaintance with the Latin, Greek, and Hebrew tongues, is not thought to be of equal importance in a liberal education, as it formerly was. Whatever may be pleaded in fupport of this opinion, the enlightened friends of chriftianity, muft reprobate the idea of a total ignorance in all its minifters, of the languages in which the Jewifh and Chriftian fcriptures were firft written. If this event fhould happen, in the prefent ftate of the Church, infidels would affume an air of higher confidence againft the defenders of divine revelation, than they have hitherto done.

WITHIN the laft hundred years, greater attention has been paid to ftyle, and compofition, than in any other period fince the revival of learning in Europe, fubfequent to the reduction of Conftantinople by the Turks, A. D. 1453. Under the reigns of Louis XIV. king of France, and Anne, queen of England, writers on various fubjects rofe to a high pitch of merit. This late Auguftan age will for ever remain as a celebrated epoch in the hiftory of the Arts and Sciences. To the productions of that time are to be afcribed, in a high degree, the improvements which have been made within a few years, on both fides of the Atlantic, in the purity, the precifion, and the elegance of ftyle. The tedious prolixity which prevailed a hundred and forty years ago, is laid afide. In departing from the extreme of the feventeenth century, there may be danger of lofing the copioufnefs, which belongs to compofitions defigned to intereft the heart ; and of falling into an unimpreffive brevity, and a dull correctnefs.

WITHIN the period in review, Mathematical learning has been carried to a high degree of perfection.

THE knowledge of the eftablifhed laws by which the natural world is governed, has been much increafed. For the advance which has been made in this, as well as in the Mathematics, the republic of

A CENTURY SERMON.

letters is much indebted to that great luminary of fcience Sir Ifaac Newton; who died a little more than feventy years ago. In natural philofophy experiments have taken the place of hypothefes; and have been multiplied far beyond what had been known in former times.

In electricity, many important difcoveries have been made. In thefe, the late Dr. Franklin led the way. To that ornament of fcience mankind are indebted, for a knowledge of the means of defence againft the lightning.

Some great naturalifts have, of late, turned their attention to Chemiftry; and have gone far in difcovering the extent and ufe of chemical knowledge. Vifionary projects in chemiftry, as in every thing elfe, cannot endure the teft of time. What is folid will abide; and what is imaginary will vanifh away.

Astronomy, has been clofely ftudied by many eminent men; and towards the clofe of the laft century, a *feventh* primary planet belonging to the folar fyftem, was difcovered by Dr. Herfchell. He has fince difcovered feveral moons which revolve round this planet.

Many new inventions in the Mechanic arts, have appeared within a few years paft.

Men who have devoted themfelves to literary purfuits, have had recourfe to firft principles; and have done much in fimplifying the more abftrufe parts of fcience. Barbarous terms have been more exploded in the courfe of the century in review, than they were in any former age. The late eminent writers in all the learned profeffions, have difcovered an uncommon degree of care, to render themfelves intelligible to every clafs of readers.

The tafte for reading among the civilized nations, has greatly increafed of late. Books have been mul-

B

tiplied within thirty or forty years, far beyond what had been feen within a period of the fame length, even fince the art of printing was invented. It has become rare in our infant nation, to find a town of much age, efpecially in the Northern States, without a circulating library. Schools, academies, univerfities, and affociations of literary men, have been multiplied, with a furprifing rapidity, in the United States, fince the clofe of the revolutionary war.

LEARNED treatifes have been written on the faculties of the human mind, and on the means of enlarging man's knowledge. The metaphyfical fubject of liberty and neceffity, has engaged the attention of writers of deep penetration, and clear difcernment. Man's relations to God, and to his fellow-creatures, and the duties which he owes to the Creator, to himfelf, and to fociety, have employed many able pens.

EXPERIENCE has taught that mathematical demonftration is not applicable to moral fubjects. Requiring the fame kind of demonftration in thefe, as can be made by figures and lines, has, no doubt, been one caufe of increafing the fceptical turn, which has of late, taken fo wide a fpread.

FOR more than thirty years paft, the principles of civil and religious liberty have been abundantly difcuffed, by men of genius and erudition. It has been clearly fhown that all men, of whatever complexion, or climate, have an equal claim to freedom. The abfurdity of the African flave-trade has been expofed ; and a more general abhorrence of this nefarious traffic in the human fpecies has been excited, than had appeared fince its commencement. The friends of humanity rejoice in the profpect of its abolition.

THE feveral forms of civil government, have engaged the pens of the learned and the contemplative; and the Republican theory has been demonftrated to be the moft confonant to man's natural rights.

CHAPTER 13

A CENTURY SERMON.

EVERY one who loves mankind, muſt deſire that as large a portion of individual liberty may exiſt, as is conſiſtent with perſonal ſafety, combined with the general welfare. This muſt be determined by the circumſtances of a people. If they are wiſe and virtuous, they are qualified to live under a mild government ; but if they are abandoned to vice, their government will aſſume a high tone, whatever be the name by which it is called. The inhabitants of the United States of America, have the faireſt opportunity to enjoy rational civil freedom of any people now on the earth. Whether we ſhall have wiſdom and virtue enough, to legiſlate by the men of our own choice, and peaceably to obey as ſubjeſts ; or whether we ſhall be rent and torn by party ſpirit and faſtion, until we fall under deſpotic rule, can be determined only by experience.

THE political diſquiſitions of our time, were occaſioned by the arbitrary and oppreſſive meaſures which Great Britain adopted, towards her Colonies in North-America. Theſe meaſures led on to a long and bloody war, which terminated in our eſtabliſhment as independent States. In that day of trouble, great and reſpeſtable charaſters were raiſed up, to guide our councils and our armies. At the head of this band of patriots appeared the late illuſtrious WASHINGTON ; whoſe high fame, as a general, and a preſident, will live as long as the hiſtoric page ſhall preſerve the memory of nations.

NOT long after the peace of 1783, France, which had taken ſo aſtive a part in the American war, diſcovered ſymptoms of a revolution. Some of the men who contemplated a reform in the French government, were, no doubt, aſtuated by laudable motives. They were influenced to attempt a change at home, by the knowledge which they had gained by their intercourſe with the United States of America. Theſe patriots, in an early period of the revolution, were expelled from the councils and the armies of

313

France; and were either put to death or driven into banifhment, by demagogues, who had been initiated in demoralizing principles, and had planned a revolution which is without a parallel in the hiftory of mankind. In purfuing their meafures, the French king and his queen were beheaded; and all the members of the royal family, together with all who were nearly allied by blood, were either difgraced, or exiled, or fell by the hand of the executioner. The nation paffed from the government of abfolute monarchy to the extreme of democracy; and is at prefent under abfolute confular fway.

Both hemifpheres have felt the fhock caufed by the French revolution. In France the ancient order of things has been overthrown, and an attempt has been made, to introduce a kind of rule which openly bids defiance to every thing facred. The national enterprize has been directed towards an object which in no inftance has been held up by the leaders of any ftate or kingdom, until near the clofe of the eighteenth century. The devaftation, the cruelty, and the bloodfhed which have attended the revolution, in France, and in the countries which have been brought under her yoke, are fhocking to humanity.

In this day of trouble, deifm and atheifm have prevailed, far beyond what they had done in any former age. In the violent attack which has been made upon papal tyranny and fuperftition, an opportunity has prefented, for the human heart to fhow itfelf without difguife; and to be impelled to action by motives, which are hoftile to all government both human and divine. The men who have led in the convulfive meafures of the day, have difplayed on a broad fcale, the fyftematical impiety and violence which were planned by Voltaire, a celebrated French writer, in an early period of the laft century. To accomplifh his defign, he affociated with himfelf literary and influential characters. This combination was ftrengthened, by the acceffion of a great number of perfons of rank and talents, in France, in Germany, and in other places, until it became powerful enough to produce the convulfions, which have aftonifhed and terrified the world.—The prefent courfe of events among the nations to whom chriftianity is known, is calculated to convince that there is no neutral ground to be taken, between evangelical doctrines and infidelity ; and to enable us to difcern more plainly than heretofore, between thofe that ferve God and thofe that ferve him not.

WE need not wonder that deifts go on to atheifm. The material philofophy, which has become fo much in vogue, is inconfiftent with the idea of an infinite Spirit. If there be nothing in the univerfe but matter, *God* and *nature* are fynonymous terms ; and it would be as abfurd, on the material fyftem, to fuppofe man accountable to a fuperior being, in a moral view, as to fuppofe our moon a moral agent, and accountable to the earth for its motions. If it be admitted that there is one eternal, independent, infinite Spirit, the Creator and Governor of all worlds with their inhabitants, it muft follow that intelligent creatures are bound to worfhip him. It muft, therefore, be defirable to know what that Spirit is who is ftiled God, that we may difcover how he is to be worfhipped. Allowing that the Deity juftly claims homage from us, it will be acknowledged, from a flight furvey of the polytheifm and idolatry of the moft fcientific heathen nations, that a fupernatural revelation is to be defired. In examining the feveral religions which have appeared among mankind, no one can be found, even by the confeffion of difcerning infidels, which deferves to be compared with the religion contained in the book called the Bible. Hence, when this is renounced, the way is prepared to adopt the horrors of atheifm.

WE have feen, within a few years, a difpofition to innovate in every thing efteemed important, which

lies within the reach of human efforts. This turn
of thinking, which fo large a part of the public mind
has received, gives a coloring to mental exertions
even of the laudable kind, far beyond what we can
at once conceive. It is rare that any man rifes wholly above the peculiarities which give complexion to
his own time ; or can judge with impartiality in his
own cafe. We have reafon to believe that we have
not lefs caufe to requeft the candor of pofterity, than
our anceftors had to requeft ours. But in whatever
age any one lives, he will, if guided by an honeft
heart, abhor principles which breathe a fpirit of impiety and violence. He will not be fwallowed up in
the vortex of diforganizing fentiments and meafures,
nor let go his hold of the plain principles which guide
and protect the upright in the moft tempeftuous feafons. Brilliant talents engaged on the fide of iniquity, may command refpect, for a time, from fome
well-meaning perfons ; but their delufion will not
be lafting. The upright will not long inconfiderate-
ly gaze on the energies which promife to accomplifh
the moft difficult things, and which brave every
danger, when fuch talents are employed to banifh
truth and peace from the earth.

IT is painful to thofe who have imbibed the fpirit
of chriftianity, to behold much the greateft proportion of the human race ftill remaining in the darknefs of paganifm. But few converts to the religion
of Jefus Chrift, have been made from among the
heathen, during the laft hundred years. Many millions of mankind, in the North, and in the South, in
the Eaft, and in the Weft, continue devoted to the
various forms of pagan idolatry.

THE religion of Mahomet, appears to have as an
extenfive a fpread in Afia, Africa, and Europe, as
it has had for feveral centuries paft. Converfions
from Mahometanifm to the Chriftian faith, have
been more rare than from Heathenifm.

A CENTURY SERMON.

THE Jews continue to reject Jefus of Nazareth, and remain difperfed among the nations. Their creed appears to be much the fame as it was, when their famous Mofes Maimonides, fix-hundred years ago, abridged the Talmud, which contains the body of their civil and canon law. They are as numerous as they have been for many centuries paft. The moft of them refide on the Eaftern Continent, and in the adjacent iflands. Their fufferings have been lefs in the laft century, than in any former one fince their difperfion.

IN reviewing the ftate of Chriftendom for the laft hundred years, we find nothing which deferves fpecial notice in the ftate of the Greek church.

IN the Latin, or Roman Catholic church, fome great changes have taken place. The religious order of the Jefuits, inftituted a little after the reformation, was fuppreffed and banifhed by Pope Gangenelli, in the year 1773. The Jefuits were warm partizans of the papal power ; and bid fair, for a feafon, by their fuperior abilities and undaunted fpirit of enter-prize, to propagate the Catholic faith through the world. But they rendered themfelves obnoxious to all the courts where they were known, by their cabals and intrigues, and brought on their own deftruc-tion. The papal church received a blow in the days of Luther, Zuingle, and Calvin, from which it has not recovered. In the century now gone, it has been greatly weakened, and its ruin appears to be at hand. The Court of Inquifition has either been annihilated, or its power has been reduced almoft to nothing, in all the Roman Catholic countries. The thunders of the Vatican have loft their ancient terror and influ-ence ; and we have lately feen a Pope plundered of his wealth, ftripped of his dominions and driven from his chair. It is not, however, to be fuppofed, when we confult the prophecies, that the Antichriftian church is to be immediately deftroyed. The laft dying ftruggles of the man of fin are yet future, and

16   A CENTURY SERMON.

will be violent ; and will form no fmall part of the battle which is introductory to the millennium. Popery addreffes itfelf to more prejudices of the depraved human heart, than any other fpecies of falfe religion which has affumed the Chriftian name. The perfecuting fpirit of infidelity, with other caufes, may operate in favor of a temporary reviving reputation of the Catholic church.

Among the Proteftants, fects have rifen up, that have difcarded the diftinguifhing doctrines of the Bible, and have endeavored to weaken its authority as an infpired book. The latitudinarian fentiments of fome profeffed Chriftians at the prefent time, reprefent articles of faith as being of very fmall importance. If individual belief be the ftandard of religious truth, as many have pleaded, it is folly to contend for the divine original of the fcriptures of the Old and New Teftaments.

The Socinians, in particular, who have become numerous, have confidered the authority and the doctrines of the Bible in fuch a light, as to give to chriftianity a complexion, highly favorable to the views of thofe, who advocate the fufficiency of the light of nature to guide man to happinefs.   Neither do the Univerfalifts, in general, admit the plenary infpiration of the fcriptures.—Individuals who have maintained the falvation of all men, and the final reftoration of all intelligent creatures to happinefs, have been found within the limits of Chriftendom, from the days of Origen, who lived in the third century. This denomination has increafed of late ; and a few years ago, for the firft time, eftablifhed churches. It has not been rare for Socinians and Univerfalifts to end in open Deifm.

It has been fhown, with great force of argument, by late, as well as more ancient Trinitarian writers, that Jefus Chrift is God, as well as man ; and that a denial of his divinity, involves a denial of the fcripture doctrine of atonement, and all the other diftinguifhing doctrines of revealed religion.

A CENTURY SERMON.

THE denial of future endlefs punifhment, has led to a critical examination of the fcriptures on this fubject. It has been demonftrated with great clearnefs, and ftrength of argument, by fome American divines in particular, that the punifhment threatened in the law of God, is not difciplinary, but vindictive ; and that a large number of texts can admit of no confiftent meaning, if the whole of mankind are to be happy after death. Thefe advocates for the faith which was once delivered unto the faints, have made it appear that there is nothing in the nature of the divine benevolence, which requires the removal of evil from the univerfe ; and that the greateft fum of intelligent happinefs, is reconcilable with the interminable mifery of the obftinate enemies of God.

THEOLOGICAL talents of a refpectable grade, have been employed in learned and elaborate inquiries, into the neceffary and immutable perfection of the divine goverment, into the nature of holinefs, and into the grounds and perpetuity of moral obligation. In thefe, and connected fubjects, the late Prefident Edwards led the way. His memory will be precious to the friends of pure religion, in ages to come. They will read with pleafure his writings on doctrinal, experimental, and practical piety. His depth in metaphyfical refearches has rarely been equalled. The diftinction made by this great man, between what is natural and what is moral in the human mind, is more and more approved by Calvinifts ; and acknowledged to be important, in reconciling with the total moral impotency of mankind, the commands, threatenings, and invitations, which are addreffed to them in the word of God.—Perhaps, the principles which have been confidered as fundamental in the Calviniftic fyftem, have been purfued farther into their confequences, within the laft fifty years, than they had been in any former period.

WE have feen within the century in review, the fame fondnefs for novelty and diftinction, among

C

18   A CENTURY SERMON.

profeffed Chriftians, as had appeared in the preceding ages. Men of genius and learning have rifen up, and have collected followers who have been called after their refpective names.—It is to be remember-ed, that truth and error in all their varying dreffes, do not change their natures. The difference between them will abide, whether the epithets applied to them be reputable, or reproachful.

As the fulfilment of prophecy affords an argu-ment, of no fmall weight, in fupport of the truth and infpiration of the Bible, we may fee, in part, a reafon why divines have of late, beftowed more atten-tion upon the prophetic writings than had been known for feveral ages. It is to be expected, be the ftate of infidelity what it may, that the prophetic pa-ges will be more clofely examined, as the time draws near in which " the myftery of God fhall be finifh-ed." We ought not to be furprifed when we reflect on the imperfection of man, the mifguided warmth to which he is liable when looking into futurity, and his fondnefs to bring every future event of great im-portance within the limits of his own life, that fome crude and imaginary notions fhould be advanced, in interpreting the prophecies. It is, however, believed that the able and candid divines of future ages, will look back with refpectful notice to many of the wri-tings on this fubject, which appeared in the eight-eenth century.

As the friends of truth are called to oppofe the enemies of the day, the infidious and violent attacks which have been made on the truth and divinity of revealed religion, have occafioned many able defences of the holy fcriptures to appear, within the century now ended. The internal and the external evidences of chriftianity, have been placed in a clear and con-vincing light. The men who remain infidels at the prefent luminous period, muft be confidered as obfti-nate in their enmity to a religion, which has been fo abundantly proved to be from heaven and not of men.

A CENTURY SERMON.

BETWEEN the years 1740 and 1745, an uncommon attention to experimental and practical piety commenced in Great Britain, and in her American Colonies. New-England shared largely in the work. It was attended, in many instances, with bodily agitations and outcries. An appearance so extraordinary attracted the attention of all sorts of people. Some condemned the whole in a mass : Others admitted error as well as truth.: Another class separated the wheat from the chaff. The events of that day have extended their influence down to the present time. Evangelical doctrines wherever preached, have, ever since that revival, been exhibited in a more experimental and discriminating strain than they had been for many years before. True religion has been delineated, and distinguished from its counterfeits, with greater clearness than usual. The errors and divisions which sprang up at the close of the foregoing memorable period, have taken a course which has served as a warning to the serious and the enlightened, " not to believe every spirit, but to try the spirits whether they are of God." Painful as have been the schisms in the churches in this land, for more than fifty years past, they have been the occasion of leading the friends of evangelical piety, to a more critical examination of its nature. They have manifested an enlightened zeal in this respect, which is worthy of the imitation of posterity.

THE divisions among Protestants in general, are as numerous, as they have been at any time ; but a spirit of mutual toleration prevails beyond what had been before seen, among the various denominations that are large, and of long standing. This is to be accounted for, in part, from a better acquaintance with the nature of religious liberty, from the conviction of the pious of different communions that they are engaged in the common cause of the Redeemer, and from feeling the necessity of their united efforts against the growing infidelity. It will not be

A CENTURY SERMON.

thought uncandid by the judicious, to attribute the increafing toleration, in part, to the indifference and fcepticifm, which have made fuch alarming progrefs among nominal Chriftians.—Some great revolution in the religious, as well as in the political ftate of the world, feems to be at hand.

NEAR the clofe of the laft century, the godly people in England, were led ferioufly to reflect on the decay of piety, and the benighted ftate of the heathen nations. They proceeded to form Miffion-ary Societies, " to fpread the knowledge of Chrift among Heathen and other unenlightened nations." The Moravians had been left, for a long time, to labor alone for the converfion of the Heathen, until within the laft eight years. Within this period, many Miffionary Societies have been formed in Great Bri-tain, and in other parts of Europe. The Miffionary Society inftituted at London, in 1795, is the moft diftinguifhed of any modern one, and has given rife to moft of the others which have been lately form-ed. Miffionaries have been fent to carry the glad news of gofpel falvation, to fome places in Africa, and in Afia, and to feveral iflands in the South Sea. The zeal of European Chriftians, hath been inftru-mental in exciting a like pious ardor in this land. Several Spcieties have been formed here, for the purpofes of " Chriftianizing the Heathen in North-America, and for the fupport and promotion of Chriftian knowledge, in the New Settlements within the limits of the United States." Preachers of the gofpel have been fent into our infant fettlements, and they have labored with great fuccefs. An effort has been made by fome of the American Miffionary Societies, to bring the Indian Tribes to the knowl-edge of a crucified Saviour. We hope that an effect-ual door is opening, for the fpreading of the gofpel among the benighted Savages on this Continent. The friends of the Redeemer are animated with the profpect, that the exertions which are now made, may be among the principal means of the ingathering of " the fulnefs of the Gentiles," in the Lord's time.

WITHIN three years paft there has been a wonderful revival of religion, in New-England, and in fome other parts of the United States. This revival has been generally free from bodily agitations and outcries ; and has, in other refpects, been remarkably pure. This work, though far from being univerfal, has been more extenfive, than had been feen in this land for more than half a century.

EVANGELICAL minifters, as well as other Chriftians, are, at the prefent time, more deeply impreffed than ufual, with the worth of the religion of Jefus Chrift, and with the importance of withftanding the powers of darknefs. They difcover an uncommon zeal, in laboring for the advancement of the Redeemer's kingdom on the earth.

FROM the foregoing brief review of the eighteenth century, we may remark,

1. THAT the events in divine providence, confirm the truth and infpiration of the holy fcriptures.

THE increafe of geographical knowledge, has removed the difficulties in the peopling of America and the iflands of the ocean, from the Eaftern Continent. By the difcoveries which have been made in the natural world, as well as by the hiftory of the nations, it appears that all mankind defcended from the firft pair who dwelt on the banks of the Euphrates ; as is affirmed in the book of Genefis. The variety of complexion and figure in the human fpecies, may be fatisfactorily accounted for, on the principle of found philofophy ; and forms no folid objection to the fcriptural account of the propagation of the human race—" That God hath made of one blood all nations of men, for to dwell on all the face of the earth."

A CENTURY SERMON.

THE improvements in the arts and fciences, evince the fuperior rank which man holds among the creatures of this lower world; and that God placed him in the exalted grade in the fcale of being, which is affigned to him in the facred writings. Man has explored this globe, from fide to fide, and he has fearched into all the works of the Creator around him. He is endowed with a mind which qualifies him to look back to the ages which are gone, and to enlarge his knowledge by their experience and refearches. The fruits of man's invention and induftry are fcattered over the face of the earth. We behold him tracing his relations to fociety, and to the Infinite Mind. We behold man forming various complicated combinations, which harmonize large communities, and lead on to convulfions, which fpread terror and difmay through ftates and kingdoms.

THE impiety and violence which have prevailed on this earth, convince more than a thoufand arguments drawn from reafon, that the human heart is deceitful above all things, and defperately wicked; as is affirmed in the word of God. The members of Adam's family have encroached upon the rights of each other, and have been mutual deftroyers. Empires have rifen up amidft violent commotions, like the ftriving of the four winds of the heaven upon the great fea, and have refembled devouring beafts. We have heard men of high rank profeffing to aim at the introduction of all the gentle and amiable manners, which can adorn the human race; we have heard them boaft of their purpofe, as well as ability, to convert this earth into a paradife; and while we have heard their fair and flattering words, we have feen them acting out all the rancour of which the depraved heart is capable; we have witneffed their outrage upon all the rights of humanity; and we have beheld them turning the world into a field of blood. Painful as thefe events are, they eftablifh

A CENTURY SERMON.

the truth of divine revelation, which predicts " that in the laft days perilous times fhall come" when the wicked are given up to felfifhnefs, covetoufnefs, boafting, pride, and blafphemy.

THE rapacity of the Affyrian monarch, exhibits the human heart, when reftraint is thrown off, and an opportunity is prefented to indulge the pride of conqueft. " He is a proud man, neither keepeth at home, who enlargeth his defire as hell, and is as death, and cannot be fatisfied, but gathereth unto him all nations, and heapeth unto him all people."*

IT is declared in fcripture, and demonftrated by events, " that the Moft High ruleth in the kingdom of men, and giveth it to whomfoever he will." In fome inftances he " fetteth up over it the bafeft of men." Jehovah accomplifheth his purpofes by what inftruments he pleafeth. He maketh the wrath of man to praife him. He ufed the Affyrian monarch as the rod of his anger, in punifhing the rebellious Ifraelites. The Lord declared, " O Affyrian, the rod of mine anger, and the ftaff of their hand is mine indignation. I will fend him againft an hypocritical nation ; and againft the people of my wrath will I give him a charge to take the fpoil, and to take the prey, and to tread them down like the mire of the ftreets. Howbeit he meaneth not fo, neither doth his heart think fo ; but it is in his heart to deftroy and cut off nations not a few."†

As the age of the world has increafed, the fum of evidence has alfo been increafed, that the world by its own wifdom knoweth not God. " Where is the wife ? where is the fcribe ? where is the difputer of this world ? hath not God made foolifh the wifdom of this world ?" Great ftrength of intellect, and high literary attainments, furnifh no guide to immortal happinefs. Men of this defcription have, in not a few inftances, fanctioned by their authority the

---

* Habak. ii. 5. † Ifaiah x. 5, 6, 7.

24   A CENTURY SERMON.

groffeft errors.   They have been feen to plunge into the depths of delufion, and to adopt the language of the fool, " There is no God."   When any have openly renounced the Chriftian faith, the enormity which has marked their fubfequent life, has afforded a dreadful warning againft the evil of apoftacy, and has exhibited proof of the excellent nature of the religion which they have abjured.

THE men of the greateft talents, who have been made fubjects of the fpecial grace of God, have been the moft abundant in acknowledging the abfolute neceffity of a fupernatural revelation.   They have labored to convince others, that mankind when left to the light of nature will never come to a right knowledge of God ; and that his word only, can be a lamp unto their feet, and a light unto their path.   The mariner in the midft of a wide ocean, inveloped in darknefs, and without the aid of a compafs, is not in fo deplorable a ftate with refpect to fteering his courfe to fome port, as apoftate man is, without the light of revealed truth, with refpect to directing his way to the world of immortal happinefs.

REMARKABLE is the fulfilment of the fcripture prophecies by the events which are now before us. The providence of God is conftantly proclaiming the truth of his word. He is ftill enlarging Japheth, and giving him to dwell in the tents of Shem.   The defcendants of Ham are, generally, either fubjected to a foreign yoke, or are fold in the market for flaves.*   Egypt, in particular, has long been " the bafeft of the kingdoms," and has been wafted " by the hand of ftrangers."† The Jews, who defcended from Shem, remain " fcattered among all people, from the one end of the earth even unto the other." The vial poured out by the fixth angel, mentioned in Revelation xvi, appears to be now running.   The

---

* Gen. ix. 25, 26, 27.   † Ezek. xxix. 15.   xxx. 12.

power of the man of fin is brought very low ; and the unclean fpirits that " come out of the mouth of the dragon, and out of the mouth of the beaft, and out of the mouth of the falfe prophet," have begun to " go forth unto the kings of the earth, and of the whole world, to gather them to the battle of that great day of God Almighty."

AMIDST the fiery trials thro' which the Church hath paffed, fince her flight into the wildernefs, fhe hath been protected from on high. The powers of the earth, though hoftile to her doctrines and laws, have been made to help her. Able and faithful men have been raifed up, to contend for the Chriftian faith. Though the witneffes have been fometimes covered with fackcloth, they have never been filent. When the enemy hath come in like a flood, the Spirit of the Lord hath lifted up a ftandard againft him ; according to prediction and promife. We now behold Jefus Chrift animating his people, to labor with uncommon activity and zeal, to extend the knowledge of his holy name, in the weft, and towards the rifing of the fun. We behold many made the willing fubjects of the Prince of Peace. We have renewed evidence that true religion is not created nor upholden by human power, but by the Spirit of the Lord. The Church is built upon the Rock of ages, and the gates of hell fhall not prevail againft it.

CAN we doubt the truth and infpiration of the holy fcriptures, when we open our eyes upon the ftate of the world, and of the Church of God ? If we are willing to receive the divine teftimony, we fhall difcern the worth of that kingdom which cannot be moved ; and when the Lord arifeth to fhake terribly the earth, our faith will be confirmed by the events, which occafion the wicked to blafpheme, and fill the nations with difmay. " The counfel of the Lord ftandeth for ever, the thoughts of his heart to all generations."

D

2. In looking back to the former age, we may learn the importance of ferving God, and of practifing the focial virtues.

Our confciences teftify in favor of no men however pre-eminent in talents or rank, who have fold themfelves to work evil in the fight of the Lord. The pious and the juft, whether among the living or the dead, have a commanding dignity of character, to which our judgments will not permit the wicked to afpire, in our moments of calm reflection.

Our moral obligations are coeval with our exiftence, and are as durable as our relation to the great Lord of all. Let us dedicate ourfelves to the Lawgiver and Redeemer of men. Let us not henceforth live unto ourfelves, but unto him who died, and rofe again, that he might be Lord both of the dead and living.

Eighteen hundred years have rolled away, fince the Son of God came down from heaven to earth, and entered on the humiliation to which he fubjected himfelf; that he might redeem a Church from among mankind, and " that the abundant grace might, through the thankfgiving of many, redound to the glory of God." On the night in which Chrift was born, the Angel of the Lord appeared to the fhepherds in Bethlehem, " and the glory of the Lord fhone round about them; and they were fore afraid. And the angel faid unto them, Fear not: for, behold, I bring you good tidings of great joy, which fhall be to all people. For unto you is born this day, in the city of David, a Saviour, who is Chrift the Lord. And this fhall be a fign unto you, ye fhall find the babe wrapped in fwaddling clothes, lying in a manger. And fuddenly there was with the angel a multitude of the heavenly hoft praifing God, and faying, *Glory to God in the higheft! and on earth peace, good will toward men!*"—May our hearts be warmed with this heavenly flame; and let us devote

our lives to the advancement of the declarative glory of God, and the happinefs of his holy intelligent
kingdom.   If the fpirit of the angelic fong governed the hearts of all men, wars and fightings would
ceafe ; and harmony and friendfhip would reign
through the world.   Governed by Chriftian love
we fhall find peace in our own fouls, though there be
" upon the earth diftrefs of nations, with perplexity ;
the fea and the waves roaring."

LET us fhun the rocks on which many have been
fhipwrecked, and direct our courfe by that wifdom
which is from above.   In this way we fhall pafs in
fafety through the ftorms of life, and fhall reach the
haven of immortal reft and joy.   If we fear God,
and work righteoufnefs, we fhall derive benefit from
the errors of thofe who have gone before us, and
fhall leave the weight of good example to our fucceffors.   Let us uphold, and inculcate the principles of religion and morality ; which are fo effential
to the fupport of the order and the happinefs of fociety.   It is of high importance that we be faithful
and exemplary, in this diforganizing period.

LET thofe who devote themfelves to reading and
ftudy, and communicate their thoughts to the public,
beware of leading their fellow-men aftray.   Pride
and ambition are dangerous guides ; and when they
reign in the minds of the fpeculative, they are often
productive of incalculable mifchief to fociety.   The
convulfions of the day are, in no fmall degree, owing
to the extravagant notions which were conceived in
the clofets of literary men.   Thefe philofophifts were
puffed up with a high fenfe of their own fuperior
knowledge, until they bewildered themfelves.   The
evil would have been comparatively fmall, had it
gone no farther : Thefe treacherous guides have un-
fettled and poifoned the minds of many others, in
the various walks of life.   The fondnefs to be
thought wifer than others, either among the living
or the dead, has been a fource of innumerable delu-

fions. To look with contempt on the knowledge of paft ages, furnifhes no evidence of an improved mind. The attainments of the prefent time, are very much indebted to the attainments of former generations.

WE are prone to make fevere remarks on the faults and foibles of others, and to be blind to our own. The fucceffive generations of men have dif-covered this partiality, when comparing themfelves with their predeceffors. We have heard much faid, in our time, of the credulity and fuperftition of our fathers ; and we have heard men make their boaft in the advent of a period, in which nothing is admit-ted as truth, except on the ground of infallible de-monftration. It is conceded that fuperftition has lefs influence than it had heretofore. The turn of the prefent age inclines to the oppofite extreme. But is there nothing at the prefent time which can be confidered as a mark of credulity ? Will thofe who are to come after us think, that all the opinions lately advanced and advocated by men of genius and learning, furnifh proof that the reign of credulity was ended ? Will they think that all the men who lived near the clofe of the eighteenth century, who were held in high repute for their talents, had taken a ftep in real knowledge beyond the former generations ? In what light will pofterity look upon the idea which contemplates a compleat recovery of the human race to virtue by political regenerations and the progrefs of fcience ? What will be thought hereafter of the opinion, which encourages the hope of expelling death from the world, by temperance, and improve-ments in the healing art ? Thefe notions, with fome other which might be named, will not imprefs fuc-ceeding generations with the idea that the reign of credulity was over, when men of high literary fame could broach fuch things, and have found admirers. It will not be found that civil freedom or fcience, will regenerate the heart ; nor that man can efcape the diffolution of this mortal frame.

A CENTURY SERMON.

WE live in the laſt days, or in one of the latter ages of the world. Events of vaſt magnitude, are brought into exiſtence in quick ſucceſſion ; and the connection of preſent events with the paſt, and the uſe to be made of them all, in the diſplay of God's juſtice and mercy, become more and more viſible and ſtriking, in the eyes of all who have wiſdom to underſtand. The work which the Lord hath been carrying on for ages, by the courſe of events, hath been brought into clear view, within a few years ; as ſtreams become broader and deeper in their near approach to the ocean.

WHILE many run to and fro, and knowledge is increaſed, let us make progreſs in every thing which contributes to the true glory of man. The wiſe and the good, of whatever age, or degree of improvement, build on the ſame foundation, and are engaged in a common cauſe. No perſon's name, however great and ſhining his talents may be, deſerves to go down to poſterity with applauſe, who encourages oppoſition to the immutable laws, by which the Supreme Ruler governs the moral world. The memory of none but the juſt is bleſſed. By faithfully ſerving God and our generation, we ſhall benefit ſociety, long after we ſhall ceaſe to be remembered among the living. In the practice of piety and virtue, let us ſtand in our lot to the end of our days.

LASTLY, As we review the paſt age, let us realize that we muſt die ; and let us feel the importance of ſecuring immortal happineſs.

OUR fathers, where are they ? " One generation paſſeth away, and another generation cometh." The ſentence " duſt thou art, and unto duſt ſhalt thou return," hath been executed upon countleſs millions of the human race. The learned and the illiterate, and perſons of every rank, age, and character, have been cut off from the land of the living. They who were public bleſſings, and they who were ſcourges to mankind, have been laid under the clods of the valley. The great and the mighty, who once made the earth to tremble, who fhook kingdoms, who made the world as a wildernefs, and deftroyed the cities thereof, have been brought down to the grave. The men who are now the chief inftruments in con-ducting the affairs of fociety, as well as thofe who are placed in humbler ftations, will foon meet in the land of filence. " We are ftrangers, and fojourners, as were all our fathers : our days on the earth are as a fhadow, and there is none abiding." There is not one now on the earth, who took an active part in the concerns of life, when the laft century commenced. There are very few individuals on this globe, who were born a hundred years ago. We meet on an oc-cafion which is new to us all. Before the return of another fuch day, every one of us muft expect to be numbered with the dead. Shall we when abfent from the body, be prefent with the Lord ? or fhall we have our portion with unbelievers ? Where! Oh where! will our fouls be found, while our mortal part lies mouldering in the duft ! May we be prepared to unite with the fpirits of juft men made perfect.

By a holy faith let us look for the fecond coming of the Lord Jefus Chrift ; who will reanimate the flumbering duft, and pafs fentence upon the living and the dead. How vaft will be the multitude that will ftand before his judgment feat ! He will change the vile body which once clothed his followers, in common with the reft of mankind, and will adorn them with one which will be fafhioned like unto his glorious body. When he fhall appear fitting on the throne of judgment before all worlds, he will make a bright and glorious difplay of his holinefs, in his conduct towards the righteous and the wicked ; and will unfold the wifdom and rectitude of his govern-ment, in ordering all the events which had taken place, in every age from the beginning of time.

A CENTURY SERMON.

THIS globe will remain, until the defigns of the
Creator in fpeaking it into exiftence, fhall be accomplifhed. Generations will be born, and will be removed by death, until all the human race be brought
into being, and the whole number of Chrift's feed
be gathered into his kingdom : Then, " the day of
the Lord will come as a thief in the night ; in the
which the heavens fhall pafs away with a great noife,
and the elements fhall melt with fervent heat, the
earth alfo, and the works that are therein, fhall be
burnt up. Seeing that all thefe things fhall be diffolved, what manner of perfons ought we to be in
all holy converfation and godlinefs ?"

*Now, unto the King eternal, immortal, invifible,
the only wife God, be honor and glory for ever and
ever.* AMEN.

Dr. Backus's Difcourfe

ON

GODLY FEAR.

A

DISCOURSE,

ON THE NATURE AND INFLUENCE OF

GODLY FEAR:

CONTAINING ALSO,

A MINISTER's ADDRESS TO HIS CHURCH AND
CONGREGATION; TOGETHER WITH A
FEW INTERESTING EVENTS IN
THEIR HISTORY:

WRITTEN IN A TIME WHEN HE WAS TAKEN OFF
FROM PREACHING BY BODILY INFIRMITIES:

PUBLICLY READ, LORD's-DAY,
January 31, 1802.

———◦❀❀◦———

BY CHARLES BACKUS, D. D.

PASTOR OF A CHURCH IN SOMERS.

———◦❀◦———

HARTFORD:
PRINTED BY HUDSON & GOODWIN.
———
1802.

A DISCOURSE, &c.

I PETER I. 17.

Pass the time of your sojourning here in fear,

IF the Holy Spirit, who dictated thefe words, fhould touch our hearts, we fhall learn the un-certain and tranfient nature of our abode on the earth, and in what manner we ought to fpend the prefent momentary ftate of our exiftence. We do but *fojourn* in this world ; and this time of our fojourning fhould be *paffed in fear*. Let thefe thoughts occupy our minds. They are of infinite importance to creatures who are foon to go into eternity, and to appear be-fore Him who doth not refpect perfons, but judgeth according to every man's work.

I. LET us confider our ftate as fojourners in the prefent world.

A SOJOURNER, in its primary meaning, is applied to one who refides in a place not as a fettled inhabitant, but as a ftranger, or as one who expects to remove from it. When there was a famine in the land of Canaan

in Abraham's time, he " went down into Egypt to
fojourn there."*   He did not expect to continue in
Egypt any longer than while the famine fhould laft :
he expected to leave the country, as foon as plenty
fhould be reftored in other places.   When Jacob, on
his return from Padan-Aram, fent meffengers before
him to Efau his brother, " He commanded them faying, Thus fhall ye fpeak unto my Lord Efau ; Thy
fervant Jacob faith thus. I have *fojourned* with Laban,
and ftayed there until now."†   Jacob lived with Laban twenty years ; but he labored with him on hire,
and expected to return to his father's houfe.

THE word *fojourning*, in the text, is applied to the
ftate of the human race in the prefent world.   Man
has no permanent abode on the earth, and he foon is
called to bid an everlafting farewell to every thing here
below.   1 Chron. xxix. 15. " For we are ftrangers
before thee, and fojourners, as were all our fathers :
our days on the earth are as a fhadow, and there is
none abiding."   Pfalm xxxix. 12, 13.   " Hear my
prayer, O Lord, and give ear unto my cry ; hold not
thy peace at my tears : for I am a ftranger with thee,
and a fojourner, as all my fathers were.   O fpare me,
that I may recover ftrength before I go hence, and be
no more."

PIOUS men have always accounted the prefent life a
ftate of pilgrimage, according to the paffages juft quot-
ed.   They have not felt themfelves to be at home
while they have tabernacled in the flefh.   They have
viewed life in its true light, in proportion to their degree of conformity to God.

WE are all of us but fojourners, while we remain
on this fide of the grave.   However ftupid any may
be, they cannot change the tranfitory nature of the
prefent life.   Like a fhadow it is void of fubftantial
happinefs ; it is conftantly changing ; it will foon

---

* Gen. xii. 10.   † Gen. xxxii. 3, 4.

come to an end, and will leave no traces behind. Earthly pleafures, riches and honors, cannot afford true felicity to creatures defigned for an immortal exiftence : they continue but a fhort time in the fame hands ; they are rapidly paffing away ; and their prefent poffeffors will be wholly ftripped of them when foul and body fhall be feparated.

THE members of the family of apoftate Adam fall victims to death, in every period from infancy to old age. The few who arrive at threefcore years and ten, are taught by experience, beyond all others, that the prefent ftate of man, is a ftate of change. They have witneffed a courfe of events very different from their calculations when they were young ; and they have feen many flattering worldly hopes dafhed in pieces, in themfelves and in others. They are furnifhed with facts without number, to prove the mutability of earthly things ; from the dealings of divine providence with individuals, with families, with neighborhoods, with towns, with ftates, and with kingdoms. When they ferioufly reflect on paft life, they feel that their progrefs was fwift from childhood to youth, from youth to manhood, and from manhood to old age. They can adopt the words contained in the prayer of Mofes, the man of God, in the xc. Pfalm—" We fpend our years as a tale that is told. The days of our years are threefcore years and ten ; and if by reafon of ftrength they be fourfcore years, yet is their ftrength labor and forrow : for it is foon cut off, and we fly away."

I proceed to confider,
II. THE manner in which we ought to pafs the time of our fojourning in the prefent world. We are commanded in the text to *pafs it in fear.* This fear is that holy fear of God which is every where inculcated in the fcriptures. Pfalm cxi. 10. " The fear of the Lord is the beginning of wifdom." A reverential fear of God is the offspring of love, and diftinguifhes his friends from his enemies. Thefe laft have fometimes, in the prefent world, fuch apprehenfions of

the vindictive wrath of the Almighty as fills them with
dread. In the world to come, the impenitent will
have a perpetual overwhelming fenfe of the vengeance
of the infinite majefty. A pious fear leads men to
draw near to God, with a humble hope of his mercy
as revealed in the gofpel. The righteous pay to him
the homage of the heart ; they rejoice that he is on
the throne of the univerfe, and ftudy to know and
obey his will in all things. To fear God and keep
his commandments is the whole duty of man. In
difcharging this, we ought to fpend all the time of
our fojourning in the prefent world.

To open and illuftrate the fear which is required, I
obferve,

I. THAT they who fear God cordially acknowledge
and adore his holy character. Revel. xv. 4. " Who
fhall not fear thee, O Lord, and glorify thy name ?
For thou only art holy." The God whom we are
commanded to fear, is glorious in holinefs ; and he
is the head of a holy kingdom which he hath eftablifhed, and will uphold forever. A view of him as
feated upon the throne of his holinefs, excites a filial
reverence towards him in the hearts of all his children.
Their knowledge and their love are fmall while in life,
but their fupreme affections are placed upon their
heavenly Father, and they defire above all things, that
the honor of his name, and the happinefs of his kingdom may be promoted. The holinefs, the juftice,
and all the other moral perfections of God, appear
to be infinitely amiable to the pious mind, and command reverence from it. God is love. Love, or holinefs, is the fum of all the excellencies which belong
to the divine nature. The knowledge, the power,
and all the other natural perfections of Jehovah, are
employed in accomplifhing the defigns of infinite love.
How deferving is fuch a God of our love and reverence ? How different is that fear which hath the glorious majefty of heaven and earth for its object, from
every other which is known by mankind ? If we, my
brethren, are governed by the filial fear of God, we

342

fhall enjoy communion with him on the earth, and fhall dwell at his right hand for evermore.

GOD hath revealed his character in his law. The commandment is exceeding broad, as well as holy, juft, and good. We fhall delight in God's law, if we fear him. It is our duty to compare our hearts and lives with God's law. If we are impartial in comparing ourfelves with it, we fhall find that we have within us a carnal mind which is enmity againft God, and which is not fubject to his law. We cannot fear him if we do not judge and condemn ourfelves, and approve of all the requirements of the lawgiver, and acknowledge the juftice of the fentence of eternal death which is denounced againft every tranfgreffor. " I acknowledge," faith penitent Dàvid, " my tranfgreffions ; and my fin is ever before me. Againft thee, thee only have I finned, and done this evil in thy fight ; that thou mighteft be juftified when thou fpeakeft, and be clear when thou judgeft."*

2. To pafs the time of our fojourning here in fear, we muft humbly feek God's mercy, as revealed in the atonement made by Jefus Chrift. No one of the human race, can have any juft ground of hope on the footing of the covenant of works, which God made with man in the day of his creation. We have all finned, and come fhort of the glory of God. Chrift is the end of the law for righteoufnefs to every one that believeth. " There is none other name under heaven given among men, whereby we muft be faved." He was delivered for the offences of his people, and he was raifed again for their juftification. The heirs of glory were not redeemed with corruptible things as filver and gold ; but with the precious blood of Chrift, as of a lamb without blemifh and without fpot. The grace difplayed in the gofpel, is wonderful grace. The divine perfections are difplayed in glorious harmony in the atonement : mercy and truth have met together ;

---

* Pfalm li. 3, 4.

B

righteoufnefs and peace have kiffed each other. If we
have tafted that the Lord is gracious, we fhall adopt
the language in the context, " Bleffed be the God and
Father of our Lord Jefus Chrift,. which according to
his abundant mercy, hath begotten us again unto a
lively hope, by the refurrection of Jefus Chrift from the
dead, to an inheritance incorruptible, and undefiled,
and that fadeth not away, referved in heaven for you."
The faved are brought out of darknefs into marvellous light—they are born again. They choofe God
the Father, for their Father; Jefus Chrift, for their
Redeemer and Saviour ; the Holy Ghoft, for their
Sanctifier, the Word of God, for their Guide ; and
Heaven for their home.

THE good tidings of great joy proclaimed in the
gofpel, will be in vain to us, if we continue to go about
to eftablifh a righteoufnefs of our own, and do not
fubmit to the righteoufnefs of God, which is exhibited
in the atonement. We muft renounce felf-depen-
dence,.and come to God in Chrift's name, and rely
only on the efficacy of his blood to deliver us from the
wrath to come, and on his obedience to render us
righteous. A juft fenfe of what we are, and of the
neceffity and worth of divine grace, will engage us to
plead earneftly with God for forgivenefs, and that we
may become heirs according to the hope of eternal life.
How earneftly did the Pfalmift fupplicate the divine favor, " Have mercy upon me, O God, according to
thy loving kindnefs ; according to the multitude of
thy tender mercies blot out my tranfgreffions."*
With what earneftnefs did Peter's hearers, on the day
of Pentecoft, when they were pricked in their heart,
inquire of him and of the reft of the apoftles, " Men
and brethren what fhall we do ?"† With what deep
folicitude did the Jailor addrefs himfelf to Paul and
Silas his prifoners, after the earthquake had burft open
the doors of the prifon, " Sirs, what muft I do to be
faved ?"‡

---

* Pfalm li. 1.   † Acts ii. 37.   ‡ Acts xvi. 30.

JESUS CHRIST is precious to them who believe as a holy Saviour. He is precious to them as a prophet, as a prieft, and as a king. Chrift's fheep hear his voice. They embrace the doctrines which were taught by him in perfon, and by thofe who were infpired to fpeak in his name. Believers look with abhorrence upon thofe doctrines which rob him of his perfonal and mediatorial honors; and which encourage the hope of future happinefs in the clofe of a life fpent in fin. The followers of Chrift feel themfelves under indifpenfible obligations, according to their abilities, to contend earneftly for the faith which was once delivered to the faints. In vain do any profefs to receive him as their Saviour, while they neither believe his doctrines, nor reft upon his atonement, nor obey his laws.

3. To maintain the holy fear enjoined in the text, we muft forfake iniquity, and obey the divine will in all things. Peter exhorteth believers in the context, " As obedient children, not fafhioning yourfelves according to the former lufts in your ignorance; but as he which hath called you is holy, fo be ye holy in all manner of converfation : becaufe it is written, Be ye holy; for I am holy.

BY the fear of the Lord men depart from evil. As the religion which is from above, is pure in its nature, it influences its fubjects to purify themfelves. However fmall the degree of fanctification be in the moment of the new birth, holinefs continues to increafe in the renewed heart, until it be completely ripened for the enjoyments of the new Jerufalem. In proportion as any fear God, they hate evil, and labor to mortify their corrupt defires. If we would obtain mercy from God we muft *forfake*, as well as confefs our fins. When falvation came to the houfe of Zaccheus the publican, he was ready to do juftice to thofe whom he had injured by extortion, and his heart was opened to give of his riches to the poor.* There was a very

---

* Luke xix.

vifible alteration in the real converts to chriftianity in
the days of the apoftles. The Jews renounced their
Judaifm, and the Gentiles their idolatry, and licentious
behaviour. To thefe laft Peter faith, in 1 Epift. iv.
3, 4. " For the time paft of our life may fuffice us to
have wrought the will of the Gentiles, when we walk-
ed in lafcivioufnefs, lufts, excefs of wine, revellings,
banquetings, and abominable idolatries : wherein they
think it ftrange that ye run not with them to the fame
excefs of riot, fpeaking evil of you." It appears that
thefe converted Gentiles difcovered fuch a ftriking
contraft in their prefent behaviour to their paft, that
their heathen neighbors looked on and wondered.
They were offended with thefe Chriftians, becaufe they
would not mingle with them in their debaucheries and
lewd idolatrous rites as in times paft. How honorable is it to Chriftian profeffors when they, by the purity
of their lives, bear teftimony to the fincerity of their
profeffion ? And when neither the threats nor the
fcoffs of the wicked deter them from maintaining their
happy fingularities. The Apoftle faith in his epiftle to
the brethren at Rome, " God be thanked that ye were
the fervants of fin ; but ye have obeyed from the
heart that form of doctrine which was delivered you.
Being then made free from fin, ye became the fervants
of righteoufnefs."*

IF my brethren, we are paffing the time of our fojourning here in fear, we fhall find much to do in
watching over our treacherous hearts, and in guarding againft temptations from without. " Watch and
pray, that ye enter not into temptation," faid our Saviour to his difciples.—He repeated the counfel and
the warning. We need often to be reminded of thefe
duties. It becometh us to be fober and to watch unto
prayer. Who would be faved were not believers kept
by the power of God through faith, unto falvation ?
Did not the promifes of God fecure the final perfeverance of the faints, they might all fit down in defpair.

Rom. vi. 17, 18.

of Godly Fear. 13

Are there given unto them exceeding great and precious promifes, then let them give diligence to make their calling and election fure. If any take encouragement from the promifes to continue in fin, they do not belong to Chrift—they never were united to him by faith. If any man think that he ftandeth fecurely by his own vigilance, let him take heed left he fall. " Be not high-minded, but fear."

WHAT a wide field of duty opens when we take a furvey of the moral law delivered at Mount Sinai, and of other particular precepts and prohibitions contained in the word of God ? Whatever we are commanded to do, we are commanded to do heartily as to the Lord, and not unto men. Read Chrift's fermon on the Mount, and you may fee clearly illuftrated the fpirituality and extent of the divine law. He caufeth it clearly to appear, that we may break the law in the eyes of God, while we may be accounted guiltlefs in the fight of men.

IN the decalogue the worfhipping of images made by the hands of men, and every other fpecies of idolatry are forbidden. We are commanded to worfhip Jehovah, and him only to ferve. Idolatry is a more fecret fin than we may be aware. We may with the name of the true God on our tongues, and with great vifible refpect to him in our external conduct, fet up idols in our hearts. Covetoufnefs is idolatry. Every inordinate affection to creatures is idolatry. We muft keep ourfelves from idols, if we would obey the divine will. We are forbidden in the moral law, to prophane God's name, and day ; and are commanded to reverence both, in our thoughts, words and actions. Numerous are the duties which are included in the command, " Thou fhalt love thy neighbour as thyfelf." There are mutual duties between parents and children, hufbands and wives, minifters and people, rulers and fubjects. Each one is commanded to do good unto all men as far as he has opportunity, and efpecially to thofe who are of the houfhold of faith. The fupreme

Lawgiver hath forbidden us to lay the hand of violence on our fellow men. We are required to feek the welfare of others, and to neglect no means in our power to preferve human life, and to augment human happinefs. If we habitually indulge a fpirit of malice and revenge, the love of God dwelleth not in us ; and if we were unreftrained, we fhould progrefs, until we had imbrued our hands in the blood of thofe whom we hate. Charity is to be maintained in our thoughts, words and actions ; and we are commanded to refrain from every kind of uncleannefs. Libidinous defires indulged, expofe perfons to fall into open debauchery, and to facrifice innocence to their brutal lufts. In the divine law a guard is placed round the eftates of individuals, which may not be invaded by theft or fraud. Neither thieves nor extortioners, nor the unjuft fhall inherit the kingdom of God. They muft repent and reform, or perifh forever. Truth is to be maintained between man and man.—The tongue, that unruly member, muft be bridled ; and not be permitted to wound innocence by flander. The holy law of God forbids us to covet the fubftance, the domeftic comforts, the gifts, or any thing that is our neighbors. It is our duty to rejoice in his profperity ; and to be contented with the portion which infinite wifdom and benevolence have affigned us in the world. All the particular inftitutions enjoined on men are to be practifed. We are commanded to pour out our hearts to God in prayer, in our clofets, in our families, and in the houfe of God. The ordinances of Chriftian baptifm, and the Lord's fupper, are enjoined upon us. We cannot follow Chrift, except we ftrive, in our places, to uphold and carry into effect the laws which he hath given to his difciples, both with refpect to their perfonal behaviour, and to the watch which they are required to maintain over their brethren in the Lord. In times of declenfion we are not to fit down in defpondency ; but are called upon to be watchful, and to ftrengthen the things which remain, that are ready to die.

of Godly Fear.

IN a review of the duties which are enjoined, muſt we not adopt the language of the Pſalmiſt,* "If thou Lord ſhouldeſt mark iniquities, O Lord, who ſhall ſtand ? But there is forgiveneſs with thee, that thou mayeſt be feared." If, brethren, we know ourſelves, we ſhall find conſtant need of repairing to the blood of Chriſt for pardoning mercy. Let us adore the riches of God's grace, who can ſave creatures as guilty as we are, from the wrath to come, and can ſanctify us, for his own ſervice in time, and for the enjoyment of himſelf in eternity.

4. To paſs the time of our ſojourning here in fear, we muſt be patient in tribulation.

MAN is born unto trouble as the ſparks fly upward. The godly are not exempted from ſuffering while in the body. They have often ſuffered much more while they have been in the body than the men of the world. No perſon's character can however be determined from the events which overtake him in divine providence, while on the earth ; but character is to be learned from the manner in which afflictions are endured.

THE people of God, in all ages, have been viſited with the rod ; and have been convinced that he hath afflicted them in faithfulneſs. They are "now for a ſeaſon (if need be) in heavineſs through manifold temptations ; that the trial of their faith being much more precious than of gold that periſheth, though it be tried with fire, might be found unto praiſe, and honor, and glory, at the appearing of Jeſus Chriſt," (verſes 6th and 7th of context.) The righteous are uſually recovered from their backſlidings by the rod. By means of its ſtrokes their ſins have been called to remembrance, and they have been brought nearer to God than ever. The Pſalmiſt, ſaith in his addreſs to the Moſt High, "before I was afflicted I went aſtray ; but

* Pſalm cxxx, 3, 4.

now have I kept thy word."*   " We glory in tribu‑
lations," faith the Apoſtle Paul, " knowing that tri‑
bulation worketh patience ; and patience experience ;
and experience hope."† Saith James, " My brethren,
count it all joy when ye fall into divers temptations ;
knowing this, that the trying of your faith worketh
patience."‡   Again he faith, " take my brethren, the
prophets, who have ſpoken in the name of the Lord,
for an example of ſuffering affliction, and of pati‑
ence.   Behold, we count them happy who endure.
Ye have heard of the patience of Job, and have ſeen
the end of the Lord ; that the Lord is very pitiful,
and of tender mercy."

PATIENCE implies a belief in the rectitude and
goodneſs of God's government, and ſubmiſſion to his
holy will.   It does not imply an infenſibility to pain ;
for " no chaſtening, for the preſent, ſeemeth to be
joyous, but grievous."   The patient man poſſeſſes a
calm and a quiet ſpirit while he feels the rod, and is
willing to wait God's time for its removal; and for the
performance of all the promiſes revealed in the cove‑
nant of grace.   When outward appearances are dark
and threatening, we may in patience poſſeſs our ſouls.
The patient man derives great benefit from his trou‑
bles while in life, and has the promiſe that his afflic‑
tion will work for him a far more exceeding and eternal
weight of glory in the world to come.   I am perſuad‑
ed, my brethren, that if we have the patient ſpirit
which chriſtianity dictates and inſpires, we ſhall be
fully convinced that our trials are as neceſſary for us,
as the outward favors which we receive.   We are lia‑
ble to ſay in our proſperity that we ſhall never be
moved, and to become remiſs in duty.   Have we not
found that we have been brought to love God more,
and to ſerve him better, when he hath been pleaſed to
viſit our iniquity with ſtripes ?   The redeemed will
bleſs God to eternity, for the peaceable fruits of
righteouſneſs which have followed their chaſtiſements.

----

* Pſalm cxix. 67.   † Rom. v. 3, 4.   ‡ James I. 2, 3.

5. To pafs the time of our fojourning here in fear, we muft think much on the end of life, place our affections on things above, and prepare to be found of our Judge in peace.

We are going the way of all the earth, and fhall foon reach the end of our days. It is appointed unto man once to die. In the war of death there is no difcharge. The godly, in all ages, have thought much on death, and have kept it in view in the actions of their lives. They have been ftudious to prepare to take leave of the world, and to imprefs on thofe around them a deep fenfe of their mortality. The patriarchs and the prophets delivered their dying charges to their families, and to the Jewifh nation. Job faith, " all the days of my appointed time will I wait till my change come." The apoftle Paul fpeaks of the time of his departure as being at hand. Peter declares, that he knew that he muft fhortly put off this his tabernacle.

With fome, whofe minds have been corrupted with falfe philofophy, death has been confidered as clofing man's exiftence. Thefe have given full indulgence to their fenfual appetites, as the only way in which they wifhed to enjoy life. They have progreffed in their brutifhnefs, until many of them have confeffed themfelves to be wretched ; and have either fallen victims to their debauchery, or have laid violent hands upon themfelves, and put an end to their lives. Thofe who have been illuminated by the wifdom which is from above, have confidered the prefent ftate of man as but the dawn of his exiftence ; and have confidered death as finifhing the feafon affigned to him for forming his character, and as introducing him to the endlefs retributions of eternity. Hence they have felt the importance of being diligent and faithful in time, and have contemplated death as a moft important event. They have viewed it as being near at hand, and as a conftant monitor to do whatever their hands find to do, with their might. " Brethren, the time is fhort," it

C

remaineth, that both they that have wives be as though
they had none ; and they that weep, as though they
wept not ; and they that rejoice, as though they rejoiced not ; and they that buy, as though they poffeffed not ; and they that ufe this world, as not abufing
it ; for the fafhion of this world paffeth away.''* Pious reflections on death, rendered habitual and familiar, will difarm it of diftracting terrors, and will diffufe a ferenity through the foul in the laft moments of
life. When we lie down on our beds at night, let us
remember that our bodies will foon fall afleep to awake
no more until the refurrection ; when we rife in the
morning, and through the bufinefs of the day, let us
not forget that our fouls will foon be in the world of
fpirits.

IF we who ftand on the borders of eternity, feek
for our fupreme happinefs in earthly purfuits and enjoyments, we fhall be guilty of the height of folly and
madnefs. Let us attend to the words of the divine
Saviour, in Matthew vi. 19, 20. " Lay not up for
yourfelves treafures upon earth, where moth and ruft
doth corrupt, and where thieves break through and
fteal : but lay up for yourfelves treafures in heaven,
where neither moth nor ruft doth corrupt, and where
thieves do not break through nor fteal." Health and
qüiet, food and raiment, houfes and lands, and all
other worldly enjoyments, call for thankfulnefs to the
Author of all mercies : But they are to be confidered
as of no comparative value, when fet over againft the
durable riches and righteoufnefs, which Chrift beftow-
eth upon his friends. True felf-denial forbids us to
withhold any temporal bleffing, not excepting life itfelf, when called to facrifice it to the intereft of God's
holy kingdom. The faithful, in view of the joy fet
before them, have been willing to part with every
thing which they held dear on the earth. Mofes
" chofe rather to fuffer affliction with the people of
God, than to enjoy the pleafures of fin for a feafon ;
efteeming the reproach of Chrift greater riches than

---

1 Corinthians, vii. 29, 30, 31.

the treasures in Egypt ; for he had refpect unto the recompenfe of the reward."* The primitive Chriftians "took joyfully the fpoiling of their goods, knowing in themfelves, that they had in heaven a better and an enduring fubftance."† They cheerfully met death in its moft dreadful forms, rather than renounce the profpects of an incorruptible crown.

IF we are working out our own falvation with fear and trembling, we fhall meditate often upon the things which God hath prepared for them who love him. There remaineth a glorious reft to the people of God. They will, in heaven, reft from fin, from temptations, from fufferings and from forrow ; and will be made perfectly holy, and perfectly bleffed in the full enjoyment of God to all eternity. They will unite with the holy angels, in the fong, " bleffing, and honor, and glory, and power, be unto him that fitteth upon the throne, and unto the Lamb for ever and ever."‡ Chriftians, is there a heaven of immortal joys before you, and will you not fix your meditations upon it ? Do not your hearts breathe after perfect conformity to God ? Do you not defire to be with Chrift that you may behold his glory ? Do you not defire the fociety of an innumerable company of angels, and of the fpirits of juft men made perfect ? Let us think of the lively hope of the apoftle Paul, " For we know, that if our earthly houfe of this tabernacle were diffolved, we have a building of God, an houfe not made with hands, eternal in the heavens. For in this we groan, earneftly defiring to be clothed upon with our houfe which is from heaven." The ftrong defires and groanings of the apoftle here expreffed did not terminate on death. He did not wifh to die, as many have, only to be cleared from trouble—He faith, " For we that are in this tabernacle do groan, being burthened : *not for that we would be unclothed,* but clothed upon, that mortality might be fwallowed up of life."§ The thought of being *unclothed,* or being ftripped of

---

* Heb. xi. 25, 26.   † Heb. x. 34.   ‡ Revl. v. 13.   § 2 Cor. v. 1, 2, 4

this body, is painful, when confidered by itfelf. We all tremble in view of death, when we reflect on its confequences, and have not a triumphant faith. But to be abfent from the body and to be prefent with the Lord, muft, to the mind of every true Chriftian, appear far better than to abide in the flefh.

How does it happen, it may be afked, that fo many Chriftians, through fear of death, are all their life time fubject to bondage : To this it may be replied,

1. THAT fome chriftians of diftinguifhed piety, have a conftitutional gloomy turn of mind, which renders them timid with refpect to every thing which can awaken fear, and efpecially renders them afraid to meet death.

2. THE general reafon why Chriftians feel fo much reluctance to dying, is, that they have fo little conformity to God, and confequently fuch a fmall degree of evidence, that they are his children. Moft Chriftians, in ordinary times, live at fuch a poor, low rate, as to render it improper that their hopes of future happinefs fhould be ftrong and lively. They have daily caufe to remember the warning of the apoftle in Heb. iv. 1, " Let us therefore fear, left a promife being left us of entering into his reft, any of you fhould feem to come fhort of it."

LET your affections be at all times, warmly exercifed towards the heavenly ftate, and your evidences will be increafed that you will live and reign with Chrift forever. By fetting your hearts on the new Jerufalem, the prefent world will have fewer charms in your eyes ; your graces will be enlivened ; your enjoyments will increafe ; and you will be ready to welcome the hour when your Lord fhall come.

To live as becometh fojourners, we muft live in a realizing belief that we muft all appear before the judgment feat of Chrift, that every one may receive the things done in his body, according to that he hath done, whether it be good or bad.* Each member of the human race is judged and fentenced for eternity on the day of his death ; but befide this particular judgment, there is a general one, when the dead will be raifed and all the inhabitants of heaven, earth and hell will be affembled before the judge of the living and the dead. Then God's righteous judgment will be publicly revealed ; to the joy and triumph of the faints and the holy angels, and to the confufion and mifery of wicked men and devils. Let our fouls be filled with a folemn awe as we look forward to the day, when the Lord Jefus fhall be revealed from heaven with his mighty angels, in flaming fire, taking vengeance on them that know not God, and that obey not the gofpel of our Lord Jefus Chrift : who fhall be punifhed with everlafting deftruction from the prefence of the Lord, and from the glory of his power ; when he fhall come to be glorified in his faints, and to be admired in all them that believe.† Banifh not from your minds the judgment to come. Words cannot exprefs the importance and weight of the fubject. Be reconciled to the divine government, and you will through endlefs ages fhout " Alleluia ! the Lord God omnipotent reigneth ! gird up the loins of your mind, be fober, and hope to the end, for the grace that is to be brought unto you at the revelation of Jefus Chrift."

As illuftrative of our ftate as fojourners, and to prepare the way to apply the foregoing fubject to ourfelves, I fhall introduce a few hiftorical facts relative to the firft fettlement of this town, and more particularly relative to the Church which has been, for a number of years, under my Paftoral care. " I will remember" faith the Pfalmift, " the works of the Lord ; furely I will remember thy wonders of old, I will meditate alfo of all thy works, and talk of thy doings."‡ We may confirm our faith and the faith

---

* 2 Cor. v. 10.　† 2 Thef. i. 7, 8, 9, 10.　‡ Pfalm lxxvii. 11, 12.

of others in the doctrine of a divine providence, by a recital of paft events ; and may bring into view motives to excite to a life of piety, both in ourfelves, and in the children who are to be born ; that they alfo may be induced to declare them to their children, that they might fet their hope in God, and not forget the works of God : but keep his commandments.

THIS town, is the fouth-eaft corner of the ancient town of Springfield, granted by the general court of Maffachufetts, to William Pyncheon and company. Springfield was fettled in 1636. This place, with the other parts of Springfield, which were covered by the Connecticut charter, remained under the jurifdiction of Maffachufetts, until about fifty years ago. It formed afterwards a part of Enfield, when it was fet off from Springfield and incorporated as a town in 1679. About the year 1724, it was formed into a fociety by the name of Eaft-Enfield. It was made a town in 1734.

IN looking back to the early fettlements in this place, correct information is not to be obtained. The firft part of our hiftory is to be learned much more from tradition than from records.

THE firft fettler in Somers, was Benjamin Jones. He came into the place from Enfield ftreet, lying near Connecticut river, about the year 1706. He erected a fmall houfe about half a mile to the eaftward of the point, where the two principal roads crofs each other, which pafs through the town from the eaft to the weft, and from the north to the fouth. He with his family refided here feveral years alone, in the fummer feafon. In the winter he ufed to return with his family to Enfield ftreet, and at other times in the year when he apprehended danger from the Indians. It does not appear that the Indians were ever very numerous in this place. The reafon doubtlefs was, that they found better ftands for raifing corn, for fifhing, and for hunting, in the neighbourhood.

THE settlement of Somers proceeded slowly. It was not until about the year 1713, that Mr. Jones was joined by other settlers. At that time removed hither Edward Kibbe, James Peafe, Timothy Root, and John M'Gregory, all of them in family state. Thefe all came from the old settlement in Enfield. Several men with their families came into the place within the next fourteen years, from Enfield, Springfield, Mendon, Hollifton, and other towns. Among thefe were Nathaniel Horton, Jofiah Wood, Benjamin Thomas, Luke Parfons, Jofeph Fifk, Thomas Purchafe, Robert Peafe, Jofeph Sexton, Samuel Felt, Samuel Rockwood, Ebenezer Pratt, and Benj. Cittron. The number of inhabitants in Eaft-Enfield, now Somers, did not exceed 170 or 180, at the time of the settlement of the firft minifter, in March 1727. By the enumerations which have been made, by order of government, at the following periods, the town has contained the numbers annexed, viz. in 1756, nine hundred ; in 1774, one thoufand and twenty-feven ; in 1790, twelve hundred and thirty-two ; and in 1800, thirteen hundred and fifty-three.

' THE church was gathered, March 15, 1727. It confifted of nine male members, their names are, Samuel Allis, Nathaniel Horton, Jofiah Wood, James Wood, Jofiah Wood, jun. Benjamin Thomas, Luke Parfons, Nathaniel Horton, jun. and Jofeph Fifk. Mr. Samuel Allis, whofe name ftands firft among thofe who entered into an explicit covenant, was on the fame day ordained the Paftor of the church. The Rev. Mr. Williams, of Deerfield, the narrative of whofe captivity is well known, preached on the occafion. Mr. Allis was born at Hatfield, Maffachufetts. After finifhing his education at Harvard College, he ftudied divinity under the famous Mr. Stoddard, of Northampton. Mr. Allis continued in the miniftry in this place about twenty years. He was difmiffed in the fpring of 1747 : I cannot afcertain the day nor the month. He continued to refide in the town until the clofe of life. He preached occafionally till a

357

few years before his death. He died December 18, 1796, in the 92d year of his age.

DURING his miniſtry, there was not a diſſenter in the town from the congregational mode of worſhip, which was practiſed in all the churches that were firſt gathered in New-England. The religious revival which took place in many parts of the country ſixty years ago, extended to this congregation. Large additions were made to this church in the year 1741 and 1742. What number it contained at the time of Mr. Allis's diſmiſſion, cannot now be known ; as no account can be found of removals from it, by death, or diſmiſſions to other churches.

MR. FREEGRACE LEAVITT, of Suffield, ſucceeded Mr. Allis in the Paſtoral charge. He was ordained July 6, 1748. He continued his miniſterial labors here until the cloſe of his life. He died, October 9, 1761, after a little more than thirteen years ſervice, in the forty-third year of his age. He was much eſteemed in life, and much lamented in death. Moſt of the records kept by him are loſt. It is not known what number was admitted into the church by him. It has been ſaid that the number was not large. Within about two years after his ſettlement, a few members of the church withdrew from his miniſtry, and began another meeting ; which continues to the preſent day. The proportion of diſſenters to the reſt of the inhabitants, is but a little larger now, than it was fifty years ago.

AFTER the death of Mr. Leavitt, a vacancy enſued of almoſt thirteen years continuance. A large part of this time was ſpent in warm altercation. In the year 1769, the church was divided into two bodies. This diviſion was of more than four years continuance. The two bodies united in December 8, 1773.

YOUR preſent paſtor, was ordained Auguſt 10, 1774. At that time the church conſiſted of one

hundred and twenty-nine members; of whom fifty-
fix were males, and feventy-three females. Since my
ordination there have been admitted two hundred and
feventy-two members. Thefe added to the members
who belonged to the church at the time of my fettlement, make four hundred and one. There have been
removed by death, and difmiffions to other churches,
one hundred and eighty-three ; which leaves two hundred and eighteen, the prefent number of communicants. Of this two hundred and eighteen, there
are eighty-three males, and one hundred and thirty-
five females. The whole number of baptifms adminiftered in this church, between my ordination and
January 10, 1802, is fix-hundred.

THERE have been in this church feven deacons.
James Wood and Nathaniel Horton, jun. were chofen
April 20, 1728. Deacon Wood ferved in his office
more than forty-five years. He was feized with a nervous
fhock, which put an end to his ufefulnefs, in the latter part of the year 1773. He died February 12, 1779,
in the eighty-fourth year of his age. Deacon Horton,
performed the duties of his office more than forty-
fix years. He refigned, September 22, 1774. He
died June 6, 1790, in the ninety-fifth year of his
age. On the fame day in which he refigned, his fon
Nathaniel Horton, was chofen to the deacon's office.
He removed to Conway, in Maffachufetts, in 1777.
June 7, 1775, Jofhua Pomry was chofen to the deacon's office. At a meeting of the church, June 18,
1777, it was refolved that it was expedient to have
three deacons in office at the fame time. The church
made choice of Jofeph Sexton, jun. and Aaron Horton,
fon of the firft deacon Horton. Deacon Aaron Horton, by reafon of ill health, refigned his office, September 30, 1796. He died Auguft 13, 1800, in
the fixty-feventh year of his age. On the fame day
in which he refigned, Jabez Collins was chofen
deacon.

D

IT has been my conftant practice fince my fettlement in the miniftry, to give to the congregation on the firft fabbath in January, an account of the number of deaths in the whole town the paft year, and to mention the particular ages of all who have died beyond the years of infancy. By means of this practice, I am able to give a correct account of the deaths which have taken place among us ; though I did not begin to keep a bill of mortality in form, until the beginning of the year 1786. The number of deaths from Auguft 10, 1774, to January 10, 1802, is four hundred and forty-three. Of thefe about one fifth were *feventy*, and upwards.

THE revolutionary war proved fatal to a few of our inhabitants. The year 1775, was a year of great mortality. The fcarlet fever and the dyfentery, carried off a number. But the diforder which prevailed moft, and was moft fatal, was a putrid malignant fever. The ficknefs began about the firft of Auguft, and raged three months. Thirty-fix perfons died in that year ; the moft of whom died within the three months after the commencement of the ficknefs. For feveral weeks about a twentieth part of the inhabitants were fick ; and about a twenty-ninth part of the whole number who were alive on the firft of the preceding January, were lodged in the grave, by the end of the year.

I WAS informed by fome of the aged fathers, who were alive when I came into the town, that within a a few years after the incorporation of the fociety, a diftreffing ficknefs prevailed among the people, which carried off fixteen perfons within a few months. Many more died, it appears, in proportion to the number of inhabitants at that time, than in 1775.

WHEN we review the proportion of old perfons on our bills of mortality, we cannot confider this place as unhealthy. There are but few places, even in New-England, and where our temperate ftyle of liv-

ing prevails, in which through a period of twenty-
feven years, about one fifth part of the number deceafed, arrived at feventy years of age.

THE malignant fever which fwept off fo many here
in 1775, feized its patients with great violence ; and
in the inftances in which it proved mortal, it frequently brought life to a clofe by the eighth day, and fometimes as early as the fixth. I have regretted that no
perfon of medical fkill has given an account of it to
the public. Two, three, four and five perfons, were
fick of it at a time in fome houfes. It rarely failed of
attacking every perfon in the houfe where it entered,
in its early ftages. The people in general were filled
with confternation. Nurfes were procured with great
difficulty, and, in a few inftances, the fick muft have
fuffered, if recourfe had not been had to legal coer-
cion. The fcenes of diftrefs which opened among the
fick and the dying, can be remembered by us who
were eye-witneffes, but cannot be defcribed. Two
and three funerals were attended for a number of
weeks in fucceffion ; and in feveral inftances two
corpfes were carried to the grave at the fame time.
Never can I forget the cry which pierced my ears, as I
entered the apartments of fome who were approaching
their laft hour,—" What muft I do to be faved !—
The Lord have mercy upon my foul !"—I defire to
blefs God that he continued to me health in that perilous feafon ; and that he permitted me to behold
with what fweet compofure fome eminent Chriftians
have been enabled to die.

As we recal paft days, we may find abundant caufe
to praife the Lord for his goodnefs, and for his wonderful works which we have feen, and which our
fathers have told us. Amidft all the afflictions which
we have endured, we have to acknowledge that God
" hath not dealt with us after our fins, nor rewarded
us after our iniquities. He hath redeemed our lives
from deftruction ; and he hath crowned us with loving kindnefs and tender mercies." Let us blefs his

28   *On the Nature and Influence*

holy name that he hath been pleafed to eftablifh a church in the world, that he hath preferved it until now, and that he hath promifed that the gates of hell fhall not prevail againft it. " The Lord is good, his mercy is everlafting ; and his truth endureth to all generations." His covenant people in this place, are called to offer to him the facrifice of thankfgiving, that he hath gracioufly remembered them in times of trouble, and that they have feen the goings of their God and King in the fanctuary. " This fhall be writ- ten for the generation to come ; and the people which fhall be created fhall praife the Lord."

A sovereign God, hath, to an unufual degree, vifited this people with the effufions of his Spirit. As has been mentioned, he revived his work here fixty years ago. This congregation has feveral times fince been favored with fpecial tokens of the divine gracious prefence. There are four feafons of remarkable reli- gious attention, which have fallen under my particu- lar notice. The firft commenced in 1774; the fe- cond, in 1783; the third, in 1797; and the fourth, in 1800. The fecond and third were the moft ex- tenfive, and caufed large additions to be made to the Church. " Not unto us, O Lord, not unto us, but unto thy name give glory, for thy mercy and for thy truth's fake."

BRETHREN OF THE CHURCH.

You have profeffed to give yourfelves up to God in an everlafting covenant. You have in the prefence of your fellow-men, before witneffing angels, and under the eye of that infinite Being who knoweth all hearts, folemnly engaged to renounce the lying vanities of this world, and to walk as the true difciples of Jefus Chrift. " Sanctify the Lord of hofts himfelf; and let him be your fear and let him be your dread."*— Live under the conftant influence of that filial fear, which diftinguifhes the children of God from the

* Ifaiah viii. 13.

362

men of the world. Contemplate the excellencies of the divine mind, and let your hearts be warmed with holy love. " Who is like unto thee, O Lord, among the Gods ? Who is like unto thee, glorious in holinefs, fearful in praifes, doing wonders ?"

WHEN we finful worms of the duft have clear views of the Lord of hofts, we fhall, in the fame proportion, abhor ourfelves, and repent in duft and afhes. No one who has the feelings of a true penitent, will remain under the dominion of a proud and felf-righteous fpirit. He will not think that he has made himfelf to differ from the ungodly world, and has caufe to fay to his neighbor—" Stand by thyfelf, come not near to me ; for I am holier than thou." " Brethren, " be clothed with humility ; for God refifteth the proud, and giveth grace to the humble."

MAINTAIN a deep fenfe of your dependence on the free and fovereign grace revealed in the gofpel. " Count all things but lofs for the excellency of the knowledge of Chrift Jefus your Lord." May he be more and more precious to your fouls. Reft not in paft attainments ; but " forgetting thofe things which are behind, and reaching forth unto thofe things which are before, prefs toward the mark, for the prize of the high calling of God in Chrift Jefus."

OUR holy religion is diftinguifhed from every other, by its pure and fublime doctrines, and its directions for holy living. In particular, it reveals an atonement, which opens a door of hope to guilty men, and it breathes a fpirit of difinterefted love. You will be unworthy of the name of Chrift's difciples, if you turn away from the truth, or liften to thofe who corrupt the word of God. If you have received Chrift Jefus the Lord in his true character, fo walk ye in him ; rooted and built up in him, and ftablifhed in the faith." Whofoever tranfgreffeth, and abideth not in the doctrine of Chrift, hath not God : he that abideth in the doctrine of Chrift, he hath both the Father and the

Son. If there come any unto you, and bring not this doctrine, receive him not into your houfe, neither bid him God fpeed : For he that biddeth him God fpeed is partaker of his evil deeds."* Let not a fear of being called rigid, illiberal, or bigots, render you afhamed of the gofpel of Chrift. It was of old, to the Jews a ftumbling-block, and to the Greeks foolifhnefs. It is not in any age, relifhed in its native fimplicity, by men that are wife in their own eyes, and prudent in their own fight. Daily look to the Father of lights by fervent prayer, and with a meek and a humble fpirit faithfully fearch the fcriptures ; and you will learn to correct your own errors in faith and in practice, and you will not be fatally deluded by the dreams of enthufiafts, by the flattery of the licentious nor by the infidious arts of infidels. Take to yourfelves the whole armour of God, and you will be enabled to withftand the fubtilty, the malice, and the power of earth and hell.

CLEAVE to the doctrine which is according to godlinefs, or you will grieve the Holy Spirit, and provoke him to withhold his influences. You have been watered with fhowers of divine grace, beyond moft churches, in years paft. By the great things which the Lord hath done for you, he hath placed you under high and peculiar obligations to maintain evangelical piety. If this fhould be loft, the glory will depart from you, and your candleftick will be removed out of its place.

WHEN God fhall call you to the choice of a paftor, may you, and the congregation, be united in one who is a fcribe well inftructed unto the kingdom of heaven ; and who fhall ferve you with much greater ability and faithfulnefs than I have done. In this important choice be not guided by a capricious temper, but by found judgment. Read attentively the holy fcriptures, and particularly the Epiftles of Paul to Timothy and Titus, that you may learn the qualifications

* 2 Epiftle of John, 9, 10, 11.

of Godly Fear. 31

of a Bifhop, or Prefbyter. Be not carried away with
fhowy talents, but have refpect rather to foundnefs in
the faith, aptnefs to teach, prudence and piety, in a
public teacher. You are not to expect that any man
will equally excel in every minifterial gift, or will be
without finful infirmities. A minifter who has an ardent love to Chrift, and to immortal fouls, will delight in taking the charge of a people who ftand faft
in one fpirit, with one mind, ftriving together for the
faith of the gofpel.

REMEMBER, my brethren, that " they who are
Chrift's have crucified the flefh, with the affections
and lufts." Jefus did not come to fave his people *in*
but *from*, their fins. Your hope is vain if it does not
incline you to purify yourfelves, and to renounce " all
filthinefs of the flefh and fpirit, perfecting holinefs in
the fear of God." You muft pafs through many con-
flicts while you are fojourners. The righteous are
fcarcely faved. They have to conflict with inward
corruptions, with an enfnaring world, and with a
fubtle and a potent enemy from beneath. Truft not
to your own hearts ; fuffer not the unrighteous mam-
mon, nor wicked men, to lead you aftray ; and refift
the temptations of fatan. " Be fober, be vigilant ;
becaufe your adverfary the devil, as a roaring lion,
walketh about, feeking, whom he may devour."*
Let not the name of God and his doctrine be blaf-
phemed by your unholy lives. Give no juft occafion
to the adverfaries of the truth to fpeak evil of you.
" Let your light fo fhine before men, that they may
fee your good works, and glorify your Father who is in
heaven."

LIVE in the conftant practice of all moral and pofitive duties, and keep yourfelves unfpotted from the
world. " I befeech you, therefore, brethren," faith
the apoftle, " by the mercies of God, that ye prefent
your bodies a living facrifice, holy, acceptable unto

---

* I Peter, v. 8.

God, which is your reafonable fervice : And be not
conformed to this world ; but be ye transformed by
the renewing of your mind, that ye may prove what
is that good and acceptable, and perfect will of God."*

LET the fear of God be at all times before your
eyes, that you fin not againft him. What thing foever the Lord hath commanded you, obferve to do it ;
not adding thereto, nor diminifhing from it. He
looketh with abhorrence upon all will-worfhip ; as
partaking of the nature of idolatry. Jehovah is a holy and a jealous God : His glory will he not give to
another. " O worfhip the Lord in the beauty of holinefs : Fear before him all the earth. O come, let
us worfhip and bow down : Let us kneel before the
Lord our maker." Let a reverential awe of the infinite majefty keep the door of your lips, that you do
not prophane his holy name. Religioufly obferve the
fabbath in your clofets, in your families, and in the
houfe of the Lord. If this day be difregarded, the
form as well as the power, of godlinefs will foon be
gone. No miracle is neceffary to remove religious
privileges. If you treat them with entire neglect, they
will ceafe to be enjoyed. A righteous God will not
continue the means of grace among a people who univerfally defpife them. As friends to divine inftitutions you will feek to enjoy them ; and God will not
forget your work and labor of love. Though he may
fubject you to trials, he will not take from you the ordinances which he hath appointed, to be obferved in
his church to the end of the world. God hath not
laid wafte any part of his vineyard, until it had firft
brought forth wild grapes.

EXERCISE the benevolence required by the law and
the gofpel, towards your fellow-men ; and exprefs
this in the difcharge of all relative duties. " Children
obey your parents in the Lord." Refift not the rightful authority which God hath given to them from

* Rom. xii. 1, 2.

whom you derived your birth ; and by whofe care you were nurfed in your helplefs years. Gladden their hearts by dutiful behaviour, and minifter to their neceffities and comfort, when either through poverty, or the infirmities of age, they may look to you for fupport. Ever keep in view the filial obedience of Chrift, and his conduct on the crofs, in commending the care of his Mother to the difciple whom he loved. " Ye fathers, provoke not your children to wrath : but bring them up in the nurture and admonition of the Lord." Addrefs the throne of grace before your houfholds, morning and evening. Inftruct your offfpring, and all under your direction, in the doctrines and duties of chriftianity, and enforce your inftructions by a pious example. Feel the worth of the fouls committed to your care, and you will open your lips to them in warning and counfel. " Wives, fubmit yourfelves unto your own hufbands, as is fit in the Lord : Hufbands love your wives, and be not bitter againft them." Conftantly endear yourfelves to each other by mutual kind offices : And walk " as being heirs together of the grace of life ; that your prayers be not hindered." Art tnou united in marriage with one who is an unbeliever, be faithful in thine attempts to win to the faith the friend of thy bofom. " For what knoweft thou, O wife, whether thou fhalt fave thy hufband ? Or how knoweft thou, O man, whether thou fhalt fave thy wife ?"

PERFORM the various duties which belong to your feveral ftations, and which flow from your relations to the church and to the commonwealth. Do juftly, and love mercy. " Let all bitternefs, and wrath, and anger, and clamour, and evil-fpeaking, be put away from you, with all malice." Abftain from all uncleannefs and covetoufnefs. " Let no corrupt communication proceed out of your mouth, but that which is good to the ufe of edifying, that it may minifter

E

grace unto the hearers.   Be ye all of one mind, having compaſſion one of another : Love as brethren, be
pitiful, be courteous.

BROTHERLY love is abundantly inculcated in the
inſpired writings.   John, in particular, in his epiſtles,
dwelleth much upon it.   " He that ſaith he is in the
light, and hateth his brother, is in darkneſs even until
now. He that loveth his brother abideth in the light,
and there is none occaſion of ſtumbling in him. We
know that we have paſſed from death unto life, becauſe
we love the brethren : he that loveth not his brother
abideth in death."*   If we have the ſpirit of Chriſt
we ſhall exerciſe the love of benevolence towards all
men, and the love of complaiſance towards his viſible
diſciples.   He declared to them when he was on the
earth, " By this ſhall all men know that ye are my
diſciples, if ye have love one to another."†   Let this
love abound in you, my brethren, and you will ad-
moniſh one another daily, and will be incited to uphold the diſcipline which our Lord hath inſtituted.
This is ſhamefully neglected in moſt churches at the
preſent day, and ſhould they perſevere in their preſent
courſe, they will continue to decline, until they become ſynagogues of Satan.   Tremble at the thought
of being reprobated of God, and provoke him not to
caſt you out of his ſight.   " Remember how you have
received and heard, and hold faſt and repent."

BRETHREN, " be like-minded, having the ſame
love, being of one accord, of one mind.   Let nothing
be done through ſtrife or vain glory ; but in lowlineſs
of mind let each eſteem other better than themſelves."
You have heretofore felt the bitter fruits of contention.   You have ſince, in a good degree, experienced
" how good and pleaſant it is for brethren to dwell
together in unity."   May you increaſe in love, and always maintain the harmony which becometh the friends

* 1 Epiſt. John ii. 9, 10. iii. 14.   † John xiii. 35.

of the bleſſed Redeemer. " Live in peace, and the God of love and peace ſhall be with you."

Bestow of your goods to feed the poor ; eſpeci-ally the poor who are found among the followers of Jeſus Chriſt. " Whoſo hath this world's good, and ſeeth his brother have need, and ſhutteth up his bow-els of compaſſion from him, how dwelleth the love of God in him ?" Beware of indulging that covetous ſpirit which renders men blind to the wants of the needy, and deaf to the cry of the helpleſs. When ſuch a temper appears among nominal Chriſtians, the avowed enemies of the croſs will glory over them, and become hardened in unbelief. In the account of the laſt judgment, contained in the xxv. of Matthew, we find the character of thoſe whom Chriſt ap-proveth, deſcribed by miniſtering to the neceſſi-ties, and alleviating the ſorrows of his afflicted diſci-ples ; whom he ſtyles his brethren. " I was hungry, and ye gave me meat : I was thirſty, and ye gave me drink : I was a ſtranger, and ye took me in : naked, and ye clothed me : I was ſick, and ye viſited me : I was in priſon, and ye came unto me—In as much as ye have done it unto one of the leaſt of theſe my brethren, ye have done it unto me." What wonder-ful condeſcenſion is here expreſſed ! " Amazing ' words ! That the meaneſt faint ſhould be owned by ' the King of glory as one of his brethren ! Irreſiſtible ' argument to thoſe that do indeed believe theſe words, ' to ſtir them up to abound in every good word and ' work ! Under this impreſſion, methinks, inſtead of ' hiding ourſelves from thoſe who ſhould be to us as ' our own fleſh by virtue of our common union to ' him, we ſhould not only hearken to their entreaties, ' but even ſearch them out in thoſe corners to which ' modeſt want may ſometimes retire, and caſt about ' in our thoughts how we may ſecure any happy op-' portunity of relieving ſome poor faints, for their ſakes, ' and for their Maſter's and even for our own. What ' if Chriſt came to us in perſon as a poor helpleſs ſtran-

' ger? What if we faw him deftitute of 'food, and
' raiment, or in want, of any other of the neceffaries
' of life? Should we not contend for it as an honor,
' which of us fhould receive him into our houfes,
' which of us fhould entertain him at our table, which
' of us fhould even ftrip ourfelves of our clothing to
' give it to him? And yet he tells us that he is in effect
' with us in his poor members; and we invent a thou-
' fand cold excufes for neglecting to affift him, and
' fend our compaffionate Saviour away empty. Is this
' the temper of a Chriftian? Is this the temper in
' which we fhould wifh to be found at the judgment-
' day?"*

WE cannot, my brethren, ever enough admire
" the grace of our Lord Jefus Chrift, that though he
was rich, yet for our fakes he became poor, that we
through his poverty might be rich." Let us imbibe
his fpirit, and cheerfully minifter of our fubftance, according to our ability, to fupply the wants of his needy
members, and for the advancement of his kingdom
in the world. How glorious will be the ftate of the
church on the earth, when the prophecy in Ifaiah lx,
9th, fhall receive its full accomplifhment? " Surely
the ifles fhall wait for me, and the fhips of Tarfhifh
firft to bring thy fons from far, their filver and their
gold with them, unto the name of the Lord thy God
and to the holy one of Ifrael, becaufe he hath glorified
thee."

THE church is to pafs through fharp conflicts before the Lord will make her a name and a praife a-
mong all people of the earth. " Beloved, think it not
ftrange concerning the fiery trial which is to try you,
as though fome ftrange thing happened unto you."†
It is predicted " that in the laft days perilous times
fhall come;"‡ and that violent commotions will arife
among the nations which had been corrupted by An-

---

* Dr. Doddridge's Family Expofitor, Vol. 2, page 398.
† 1 Peter, iv. 12.   ‡ 2 Timothy, iii. 1.

of Godly Fear.

tichrift. Let us not be difmayed in this day of rebuke and blafphemy ; but in patience may we poffefs our fouls. May our faith in the holy religion of Jefus Chrift be confirmed, while infidels amidft their profeffions of feeking the happinefs of the human race, may become as cruel as inquifitors, and may fill the earth with violence.

BE not furprized that apoftates fhould appear at the prefent time. They have appeared in every age ; and have always difcovered a bitter enmity to the truth, and to thofe of its friends in particular, with whom they had formerly affociated. " They went out from us," faith the Apoftle, " but they were not of us ; for if they had been of us, they would no doubt have continued with us ; but they went out that they might be made manifeft that they were not all of us."* In days when your faith and conftancy are tried, be excited to watch and keep your garments. The difappointments, forrows, pains, and all the fufferings of this life are but for a moment. Be patient, brethren, ftablifh your hearts ; for the coming of the Lord draweth nigh. The faithful will foon enter into the reft which remaineth to the people of God. Man's life is even a vapour that appeareth for a little time, and then vanifheth away. The fathers of this church and town are all laid in the grave. But here and there one of their immediate defcendants remain ; and a large part of the third generation are removed into the land of filence. Many whom we in elder life once met at the communion table, are gone into the eternal world. How happy are they if affociated with the fpirits of juft men made perfect ? Glorified faints are beyond the reach of fin and forrow ; they are before the throne of God, and ferve him day and night in his temple, and he fhall wipe away all tears from their eyes.

---

* 1 Epift. John, ii. 19.

You will hope in vain for immortal joys, if you only call Chrift, Lord, Lord, with your lips, and eat and drink in his prefence. To many fuch he will declare in the day of retribution, " I never knew you: depart from me, ye that work iniquity." It is through faith and patience that the redeemed inherit the promifes. " Examine yourfelves whether ye be in the faith ; prove your ownfelves : know ye not your ownfelves, how that Jefus Chrift is in you, except ye be reprobates ?" Make the ftatutes of the Lord your fongs in the houfe of your pilgrimage ; and let your converfation be in heaven. I pray that Chrift may prefent you to himfelf a glorious church, not having fpot, or wrinkle, or any fuch thing ; but as holy and without blemifh.

THOSE to whom I have been called to minifter in this place, who have not as yet publicly covenanted with God, will fuffer the word of exhortation.

I have reafon to believe that fome of you, my friends, have come to a fixed purpofe of confefling Chrift before men without delay ; and that others have fuch ferious fearchings of heart with refpect to their duty, as will not permit them long to withhold appearing openly on the Lord's fide, fhould their lives be continued. I would enquire of the perfons of this laft defcription, whence is it that if you really fear to offend God, you do not obey his commands ? Why do you not obey the command to remember Chrift by coming to his table ? You will fay that you are unworthy. I would be far from encouraging hypocritical profeffions, but would obferve, that if you have a juft fenfe of your unworthinefs—if you can pray with all your heart, as did the Publican, " God be merciful to me a finner," Chrift will make you welcome at his table. If you have had the idea that gracious communicants think themfelves able to fay to Chrift, " We feel ourfelves to be worthy to have a place among thy difciples," you have miftaken the nature of true religion.

of Godly Fear.

A broken and a contrite heart, God will not defpife. Do you find this within yourfelves ? If you poffefs, delay not openly to commemorate the love of the divine Saviour, who died that penitent finners might be pardoned, and live. The time for ferving God is fhort : You will foon be lodged in the grave. Can you endure the thought of reflecting in a dying hour that you did not confefs Chrift before men ?

ARE there not thofe in this congregation, who have grown up, and grown old, in fin ? Do not your words and actions bear witnefs that you have not the fear of God before your eyes ? You have remained obftinate under the many calls which you have had, from the word and providence of God. You have often been warned to flee from the wrath to come, and to lay hold on the hope fet before finners in the gofpel. Your hearts have remained impenitent, while you have feen fome around you preffing into the kingdom of God. The pious of your age are about to be received into the heavenly manfions, while you appear to be ripening for the world of endlefs mifery. Wake up from your dangerous fleep—look back on paft life—and look forward to the judgment to come. You ftand upon the threfhold of the eternal world. O realize the worth of your immortal fouls ! Feel the worth of time ! And devote its few remaining days to the fear of the Lord. Contend no longer with the divine government—be reconciled to God—build your hope on his fovereign mercy as revealed in the gofpel—and by patient continuance in well-doing, feek for glory, and honor, and immortality, and you will obtain eternal life.

LET the middle-aged who have hitherto lived without God in the world, be warned of their danger, and be exhorted to choofe the good part which will not be taken from them. Be not fwallowed up with the cares of this life, and the deceitfulnefs of riches. " What is a man profitted, if he fhall gain the whole world, and lofe his own foul ? Or, what fhall a man give in exchange for his foul ?" Let not your hearts be charmed with the honor which cometh from men ; but feek that honor which cometh from God only. In your prefent active period of life, devote your talents to the divine fervice. Know and fee that it is an evil thing and bitter that you have forfaken the Lord, and that his fear is not in you. Turn unto him by unfeigned repentance, and be obedient to his holy will in all things. Let a crucified Saviour be your hope and joy, in life and in death. To him dedicate yourfelves, and every thing which you hold dear.

In the late religious revivals in this and in other places, prayer has been introduced into many houfes, in which a worldly and vain fpirit had heretofore exc`ided even the form of religion. Parents have publicly dedicated themfelves and their children to God. Can you look on thefe things and remain unmoved ? After every attempt to find hypocrify in Chriftian profeffors, do not your confciences tell you in the hour of reflection, that your pious neighbors and friends are acting a wife part ? And that they will be fwift witneffes againft you at the bar of God, if you fpend your lives in fin ? Provoke him not to pour out his fury upon you ; but humbly feek his gracious prefence. " The curfe of the Lord is in the houfe of the wicked : But he bleffeth the habitation of the juft."

FLATTERING as may be your worldly hopes, they may be cut off in a moment. In the midft of your exertions, and while you are in your full ftrength, death may be commiffioned to do its work upon you. It is of infinite importance to be prepared to depart from this world in peace. Of what avail will be earthly glory in a dying hour ? Would you die the death of the righteous, and have your laft end like his, now die unto fin and live unto God.

of Godly Fear.

LET the young people of this congregation, obey the command given from on high—" Remember now thy Creator in the days of thy youth." It affords matter of abundant thankfulnefs that a number of your age are hopefully devoted to God. It is peculiarly pleafing to meet them at the communion-table, and to witnefs their fobriety. O that you all were engaged to renounce the follies and vanities of the world, and to pafs the time of your fojourning in fear !

You are, my young friends, in the forming period of life; in which a lafting character is ufually formed, both with refpect to the prefent world, and the world to come. But a few of thofe who wafte the morning of their lives in folly, ever become the fubjects of heaven-ly wifdom. Now while your paffions are warm, and your imaginations are lively, you are very liable to yield to temptations, and to be carried on in the broad road which leads to eternal death. At the prefent time licentioufnefs in thinking, and in conduct, are awful-ly prevalent. Many perfons in elder life, and of bril-liant talents, are openly engaged on the fide of infidel-ity and wickednefs. To quiet their own confciences in fin, and, like the builders of Babel, to make to themfelves a name, they fpare no efforts to corrupt all around them. They are ftriving, in particular, to gain over the young, as the beft means to perpetuate their opinions and practices. Thefe fons of Belial will treat you with great attention—they will invite you to mingle with their convivial affemblies, and will ftrive to amufe and diffipate your minds by various arts. They will profefs to be your warm friends and admi-rers, and that they are devoted to your happinefs. They will tell you that you have been laid under un-reafonable reftraints by bigotry and fuperftition ; and that they wifh to deliver you from the yoke of bond-age ; and that if you will liften to them, they will guide you to a freedom and a liberality which become the dignity of man. With fuch fair fpeeches in their

F

mouths, they will endeavor to root out all moral and religious principles from your minds, and to fix you in the belief that the bible is a forgery, and that nature is the only guide to happinefs. If you have a tafte for reading they will put into your hands fuch novels, or other books, as are fuited to inftil the poifon which they wifh to infufe. If you liften to fuch apoftles of Satan, your minds and manners will be debauched, and you will bring endlefs mifery upon yourfelves.

DEAR YOUTH,
" TAKE faft hold of inftruction ; let her not go : keep her ; for fhe is thy life. Enter not into the path of the wicked, and go not in the way of evil men. Avoid it, pafs not by it, turn from it, and pafs away." Be not the companions of fools, but walk with the wife. Be convinced of your fins, confefs them to God, and feek for pardoning mercy through the Son of his love. Spend your days under the influence of holy fear, and you will experience the divine protection in life and in death. " Like as a father pitieth his children, fo the Lord pitieth them that fear him." Jofeph, Samuel, David, Obadiah, Daniel, Timothy, and other pious youths, are witnef-fes of the gracious care which the Lord taketh of his people in times of temptation, and under all the circumftances of life. Forget not that you are mortal, and that you may be cut down in the bloom of youth. Prepare to die. I pray that you may long be continued in the world, and be made bleffings to fociety. You are the hope of the commonwealth, and of the church of God. May you be faithful in both thefe relations ; and be highly inftrumental of promoting the caufe of righte-oufnefs and peace, when we who are now in the meridian, or in the decline of life, fhall be numbered with the dead.

DEAR CHILDREN,
WHILE I am addrefing the people of my charge, I cannot forget you. Remember the texts which I

of Godly Fear. 43

have often charged you to treafure up in your minds and hearts. The two following I have mentioned to you oftener than any other. The firft is in Pfalm xxxiv. 11. " Come, ye children, hearken unto me ; I will teach you the fear of the Lord." The other is in Matthew xix. 14. " But Jefus faid, fuffer little children, and forbid them not to come unto me ; for of fuch is the kingdom of heaven." If you do not fear God, he will be angry with you every day ; and if you do not fear him while you live, you muft be miferable after death. You were born in fin ; and you muft repent of your evil defires, thoughts, words and actions, and come to Chrift, if you would go to heaven. May the bleffed Saviour take you into the arms of his mercy, and fanctify your hearts by his fpirit. Obey your parents, as Chrift did his, and keep all God's commandments. Every day retire, and pray to God that he would make you his children, and fit you to ferve him in time, and to enjoy him in eternity. You do not know how foon you may die. Begin to prepare for death, without delay ; and it will be well with you, whether you are laid in the grave in childhood, or in whatever age. Read daily in the bible. It is the book of God ; and may it be bleft to make you wife unto falvation.

My Brerhren and Friends,

I have fet before you the manner in which we ought to fpend life ; I have taken a brief view of the dealings of divine providence with this Church and Congregation ; and have warned and counfelled you with unreferved freedom. May God, by his fpirit, imprefs your hearts with the truths and duties which have been inculcated, and engage you to pafs the time of your fojourning here in fear.

It is more than twenty-feven years fince I was confecrated to the work of the gofpel miniftry, and to the paftoral care of this church. I defire to thank Chrift Jefus our Lord, for putting me into an office

which is more important than any other which has
been committed to man ; and for continuing me in it
fo long. I feel myfelf to be unworthy of the facred
truft ; that I have very imperfectly illuftrated and enforced the religion of the gofpel in my difcourfes, and
that I have fallen awfully fhort in a practical conformity to it. I can at the fame time declare to you, that,
in my neareft views of the eternal world, the religion
which I have preached, is the religion by which I
wifh to live, and to die. The doctrine which I have
taught, I am fully perfuaded, is the doctrine which
is according to godlinefs. Daily fearch the fcriptures,
as did the ancient Bereans, with a humble and devout
frame of mind, that you may become firmly eftablifhed in the faith.

I TRUST that I have not labored among you wholly in vain. That the feeble efforts of a finful worm
of the duft, fhould, in any inftance, be crowned with
fuccefs, can be attributed to nothing but rich and fovereign grace. Accept my unfeigned thanks for the
many tokens of refpect and friendfhip which I have
received from you, in the courfe of my miniftry. I
can never forget the tendernefs and fympathy which
you have manifefted towards me, during my prefent
long and threatening bodily infirmities. In this time
of affliction, I have received from you as a people, and
from numerous individuals in this place, liberal tokens
of love. I pray God to reward you with fpiritual and
everlafting bleffings. To Him who hath the hearts of
all men in his hand, be the glory, for rendering you
the inftruments of difpenfing his favors. Whether I
am to realize a recovery to health, and a return to my
public labors, or whether the prefent illnefs will terminate in my removal from the world, is to us unknown.
Let it be the daily prayer of all who feek God, that
" Chrift may be magnified in my body, whether it
be by life or by death."

OUR entrance into the invifible world, and on our eternal ftate, is fwiftly approaching. Like the former generations we muft fleep in the duft of the earth, and with them, and with all who fhall go down to the grave, we fhall be awakened at the refurrection, by the voice of the archangel, and the trump of God. With all the living and the dead, we muft appear before the judgment feat of Chrift, and receive our final fentence. We muft, before the affembled univerfe, give an account to him of our conduct towards each other as minifter and people, and of all the actions of our lives. I pray God, that you may all be my joy, and crown of rejoicing, in the day of the Lord Jefus. "Now unto him that is able to keep you from falling, and to prefent you faultlefs before the prefence of his glory with exceeding joy, to the only wife God our Saviour, be glory and majefty, dominion and power, both now and ever." AMEN.

A

DISCOURSE,

UPON

BAPTISM.

By AARON PUTNAM,
PASTOR, OF THE FIRST CHURCH IN POMFRET.

HARTFORD:

PRINTED BY

HUDSON & GOODWIN.

1801.

A SERMON, &c.

ACTS II. 38, 39.

Then Peter said unto them, Repent, and be baptized
every one of you in the name of Jesus Christ, for the
remission of sins, and ye shall receive the gift of the
Holy Ghost. For the promise is unto you, and to
your children, and to all that are afar off, and to
as many as the Lord our God shall call.

THESE are the words of the apostle Peter, ad-
dressing his discourse to his hearers, upon the
day of pentecost, upon that remarkable season, when
so many were persuaded to comply with the word
of the Lord, and an addition of three thousand was
made to the Christian church, of which we have
account in the 41st verse of the context, " Then
they who gladly received his word, were baptized ;
and the same day, there were added unto them,
about three thousand souls." And considering the
number of those who were then baptized, I can
scarcely think, that they were baptized by being
dipped ; and this I think, we may suppose was not
the mode in which the jailer and his family were
baptized ; account of which we have in Acts xvi.
33. " Then took he them the same hour of the night,
and washed their stripes, and was baptized, he and
all his, straitway." We have no account of his being by a pond, a river, or fount of water ; and in
it (*i. e.* the baptism) was performed in the house, as
most likely it was, there then must have been some
time for making preparation for its being done by
dipping ; but instead of that, we are told, that he
and his were baptized straitway, (*i. e.* forthwith in

the fame hour of the night in which he wafhed the apoftle's ftripes.)

There are fome who do very confidently affirm, that baptifm, performed by plunging, is the only fcripture mode, in which the ordinance of baptifm is performed, and ought now to be performed ; and they ground their affertion upon fundry inftances of baptifm we have account of in fcripture. I fhall not here notice the feveral inftances they ufually alledge; fuffice it for me here to mention the baptifm of the Eunuch by Philip, which is much infifted upon by them in fupport of that fentiment. We have account of that baptifm in Acts viii. 38. "And they went down both into the water, both Philip and the Eunuch, and he baptized him." But here it is to be obferved (as in feveral other inftances alledged) that it depends on a fingle word in the Greek original, which may as well be rendered *unto* as *into ;* in the former fenfe only, can it be underftood. Matt. v. 1. "And feeing the multitude, he went up *into* a mountain, and taught :" *i. e.* he went up *upon* a mountain, and taught ; and when as before recited, Acts viii, they are faid both to come out of the water, the word (the prepofition) in the Greek original, may be rendered *from,* as well as *out of ;* in the former fenfe only, can it be underftood. In Luke xi. 31. where our Saviour ufes the fame word, when fpeaking of the Queen of Sheba ; that fhe came from the uttermoft parts of the earth, to hear the wifdom of Solomon.

As to the mode of baptifm (though I freely own, that to me, it does not appear effential to the ordinance) yet I may obferve fome further ; no one, I fuppofe, will think that he can authentically baptize himfelf, but that there muft be fome perfon vefted with proper authority to adminifter that ordinance upon him. Now fuppofing the perfon to be baptized, fhould wade into the water up to his eyes, and he who is to baptize him, has only to dip into water, that fmall part which is out of the water ; it muft be put by a figure (a part for the whole) if it be called baptifm by plunging. And why may not the like figure be allowed, when baptifm is performed by fprinkling ? A great and good man faid, that as to the mode of baptifm, it did not fo ftick in his confcience, but that he could perform it by plunging, when perfons appeared confcientioufly to think that that way was moft agreeable to fcripture ; and once he did it in that way, for one and his family, whom he thought to be really confcientious in the matter ; but he thought he would not do fo again ; for he thought, by the perfon's conduct afterwards, that there was more of corrupt will, than real confcience in the matter.

Thus much concerning the mode of baptifm.

In the text we find the apoftle exhorting his hearers unto duty ; particularly the duty of repentance. Repent (faith he) be heartily forry for what ye have done amifs ; particularly in crucifying Chrift. Let the confideration of it, as being a very high crime againft God and againft his Son Jefus Chrift, influence and excite you to a godly forrow for that, and for all your other fins ; for there is no fin, but it is committed againft God, and againft the compaffionate Saviour of finners, Jefus Chrift. Let the confideration of your having, by your fins caft difhonor upon the divine character, fill your hearts with unfeigned grief and forrow, that you have committed them ; and difpofe you to leave them, in unfeigned converfion and amendment, and if you do (as thus exhorted) repent, ye fhall receive remiffion of your fins, how many, and great foever they have been ; for fo the word affures us, Acts iii. 19. " Repent therefore, and be converted, that your fins may be blotted out, when the times of refrefhing fhall come from the prefence of the Lord ;" but, perhaps, it will here be objected that infant children ought not to be baptized, becaufe they do not manifeft repentance : The Apoftle was not addreffing this his exhortation to fuch children ; but unto adults, who ought to repent, and to manifeft their repentance ; he was addreffing this his exhortation,

6

to thofe who were pricked to the heart, for having crucified the Lord of life and glory, and for their other fins, committed againft God.

It affords no juft argument, at all, againft the baptifm, of the infant offspring (or children) of covenant parents, that their children in infancy, are not capable of the exercife and manifeftations of repentance towards God, nor of faith towards our Lord Jefus Chrift.

It is by fome, faid, believe and be baptized; it is not fo faid, as I remember, in the word; indeed Philip faid to the Eunuch, Acts viii. 37. " If thou believeft with all thine heart, thou mayeft be baptized :" But he faid it to an adult perfon, and not to an infant child.

Repentance, and faith are terms of falvation, eftablifhed in the gofpel, to adult perfons, enjoying it ; but who may fay, they are terms of falvation, to infants ? Without which, and the exercife and manifeftation thereof by them, they muft be loft forever ! Repentance and faith, are terms of falvation, to the capable, not to the incapable fubjects thereof.

It was neceffary in the order of things, that the Apoftles, who were fent forth, to preach the doctrines of the gofpel, and to perfuade perfons to embrace Chriftianity, fhould teach thofe who were capable of being taught, and to indoctrinate thofe who were to be added to the Chriftian church ; and perfuade and bring them openly to profefs their faith in Chrift, acceptance of the gofpel, and fubjection to his laws and ordinances therein eftablifhed : But how unreafonable muft it be, to make thofe things which infants are not capable of, and which the Apoftles never propofed as terms of their baptifm, to be now objecting againft it.

We may in further confidering the text, obferve the words of encouragement therein, by the Apoftle mentioned, faying, the promife is to you, and to your children ; Jewifh covenant parents might juftly object againft their embracing Chriftianity, if it made no provifion for their children to be brought into any fpecial covenant relation to God; they might juftly object, and fay, we fhall be worfe off than we were, under the former difpenfation; for therein provifion was made, for our children being (with us) taken into a covenant relation to God; and if no fuch provifion be made in the gofpel difpenfation, inftead of being gainers, we fhall, in that refpect, be great lofers, in renouncing Judaifm, and embracing Chriftianity.

This objection, methinks, the Apoftle doth fully obviate, by his faying, as in the text, the promife is to you, and to your children; we cannot produce an inftance of God's covenant dealing with his people, in the Jewifh church, but he was pleafed alfo to take their children into a vifible covenant relation to himfelf, what warrant then, have any to cut them off? Where do we find, in all the gofpel, that right and privilege of the children of covenant parents taken away? And if not taken away, by fome exprefs order of God, who only can give, and take it away, may we not, muft we not, thankfully confider and acknowledge, that it ftill continues, under the gofpel difpenfation of the fame covenant of grace? It is a great miftake indeed, for any to conclude, that the Jewifh and Chriftian church, ftands founded upon a different covenant: Difference there evidently is, as to the mode of adminiftration of it; in the Jewifh, and Chriftian church; under the Jewifh difpenfation, circumcifion, and the paffover, were the two fpecial facraments; under the Chriftian difpenfation, baptifm and the Lord's fupper, are the two ftanding facraments; but though there is this difference, it makes no odds (or alteration) in the covenant itfelf; it then was and now is, the covenant of grace, which is everlafting, an unchangeable covenant.

Another thing here neceffary to be obferved, is, that the children of covenant parents, are only bro't under the vifible, or external adminiftration of the covenant; and not that by the external token of the

covenant, put upon them, though of divine appointment, that thereby they are admitted to the fpecial
and faving grace and bleffings of the covenant, or
any way thereby, infallibly made partakers thereof ;
we cannot fuppofe that all who were circumcifed,
were admited to the faving grace and bleffings of the
covenant, though thereby they received the token
of God's covenant, and were brought under the
external adminiftration of it ; and now the children
of Chriftian covenant. parents, are, by baptifm
brought under the vifible, or external, difpenfation
of the covenant, nor do we pretend to hold (though
fome tax us with holding) that baptifm doth preclude the neceffity of regeneration, to all who are
baptized (as well as to every one elfe) in order to
their future and everlafting happinefs.

It is objected, that as the church of the Jews,
was a national church ; but it not being the cafe with
the church now, under the gofpel difpenfation ;
therefore it is very unjuft to argue from God's conduct towards his covenant people and their children
then, to prove the right of the children of covenant
parents, now, when it is not the cafe of the Chriftian church to be a national church, as was the Jewifh church ; as to this objection, I think it need not
trouble our minds and confciences any ; if God was
pleafed to deal with his church, and their children,
in that national capacity, who of us, may dare fay
nay to that his conduct? And if he was pleafed in
his conduct towards his church and people then,
to eftablifh a right to the children of Chriftian covenant parents now, to an external token of his covenant ; though the church be not now national, as
was the Jewifh church ; may we (or any) from hence
argue, and fay that his conduct towards his church
and people was, and is, unwife and unfuitable ? It
ought, certainly, to be our great concern, defire
and endeavour to fubmit, and fuitably to behave
under the gracious dealings of his hand (in this matter) towards his church, both then and now.

It will further perhaps be faid, that the Jews, devoted, by circumcifion, only, their male children, and left out their female children ; and that if we. fay that baptifm fucceeds to circumcifion, it feems that female children are not to be baptized, as they, as well as male children, are.

To this it muft be obferved, that they who by circumcifion, did devote to Jehovah, their male children (who only were naturally capable of that token of the covenant, which God had enjoined) did alfo devote their female children, to be his, in the fame covenant, and to be therein, in the like covenant relation to him, as their male children were : Hence we fo often read of the circumcifion, and of the uncircumcifion ; the circumcifion meant the Jews including their females, as well as their males ; the uncircumcifion, meant Gentiles : And now under the gofpel difpenfation, female, as well as male children (of covenant parents) are baptized, and that by his order, who hath inftituted baptifm, to be adminiftered, without diftinction of fex ; and baptifm, doth either fucceed to circumcifion, or the Christian difpenfation, is lefs complete, as to external facraments, than was the Jewish difpenfation ; which can hardly be fuppofed. That the facrament of baptifm fucceeds to that of circumcifion may juftly I think, be concluded, from what the Apoftle fays, in Coloff. ii. 10, 11. " But ye are complete in him, which is the head of all principality and power. In whom alfo ye are circumcifed, with the circumcifion made without hands, in putting off the body of the fins of the flesh, by the circumcifion of Christ." By the circumcifion, made without hands, we are doubtlefs, to underftand, the regeneration of the foul, by the fpirit ; the circumcifion of Christ, there mentioned, means baptifm, under the Christian difpenfation ; and this feems to be apparently the cafe, becaufe the Apoftle goes on, in the next words, to fpeak of baptifm.

In my text the Apoftle faith, the promife is unto

B

you, and to your children. What promife, in particular, is there intended, is not exprefsly faid; however, I think, it is moft likely, that promife God was pleafed to make, when he entered into covenant with Abraham ; Gen. xvii. 7. "And I will eftablifh my covenant between me and thee, and thy feed after thee, in their generations, for an everlafting covenant ; to be a God unto thee, and to thy feed after thee." But fome will fay, let that, or fome other, be the promife, therein fpecially intended, it will be made good, when God calls them and not before ; but to this it muft be obferved that when God doth call any, by his word and fpirit, to repentance and converfion, they, as perfonal penitents and converts, receive remiffion of fins, and become favingly interefted in all the promifes of the covenant of grace (and all this to them as perfonal penitents and converts) whereas the Apoftle here doth fpeak of a promife belonging to them, as their children ; importing, (as I think) a manifeft diftinction ; the promife is to you, of remiffion of fins, who do repent and profefs your fubjection to the laws and ordinances of the gofpel ; and not only to you, as thus perfonal penitents and converts ; but there is a promife which doth belong to your children ; and if a promife doth belong to them, what warrant have we, or any to cut them off ? and leave them, as the children of Heathens, and the uncovenanted world ?

It is often objected, by fome againft infant baptifm, that there is, in the gofpel, no exprefs command for, nor example of it, therefore infants ought not now, to be baptized :

In anfwer hereto, I would obferve, that I can fee no neceffity of an exprefs command for, or example of infant baptifm, in the gofpel, in order to warrant it now : I think it can be proved, that the infant offspring, of covenant parents, have, by God, been admitted into a covenant relation to himfelf, in having the external token of his covenant, put upon them ; and if by his order, the right of the

children of Chriftian covenant parents to an external token, or fign, of God's covenant be not, by
him, or by his order, taken away, it ftill continues,
under the Chriftian difpenfation ; and as there is no
other facrament, of divine inftitution, in the Chriftian difpenfation, as an external token, or fign of
God's covenant, which infants now are capable of,
but baptifm, therefore they are, by it, to be dedicated to God, as a covenant God : In the objection,
it is faid, that there is no exprefs command, in the
gofpel, for infant baptifm. And is there any exprefs
command for adult baptifm ? Is there an exprefs
command for obferving the firft day of the week, as
the holy fabbath ? Is there an exprefs command, that
women fhould partake of the Lord's fupper ? But
who of us, pretends to object againft duty, in
thefe particulars, though there is not an exprefs
command therefor in the gofpel ! In the inftitution
of baptifm, it is not faid, that adults only are to be
baptized ; but no infants: Let them take heed, who
confine it only to adults, and exclude all infants ;
as to a command for infant baptifm, though not exprefs, yet it may be confidered, as implied, in the
order which Chrift gave his Apoftles, when he inftituted the ordinance, Matt. xxvi. 19. " Go teach
all nations, baptizing them in the name of," &c.
How could they obey, or act according to that order, if the children of thofe who profefs their faith
in Chrift, and fubjection to his laws, were by them
to be excluded from baptifm, feeing that they do,
at leaft, make up a part of all nations.

It is further alledged in the objection, that there
is no exprefs example, in the gofpel, of infant baptifm ; and for the reafon, before mentioned, I fee
no need there fhoud be any; however, I think, it
can never, by any, be proved, that the Apoftles did
not, purfuant to the order which their divine Lord
gave them, baptize the infant children of thofe,
who did among all nations, where they went, profefs the Chriftian faith ; I think it can never, by any,
be proved, that there were no infant children, in the

391

jailer's · or in Lydia's family, or none in them, who were baptized, on his, or her profeffed faith : I don't pofitively fay there were any ; yet I think it very unwarrantable for any to affert that there were none.

It is often objected, by fome, and faid that as infant children are uncapable of the manifeft exercife of faith and repentance, therefore they are not to be baptized : To this it muft be obferved, that Jewifh parents might, on the fame account, have objected againft their children's being circumcifed, at eight days old ; their parents might object againft it, and fay, that at that age, their children knew nothing of the obligations of the covenant, or of the defign of circumcifion, and therefore ought not to be circumcifed ; would God have taken this well at their hands ? When he had made known to them his will, that their male children fhould be circumcifed at that age : Did not he who had inftituted the ordinance of circumcifion, fully know the capacity of children at eight days old ? Will any fay that his conduct towards them, was unwife and unfuitable, in ordering that at that age they fhould receive the appointed token of his covenant, though at that age they knew nothing of the obligations of the covenant, or of the defign of circumcifion ? If he was pleafed, in his conduct towards his covenant people of old, to fettle the right of the children of covenant parents to an external token (fign) of his covenant, which can no where be found, in his word, taken away ; why fhould it be made, and by fo many confidered, fuch a mighty objection, againft the baptifm of children, that they are (in their infancy) ignorant of the ends and defigns of baptifm ? Will parents, will children of covenant parents, eafily give up that right, and privilege, belonging to them, to baptifm, as an external token of God's covenant ; or having received it, in their infancy, will they renounce it as if it were fomething infignificant, null and void.

Let parents confider, the wonderful grace and condefcenfion, which God hath manifefted in his

13

covenant, and in his conduct towards his covenant people, in thus making provision for them and for their children ; herein surely he hath done that which calls for their religious and hearty thankfulness, and praise to him ; and after all that he has been pleased to say, and to do in this matter, will covenant parents think and say, that he hath done no more for their children, than for the children of Heathens, and the uncovenanted world ? Oh let covenant parents take heed, left in so doing they despise the Lord's kindness, and provoke his anger against them : And let the children of the covenant, seriously confider the obligations of the covenant of God, that are upon them, by virtue of their infant baptism ; can you think to be wiser than the provision, which God in his word hath made ? Can you think, to be wiser, in this matter of concern, than the Christian Church hath been, for ages past ? And here I might, did time and room permit, or necessity require, mention many, and large testimonies from the fathers, concerning the belief, and usage of the Christian church, in respect of infant baptism : But I shall here only mention the testimony of Calvin the reformer, whose praise is in the churches at this day, and who was well acquainted with the practice of the church, in regard of infant baptism, not only in his day, but long before ; " I affirm," faith he, " that this holy ordinance of infant baptism, " hath been perpetually observed in the Christian " church ; for there is no ancient Doctor, that doth " not acknowledge, that infant baptism, was con- " stantly administered by the Apostles."* Indeed as to all religious faith and practice, and particularly as to this matter, we must take our warrant, from the word of God, (in the holy scriptures) yet it may be of great and special use to us, to see what has been the belief and practice, in this matter, of the Christian church, in ages before our time ; and how it has been, I might produce many testimonies, con-

* Marshall, p. 60, 61.

cerning it ; the teftimony juft now mentioned, is very exprefs and full ; and after all, will any fay, that
they were quite miftaken, who have borne teftimony
in this matter ? Will any now fay, that they can
judge of their duty and practice, in the matter, better for themfelves, than the Chriftian Church, for
paft ages has ? Be not thus deceived ; they who
have gone before us (advocates for infant baptifm)
were as wife and confcientious, as thofe at the prefent day, can pretend to be : We cannot fuppofe that
they meant to be enfnared themfelves, or to enfnare
us ; (in this matter) we cannot without great arro-
gancy, think, that we are better able than they were
to guard againft, and to avoid dangerous fnares and
errors, in this matter ; certainly it is not a matter to
be trifled with ! No doubt but there are many precious fervants of Chrift, and children of God, of
the anabaptift perfuafion ; but that doth no ways
oblige us to approve of the fyftem of their principles and line of conduct, particularly in denying infant baptifm ; and it muft be affecting to us, to hear
and know of fo many renouncing their infant baptifm. I have endeavoured in this difcourfe, to anfwer and remove objections and difficulties which are
commonly thrown in the way (by Anabaptifts, and
by them ufed to perfuade perfons to renounce their
infant baptifm, as being a nullity) I have endeavoured herein to fhew from the word of God, that the
infant offspring of covenant parents have a right,
under the Chriftian difpenfation, to baptifm, as an
external fign and feal of the covenant. Let not what
the Lord has been pleafed in his word to do, (in this
matter,) appear to covenant parents, or to their children, to be but a fmall matter.

Hath Chrift, by his Apoftle (as we fee in the text)
affured us, that the promife is unto you and to your
children ; and fhall we after all fay, that there is no
divine promife, belonging to the children of covenant parents at this day ? Let the baptized children
of the covenant, in this place, be directed and exhorted, to realize, and to endeavour to live agreea-

bly to the obligations of the covenant, that are upon them, by, virtue of their baptifm ; much may be drawn from the confideration of Baptifm, againft fin ; I remember, reading of one, who had been baptized, being tempted to a particular fin, anfwered *baptizata fui* (I have been baptized ;) and with that fhe overcame the temptation : Oh ! How many have, at one time and another, efcaped the dangerous fnares of Satan, by appealing unto and making proper improvement of their baptifm ? When therefore you are tempted to fin, of any kind, be directed to have ferious recourfe to your baptifm ; whereby you were laid under folemn obligations to renounce fin, and the fervice of Satan : Improve it, for your excitement to, and encouragement in the fervice of God ; to him and to his fervice you were in baptifm devoted, and will you leave his fervice, for the devil's fervice ? As you do, in effect by every fin that you knowingly and wilfully commit ! When therefore you are tempted to omit covenant duties, or to tranfgrefs the laws of God's holy covenant, remember, that in baptifm you were devoted, not only to the grace, but to the fervice of God ; and when you vifibly conduct contrary to the laws and rules of God's holy word and covenant, you oblige the church to call you to an account, and to deal with you therefor, and this by virtue of your covenant relation to God, and to his people, by your baptifm ; and the confideration of this your accountablenefs to the church ought in reafon, to have fome reftraint upon you, from fuch overt acts of tranfgreffion of the facred laws of baptifm ; but above all, fhould the confideration of your being the Lord's, and that his eye is conftantly upon you, obferving your conduct ; this fhould in a more fpecial manner reftrain you from finful acts and violations of the laws of his covenant, and the facred defigns of your baptifm ; this ought in a peculiar manner to excite you to the obfervance and practice of the duties required of you, as baptized ones.

And here confider of the fpecial obligations you

are under, to take the bonds of the covenant, and so of your baptifm, upon yourfelves ; publicly fubmitting thereto, owning the fame and waiting upon Chrift at his table, in attendance upon the holy ordinance of his fupper ! That other facrament, of his appointing, though I think, you are not to confider yourfelves, as intitled to partake of that ordinance, merely by virtue of your baptifm, yet certainly your baptifm, as one of the figns and feals, by divine appointment, put upon you, ought to excite in you fuch ferious confiderations, as much tend to qualify you, in a fincere, and hearty and public manner, to enter into covenant with God, through Chrift, and to become members in full communion, in his church, and fo to partake of that other fign and feal of the covenant, even the Lord's fupper.

It is melancholy indeed, that fo few among us, who have been baptized, are perfuaded to make profeffion of Chrift, and are difpofed to wait upon him, at his table, in an ordinance of his appointing, Oh! remember that he will be afhamed of thofe, who are afhamed, to own him before men, and to obferve the duty he has commanded and directed unto, of fuch he will be afhamed, in the end of the world, when he will come in great glory to judge the world.

And is there a promife, plead it with God in earneft prayer, that he would be pleafed to remember it for, and fulfil it to you ; let not the promife God has been pleafed to make, lay by you, ufelefs and unimproved; feek and ftrive by repentance, faith and an holy life, to anfwer the facred defigns of your baptifm.

May you ! May we all ! who have been baptized, be difpofed and enabled to live agreeably to the duty pointed out and enjoined, in 1 Pet. iii. 21, "The like figure whereunto baptifm doth now fave us, (not the putting away of the filth of the flefh, but the anfwer of a good confcience toward God,) by the refurrection of Jefus Chrift :" To whom, with the Father and the Holy Spirit, be afcribed, all religious honour and praife forever. AMEN.

Mr. ROWLAND's

THANKSGIVING DISCOURSE.

November 27th, 1800.

A
DISCOURSE,

DELIVERED

NOVEMBER 27th, 1800 ;

A DAY OBSERVED AS AN

ANNIVERSARY THANKSGIVING.

By HENRY A. ROWLAND,

PASTOR OF THE FIRST CHURCH IN WINDSOR.

PUBLISHED BY DESIRE OF THE HEARERS.

HARTFORD:

PRINTED BY HUDSON AND GOODWIN.

1801.

A Thanksgiving Sermon.

———◆———

PSALM cxlv. 10.

*ALL thy works praise thee, O LORD, and thy Saints
shall bless thee.*

WE are assembled, my brethren, at this
time, to pay our devout adorations to the great author of our beings ; and to offer thanksgiving and
praise to his holy name.   This is a · duty both pleasant and profitable.   It is pleasant to a grateful heart,
because it is the expression of that which it feels,
and wishes to utter ; and profitable because it culti-
vates a spirit of devotion and · accustoms it to those
exercises which are to be its eternal employment.
A grateful heart will never want motives to call it into exercise.   It will see the goodness of GOD, even

6   THANKSGIVING SERMON.

in times of the deepeſt diſtreſs and feel its obligations *to give thanks to* GOD, *always, for all things.*

IF thoſe whoſe hearts are thus diſpoſed will *rejoice in the* LORD *and joy in the* GOD *of their ſalvation,* when the *fruits* of the *vine* and *fields*—the *labor* of the *olive* and the *herd* of the *ſtalls* all fail, and their worldly proſpects are the moſt gloomy ; how muſt grateful emotions ariſe and ſwell your boſoms, when the bounties of divine providence are continually of-fering freſh motives to this duty. The devout ex-erciſe of praiſe, in earthly communities, will bring them to a near reſemblance to the bleſſed ſociety above, where all hearts are filled with gratitude and all the work is praiſe. Suitably to appreciate the goodneſs of God, to have the heart filled with grat-itude, and to expreſs it in all ſuitable ways, will bring men to bear the greateſt likeneſs to his moral image, and therefore to enjoy the greateſt happineſs. It is a work begun, which will be perfected in glory.

BUT if we draw aſide the veil which is ſpread over ſome, who appear in the forms of devotion, and look at the inward temper and diſpoſition of the ſoul, what inconſiſtency is there exhibited ! The emotions of the heart are altogether oppoſed to the outward ſhow of piety.

THOSE, who wiſh to unite their devotions with the celeſtial orders, muſt have a heavenly temper formed within ; muſt fix their ſupreme affections on GOD, and conſecrate themſelves forever to his ſervice. If we hope one day to be admitted to the heavenly courts, to join the company of pure fpir-its, to be happy in the fociety of angels, we muft be formed to a temper of gratitude to the fupreme JE-HOVAH for the wonders of his love. It is the com-mon felicity of glorified fpirits in heaven and thofe who love to contemplate the divine goodnefs here on earth.

ALL GOD's *works praife* him ; and fhall man, the nobleft of his works on earth, be filent ? Surely his *faints fhall blefs* his holy name. " Praife ye the LORD for it is good to fing praifes to our GOD ; for it is pleafant and praife is comely for the upright. Praife the LORD, O Jerufalem. Praife thy GOD, O Zion. Let us come before his prefence with thankf-giving and make a joyful noife to him with pfalms. For the LORD is a great GOD and a great King above all Gods.—O come, let us worfhip and bow down ; let us kneel before the LORD our maker ; for he is our GOD and we are the people of his pafture.—His mercy is everlafting and his truth endureth to all generations."

" ALL thy works praife thee, O LORD, and thy faints fhall blefs thee."

THESE words, my brethren, which are a fuita-ble theme for our meditations to day, in their moft extenfive import, may be confidered as imply-ing the works of Creation, Providence and Re-demption, in each of which are involved truths fuf-

8   THANKSGIVING SERMON.

ficiently myfterious and fublime, to excite the admiration of all created intelligences. From thefe in-
exhauftible fubjects, new wonders will arife and increafe through interminable ages.

IN attending to this fubject we will make fome remarks on each of thefe works of GOD which praife
him—and on the obligations of the faints to blefs
him.

GOD'S works of *creation* praife him, who in wifdom made them all. They declare the glory of the
fupreme architect. By him were all things created
that are in heaven and that are in earth, vifible
and invifible. "He fpake and it was done; he commanded, and it ftood faft;" He faid let there be
light and there was light. "He made heaven, the
heaven of heavens with all their hoft; the earth and
all things that are therein. The LORD by wifdom
hath founded the earth; by underftanding hath
he eftablifhed the heavens; by his knowledge the
depths are broken up and the clouds drop down
dew. The heavens declare the glory of the LORD
and the firmament fhoweth his handy work." Supreme power, wifdom and goodnefs are every where
difplayed. None but a being of infinite power
could have made all things out of nothing. None
but a being of infinite wifdom could have planned
the vaft machines—could have hung them in empty
fpace and balanced worlds and fyftems; and caufed beauty, harmony and order to fhine in all.

THE works of *Providence* praife him. He pre-
ferveth and upholdeth all things by the word of his

THANKSGIVING SERMON. 9

power; and they continue to this day according to his ordinances. His creative power is conſtantly exerciſed in the ſupport of all worlds and creatures to which he hath given exiſtence. He ruleth in the kingdoms of men and giveth the dominion to whomſoever he will. At what inſtant he ſpeaketh, he enlargeth and ſtraiteneth, increaſeth and deſtroyeth the nations. He changeth times and ſeaſons. He ſets up and puts down. He worketh all things after the counſel of his own will, and he giveth not account of any of his matters. His unremitting energy upholds all beings and maintains a beautiful harmony in all his works—and ſhould it ceaſe but for a moment the wildeſt diſorder would enſue. His creatures, rational and irrational, depend entirely on him. The " young lions roar and aſk their meat of GOD"; and the eyes of all wait on him, that he may give them their meat in due ſeaſon.

BUT if we look at all GOD's creatures throughout the earth, we find that man appears to be marked as the favorite of Providence. He who made has given all the endleſs varieties of the earth and ſea, to the children of men. That the earth may be ſubſervient to them and conduce to their comfort and happineſs, he viſits, waters and greatly enriches it with the river of GOD which is full of water; he maketh it ſoft with ſhowers; he bleſſeth the ſpringing thereof; he crowneth the year with his goodneſs, and his paths drop fatneſs. All who are upheld by the energy and cheered by the munificence

B

10   THANKSGIVING SERMON.

of GOD ; and efpecially thofe who are comforted
by the gracious and vital influence of his holy fpirit,
are under the ftrongeft obligations to devote themfelves to him in holy and grateful obedience.

In the natural, moral and political world the
divine agency is, in a thoufand ways, difplayed.

In the natural world, every attentive obferver is
ftruck with wonder and aftonifhment, and acknowl-
edges the operations of a divine hand.   All nature
difplays the perfections of nature's GOD.   He maintains the beauty and harmony which are fo vifible in
all his works.   The luminaries of heaven praife him,
who in wifdom directs their revolutions and periods,
who hath " fet a tabernacle for the fun whofe going forth is from the end of heaven and from whofe
heat nothing is hidden.".   He fcattereth his diffufive
rays through the fyftem and cheers with light the inhabitants of various worlds.   From this fource the
earth derives her light, her heat and her prolific virtue.   Every tree, plant and flower feels his genial
influence.   By his attractive power, the waters are
exhaled, which under divine direction are balanced
in the air and poured in copious fhowers on the
thirfty ground.

" Sing unto the Lord with thankfgiving who
covereth the heaven with clouds, who prepareth rain
for the earth, who maketh grafs to grow upon the
mountains—who giveth to the beaft his food and to
the young ravens which cry."   Pfalm cxlvii. 7.

THANKSGIVING SERMON. 11

THE revolving feafons witnefs ; fummer and winter, feed time and harveft own, as they roll in fucceffion, his care and wifdom. The day is his, the
night alfo is his—he hath prepared the light and the
fun—he hath fet the borders of the earth ; he hath
made fummer and winter ; and while the earth remaineth, they fhall not ceafe becaufe he hath faid it.
He hath created and employs inftruments to anfwer
his defigns ; winds and feas, funfhine and rain are
ordered to produce thofe effeds which fhall be moft
for his glory and the good of his rational offspring.
No ray of light—no particle of air or dew-drop of
the night moves but by his adive will—and in what
place or at what time foever he exerts this energy,
he does it in the moft wife manner, and to effed the
beft moral purpofes in the hearts of his rational creatures, who are thereby affeded and in whofe affliction or advantage they are primarily defigned to iffue.
When the atmofphere preferves a fuitable temperature and the earth is happily watered from the river
of GOD and the year is crowned with his goodnefs—
when noxious vapors are diffipated—when thunder
and lightning, fnow and hail and ftormy winds, which
fulfil his word, are made to fubferve the health and
profperity of his people ;—and, when he blafts the
malevolent defigns of his enemies, however men improve thefe things, either as mercies or judgments,
the counfel of the LORD fhall ftand, and he will, in
a variety of ways, bring about his wife purpofes and
advance his own glory.

IN the moral world, the agency of GOD is employed with refpect to his intelligent creatures, who are under the ftrongeft moral obligations. Of this the fcriptures afford the higheft proof. It is likewife proved by the perfections of GOD. He is felf-exift-ent, all-fufficient, independent, omnipotent, infinite-ly wife and holy, juft and good. The moral per-fections, the juftice, goodnefs and truth of GOD, are illuftrated in adjufting the difpenfations of his providence, not only to the circumftances and con-ditions of men, but to the real advantage of his Church.

IN the political world the works of GOD praife him. He orders the birth, the rife and decline of empires with all the circumftances of their elevation, and their deftruction. Through what aftonifhing fcenes, changes and revolutions have moft of the nations and kingdoms of men paffed, becaufe GOD puts down and builds up as he pleafes. At what in-ftant he fpeaketh concerning a nation to plant and to build it, or to pull down and deftroy it, it is done. Where are now the Perfian, the Affyrian, the Medi-an and Babylonian kingdoms which made fuch a fig-ure in the eaft ? How have they been brought down and deftroyed, fo that not one ftone is left upon another ! What has become of the once flourifhing empire of Greece which rode in triumph and made the nations tributary ? What furprifing revolutions did the Roman empire undergo, notwithftanding her long and unexampled profperity ! When her vir-tue became only a name and her luxury and diffipa-tion realities, fhe fell and all her glory was proftrated

in the duft! Are we not to look beyond all feconda-
ry caufes and to afcribe fuch important changes to
HIM, by whom kings reign and princes decree juftice, who will punifh the nations that rebel againft
him, with a rod of iron and dafh them in pieces like
a potter's veffel ?

THE magnificent empires of the world, ingeneral,
have, after a fhort period, reached the meridian point
of their glory, and then declined and fell.　Of many of them there is hardly a veftige to be found.

AMONG the moderns, how have the nations of
Europe revolutionized and in what torrents of blood,
for feveral years paft, have her pleafanteft fields been
deluged.　With regard to our own nation, fhe has
undergone great and furprifing changes ; but all have
tended to accelerate her rifing glory.　Our beginning was fmall, and GOD defended us in our infant-
ile ftate from numerous favage foes ! When the nation from which we fprang, envious at our growing
profperity, fought to bring us under a more galling
yoke of bondage, their counfels were turned into
foolifhnefs and their haughty looks were brought
down.　GOD raifed a Wafhington to lead our armies on to victory and triumph.　When Independence was gained, it became neceffary to fecure it by
the adoption of a conftitution of federal government.
The remarkable unanimity in its adoption—the general agreement refpecting its fuperior excellency, and
the happinefs of the people in having two of the
beft characters in fucceffion at the helm of government, manifeft a kind fuperintending providence.

14   THANKSGIVING SERMON.

So numerous have been the interpofitions of heaven in our behalf, and fo plainly are his footfteps to be feen, that, however pleafing the tafk, it would be almoft endlefs to recount them. I have only hinted at fome of the moft remarkable, and fhall leave the reft to be fupplied by your own reflections.

I PROCEED to obferve that REDEMPTION is the moft glorious of all GOD's works, and that in which we are moft deeply interefted. This is indeed a boundlefs theme and can never be exhaufted. Of all the works of GOD, this praifes him the moft. And when all the works of creation are diffolved, the effect of this will continue, and be a theme of praife to eternal ages. *Worthy* is the *Lamb that was flain to receive bleffing and honor and glory and power,* for *thou waft flain* and *haft redeemed us unto* GOD, by *thy blood,* will be the fong of faints in everlafting glory.

THE faints are under the ftrongeft obligations to blefs GOD, not only for the works which he hath wrought but for the glorious perfections of his nature. If the works of nature, providence and grace, praife the LORD, furely man fhould not be filent, for whom they were wrought and who is moft deeply interefted! Created with fuch noble powers of foul as are capable of enlargement—formed for exalted happinefs in the enjoyment of GOD, it is not only the duty of man, but a duty than which nothing better becomes him, to make it his greateft care to em-ploy the nobleft faculties of his nature in the beft

410

work, and look up to GOD the fountain of perfection. What is there that can better employ the thoughts of rational creatures, and the moſt ſerious contemplations of pious men, than the ſublime and glorious attributes of the infinite author of all good ? A ſaint may improve his genius in expatiating the fields of literature ; he may ſtudy the works of nature ; but ſtill more noble objects ought to engage his chief attention, and through theſe he ſhould look up to the great firſt cauſe. He ſhould " elevate his heart above the low region of terreſtrial things to the bright abode of the immortal God."

ALL rational beings are bound to bleſs the LORD, as they are partakers of his bounty, receive from him innumerable benefits and are objects of his particular care : But ſaints above all are objects of his ſpecial notice and partakers of his richeſt grace. The former may poſſeſs the exterior of devotion and profeſs to be grateful, but the latter only are ſincere in their aſcriptions of praiſe ; they only truly admire the divine goodneſs, and feel the riches of his love in the great work of redeeming grace ; and have already begun that new ſong of praiſe which ſhall continue through the endleſs ages of eternity.

WE ſhould doubtleſs be grateful to GOD both for temporal and ſpiritual mercies, and not forget any of his benefits.

SOME of thoſe which we are bound particularly to recognize on this Anniverſary let us endeavor to recount.

THE fmiles of heaven on our American land have impofed on all our citizens, the ftrongeft obligations to this important and pleafing duty. Not to mention the countlefs favors and interpofitions of kind providence to our fathers; the land in which we live is now a cultivated, pleafant, fruitful country and the garden of the world.

OUR country is happy as to its climates; the agreeable temperature of its atmofphere; the health to which it conduces and the plenty which it every where pours forth to reward the hand of induftry. Here fcience has diffufed her cheering beams.—Our citizens are making continual improvement in the ufeful and fine arts, and liberty and independence crown all our enjoyments. We fit under the hallowed fhrine of religion's glorious temple, where the glad tidings of the bleffed gofpel are conftantly heard, and are indulged with the ineftimable privilege of worfhipping GOD according to the dictates of our own confciences, the rules of his infpired word, and the emotions of his holy fpirit. While thoufands in different parts of the world ftupidly proftrate themfelves before fenfelefs idols, while they groan under the hard hand of religious tyranny and are worn out with abftinences and pilgrimages, we glory in a religion which is mild and merciful as its divine author; and worfhip the LORD who made heaven and earth, and who requires no other facrifices but thofe of devout and pious hearts.

No nation fince the days of miracles and infpiration could ever trace more clearly the veftiges of providence in their favor than we can trace them in ours. The nation of the Jews were a living monument of GOD's goodnefs. He reared and made them a great people, that his declarative glory might be difplayed among the heathen. We too have large experience of his heavenly interpofition, and are in point of privilege, diftinguifhed from all the other nations of the earth. They could trace the hiftory of Providence from the calling of Abraham from the plains of Mefopotamia and Ur of the Chaldees to their happy eftablifhment in the promifed land of Canaan. We can tell of the adventurous flight of our pious fathers from their native country, acrofs the flood of the Atlantic to a land that they knew not, and recognize a feries of happy providences, which have attended their fons, down to the termination of our revolutionary war, the eftablifhment of our federal government, and the profperous courfe of our national affairs to the prefent day. While they applaud their Jofhua and recount his immortal deeds ; we can fpeak of our beloved, Wafhington, of the aftonifhing wifdom and fortitude with which he commanded in the field, fuftaining the trying viciffitudes of dubious war. Prompted by the moft difinterefted love for his injured country, this friend of liberty, virtue and mankind, quitted his favorite retirement and the endeared fcenes of domeftic life, and graced the firft feat in our public councils. In the alarming incidents of war, when his foul trembled for the fate of his country, addref-

C

fing the Moſt High, he was often heard to ſay, THY
WILL BE DONE. Unmoved by the beſt gift—the
higheſt praiſes and moſt affectionate gratitude of his
fellow-citizens, he modeſtly received the ſincere ex-
preſſions of their cordial wiſhes, reminding them of
the great Author of their bleſſings and his ſucceſſes.
" I was but the humble agent of favoring heaven to
whom alone the praiſe of victory is due." That
ſuch were the ſentiments of his heart the whole of his
life declared ; and they compoſe a brighter gem in
his crown than all the conqueſts he has won.

HERE is a character which no preceding age can
boaſt. Its intrinſic luſtre ſpreads a dark cloud over
the moſt diſtinguiſhed, uninſpired perſonages, ancient
and modern, and has ſecured to itſelf a deathleſs
fame. While we pay a tribute of reſpect, juſtly due
to the friend, the father and deliverer of his country,
let us imitate his pious example in aſcribing all the
glory to Almighty GOD. If we are ungrateful to
him we deſerve to have our names blotted out from
under heaven.

LET us recognize his goodneſs, in all our victories, in the civil privileges we enjoy—in the excellent conſtitution of our government—in giving one
to ſucceed our beloved Waſhington in the Preſiden-
cy who is a tried patriot—the friend of his country,
and whoſe reputation for wiſdom and integrity, the
pen of impurity and malice has not been able to blaſt.
Let us praiſe GOD, that he has made us happy at
home, reſpected abroad and comforted our hearts
with all ſpiritual bleſſings through our LORD JESUS
CHRIST.

THANKSGIVING SERMON.

RECOLLECT, my brethren, your private and perfonal favors as fo many inducements to blefs the LORD. Some of you have been profpered through the whole courfe of the year—your ground has brought forth abundantly ; the Lord hath made a hedge about you and your houfes, and given you uninterrupted health, profperity, and the pleafures of friendfhip and love. Others among you have recovered from threatning difeafe. When you found your fpirits finking ; when you trembled on the verge of the grave ; when the folemn bufinefs of taking a long farewell of all your dear conne&ions here had overwhelmed your troubled minds, heaven interpofed, healed your difordered frames, and reftored you to the bofom of your friends whofe aching hearts had given up all hopes of your recovery. Others can recognize fpiritual bleffings. GOD has taught you the folly of fin and infpired you with the love of holinefs. When you trembled under a fenfe of the horrible guilt of your hearts and the dreadful confequences of this ftate of oppofition to GOD, in the fweet whifpers of his love he faid to your fouls, " Thy fins be forgiven thee." In the gloomy hours of defertion light has fprung up, and you have been led to the willing arms of the Almighty Redeemer, who has filled you with the unfpeakable joy and peace of believers ; and given you the kindeft affurances that he will receive you to himfelf, where all fin and forrow fhall ceafe, and tears fhall be wiped forever from your eyes !

CAN you retire from the fan&uary of praife to the focial repaft, where you expe& to meet your friends, without hearts beating high with thankfulnefs to your Almighty BENEFACTOR, without fending portions to the poor and needy, that they alfo may participate in the general joy ; and, without fympathizing with the afflicted, who have the empty feat of a hufband, wife, child, or friend to lament ?

You who are heads of families relate to your off-fpring the kind interpofition of providence to our forefathers and us down to the revolution—and from thence to the prefent time. Imprefs their tender minds with a fenfe of their dependence upon GOD, the author of all thefe bleffings ; and urge them to remember their Creator in the days of their youth.

THANKSGIVING is a religious feftival ; and you who are parents might make a lafting impreffion on the minds of your children by a religious obfervance of it. Thofe who are now children are to be the future legiflators, ftatefmen and minifters of our country ; and the good education they receive in the morning of their days, will influence them through life, and render them bleffings in their day.

LET us implore the forgivenefs of our national and private tranfgreffions ; befeech the Almighty to fmile on the United States of America ; to diffufe knowledge and political and religious liberty, free from licentioufnefs, to all mankind ; and manifeft the gratitude of our hearts, by lives conformed to the revealed will of GOD, and holy anticipations of the bleffednefs, prepared for his children, in the world of eternal praife.

BLESSED be the LORD GOD of Ifrael, from everlafting to everlafting ; and let all the people fay, AMEN.

Doctor Dana's

SERMON

AT THE

ORDINATION

OF THE

Reverend Andrew Yates.

THERE IS NO REASON TO BE ASHAMED OF THE

GOSPEL.

———◦❖◦———

A

SERMON

PREACHED AT EAST-HARTFORD,

IN THE

STATE OF CONNECTICUT,

December 23, 1801,

AT THE ORDINATION OF THE

Rev. Andrew Yates,

AS A COLLEAGUE-PASTOR WITH THE

Rev. Eliphalet Williams, D. D.

———◦❖◦———

BY JAMES DANA, D. D.

Paſtor of the firſt Congregational Church in New-Haven.

◦◦❂◦❂◦❂◦❂◦◦

HARTFORD :

PRINTED BY HUDSON AND GOODWIN.

———•———

1802.

A SERMON.

EPISTLE TO THE ROMANS,
CHAP. I. VERSE 16.

FOR I AM NOT ASHAMED OF THE GOSPEL OF CHRIST: FOR
IT IS THE POWER OF GOD UNTO SALVATION TO EVERY
ONE THAT BELIEVETH; TO THE JEW FIRST, AND ALSO
TO THE GREEK.

THE *gofpel of Chrift* was firft tendered to the Jews.
The Jewifh converts fuppofed, that the Gentiles could be
admitted into his church on no other condition than a previous compliance with the mofaic ritual. It therefore became neceffary, that the apoftle of the Gentiles fhould affert
their right to the privileges of the Meffiah's kingdom, dif-
entangled from any Jewifh ceremony. Obfervable, at the
fame time, is the caution with which he touches a fubject,
wherein he had to encounter the ftrong prejudices of his
countrymen. He reminds them, that although to them per-
tained the priority of admiffion into the church, the gofpel
knows no difference between the Jew and the Greek: There
is with God no refpect of perfons or nations. " Is HE
the God of the Jews only ? Is he not alfo of the Gentiles?
Yes." *The gofpel is falvation—to the Jew firft, and alfo to
the Greek.*

6   *There is no reason to be ashamed of the Gospel.*

The defcription which the apoftle gives of the gofpel firft claims our attention.   *It is the power of God to falvation.*

It is the power of God : For it was " confirmed by figns and wonders, divers miracles, and gifts of the Holy Ghoft." A Jewifh ruler reafoned conclufively, when he faid, in his conference with Jefus, " We know that thou art a teacher come from God : For no man can do the miracles which thou doeft, except God be with him." His minifters per-formed the fame works ; but affumed nothing to themfelves. " Why look ye fo earneftly on us, as though by our own pow-er or holinefs we had made this man to walk ? Be it known to you all, that by the name of Jefus Chrift of Nazareth, whom ye crucified, whom God raifed from the dead, even by him doth this man ftand before you whole."   Our Lord, before he afcended, directed his difciples to tarry in Jerufa-lem, until endowed with power from on high.   On the day of pentecoft they were thus endowed ; and, going into all the world, approved themfelves as the minifters of God. They were witneffes of the refurrection ; and could add, *So is the Holy Ghoft.*   All who were witneffes of the miraculous gifts of the Spirit, faw that the gofpel was the power of God—that the fubjects of thefe gifts declared the teftimony of God.   Infernal fpirits certainly have not the power of the Spirit of God.   They cannot raife the dead, caft out devils, and endow the unlearned with the gift of tongues.   God only can give fuch power unto man.   A religion thus attefted has his feal—the higheft witnefs.   Faith, grounded on fuch teftimony, *ftands in the power of God.* Says St. Paul, " Moft gladly will I glory in my infirmities, that the power of Chrift may reft upon me.   Truly the figns of an apoftle were wrought among you—in figns and wonders and mighty deeds." If miracles are beyond the powers of nature, fhall we pronounce them impracticable ? Is the author of nature bound down by its laws ?

" My preaching," fays our apoftle, " is in demonftration of the Spirit, and of power." Had he preached with excel-lency of fpeech, he might have gratified the polifhed tafte of that age.   His aim was not to commend himfelf to poets, orators and philofophers ; but to commend himfelf to every man's confcience, by a plain declaration of the truth, as it is in Jefus.   The doctrine of a crucified Saviour has nothing of the enticing words of man's wifdom—no marks of human contrivance.   To the faftidious infidel it is foolifhnefs.

The gofpel makes difcoveries which reafon could not, and contains doctrines which reafon cannot comprehend. Admitting the poffibility and reality of revelation, it muft contain things which could not otherwife have entered into the human mind. The foundation truth of Chriftianity, the INCARNATION, as much tranfcends our underftanding as the heavens are higher than the earth. *The WORD was made flefh.* The WORD, who *was in the beginning with God,* and *by whom all things were created, HE took part of flefh and blood. The Son of THE BLESSED* was conceived and *born of a virgin.* To the myftery of GOD MANIFEST IN THE FLESH, add *divine foreknowledge and election, the trinity and atonement, the agency of God in regeneration, the identity of the refurrection body.* Thefe are not doctrines which man's wifdom teaches. They are *very deep,* as are HIS thoughts upon whofe authority we receive them : For they are all declared in the gofpel. We have proof of the myftery of the gofpel fimilar to that which we have for an author of nature and a fuperintending providence. The gofpel has like fignatures, in its miraculous confirmation, as the frame and confervation of the univerfe. We may difbelieve a God, if we may difbelieve the gofpel.

Our condemnation and death through man's firft offence—reconciliation by the crofs of Chrift—faith in his blood for juftification—renovation by the Spirit of life in him—and the change of our body of humiliation into the likenefs of Chrift's glorious body, are doctrines which Paul inculcated. The moral fyftem of Chriftianity, excellent, and fuperior to every other, would have been unadapted to our fallen race, had not the evangelical doctrines and promifes been connected with it. The whole guilty world need mercy to pardon, and grace to renew them. Thefe are derived through a Mediator.

Free grace, the atonement in the blood of Chrift, and the energy of the Holy Ghoft are exalted, when we contemplate them as infeparably *connected.* Our ideas of grace, to be juft, muft not preclude a Mediator, or the neceffity of the Spirit's influence. Our ideas of atonement muft not enervate the grace which provided it, or exclude the fupernatural agency which applies it. Our ideas of the operation of the Holy Spirit, if juft, embrace the redemption of the crofs, and the free grace which juftifieth through that redemption. We may not rely on grace to the contempt of the plan, through which grace fuperabounds where fin abounded. Nor may we have confidence in Chrift, at the expence of the honor and gratitude which we owe to the Father of mercies, who firft loved us ; and, as the higheft inftance of his love, gave his only begotten Son to be the propitiation for our fins. If any who rejeƈt the atonement, and the riches of grace which it exhibits, yet fuppofe that they are *filled with the Spirit*, they *fay that they have no fin, and make God a liar.* His grace is the fource of redemption : It found a ranfom for our apof-tate world. The voluntary facrifice of Chrift is the meri-torious ground, in confideration of which the fins of peni-tents are not imputed. The fanƈtification of the Spirit unto obedience is the qualification of the gofpel. What God hath joined, let not man put afunder.

The divine defigns are known by revelation, and no fur-ther than revealed. It is arrogance to difcufs the queftion, Whether there might have been falvation otherwife than by Chrift ? Our duty is to acquiefce and rejoice in his falvation. Neither humility nor wifdom permit us to attempt an ex-planation of the reafons of it. If the mighty works and the wifdom of Jefus and his firft minifters were from above, then the gofpel is the power of God, and the wifdom of God.

Further, the gofpel is the power of God in its *fanƈtifying influence.* To this evidence of its truth the apoftle refers, 1. Theff. ii. 13. " When ye received the word of God which ye heard of us, ye received it not as the word of men, but (as it is in truth) the word of God, *which effeƈtually worketh alfo in you who believe.*" To the fame purpofe are the words of St. John : *He who believeth on the Son of God hath the wit-nefs in himfelf.* The transforming power of the gofpel is, to the fubjeƈt of it, a witnefs which fuperfedes all other evidence.

The human race, naturally, " have the underftanding dark-ened, and are alienated from the life of God." When the gofpel is cordially embraced, they, " who were fometime darknefs, become light in the Lord. Turned from the power of Satan, every thought being brought into captivity to Chrift," great is the change in their views and affeƈtions. " Old things are paffed away ; behold, all things are be-come new." This renovation fuppofes native depravity. " From within, out of the heart of man, proceed murders, adulteries, fornications, thefts, falfe witnefs, blafphemies.",

Ignorance of the corruption of human nature is a melancholy proof of the thing, and a moft threatening fymptom. He who faith, " I am rich, and have need of nothing," will not regard the counfel of Chrift, " Buy of me gold tried in the fire, and white raiment." There is no occafion to enquire how far the depravity of mankind may be owing to education, example or habit. For if there is not a juft man living who doeth good, and finneth not, the evil muft be traced to a common fource. " A thoufand allegories, diffufed over all nations, atteft the felicity and the fall of the firft man."

Redemption teaches the neceffity of the crucifixion of the old man, or the deftruction of the body of fin. " Ye are bought with a price ; therefore put off the old man which is corrupt ; and be renewed in the fpirit of your mind." This renovation is afcribed to *the power of God.* " We are his workmanfhip, created in Chrift Jefus." No eftablifhment of fecond caufes in the natural world, nor means in the moral, preclude HIS agency *who worketh all in all.* Means, knowledge and exertions, unaccompanied with a divine energy, are vain. " You hath he quickened, who were dead in trefpaffes and fins." Gofpel faith is *the faith of the operation of God. He fulfilleth* in the heart the *work of faith with power.* Hence believers " know the things which are freely given them of God." Feeling the weight of his truth, they magnify his grace.

The gofpel is improved as the *medium* of moral renovation and falvation to believers.

" Faith cometh by hearing, and hearing *by the word of God.* The *preaching* of the crofs is the power of God. Of his own will begat he us, *with the word of truth.* Being born of incorruptible feed, *by the word of God.*" His co-operation is to be expected with the ufe of appointed means ; not otherwife. Thus God *magnifieth his word.* However he *might* make known the riches of his glory on the veffels of mercy, without any intervening medium, the *encouragement* is annexed to means and human endeavors. The neglect of thefe is contempt of God. And the defpifers of him fhall be lightly efteemed.*

----•+•----

* The pious and learned Mr. Howe obferves, that an unregenerate perfon, tho' he " cannot act *holily* as a faint, can act *rationally* as a man. You can attend

B

10   *There is no reason to be ashamed of the Gospel.*

From his own experience, Paul knew and declared, that the gospel, in its sanctifying influence, is the power of God to salvation. While in the full career of persecuting zeal, God was pleased to reveal his Son in him. From that time he determined to know and preach Jesus Christ, and him

———◦+◦———

upon the dispensation of the gospel, which is *God's power unto salvation*, the seal by which he impresseth his image; the glass through which his glory shines to the changing of souls into the same likeness. You are as able to sit in the assembly of *saints* as of *mockers*. You can consult the written word of God, and thence learn what you must be and do. Your eyes will serve you to read the bible as well as a gazette or play-book. You can enquire of your minister, or of an understanding neighbor, concerning the way and terms of blessedness. Your tongue can pronounce these words, *What shall I do to be saved*, as well as those, *What news is there going*. You can apply your thoughts to what you meet with suitable to your case, in your attendance upon preaching, reading, or discourse. You can select an hour on purpose, wherein to sit alone, with this resolution, Well, I will now spend this hour in considering my eternal concernments. True, you cannot think a good thought without God. But ask thy conscience, Whether upon trial thou findest not an *assistance sufficient* to carry thee thus far? Possibly thou wilt say, Yea, but what am I the better? I am only brought to see myself in a distressed perishing condition. 'Tis well thou art got so far. What course wouldst thou take in any other distress, wherein thou knowest not what to do to help thyself? Would not such an exigency force thee down on thy knees, and set thee to cry to the God of mercy for relief and help? Represent then the deplorable case of thy soul before him that made it, and crave his merciful relief—Shouldst thou, when the great God sends abroad his proclamation of pardon and peace, refuse to attend it, to consider the contents of it, and thy own case in reference thereto, and thereupon to sue to him for the life of thy soul? Thy refusal must needs be more provoking than thy defective performance. This speaks *disability ;* but that *rebellion* and *contempt*.

Canst thou pretend, though thou hast no pre-assuring promise, thou hast no hope? Is it nothing to have heard so much of God's gracious nature?—Do his giving his own Son, his earnest unwearied strivings with sinners, his long patience, the clear beams of gospel light, the amiable appearances of his grace, give ground for no better, no kinder thoughts of him? Yea, hath he not expresly stiled himself *the God hearing prayer*, taken a name on purpose to encourage *all flesh to come to* him? Wilt thou then dare to adopt those profane words, *What profit is it to pray to him ?* and say, It is better to sit still, resolving to perish, than address to him, or seek his favor ; because he hath not by promise assured thee of the issue ; and that, if he suspend his grace, all thou dost will be in vain?

How wouldst thou judge of the like resolution? If the husbandman should say, when I have spent my pains and cost, in breaking up and preparing the earth, and casting in my seed ; if the sun shine not, and the rain fall not in season ; if the influences of heaven be suspended ; if God withhold his blessing ; or if an invading enemy anticipate my harvest, all I do and expend is to no purpose: And God hath not ascertained me of the contrary, by express promise: 'Tis as good therefore sit still. Censure and answer him and thyself both together."

Howe's blessedness of the righteous.

426

crucified. " I account all things but lofs for the excellency of the knowledge of Chrift Jefus my Lord—that I may be found in him, not having mine own righteoufnefs, which is of the law ; but that which is through the faith of Chrift—That I may know him, and the power of his refurrection, and the fellowfhip of his fufferings, being made conformable unto his death."

The Holy Spirit was given to confirm the gofpel ; to turn the difobedient to the wifdom of the juft ; to direct, fupport and fucceed our religious enquiries and labor. The Spirit fhews the things of Chrift to his difciples. Through him ftrengthening us, we can do all things. By the refurrection of our Lord, we are begotten to a lively hope of an inheritance incorruptible and undefiled in heaven. This hope influenceth to purify ourfelves even as he is pure. To a well placed confidence in Chrift, it is unalterably requifite, that we poffefs his Spirit. To no others is the gofpel the power of God to falvation. " There is no condemnation to them who are in Chrift Jefus." The following words point out their character : " Who walk not after the flefh, but after the Spirit." The atonement is the purchafe and medium of juftification and life. " God hath made him, who knew no fin, to be a fin-offering for us, that we might be made the righteoufnefs of God in him." Faith in his expiatory facrifice is the term of acceptance. *Through faith in his blood.* Faith involves the love of the truth, an heart purified by obedience. " When the truths, promifes and precepts of the gofpel influence the affections and actions, this gives new ftrength to all the proofs alledged in favor of Chriftianity. It collects every ray of evidence in the heart, and excites that calm fatisfaction and anticipation of future felicity, which none but the Chriftian can feel. He has an intimate conviction, that the gofpel is not the fruit of error or impofture, but the offspring of heaven." While his temper and life exemplify the power of the gofpel, let infidels confefs, that God is in him of a truth.

To proceed. *I am not afhamed of the gofpel of Chrift.* We enquire, Is there any reafon to be afhamed of it ?

Bleffed is he whofoever fhall not be offended in me. The Saviour forefaw that the gofpel would be an occafion of offence. As was prophecied of him, He was defpifed and rejected of men. He was to the Jews a ftumbling-block,

and to the Greeks foolifhnefs.   Authority, fuperftitious zeal,
artifice and ridicule were all employed againft the gofpel in
the beginning, though it was *preached with the Holy Ghoſt
ſent down from heaven.*   Scoffers, in every age, have poured
all kinds of obloquy upon it.

When the gofpel was introduced, the nations were in
grofs darknefs on the fubjects of a future life and the way
of conciliating the favor of God.   The gofpel enlightened
and relieved them in this perplexity.   It gave them juft and
clear views of the attributes and providence of God ; the
way and terms of reconciliation : It changed their principles
and their hearts.   They no longer enquired, *Shall I give my
firſt-born for my tranfgreffion ?*   The humble Chriftian knows
the true God, and is wife to falvation.   On the fureft ground,
he hopes for pardon, grace and glory.   All things are plain
and poffible to him.   His peace paffeth underftanding.   Did
human wifdom enlighten or reform mankind ?   It rather
plunged them deeper in ignorance of God, and in all manner of pollution.   In proof of this, you are referred to the
multiplicity and character of their deities, and their religious rites.

The author of our faith " looked not on his own things."
He dwelt on earth " full of grace and truth, went about
doing good, and was made in all things like unto us, except
fin.   He endured the crofs, defpifing the fhame ;" that he
might reconcile the fallen human race to God, and to one
another.   " He was rich ; but for our fakes he became
poor."   His religion " is righteoufnefs, and peace, and joy
in the Holy Ghoft."   To lay the foundations of his church,
and propagate the gofpel, he chofe twelve men, from whofe
talents, circumftances and rank in life nothing, in an human view, could have been expected, but fhame and confufion to him and them.   They, however, overfet fuperfti-
tions which had the fupport of civil government, and were
fanctioned and venerable from their antiquity.   The apoftles' doctrine enlightened, reformed, and filled the world.
No dangers or fufferings extinguifhed or abated their love
and zeal.   They efteemed reproach for Chrift their glory ;
becaufe they *looked for the bleffed hope.*

If we fuppofe that we fhall be miferable hereafter, or that
death will terminate our exiftence, can we be reconciled to
death, or enjoy life ?   On the latter fuppofition, the believer

cannot be afhamed, nor can any reproach him with his credulity, after death. Should he, on the contrary, exift hereafter, he has embraced the only way to make his pofthumous life happy. His faith will be applauded, when all his hopes fhall be accomplifhed, exceeding, abundantly above all he can now imagine. Remark the great difference between the believer and the fceptic. If the former is deluded, he is yet no lofer, but rather a gainer, by his delufion ; as is evident from his prefent peace and hope. And if not deluded, he fhall receive the end of his faith, the falvation of his foul. The fceptic, if right in fpeculation, is practically wrong. He finds no fatisfaction in vain imaginations, which exalt againft the knowledge of God; or in any fecular purfuits. He travaileth with pain all his days. Without God, he is without hope. Should he exift hereafter, he will find to his coft, that the gofpel, which he ventures to treat as a fable, and loads with reproach, came from God, and that irretrievable ruin is the confequence of defpifing it. With fallen angels, he will *believe and tremble.*

They who are juftified by faith, and have therefore all joy and peace in believing, have no reafon to be afhamed of Chrift, through whom they have attained to their happy ftate—no reafon to be afhamed of the gofpel, which manifefts plenteous redemption by the well-beloved Son of God —no reafon to be afhamed of the perfect rules, and perfect pattern of Chrift.

Believers unto life hold faft their profeffion in all circumftances of trial. Their final perfeverance is a doctrine fupported by fuch fcriptures as thefe : " The path of the juft fhines more and more unto the perfect day. Whom he juftified, them he alfo glorified. I give to them eternal life, and they fhall never perifh. Neither death, nor life, nor angels, nor principalities, nor powers, nor height, nor depth, nor any other creature, fhall be able to feparate us from the love of God, which is in Chrift Jefus our Lord." If a believer may fall away totally and finally, how then is that declaration of the apoftle to be underftood, *Whofoever believeth on him fhall not be afhamed ?* The believer is liable to fuch defections as deeply wound religion : But he is recovered ; and, when converted, he ftrengtheneth his brethren. *The covenant of God ftandeth fure.* The faints are *kept by his mighty power, through faith unto falvation.* They cannot be *moved away from the hope of the gofpel.* If fcoffed at for their

14   *There is no reason to be ashamed of the Gospel.*

faith, *to* them *it is given,* as a peculiar honor, *to suffer shame for* Chrift's *name.* The gofpel which brings immortality to light, gives them a fuperiority to the world which philofophy never gave. Prefent afflictions "work out for them a far more exceeding eternal weight of glory." Their joy may be higheft, when, judging from their outward ftate, they muft be thought moft miferable. "In the world ye fhall have tribulation ; but be of good comfort, I have overcome the world. Peace I leave with you ; my peace I give unto you. Let not your heart be troubled, neither let it be afraid."

That believers are not afhamed of the gofpel is owing to no imbecility of underftanding. They can *give a reafon of the hope that is in* them.

Faith confifts in receiving the teftimony of God. We may abfolutely rely on this. Can we always rely on the deductions of human reafon ? Thofe who wifh well to our fallen world, or would find reft to their own fouls, muft wifh to find the gofpel true ; nor will they long be in doubt.

If Chrift hath the words of eternal life, he is worthy of the higheft efteem and reverence—efpecially as, upon this fuppofition, there is falvation in no other. But, if his divine miffion is denied, where is the way of peace ? Shall we go to thofe who "feek the Lord, if haply they may feel after him and find him" in the volume of nature ? Shall we fearch the writings of heathen philofophers and moralifts, who, " profeffing themfelves to be wife, became fools ?" Shall we go to Jewifh rabbies, ftill looking for the Meffiah ; although, by their own conceffion, the period fixed in prophecy for his advent was eighteen centuries ago ?—although the defolation of their temple, nearly as long fince, put an end to their ritual ?—although their difperfion, from that time to this, has rendered it impoffible for them to meet in the place of their folemnities, had the temple remained ? Or fhall we go to modern philofophifts, whofe miferable and only refuge is, that death may prove an eternal fleep ? To fupport their fyftem, they would deftroy all government, all focial ties, and bring the Creator and Ruler of the world to their feet. Their blaze is no other than " illumines hell." To them *is referved the blacknefs of darknefs forever.*

Shall incenfe be offered to the talents of men, whom the
fimplicity of the gofpel offends ? They do not point out a
way of pardon to finners, nor fhew how the dominion and de-
filement of fin may be removed. They do not difcover a
refurrection and immortality. They do not remove the
darknefs, impotency and death under which we labor.
Why, in the name of reafon and gratitude, do they reject a
religion which accomplifhes all thefe ends? We honor our
own underftanding, when it bows to the wifdom of God.
" He who doeth truth cometh to the light : But every one
who doeth evil hateth the light." Piety cafts a radiance on
genius and talents. Impiety cafts darknefs on the talents of
the infidel and profligate. Atheiftical philofophers have con-
fpired to crufh Chriftianity, deftroy the belief of a God, and
demoralize the world. It is beyond us to fay how long or
how far that confpiracy may continue and extend, which
fo many influential characters, in different countries, have
undertaken to patronize. The united voice of all the friends
of virtue is, " Alleluia : The Lord God omnipotent reigneth. Juft and true are thy ways, thou King of faints. The
Heathen raged ; the kingdoms were moved. The God of
Jacob is our refuge, a very prefent help in trouble. Be ftill,
and know that I am God. I will be exalted in all the earth.
The King on Zion's hill will dafh them in pieces like a potter's veffel."

The moft learned and virtuous characters are, and have
been, the friends of the gofpel. The believer is reproached
by the foes of God and goodnefs, the heirs of everlafting
contempt, who will wifh, when the Lord cometh, to be hid
under the rocks and mountains. Loft as they are to truth
and virtue, honor and good breeding, abhorred by God, and
by all holy, benevolent beings, fhall they feduce the believer
to facrifice his hope in Chrift, who was crucified even for
revilers ? *Scoffers, walking after their own lufts, trample under
foot the Son of God, do defpite to the Spirit of grace,* and fay in
their hearts, *No God.* Every fentiment of found wifdom
revolts at the thought, that fuch characters fhould make the
believer afhamed of the gofpel. He has no reafon to be
afhamed, that it has proved, through divine concurrence,
the medium of his heavenly birth—that he is conformed to
the image of Chrift, and has imbibed from him the fpirit
of humility, meeknefs and charity, purity and felf-denial,
devotion, zeal and refignation—that he endures temptation,
has peace always, by all means, and the hope which is as an

anchor to the foul, fure and ftedfaft.   He fees caufe to be
afhamed, that he is not more conformed to Chrift in temper
and life.   Others obferve many things in him unworthy of
his high calling.   He bewails indwelling fin ; and is humbled in reflecting on the weaknefs of grace and ftrength of
corruption.   He fees great occafion for ftronger faith, warm-
er love and zeal, a ftricter watch, a renewed converfion.
Having *laid the foundation of faith and repentance,* he *goes on to
perfection.*   By *waiting on the Lord* he *renews his ftrength.*
His infirmities and blemifhes notwithftanding, his confcience
teftifies, and its teftimony is his rejoicing, " that in fimplicity and godly fincerity, not with flefhly wifdom, but by the
grace of God, he has his converfation in the world."   He
accounts it his higheft honor, that God is in Chrift his reconciled friend and Father.   It is his ftrong confolation,
that in all events he fhall obtain the end of his faith.

Could falfe religion be the mean of forming the temper
of heaven in the heirs of fin and fhame ? The believer, a
witnefs to the truth of the gofpel, manifefts his wifdom in
owning Chrift, and defending the glory of his crofs, whatever facrifices it may require.   Delivered from the tyranny of
Satan, the prefages of confcience, and the fear of death,
believers juftly infer, that Jefus their deliverer, is the Chrift
of God.   Renewed in knowledge and holinefs, they " go
on their way rejoicing, through honor and difhonor, evil
report and good," plenty and want, forrow and joy.   " Being reviled they blefs ; being defamed, they intreat ; being
perfecuted, they fuffer it."   They have not been the authors
of this change of ftate and character in themfelves—a change
from enmity, fin and wrath, to a ftate of divine acceptance,
righteoufnefs and comfort.   This has been effected through
the operation of God with the gofpel.   They may then be
affured, that the gofpel is *the mighty power of God.*   It is no
matter of fhame, that the weapons of our warfare are mighty, through God, to pull down ftrong holds—that finners
are converted from the error of their way—that refrefhment
comes to them from the prefence of the Lord—that their
hope is fure and ftedfaft—that angels applaud them—that
the Father of angels views them with complacency—that he
is their chief joy, the reft of their fouls.   They walk not by
fight, but by faith ; the faith which is the evidence of things
unfeen.   Waiting for the hope of righteoufnefs by faith,
they can have no reafonable objection to pafs the valley
which intercepts our view of heavenly light and glory.   They

can have no objection to a joyful meeting, an inseparable union, with departed friends, who were dear in the flesh, but dearer in the Lord—an union also with the spirits of all just men made perfect, and infinite hosts of superior beings, who rejoiced at their conversion, and minister for their salvation. They can have no objection to enter into the joy of their Lord. When he shall appear, their station on his right hand will assure them of his unerring plaudit. Before the assembled world he will say, " Come, inherit the kingdom prepared for you." The believer will not be ashamed, when the whole universe of intelligences shall applaud him —when all who reviled him shall be confounded ; when the King of glory shall place an unfading crown upon his head.

We rejoice in the accomplishment of our earthly hopes. With much more reason will the believer rejoice in the accomplishment of his heavenly hope. " The things which are seen are temporal ; but the things which are unseen are eternal." This is a forcible reason for giving the preference to the objects of faith. If the soul is immortal, if this corruptible shall put on incorruption, there is inexpressible weight in the injunction, " Set your affection on things above."

Hopes, not founded on the gospel of Christ, will cover men with shame, sooner or later. The means of worldly good may not be within our reach. Or some unforeseen event may defeat the most promising, at a time when the proposed end was eagerly looked for. Or the expected rest is not found in the enjoyment. Riches and honor say not, *It is enough.* Pleasures, pursued beyond certain limits, lose their end. Change of circumstances may alter the ability, opinions or disposition of friends. Besides, riches fly away. Man in honor abideth not. Health may be impaired. Pleasures are but for a season. Friends go to their long home. The fashion of the world passeth away. We have no security of to-morrow. Our soul may be required this night. If then we build on earth for happiness, our hope will end in disappointment, vexation and shame. Envy not the prosperity of sinners : Choose none of their ways. Their triumph and joy are short and superficial. But *thy expectation,* if thou believest with the heart unto righteousness, *shall not be cut off.*

C

18   *There is no reason to be ashamed of the Gospel.*

Compare two sorts of characters—those who pursue some earthly object as their portion, and die without hope ; and those who have learnt moderation to sublunary things ; who shun the vices, and despise the vanities of the world ; who believe the gospel of our Saviour, and the immortality which he brought to light ; who follow him whithersoever he goeth, and shall have eternal life through his name. These walk in the light of God's countenance. They say to the last enemy, " O death, where is thy sting ?" They obtain " the victory through our Lord Jesus Christ. They shall behold his face in righteousness, and be satisfied, when they awake, with his likeness." The men of the world receive all their good things here, and die fools. Believers receive all their evil things in the present life, and lay up in store for themselves a good foundation against the time to come. They press toward the mark for the prize of the high calling of God in Jesus Christ our Lord. They aspire to the height of Christian perfection, the measure of the stature of the fulness of Christ. Have they cause to be ashamed ? To whom belongeth shame, but to the ungodly and unbelieving ? " Madness is in their hearts while they live ; and after that they go down to the dead."

At such a day as the present, and on such a solemnity, this respectable auditory will not judge, that the subject which has been selected, is unseasonable.

By the consent of all mankind, *some* religion is necessary. Who ever read or heard of a nation of atheists ? The believer in " twenty gods" may be preferred to the believer in " no god." Were the evidence of the truth of the gospel much less than it is, it should be deliberately weighed ; for the subject is highly interesting. Will any one, who is inclined to receive truth, want satisfactory evidence of it ? Men are disbelievers and scoffers, not because there is no evidence for religion, or none that is sufficient ; but because they have a strong bias to infidelity. And they have this bias, *because their deeds are evil.*

Those who revolt from a Christian education, are usually more malignant foes to the gospel, than such as have been educated in infidelity—more distinguished for evil communications, which corrupt good morals. The infidel should be so just as not to reproach the gospel for the errors or vices of its professors,—unless it can be made to appear, that their profeſſion contains thoſe errors, and countenances thoſe vices. How did Jeſus himſelf teach and live? What is it to abide in the doctrine of Chriſt, and to follow him? Thoſe muſt be foes to truth, who reproach *the doctrine according to godlineſs*. Thoſe muſt be loſt to a ſenſe of moral excellence, who reproach the maxims of the goſpel, and pattern of its author.

The ſcoffer affronts the good ſenſe of all who have been bred to *decency*. For this dictates reverence of God, of his providence, and of ſound morals. The ſcoffer violates all duty and decorum; and, as far as in him lies, ſaps the foundation of ſociety.

An Engliſh divine, of great eminence, in the 17th century, expreſſes himſelf in this forcible manner : " One would be aſhamed to be of that ſort of creature, called MAN, and count it an unſufferable reproach to be long unreſolved, *whether there ought to be ſuch a thing in the world as religion,* yea, or no. Whatever came of it, or whatſoever I did or did not beſides, I would, drive this buſineſs to an iſſue. I would never endure to be long in ſuſpence about ſo weighty and important a queſtion ! But if I inclined to the *negative*, I would reſt in nothing ſhort of the plaineſt demonſtration : For I am to diſpute *againſt mankind*, and eternity hangs upon it ! If I misjudge, I run counter to the common ſentiments of all the world, and I am loſt for ever !—If I conſider the unrefuted demonſtration brought for it, with the conſequences, religion is the laſt thing in all the world, upon which I would adventure to break a jeſt.— And I would aſk ſuch as have attempted to argue againſt it, Have their ſtrongeſt arguments conquered their fear? Have they prevailed upon themſelves *firmly to believe* things are as they would wiſh ? Have they no ſuſpicion left, that the other ſide of the queſtion may prove true ?

They have done all they can, by often repeating their faint deſpairing wiſhes, and the mutterings of their hearts, *no God ! no God !* to make themſelves believe there is none— Yet the reſtleſs toſſings to and fro of their uneaſy minds, their taſking and torturing that little reſidue of wit and common ſenſe, which their riot has left them—to try every *new method* and *ſcheme* of atheiſm they hear of, implies their diſtruſt of *all;* and their ſuſpicion, that, do what they can, things will ſtill *be as they were ;* i. e. moſt adverſe and un-

29   *There is no reason to be ashamed of the Gospel.*

favorable to that way of living, which, however, at a venture, they had before refolved on. Therefore they find it neceffary to continue their contrivances, how more effectually to difburthen themfelves of any obligation *to be religious ;* and hope, at leaft, *fome* or *other great wit* may reach further than *their own ;* and that either by fome *new model of thoughts,* or by *not thinking* it may be poffible at length to. *argue* or *wink,* the DEITY into nothing, and *all religion out of the world*—They think it an *eafier* thing to laugh away the fear of any future account, than to endure the feverities of a ferious repentance, and a regular life."*

While men of low and high degree reproach the gofpel, we who are fet for its defence may not be afhamed of it. We have much caufe to be *wife as ferpents, and harmlefs as doves, amidft a perverfe and crooked nation, fhining as lights in the world, holding forth the word of life.* We have for our example the preacher whofe words have been under confideration—the example alfo of his fellow-laborers. "Giving no offence in any thing, that the miniftry be not blamed : But in all things approving ourfelves as the minifters of God, in much patience, in afflictions, in neceffities, in diftreffes, in tumults, in labors, in watchings, in faftings ; by purenefs, by knowledge, by long-fuffering, by the Holy Ghoft, by love unfeigned, by the word of truth, by the power of God, by the armor of righteoufnefs on the right hand and on the left ; by honor and difhonor, by evil report and good report ; as deceivers, and yet true." Efpecially fhould we look to our Lord and Mafter. "If when ye do well, and fuffer for it, ye take it patiently, this is acceptable with God. For even hereunto were ye called : Becaufe Chrift alfo fuffered for us ; leaving us an example, that ye fhould follow his fteps—Who when he was reviled, reviled not again ; when he fuffered, he threatened not ; but committed himfelf to him who judgeth righteoufly." In preaching a crucified Saviour whatever offence may be taken at his crofs ; in conftantly affirming, that believers fhould maintain good works ; and in being examples to his flock, minifters are *the glory of Chrift.*

An ancient faint, warned of God that he muft be gathered unto his people, interceded for a fucceffor : "Let the

---

* HOWE's living temple. Few defences of religion againft the fceptics have the merit and excellence of this treatife..

Lord, the God of the fpirits of all flefh, fet a man over the congregation, who may go out before them, and who may go in before them, and who may lead them out, and may bring them in ; that the congregation of the Lord be not as fheep who have no fhepherd." God heard this prayer, and " provided a man in whom was the fpirit." Knowing that fhortly he muft put off his earthly tabernacle, naturally caring for this flock, of which he has had the overfight *fifty-four* years, its aged minifter fees his prayer anfwered. We blefs God, that he hath continued the life and labors of our much efteemed father, and made him an ornament to the miniftry. We participate in the fatisfaction it gives him, that one, in whom is the fpirit, is this day introduced with perfect unanimity to the facred office with him, now that he himfelf can but fay, *The hour of my departure is at hand*. It is the fupport of his advanced age, that he can *take* thofe *to record, among whom* he *has fo long preached the gofpel, that he is pure from the blood of all men, not having fhunned to declare the whole counfel of God*. May he not add, " According to my earneft expectation and my hope, that in nothing I fhall be afhamed ; but Chrift fhall be magnified in my body, whether it be by life or by death." He thus addreffeth his flock : " My brethren, dearly beloved and longed for, my joy and crown, fo ftand faft in the Lord, my dearly beloved." He exhorteth the paftor elect ; " Stir up the gift of God which is in thee. For God hath not given us the fpirit of fear ; but of power, and of love, and of a found mind."

We are perfuaded, DEAR SIR, that, as conftrained by the love of Chrift, you have preferred the work of a gofpel minifter to any other. You therefore can fay, from your own experience, with the chief of the apoftles, The gofpel is the power of God to falvation. You have taken laudable pains to acquire the qualifications which may render you a workman who needeth not to be afhamed. The tokens of efteem and refpect from this Chriftian fociety will animate your exertions for their fpiritual interefts. They expect that you will come to them in the fulnefs of the bleffing of the gofpel of Chrift.

Abftrufe fpeculations conduce not to godly edifying. Amidft the controverfies in the church, a Chriftian may be perplexed to know on which fide truth lies. One thing he may always obferve, and in obferving it may always fatisfy himfelf : "Only let your converfation be as it becometh the gofpel of Chrift."

Other foundation can no man lay, than Jefus Chrift. Let every man take heed what he buildeth thereon. Do any imagine that, in every refpect, they make choice of the beft materials, and difpofe them in the beft order?—that in all their labor, they are *wife mafter-builders?* This is to affume an exemption and diftinction appropriate to builders under the immediate direction of the Holy Ghoft. Have any the fulleft confidence in their own views and abftractions? They may confefs in heaven, what they feem not to acknowledge on earth, *God is great, and we know him not.* In our folly and weaknefs, we *fpake not of him the thing that is right.* They may be furprifed at the temerity of thofe fyftems, which are now prefumed to be of greateft moment, and have the force of demonftration. The time and coft beftowed on thefe would have been much better beftowed in *teftifying repentance toward God, and faith toward our Lord Jefus Chrift*—in inculcating *charity, the bond of perfectnefs.* This would beautify, ftrengthen and enlarge the fpiritual edifice.

The friends of Chrift are not exempt from miftakes, infirmities and paffions. They are liable to encumber and deform the gofpel with the doctrines and commandments of men—to obftruct the improvement of faith, hope and charity, by unworthy emulations, by the wrath of man which worketh not the righteoufnefs of God.

On myfterious doctrines, we know not how to order our fpeech by reafon of darknefs. It is our wifdom, therefore, to treat thefe in the language of the oracles of God, rather than to adopt human refinements.

Says the Apoftle, " We are not as many who corrupt the word of God : But as of fincerity, but as of God, in the fight of God fpeak we in Chrift." Our Mafter fpake and lived as never man did. But an hoft of enemies, as bold as they are malignant, are confederate to pull down and deftroy. All our wifdom is required, I fay not to convince, but to filence, fuch foes. All our wifdom is required, to warn every man, and teach every man, would we prefent every man perfect in Chrift.

There is no reason to be ashamed of the Gospel.   23

Arduous as your work is, especially at this day of treading down ancient institutions ; it is yet pleasing to think of entering on public life, and spending it, in the very honorable and useful employment of " preaching the kingdom of God, and teaching the things which concern the Lord Jesus Christ." With pleasure does the minister, whose heart is in his work, sit at the feet of Jesus, to receive his instructions, *in whom are hid all the treasures of wisdom and knowledge : The entrance of* his *word gives light and joy.* Your encouragement and your gifts are from him. *My grace is sufficient for you,* said Christ to his apostle, inquiring, " Who is sufficient for these things ?" professing, " We are insufficient of ourselves to think any thing as of ourselves." Go forth in his strength who hath called you to preach the gospel. " We have this treasure in earthen vessels, that the excellency of the power may be of God, and not of us." May you be *endowed with power from on high.*

You know how to appreciate, in the beginning of your ministry, the counsel of a venerable and much esteemed father. It gives you pleasing sensations, that the choice this people have made of you accords with his sentiments and wishes. May the harmony, with which you have been here called to the ministry, continue. Preach with all confidence the unsearchable riches of Christ. Great is the reward of a faithful minister. The Lord make you a rich and lasting blessing to this people, and to the churches. May you be glorious in his eyes. This is all your salvation.

BRETHREN OF THIS CHRISTIAN SOCIETY,

The advanced years of the minister, who for more than half a century has testified among you the gospel of the grace of God, have awakened a seasonable care to obtain the settlement of another. It is matter of thanksgiving to God, that he hath directed you to, and united you in, the choice of our young brother. The office he sustained, and filled with dignity and advantage, in the public seminary of a neighboring state,* and his acceptance in the churches where he has officiated as a candidate for the ministry, are honorable testimonies to his character. Your unanimity is a ground of encouragement, that his service in the gospel will not be in vain. Esteem and honor him for his works' sake. *Let him be among you without fear.*

———————

* Professor in Union College, Schenectada.

24   *There is no reason to be ashamed of the Gospel.*

You are not infenfible, brethren, that to many in thefe days *the word of the Lord is a derifion.* His friends muft walk circumfpectly, or they will expofe his caufe. When you reflect, that the kingdom of God is not in word, but in power, you will not be afhamed of the gofpel. The fub-jects of its fanctifying influence imitate the apoftle : " God forbid that I fhould glory, fave in the crofs of our Lord Je-fus Chrift ; by whom the world is crucified unto me, and I unto the world."

Take heed how ye hear and improve a preached gofpel. When the preacher feeks to find out acceptable words, even words of truth, as we believe our brother will, every hearer will have a portion, and in due feafon. Come up to the fanctu-ary, from fabbath to fabbath, determined to apply, each one, what may be fuited to his own cafe. Account not your min-ifter an enemy, but a friend, becaufe he preaches the truth as it is in Jefus—becaufe he is made manifeft unto God, and ftudies alfo to be made fo in your confciences. It will be his endeavor to manifeft the favor of the gofpel in a manner which can give no juft offence. *For the gofpel's fake,* he will *become all things to all men.*

When the word of the Lord is efteemed precious, a pro-feffing people fay with one voice, " Let us go up to the houfe of the Lord ; he will teach us of his ways, and we will walk in his paths." The religious affemblies are crouded : The worfhip is devout. Obferving the readinefs of mind in the hearers, the minifters of the word are animated. While they thus *appear before God in the gates of Zion,* they *go from ftrength to ftrength.* Your minifter will have it in charge, to watch for fouls, under a folemn fenfe of the account he muft render to the chief Shepherd. Should not you hear under the fame folemn fenfe of your final account ?

A warm and united affection of a Chriftian fociety to their minifter may change. Paul faid of the Galatians, " If it had been poffible, ye would have plucked out your own eyes, and have given them to me." But he had occafion to change his voice, and to afk, " Where is then the bleffednefs ye fpake of ?" You who experience *how good and pleafant it is to be of one accord, of one mind,* will fuffer a caution, which fo-cieties, who are moft happy in their minifter, need. *Stand faft in one fpirit—ftriving together for the faith of the gofpel.*

440

Public chriftian affemblies ever have been, and will be, the principal means of preferving and fpreading the knowledge of the fcriptures, the obfervation of the Lord's day, and the profeffion of the gofpel.

Teftify your affection to religion and to your minifter by a good converfation in Chrift. Thofe value the gofpel, who bring forth the fruit of it, in all goodnefs, righteoufnefs and truth; who are followers of God as dear children; and walk in love, as Chrift alfo loved us.

Pray for the divine influence and bleffing on the word. Build up yourfelves on your moft holy faith. When in your families and clofets you bow your knees to the God and Father of our Lord Jefus Chrift, remember both your aged and your young minifter. " The God of confolation grant you to be like-minded one towards another, according to Chrift Jefus : That ye may with one mind and one mouth glorify God, even the Father of our Lord Jefus Chrift.

The Lord build up this part of Zion, in a fucceffion of fuch as fhall experience, that the gofpel is the power of God to falvation. May the fon in the miniftry reap the harveft of the feed fown by the father; and the fower and reaper rejoice in the fruit gathered to life eternal.*

This large affembly will, we hope, bear in mind, that, if the gofpel is the wifdom of God, and the power of God, a faving faith in its divine author is of the higheft importance —*faith which worketh by love*. In religion, if in any thing, we ought to be decided. The double-minded furely are not wife. It is melancholy to fee intelligent and accountable creatures wavering in the concerns of eternal falvation— fometimes almoft perfuaded; at other times wholly carelefs and indifferent—Sometimes prefuming that they fhall die the death of the righteous; at other times juftly apprehending that their fouls fhall be gathered with finners. Ye who have not known the power of the gofpel of Chrift, unto you

---

* Succeffion of paftors in EAST-HARTFORD firft church.
I. Reverend SAMUEL WOODBRIDGE, ordained 1703. Died June 9, 1746, æt. 63.
II. Reverend ELIPHALET WILLIAMS, D. D. ordained March 30, 1748. He is in the 75th year of his age.
III. Reverend ANDREW YATES, ordained December 23, 1801.

D

26   *There is no reason to be ashamed of the Gospel.*

is it preached for a witnefs. " God fo loved the world, that he gave his only begotten Son to fave it. Whofoever be-lieveth on him fhall not perifh, but have eternal life. But how will you efcape, if you neglect fo great falvation ?"

While infidels reproach the gofpel, its friends fhould re-commend it by the light of their Chriftian example. This, if any thing, muft cut off occafion from thofe who watch for it. To this we are conftrained by love to Chrift, to our own fouls, and to the fouls of defpifers. " Whofoever fhall be afhamed of me, and of my words, in this adulterous and finful generation ; of him alfo fhall the fon of man be afham-ed, when he cometh in the glory of his Father, with the holy angels. But whofoever believeth on him fhall not be afhamed. In them he will be admired and glorified in that day."

Before that day fhall come, *this gofpel of the kingdom fhall be preached in all the world.* The faithful and true witnefs hath faid it. The prefent triumph of earth and hell cannot prevent it. When Herod and Pontius Pilate, with the Gen-tiles and people of Ifrael, combined, and crucified THE LORD OF GLORY, *it was* their *hour, and the power of darknefs.* This wrath, far from defeating the divine defigns, was overruled to accomplifh them. Glory to God in the higheft, peace on earth, and good will to men. The church is founded on a rock ; and refts affured, that no combination of enemies fhall prevail againft it. The kingdoms of men are divided and perifhable : That of Chrift is uniform in power : It *fhall break in pieces and confume all* oppofing *kingdoms, and fland for ever. The Lord fhall be King over all the earth : In that day there fhall be one Lord, and his name one.*

The God of all grace, who hath called us to his eternal glory by Jefus Chrift, after that ye have fuffered awhile, make you perfect, ftablifh, ftrengthen, fettle you. To him be glory and do-minion for ever and ever. AMEN.

Dr. WEST's

SERMON

AT THE ORDINATION OF THE

Rev. AMASA JEROME.

A

SERMON,

PREACHED AT THE

ORDINATION

OF THE

REV. AMASA JEROME,

TO THE PASTORAL CARE OF THE CHURCH IN

NEW-HARTFORD,

AUGUST 18TH, 1802.

BY STEPHEN WEST, D. D.
Pastor of the Church in Stockbridge.

TO WHICH ARE ADDED,

THE CHARGE, AND RIGHT HAND OF FELLOWSHIP.

———◆———

HARTFORD:

PRINTED BY HUDSON & GOODWIN.

—1802.—

THE GOSPEL MINISTRY A GOOD WORK.

An Ordination Sermon.

I TIM. III. I.

" This is a true saying, If a man desire the office of a bishop, he desireth a good work."

THE terms, *Bishop* and *Elder*, are indifferently used in the sacred writings, to denote one and the same office. An instance of this we have, Tit. i. 5—7. " For this cause left I thee in Crete, that thou shouldest ordain *elders*, in every city, as I had appointed thee. For a *bishop* must be blamelefs, as the steward of God." The character and the duties, which are essential to the *one*, are also, to the *other* ; and the same terms—the same impressions, are made use of, to describe them. And it will not be denied, that the office of an *Elder* is the same, as that of a *gospel minister*. The purport of the text is, therefore, this, " If a man defire the office of the gospel ministry, he desireth a good work." It is not faid, that he desires any *worldly emolument*, as though *this*, and not the employment, were to be his object. But he desires the *work*, let the worldly honors and emoluments of it be what they may. *Desiring* supposes, that the work itself, is felt to be

447

6 AN ORDINATION SERMON.

agreeable ; and that he who defires it, will engage heartily in it, and delight himfelf in the duties and bufinefs of it—that there appears fomething pleafing and animating in the employment. The words of the text therefore, clearly hold forth this truth, viz. That the office of the gofpel miniftry is a good work.

The words naturally enough, lead to a few obfervations refpecting, both the *nature* and the *excellence* of the work.

I. Refpecting the nature of it. Unlefs this in general, be underftood, a man will be but poorly qualified to enter upon the office. And though he may thirft for fome temporary advantages from it, he can with no propriety, be faid to defire the work. The refponfibility of the office is great ; and no man in his fenfes will defire to take it upon himfelf, without, *at leaft*, a general underftanding of its nature and duties. And,

1. It is a work, which has for its grand object, the intereft and glory of the kingdom of Chrift. To this great end, all its duties directly and immediately relate. The duties of the Chriftian life in general, have this for their ultimate object ; but yet in many things, more indirectly. But, this is a work, in which every talent is to be employed, and every power exhaufted, in the immediate fervice of Chrift. The Great Head of the church carries on his kingdom in this world, and manages the affairs of it, by the miniftry and inftrumentality of men. Therefore, the apoftles, as his minifters, fo often ftile themfelves, the *fervants of Chrift.* Paul, fpeaking of the church, ftiles it, God's hufbandry —God's building ; and himfelf and other minifters of Chrift, fellow-laborers with God. 1. Cor. iii. 9. " For we are laborers together with God : ye are God's hufbandry, ye are God's building." Minifters are ftiled *overfeers,* whofe bufinefs it is to feed

the church of God. Acts xx. 28. "Take heed
therefore unto yourselves, and to all the flock, over
which the Holy Ghost hath made you overseers, to
feed the church of God, which he hath purchased
with his own blood." It must be of great importance, that the nature, the laws, and the interest
of this kingdom, be well understood by those, who
enter upon the ministerial work, lest they pull down
and destroy, instead of building up. No where are
mistakes respecting the duties of office, of so dangerous and fatal a tendency, as in the work of the
ministry. It was a law of God to every king of
Israel, that he should have a thorough understanding of the laws and interest of God's then visible
kingdom; and thus be qualified to gather, and
feed, and protect his people. Deut. xvii. 18, 19.
"And it shall be, when he sitteth upon the throne
of his kingdom, that he shall write him a copy of
this law in a book. And it shall be with him, and
he shall read therein all the days of his life : that
he may learn to fear the Lord his God, to keep all
the words of his law, and these statutes, to do them."
So Christ directs his ministers now, 1 Tim. iv. 15,
16. "Meditate upon these things, give thyself wholly to them; that thy profiting may appear to all.
Take heed unto thyself, and unto thy doctrine;
continue in them : for in doing this thou shalt both
save thyself, and them that hear thee." Unless the
duties of the office, and the laws of Christ's kingdom
be understood, the most laborious exertions may
be expected to be of little advantage to the cause.
The servant is ever to take directions from the
master, and follow them ; otherwise, his labor is
unprofitable. Nor can a minister expect to be useful in the service of Christ, any further, than he follows his directions, and labors in conformity to the
laws and rules of his kingdom. What a melancholy
thing will it be for one, the whole business of whose
office is, to serve Christ, yet to be found, a stranger
to the interest and laws of his glorious kingdom !

8   AN ORDINATION SERMON.

And how awful, to be a betrayer of this intereſt, and of the truſt repoſed in him! Who would dare to venture on this arduous work, were it not for the precious, gracious promiſe of the glorious head of the church, " Lo I am with you always !"

2. It is a work, which directly and intimately concerns the ſpiritual and everlaſting good of men. It was inſtituted for edifying the body of Chriſt, and enlarging his glorious kingdom. The adminiſtration of the affairs of civil government, is of great importance, becauſe they reſpect the concerns, and involve the intereſt of multitudes, even, of ſucceſſive generations : ſtill, it is only temporal intereſts, which are concerned. But theſe are ſo infinitely tranſcended by thoſe of men's immortal ſpirits, that they are all to be renounced and given up for Chriſt, and ſacrificed in his glorious cauſe. Here is an intereſt of men, to which the attention of miniſters is called, which extends far beyond the narrow bounds of time ; and which, in its nature and its magnitude, will be continually growing and increaſing to eternity. And this vaſt and eternal intereſt of men is, in an important ſenſe, intruſted to the care of the goſpel miniſter, and to be required at his hand. Thus Ezek. xxxiii. 7, 8. " So thou, O ſon of man, I have ſet thee a watchman unto the houſe of Iſrael : Therefore thou ſhalt hear the word at my mouth, and warn them from me. When I ſay unto the wicked, O wicked man, thou ſhalt ſurely die ; if thou doſt not ſpeak to warn the wicked from his way, that wicked man ſhall die in his iniquity : but his blood will I require at thine hand." Of what great moment then, is it, that the goſpel miniſter well underſtand the ſpiritual intereſts of men, and ſuitably feel their vaſt importance—that he rightly apprehend the character of mankind in their natural ſtate—that he be acquainted with the diſeaſes of the human mind, the dangers, to which men are expoſed, and the only me-

thod of their recovery and falvation by Chrift! Not
only fo, but that he have a good underftanding of
the nature of experimental religion, that he may
know how to fpeak a word in feafon to him, that is
weary, as well as to him, that is out of the way!

The holy fcriptures reprefent mankind, as being
in a ftate awfully fallen, and deplorably wretched.
And the gofpel points out the only, yet an all-fufficient remedy; at the fame time declaring, that *ftrait
is the gate, and narrow the way, which leadeth unto
life, and few there be that find it.* Therefore, the
apoftle directs the minifter, 1 Tim. iv. 16. " Take
heed unto thyfelf, and unto thy doctrine ; continue in them : for in doing this thou fhalt both fave
thyfelf, and them that hear thee." It is the truth,
that people muft *hear*, in order to be faved. Such
confiderations may give us to fee, that unacquaint-
ednefs with the duties of the minifterial office, or
inattention to them, or even one falfe ftep in profe-
cuting them, may be followed with never ending
and infinite mifchief to men. Under the fenfe,
which Paul had of thefe things, and of the vaft
efficacy, and the feveral different effects, which divine truth would have upon men, no wonder he
exclaimed, as in 2 Cor. ii. 16. " To the one, we
are a favor of death unto death ; and to the other,
the favor of life unto life : and who is fufficient for
thefe things?" He knew too, that when any one
undertook this great work, it was at a moft awful
peril, that a faithful difcharge of the real duties of
it was required at his hand. In reference to this
therefore, it was, that he faid, 1 Cor. ix. 27. " But
I keep under my body, and bring it into fubjection:
left when I have preached to others, I myfelf fhould
be a caft away." Who that had a proper underftanding of the nature, the duties, and the importance of this folemn office, would ever enter upon
it under any, but fo glorious a head and leader, as
the Lord Jefus—fo all-fufficient a guide, as the Ho-

B

ly Spirit ! How comforting, and fupporting to the humble, faithful minifter of Chrift, will be thofe gracious words of his, which he once fpake to an eminently faithful fervant, who was crying to him for help, " My grace is fufficient for thee : for my ftrength is made perfect in weaknefs."* But we muft proceed,.

II. To obferve a few things refpecting the excellence of this work. The apoftle, in our text, ftiles it, a *good* work. There are various accounts, on which the work of the gofpel miniftry may, with much propriety, be faid to be a good work: fuch as,.

1. It is an exceedingly benevolent work. Nothing is fo pleafing to the benevolent heart, as to do good, efpecially to the fouls of men ; and nothing more animating and enlivening, than the profpects which open for it. In this refpect, it is a god-like employment : for it is the very work and delight of God himfelf, to do good. In this, he has been engaged from eternity, and is continually engaged. For this, he made, upholds, and governs the world. For this, he was manifeft in flefh, and died, and rofe, and lives, and reigns, and will reign for ever. For this, he inftituted the minifterial office, and raifes up, and fends forth his faithful fervants, and promifes to be with them. In the exercife of a portion of the fame fpirit, it was that Paul faid, " I will very gladly fpend and be fpent for you, though the more abundantly I love you, the lefs I be loved."† No bufinefs in life, gives fuch fcope to benevolence, as the gofpel miniftry. For here a field opens for the employment of every moment, and every talent and power ; uniting in every exertion, the glory of Chrift, and the everlafting good of fouls. The object and end of the gofpel miniftry is, to win fouls to Chrift, that they may be everlafting-

* 2 Cor. xii. 9.   † 2 Cor. xii. 15.

ly happy in him ; and in this way advance the intereft of his glorious kingdom. What can be more
delightful to the benevolent heart, than to be appointed by the Lord Jefus himfelf, to call finners
back from their awful wanderings, and point them
to the way of life and fafety—to feed Chrift's fheep,
and to feed his lambs—to tend the flock of Chrift,
and be their fervant—to break the bread of life, and
to divide the word of truth to his dear people !

2. In this work, we have the greateft advantages,
and are furnifhed with the richeft variety of means
for doing good ; fo that there needs nothing, but a
diligent improvement, and prudent application of
them, to give affurance, that our labors fhall be acceptable, and bleffed, in fome way or other, to the
advancement of the glory and good of Chrift's kingdom. Should we be at a lofs in any cafe, how to
apply the means put into our hands, the Lord himfelf is ever at hand, and ready to give the teach-
ings of his Holy Spirit upon humble application to
him. It is a defirable circumftance, refpecting any
work, or employment, to be furnifhed with the neceffary means for accomplifhing it to advantage.
The phyfician may feel bowels of tendernefs toward
his patient; but ftill, find all his fkill baffled by the
nature of the difeafe ; or not know where the healing medicine is to be obtained. But not fo, with
the able, faithful minifter of Chrift. He finds himfelf fufficiently furnifhed with all neceffary means of
acquaintance with every difeafe of the human mind,
and balm provided for every wound. The minifter
of Chrift has a large fund for application, both to
the confcience and to the heart. The word of God
furnifhes him with motives, which apply to every
fpring of action in the human mind—to aroufe the
attention,—to alarm the fears,—to pierce the confcience, and to reach the heart. He has advantages to fhow the awful evil and danger of fin—to fet
the terrors of the Lord before finners—to open the

fcenes of the invifible world, to bring judgment
and eternity into view, and make the eternal God,
and heaven and hell, all, as it were, now prefent
to the human mind; and this too, with fuch force
of evidence, as muft baffle and confound all the
art and malice of gainfayers.

3. The fuccefs of minifterial labors, in the converfion of fouls through the power and bleffing of
divine grace, is exceedingly comforting and animating. Does the hufbandman patiently wait for the
harveft, and rejoice in it? Does the tender mother rejoice in the growth and flourifhing of her
little nurfery of children ? The faithful minifter
feels a higher and more fincere joy in witneffing
the converfion of fouls, and the growth and increafe of grace in their hearts. The faithful minifter delights to fee the power and efficacy of divine
truth on the confciences and hearts of men. When
he can fee the attention of finners all awake to divine and eternal things, and their confciences pierced with divine truth ;—when he finds them beginning to know the plague of their own hearts, and
become fenfible of their enmity againft God—when
he fees, that they feel their way hedged up on every
fide, and tremble before the great God ; how does
it animate his hope, and engage his labors and prayers for them ! And then, to fee the new life begin
to bud and open in the finner—to hear him condemn himfelf, juftify God, admire his patience,
and adore his goodnefs, his marvellous love and
grace; what a fatisfying reward, what a heart-felt
joy does it afford ! He feels the force of the apoftle's
expreffions, " My little children, of whom I travail
in birth again until Chrift be formed in you. For
what is our hope, or joy, or crown of rejoicing ?
Are not even ye in the prefence of our Lord Jefus
Chrift, at his coming? For ye are our glory and
joy."*   Oh, what a felicity, to be inftrumental of

* Gal. iv. 19.   1 Theff. ii. 20.

faving, even *one foul*—of turning *one* from darknefs
to light, and bringing him to the enjoyment of the
glorious fum and fountain of all good for ever and
ever. Surely that muft be a good work, which
has *this* for its object, and is many times, attended
with fuch bleffed effects.

4. It is a good work, becaufe it is the fame,
which engages the attention and labors of all good
beings in the univerfe ; and the great God and Saviour gracioufly affociates his minifters with himfelf
in it. Therefore, the apoftle faith, *We are laborers together with God.* And the faithful minifter
enjoys the favor and friendfhip of all good beings in
it,—the prayers of God's children, the interceffion
of Chrift, and his promifed prefence. It is the work,
in which Chrift, and all the angelic hoft are employed ; for *they are all miniftering fpirits, fent forth
to minifter for them, who fhall be heirs of falvation.*†
What a bleffed thing to be employed immediately
in that work, which the heart of God has been
upon from eternity ; and in which it is fo infinitely
engaged, that he has been manifeft in flefh, and
died, and rofe and lives, and reigns for its accomplifhment,—and to the advancement of which, he
makes every thing in the univerfe fubfervient !—
a work, immediately relating to that great object,
in which divine, infinite love will more fully and
glorioufly appear, than in any thing elfe,—in which
the bleffed Redeemer will fee of the travail of his
foul and be fatisfied, and the heart of the eternal
God reft for ever and ever ! What a mercy, that
we may be employed by the great God, in that
very work in which his almighty power, unfearchable wifdom, and infinite love and grace are all engaged ; and be made inftrumental of forming materials for that glorious building, which GOD will
inhabit, and in which he will dwell for ever and

† Heb. i. 14.

ever,—to be united to fuch glorious, bleffed company in our work; and more than in any other
employment in life, have our communion with
the Father, and with his Son Jefus Chrift! That
muft be a good work, in which infinite goodnefs,—
the eternal God and Saviour is engaged; and in
which we may be laborers together with God.
Once more,

5. It is a good work, as it is a caufe which will
certainly be fuccefsful. There are many difcouragements to exertion in a caufe, the fuccefs of
which, after all, remains doubtful. But this is infinitely far from being the cafe, refpecting the caufe
of Chrift. This can no more fail, than the eternal
God himfelf can change. This is a caufe, which
everlafting fuccefs and triumph moft affuredly await;
and he who ftrives lawfully, will certainly be crowned. It is true, there is no abfolute promife to the
faithful minifter, that he fhall be inftrumental of
converting finners. The prophet Ifaiah, was fent
to harden; and fo may the faithful minifter be.
It will be for the glory of Chrift, and will prepare
the way for a bright difplay of it, for his faithful
minifters to be a favor of death unto death in fome,
as well as of life unto life in others. And in one,
or the other of thefe ways, all the faithful labors of
the minifters of Chrift will ferve to advance the beft
intereft of his dear and glorious caufe. God's
chofen ones, they will be the means of ripening and
maturing for happinefs and glory;—others, for
mifery and torment; and thus prepare the way
for the glory and triumph of, both righteoufnefs
and mercy, to be more illuftrious on the day when
Chrift fhall judge the world. The faithful labors
of the fervants of Chrift will all ferve, as the occafion of a clearer and brighter difcovery of the
righteoufnefs of God, in executing vengeance upon
the enemies and rejectors of Chrift; and, of the
unfearchable riches of his glorious grace in the

eternal falvation of thofe who believe. Every part
of the minifterial work, when faithfully performed,
will be made, in fome way or other, to fubferve the
beft intereft of the kingdom of God. Here is an
employment, in which none of our labors need be
loft, not one exertion, but will turn to good effect,
—not a blow ftruck in vain ; but every one ferve
in fome way or other, to advance the building of
God. All that is wifely and faithfully done in this
great work, ferves to provide and lay up matter for
everlafting adoration, thankfulnefs, and praife to
Him, who fits upon the throne, and to the Lamb.

APPLICATION.

1. With what holy courage, and humble confidence and truft, may we enter upon, and go forward with this great work under fuch a Captain
and Leader, as the Lord Jefus Chrift!—a work in
itfelf, fo benevolent—fo defirable and excellent,—
in a caufe which fhall fo furely be triumphant ;
and in fuch bleffed fociety and company, as we are
called to labor with ! In fuch a work as this, what
can appal the heart of him, who is prepared by divine grace for it, and trufts in Chrift ! How applicable to him, are the words which God fpake to a
fervant of his of old, " Have not I commanded
thee ? Be ftrong and of a good courage, be not
afraid, neither be thou difmayed ; for the Lord thy
God is with thee whitherfoever thou goeft."*
When God commands, what is there to fear ?
God's prefence finks mountains into vallies, makes
rough places plain, and the moft difficult work eafy.
But the minifter is to remember, that the preceding
words are equally applicable. The work of the miniftry, though fo very defirable a one, is yet an exceedingly folemn one. It is folemn, not only in refpect to the effect it will have upon the everlafting

---

* Jofhua i. 9.

ftate of thofe, to whom we minifter, but as to the
awful confequences to ourfelves, as well as to others,
of an unfaithful performance of its duties, or an un-
fkilful application of the talents committed to us.
Minifters are required on their peril, not to preach
for doctrine the commandments of men, but the
very truth as it is in Jefus, not fhunning to declare
all the counfel of God. Minifters are fervants,—
they have a commiffion, and to that, they are ftrictly to adhere in all their miniftrations. In vain will
it be to plead, we miftook, either the doctrines, or
the duties of the religion of Jefus. There is neceffity laid upon us ; and if we do not, in good meafure, both preach, and live the religion of the
Lord Jefus, we fhall be blind leaders of the blind,
and, both we, and our people fall into the ditch.
How will a minifter, who has any proper fenfe of
the weight of the work in which he is engaged,
and has much acquaintance with his own heart,
prize the infinite atonement, the worth and efficacy of which he fo often recommends to his people !
Feeling the neceffity of it for them, how much more
fenfibly will he perpetually feel the need of it for
himfelf !

2. What a wonder is it of fovereign, infinite
mercy, that the Lord ever makes the labors of
fuch poor, weak, vile worms fuccefsful ; gracioufly
caufing them to advance the intereft of his glorious
kingdom, and bleffing them to the everlafting falvation of finners ! How obvious, that he gives to
his church, the treafure of his faving truth in earth-
en veffels, that the excellency of the power may be
of God ! In the inftruments, which God is pleafed
to make ufe of in carrying on his glorious work
among men, how manifeft is it, that the weaknefs
of God is ftronger than men ! Are we to put on
airs of importance—are we to glory in ourfelves,
becaufe the weapons of our warfare are fometimes,
mighty through God to the pulling down of ftrong

holds ? As well might the axe boaft itfelf againft
him, that heweth therewith. Rather, much rather,
is any gracious effect, which may follow our miniftrations, fitted to carry our reflections back to the
mighty difplay of divine power, when the ftrong
walls of a city fell at the founding of ram's horns.
What are we, hell-deferving worms, that we fhould
exult, when, if our labors are ever made fuccefsful, we are but the witnefs, that God choofes the
foolifh things of the world, to confound the wife,
and the weak things of the world to confound
the things which are mighty! But who of all men,
have fuch advantage deeply to feel, and clearly
to difcern the grace, the glory, and the all-fuffi-
ciency of Chrift, if *our* labors are, in any inftances, bleffed to the converfion of finners ! And
this, are we the true minifters of Chrift, will be
the moft fatisfying reward. Who need fuch deep
humility, fuch lowlinefs of mind, as the minifters
of Chrift,—who, to feel the fpirit, and act continually the part of *fervants !*

3. What has been faid, may lead us to contemplate the folemn, awful account, which unfaithful
minifters will have to give another day. Great and
precious are the advantages, which fuch of us, as
are fuffered to be in the work of the gofpel miniftry, enjoy, that our whole employment may be
about the things of God, and his fpiritual kingdom
—fearching into thofe glorious things, which angels
defire to look into—having thofe treafures and
fources of divine knowledge open to us, and continually before us, where new beauties and glories
are unfolding every ftep we take in our progrefs
forward. Yet after all, to be found ftrangers to
the truth, as it is in Jefus, enemies to him, and
betrayers of the truft committed to us, muft be followed with an aggravated condemnation. Oh !
how awful for us to go to hell, and draw our people after us ; and to find, at laft, that we cannot

C

be damned at fo cheap a rate as others! May thefe folemn thoughts be much upon our minds, and deeply affect us. May the affecting and awful fcenes of that great day, when we muft appear at the bar of Chrift with thofe, the charge of whofe fouls is, in an important fenfe, committed to us, be continually before our eyes. And under the influence of thofe weighty and powerful motives, fuggeft- ed in thofe oracles of divine truth which we are to make our daily and continual ftudy, may we be engaged to that humble zeal and fidelity, which may be for the glory of Chrift, and the good of fouls. In this way, and in this alone, we may humbly hope for his merciful and gracious accep- tance.

But it is time to conclude with fuch addreffes, as are ufual and proper on fuch occafions as this. And,

1. To you, Dear Sir, who are now about to en- ter upon that great and good work, of which we have been fpeaking. We hope you will ever cher- ifh a grateful fenfe of the wonderful goodnefs and grace of the Lord toward you, in preparing the way, and opening a door in his providence, for you to be a laborer in his vineyard—a preacher of the glad ti- dings of falvation by Chrift. And how highly fa- vored are you of the Lord, that you may be admit- ted, as a laborer in his vineyard, in fo propitious a day as this!—a period, when the great Lord of the harveft fo remarkably and glorioufly appears to favor and plead his own caufe—to aid, and affift his faithful fervants, and to blefs and fucceed their la- bors! Never forget the vaft weight of obligation there is upon you, to be faithful in the fervice of him, who has called you; nor count your own life dear to yourfelf, fo that you may finifh your courfe with joy, and the miniftry you receive of the Lord Jefus, to teftify the gofpel of the grace of God. We hope and truft, you in fome meafure, fuitably feel the

AN ORDINATION SERMON.

very great importance of the work on which you are now entering, and your own insufficiency for it ; and that you have set down and carefully counted the cost. If you enter upon the work with the views by which we hope you are influenced, you will sensibly feel, and solemnly contemplate the extensive influence which the transactions of this day, and your consequent labors will have, not only on your own, but the eternal state of this people. To reflect how far the eternal salvation of a number of immortal souls may be suspended upon your wise and faithful discharge of the duties of the ministerial office, must be enough, one would think, to solemnize any mind, and make a poor, weak worm tremble. But then we may remember (blessed be the glorious head of the church) in whose name and strength we may go forth to the arduous work ; and who it is, that has said to his faithful servants, " My grace is sufficient for you : for my strength is made perfect in weakness." We may be weak in ourselves (and never shall we be too deeply sensible of it) but strong in the Lord and in the power of his might. You now undertake to serve Christ in the great work of the gospel ministry—to minister to the people in holy things, and to preach to them the truth as it is in Jesus. What awful consequences will follow, both to yourself, and them, if you pervert the glorious gospel. Should your great object be to please men, you would no longer be the servant of Christ. Therefore, " take heed unto thyself, and unto thy doctrine : continue in them ; for in doing this, thou shalt both save thyself and them that hear thee." Look, Sir, on this people, and remember, that the charge of their immortal souls is about to be committed, under God, to you, and that they will be, in an important sense, required at your hand. Let this thought be continually upon your mind, that you may feel for them, as you do for your own soul. And the Lord give you wisdom

20 AN ORDINATION SERMON.

and grace, to be a worker together with God. May you go forth in the ſtrength of the Lord, humbly expecting his preſence to be with you, his Spirit to guide you, and his bleſſing to attend you: for without him you can do nothing. How willingly may you ſpend and be ſpent, and exhauſt all your powers and ſtrength in ſo glorious a cauſe! May you labor for Chriſt, and for the ſalvation of periſh-ing ſinners. May you hope to be an inſtrument in his hand, of enlarging, in ſome degree, the bounds of his glorious kingdom, and, of the ſalvation of ſome periſhing ſinners. What more can you wiſh for, to awaken your zeal, and animate you to dili-gence? But can you think of entering upon ſuch a work as this, without a fixed determination to devote yourſelf wholly to the duties of it? Can you think of neglecting your ſtudies, and leading an idle life, ſo that your profiting and improvement will be viſible to none? We hope better things of you. And may the Lord continually impreſs your conſcience, and your heart with a ſenſe of the weight and importance of this great work—make you watchful and prayerful, humble and laborious in the vineyard of the Lord. Bear this people contin-ually on your heart; and may he, who is able to keep you from falling, in his good time, preſent, both you and them, faultleſs before the preſence of his glory with exceeding joy.

2. To the Brethren of this Church. We may ſurely ſay to you, as the apoſtle did to the Hebrews, " Obey them that have the rule over you, and ſub-mit yourſelves: for they watch for ſouls, as they that muſt give account; that they may do it with joy, and not with grief; for that is unprofitable for you."* How painful will be the work of your miniſter, ſhould you not approve yourſelves faith-ful followers of Chriſt!—and if you do not unite,

---

* Heb. xiii. 17.

by your pious care and influence, to ftrengthen his
hands and encourage his heart! You will remember,
that like yourfelves, he is but a man, that he will
need your candor, your friendfhip, your help.   It
is not from him, that you are to hope that his labors may be a blefling ; but from that glorious Being who fends him to you, whofe power and grace
can caufe him, out of weaknefs, to wax ftrong.
And if you wifh him to be a blefling, remember
him continually at the throne of divine grace.   No
men need the prayers of God's people more than
minifters.   In anfwer to the prayers of God's people, thefe cifterns are often filled, that it may be
drawn out unto the people.   Pray to the glorious
Head of all power and influence, that he would pour
oil into this lamp, that it may give light to you—
that he would fhower down grace into his heart, that
he may come to you in the fulnefs of the blefling
of the gofpel of Chrift.   If he be a true minifter
of Chrift, he will have a weight continually upon
his heart.   Be tender then toward him, and pity,
and pray for him.   And may God of his infinite
mercy in Chrift, grant, that you and he may be
mutual helps and bleffings to each other, be built
up together in the moft holy faith ; and your church
be as a city fet upon a hill, and be enriched more
and more with divine grace !

Finally : To the congregation in this place. How
does it become you all to feel, that this is a folemn
day, and a folemn tranfaction ! God and angels
are fpectators.   The events of this day will be followed with vaft confequences, as to the ftate of
your fouls—confequences which will reach to eternity.   The tranfactions of this day will all rife up
before the throne of God and the Lamb, and however eftimated now, will then appear in all their vaft
importance.   The Lord Jefus is this day, once more
coming to you by an ambaffador, to befeech you to
become reconciled to God.   Whether it were for

AN ORDINATION SERMON.

difregard paid to his meffage, that the holy God was pleafed in his providence, to call off a former meffenger, whom he had fent to you, another day will reveal. But be this, as it may, God now in his merciful providence, fays to this people, " how fhall I give you up !" He has pity, and fends another ambaffador with meffages of grace. Confider then, that the tranfactions of this day will be remembered and recorded in heaven, as a fwift witnefs againft you, if you reject the bleffed treaty of peace, which is now brought to you. This day may be awfully decifive to fome of you, turning the fcale, and fixing your ftate for eternity. And oh! what an awful prefage of future hardnefs of heart, and utter ruin will it be, if, inftead of that ferious and devout confideration and behaviour, which the folemnities of this day require, any fhould indulge to vanity and mirth! Would this invite the prefence and bleffing of God, without which the moft precious truths of the glorious gofpel will be but a favor of death unto death? Will it not rather provoke the holy God to fwear in his wrath, that you fhall never enter into his reft? May the good Lord therefore, grant you all a lively fenfe of his power and prefence to day, that you may be prepared to welcome the meffages of his grace, and to receive with joy the ingrafted word, which is able to fave your fouls! In this way may you be made joyfully to meet and welcome the coming and day of the Lord! AMEN.

AN ORDINATION HYMN,

Sung previous to the imposition of hands.

1. JESUS, to whom all pow'r is giv'n,
   Made Lord of earth, and King of heav'n,
   Gives his apoſtles, this command,
   Teach, and baptize through every land.

2. He ſends his heralds to proclaim
   Salvation through his worthy name,
   To call loſt ſinners to return,
   To comfort humble ſouls that mourn.

3. The ſacred office ſhall extend,
   Through every age, till time ſhall end,
   Thus here, the glorious goſpel's come,
   And preach'd within this ſacred dome.

4. This flock without a ſhepherd left,
   Of inſtituted means bereft,
   Expos'd to ſcatter, and to ſtray,
   Expos'd to diſcord's dangerous way.

5. But now, united in their choice,
   With hopeful proſpects, all rejoice
   In one, who here elected ſtands,
   Waiting the confecrating hands.

6. Thy gifts and grace, Lord, we invoke,
   To fit thy ſervant for this work.
   May he declare thy counſel, Lord,
   And preach the doctrines of thy word—

7. Explain thy pure and holy law,
   And ſinners with thy threat'nings awe ;
   Man's loſt, and ſinful ſtate proclaim,
   And pardoning grace through Jeſus' name.

8. Lord, may thy ſervant faithful prove.
   To warn, inſtruct, reprove in love.
   Great God, this flock, and ſhepherd own,
   And both, at laſt, in glory crown.

24

THE CHARGE,

Given by Rev. AMMI R. ROBBINS.

REV. SIR,

YOU having been now confecrated to the work of the gofpel-miniftry, and folemnly ordained paftor of the flock of Chrift in this place; agreeably to apoftolic direction and example; by folemn prayer and the laying on of the hands of this Prefbytery : It remains that we exhort and *charge* you to take heed to the miniftry which you have received of the Lord Jefus, that you fulfil it.

We do now therefore, before GOD and the Lord JESUS CHRIST and the elect Angels ; and in the view of this numerous affembly, folemnly *charge* you to be faithful and diligently to attend to every branch of your minifterial work.

Take heed, therefore, to yourfelf—to your doctrine and conduct, and to all the flock over which the Holy Ghoft hath made you overfeer.

Take heed to *yourfelf.* See that you are indeed a friend and difciple of the Lord Jefus. As Chrift faid to *Peter,* fo fay I to you, *Amafa*—loveft thou the Lord Jefus Chrift ? Then feed *thefe* his fheep and feed his lambs. Look well to your own heart, and maintain a humble and clofe walk with God. Be a man of prayer, and labor to keep up a holy intercourfe with heaven. Let your converfation be in heaven, whence you look for the Saviour. Keep yourfelf pure, and while you are the keeper of the vineyard of others, neglect not your own.

Take heed, alfo, to your *doctrine.* Preach the word—be inftant in feafon and out of feafon. Ufe great plainnefs of fpeech—preach boldly, the doc-

466

trines of the gofpel, and in fuch manner that you may be underftood by your hearers, and not with ambiguous words and uncertain or unmeaning found. Open up to view the character of God—his holy Law—and the infinite obligations finners are under to be conformed to it. Shew to them their tranfgreffions, and that by the deeds of the law there is no hope for the finner.—Alarm the fe-cure and carelefs by the terrors of the Lord, and by exhibiting the awful punifhment that awaits the impenitent and ungodly.

Preach the *gofpel.* Urge the precious—the all-important doctrine of *atonement* by a crucified Sa-viour as the only ground of hope ; and exhibit the gracious calls and invitations of the gofpel, in a moving and affecting manner, as becomes their na-ture and defign. At the fame time, let the finner know, that through the obftinacy of his own heart and his criminal oppofition, he will not comply—that he is entirely dependent therefore on the mere mercy of that God, who " hath mercy on whom he will have mercy"—and that unlefs this is dif-played in bowing his will, and fubduing his hard heart, he is forever undone.

Comfort alfo the feeble minded. Exhibit the in-finite freenefs of the love and grace of Chrift to the broken-hearted penitents, and invite the weary and heavy-laden to him that they may find reft.

Speak comfortable things to the children of Zion—urge the neceflity of holinefs and perfeverance in all holy obedience to the end. In a word,—" fpeak the things which become found doctrine"—giving to every one a portion in due feafon—and declare the whole counfel of God, whether they will hear or whether they will forbear.

D

Take heed alfo, that you be an *example* to the flock, " in word, in converfation, in fpirit, in faith, in purity." Let them fee that you *feel* and *live* the religion which you preach. Watch over them as a faithful fhepherd, and as much as in you lies, guard them from going aftray, warning them againft falfe teachers and erroneous doctrines.

Vifit the fick and thofe who are in trouble and diftrefs, whether of body or mind. Inftruct, warn, counfel, encourage and pray with and for them.

Moreover, we charge you, to adminifter the holy *feals* of the covenant of grace, *Baptifm* and the *Lord's Supper* to thofe who appear to be the proper and qualified fubjects of them. But take not " children's bread to give to dogs." Meet Chrift's people around his table, and there exhibit the fweet memorials of his dying love.—And *blefs* the people in the name of the Lord.

Finally we give it in charge to you, that whenever you fhall be called to induct others into this holy miniftry ; you ftrictly adhere to the direction of our Lord, and " commit this power to faithful men, who fhall be able to teach others alfo." Look into their qualifications, and " lay hands fuddenly on no man." But fuch, and fuch only, as you truft, in a judgment of Chriftian charity, are really called of God.

And now dear Brother, if you fhall be enabled by grace to keep this *charge* and approve yourfelf a faithful minifter of the Lord Jefus ; you will not, " after having preached to others be caft away ;" but fhall finally be accepted of your Lord. " And when the chief fhepherd fhall appear," you fhall " receive a crown of glory." AMEN.

The RIGHT HAND of FELLOWSHIP,
By Rev. Jonathan Miller.

Rev. and Dear Sir,

THE kingdom of our divine Redeemer is founded on the fimple principle of the moft extenfive and difinterefted benevolence. Its members, in every office they fuftain, are directed to exert their whole abilities to promote the common intereft. This principle is a folid foundation for perfect love and fellowfhip. Entire union and harmony will continue in this bleffed fociety forever ; while all affociations, formed on other principles, will fhortly find themfelves in everlafting anarchy and difcord.

Agreeably to the fpirit of this fociety, and in conformity to apoftolic practice, we, the Elders of the Churches, now convened in Council, prefent you with this right hand. It is a fignificant ceremony. By this we publicly receive you as a brother, and an equal in the holy miniftry. And we do folemnly covenant and engage to watch over you in Chriftian faithfulnefs : And with humble dependence on the aid of divine grace, we pledge ourfelves to affift you, on every occafion, in the difcharge of all the duties of your facred office, as we fhall have opportunity.

We alfo accept your right hand, our dear brother, with much pleafure, as your pledge of fimilar engagements to us.—And may our mutual exertions, through the bleffing of our common Lord, be productive of reciprocal advantages. We commit and commend you, and ourfelves, and the miniftry which we have received of the Lord, to the mercy of God, through Jefus Chrift. Amen.

Mr. FLINT's SERMON

AT THE

ORDINATION

OF THE

Rev. JOSIAH B. ANDREWS.

A

SERMON,

DELIVERED AT THE

ORDINATION

OF THE

Rev. JOSIAH B. ANDREWS,

TO THE PASTORAL CARE

OF THE

SECOND CHURCH IN

KILLINGWORTH,

APRIL 21, 1802.

By ABEL FLINT,

Pastor of the South Church in Hartford.

HARTFORD:

PRINTED BY HUDSON & GOODWIN.

1802.

A SERMON, &c.

ACTS xxviii. 31.

Preaching the kingdom of God, and teaching those things which concern the Lord Jesus Christ, with all confidence,——

THE apostle Paul was distinguished from the other apostles of our Lord Jesus Christ, by the ardor of his zeal, by the abundance of his labors in the service of his great master, and by the cruel persecutions he met with from the enemies of the Christian cause. Impressed with a lively sense of gratitude to God, for interposing, in a miraculous manner, to bring him to a knowledge of Jesus Christ and of the way of salvation through him, he devoted his life to the propagation of that glorious system. To an object so momentous he sacrificed all that the world calls dear, his ease, his interest, his reputation, and in the end life itself. This illustrious child of wisdom triumphed in the midst of persecution;—he gloried that he was accounted worthy to suffer for the cause of Christ; and desired to spend and be spent in disseminating that religion which is in fact, and which he firmly believed to be " the power of God to salvation to every one that believeth."

DEEPLY impressed himself with a sense of the excellency of the knowledge of Christ Jesus, he wished to be made instrumental of communicating this knowledge to others ; and therefore, he improved

6   AN ORDINATION SERMON.

every opportunity afforded him " to teftify the gofpel of the grace of God." Undaunted by the fear
of perfecution, unmoved by the threatenings of his
enemies, undifmayed by the profpect of bonds and
imprifonment, which he knew awaited him, he ftill
perfevered in preaching a crucified Saviour to Jews
and Gentiles.

HAVING, in the difcharge of a commiffion entrufted to him by his great mafter, incurred the re-
fentment of the Jewifh rulers and people, they would
have barbaroufly murdered him, had he not been
protected by the Roman troops then ftationed at Jerufalem. Being permitted to fpeak in his own defence, he delivered an eloquent apology for himfelf,
ftating what had been the manner of his life, and
giving a hiftory of his miraculous converfion to the
Chriftian faith, with an account of his fubfequent
conduct. The Jews ftill perfifting in their enmity,
exhibited a number of charges againft him before
the Roman governor and infifted upon his condemnation. In confequence of this, the apoftle, thinking it his duty to ufe all lawful means to preferve his
life, claimed thofe privileges to which he was entitled as a Roman citizen, and appealed from the tribunal of the Roman governor in Judea, to the judgment of Cæfar. He was accordingly fent as a prifoner to Rome. Having arrived in that city, divine
Providence fo ordered it, that inftead of being caft
into a prifon he was permitted to refide in his own
hired houfe guarded by a fingle foldier. Here Paul
" received all thofe who came unto him ; preaching
the kingdom of God, and teaching thofe things
which concern the Lord Jefus Chrift, with all confidence."

FROM the hiftory of this apoftle, contained in the
book of Acts, and from his epiftles, which form
fo important a part of the canon of the new teftament, we learn that our text contains, in few words,
the great fubjects which St. Paul thought it his duty,

AN ORDINATION SERMON. 7

as a minifter of Chrift, to inculcate on thofe to whom he was fent to preach the gofpel. He uniformly preached *the kingdom of God,* and *the things concerning Jefus Chrift.* And this he every where did with *great confidence ;* boldly declaring the whole counfel of God, that the blood of thofe fouls to whom he difpenfed the everlafting gofpel might not be required at his hands.

As God is immutable, without any variablenefs or fhadow of turning, the truths of his holy word will forever remain the fame ; and it will ever be the duty of Chriftian minifters to preach the fame fyftem of doctrines and precepts which was taught by the great apoftle of the Gentiles ; and in imitation of him to preach them " with all confidence." There is but one gofpel,—but one way of falvation ; and tho an angel from heaven were to preach another gofpel than that preached by Paul, a folemn curfe is denounced againft him. How important then that the minifters of Chrift preach the truth ! How important that they take for their pattern thofe primitive teachers who were immediately infpired by the Father of lights and commiffioned by him to proclaim to mankind the only way of falvation ! How important that " we preach not ourfelves but Chrift Jefus the Lord !"

THE attention of this numerous and refpectable audience is requefted, while I recommend to my Reverend Fathers and Brethren, and particularly to my young Brother, who is this day to be folemnly confecrated to the work of the gofpel miniftry, the example of the apoftle Paul, as mentioned in the words of our text.

THE paffage contains three leading ideas which I fhall endeavor to illuftrate and apply to the prefent occafion.

I. IT is the duty of Chriftian minifters to " preach the kingdom of God."

8   AN ORDINATION SERMON.

II. It is their duty to " teach thofe things which concern the Lord Jefus Chrift."

III. It is their duty to do this " with all confidence."

I. In the firft place, It is the duty of Chriftian minifters to " preach the kingdom of God."

" The kingdom of God," or " the kingdom of heaven," is a phrafe which frequently occurs in the holy fcriptures, and it is ufed in different fenfes. Sometimes it denotes God's univerfal kingdom, or that dominion which he exercifes over all the works of his hands—as—that expreffion of the Pfalmift, " They fhall fpeak of the glory of thy kingdom and talk of thy power ; to make known to the fons of men his mighty acts, and the glorious majefty of his kingdom. Thy kingdom is an everlafting kingdom, and thy dominion endureth throughout all generations." By the kingdom of God is fometimes meant a principle of true religion feated in the heart ;—as, " The kingdom of God is not in word but in power." " The kingdom of God is not meat and drink, but righteoufnefs and peace and joy in the holy ghoft." " The kingdom of God is within you."—Sometimes the phrafe denotes the Chriftian difpenfation, in diftinction from the Jewifh—as—where John the Baptift fays—" Repent for the kingdom of heaven is at hand." And fometimes, " the kingdom of God," means that ftate of glory and bleffednefs into which the righteous will be admitted in a future ftate of exiftence ; as in our Saviour's difcourfe with Nicodemus,—" Except a man be born again he cannot fee the kingdom of God."

As underftood in all thefe fenfes, the kingdom of God is to be preached.—Under this general idea are comprifed many particulars, fome of which will be briefly mentioned.

AN ORDINATION SERMON.   9

A TRUE knowledge of God is the foundation of all religious truth.   If on this fubject the ideas of men are effentially wrong, their whole fyftem of doctrines will be erroneous.   Faithful minifters will, therefore, endeavor often to delineate the true character and perfections of the ever bleffed God, as thefe are difcovered in the works of creation, in the difpenfations of providence, and particularly in that revelation which God hath made of himfelf; together with the mode of the divine exiftence in a trinity of perfons, fo far as this myfterious fubject is opened to the comprehenfion of men in the holy fcriptures.—They will defcribe the feveral relations which man ftands in to God, as his creator, preferver and judge, with the various duties refulting from thofe relations.   They will inculcate the doctrine of God's univerfal and particular providence, in fulfilment of his eternal decrees, foreordaining whatfoever comes to pafs ; and that the divine being will over-rule all things to the advancement of his own glory, and the greateft good of his intelligent univerfe.—They will defcribe that holy, juft and good law, which is a tranfcript of the moral perfections of its divine author, and which all rational beings are under infinite obligations always to obey ; with the perfectly reafonable penalty annexed to the violation of this law ; and the certainty of this penalty's being inflicted on finally impenitent tranfgreffors.   This will lead them often to fpeak of the general refurrection, of the day of judgment and that future ftate of retribution which is to fucceed.   They will delineate the character of the true fubjects of God's fpiritual kingdom in this world, and the glories of the heavenly kingdom, fo far as they are unveiled in the facred volume.   They will confequently be often led to defcribe true religion as confifting in holy love,—fupreme love to God, and univerfal benevolence to man ;—acted out in a life of uniform obedience to the divine precepts.

B

10   AN ORDINATION SERMON.

In a word, preaching the kingdom of God denotes preaching that fyftem of religion which God
hath revealed.   The bible is the great ftandard of
truth and duty.   From that fource are to be derived
our articles of faith and rules of practice.   To the
law and to the teftimony muft we ever appeal for the
truth of our religious fentiments ; and not to the
dictates of reafon corrupted by paffion and biaffed by
prejudice.

Those therefore who inftruct their hearers only in
what is called the religion of nature, and in the fyftems of morality taught by uninfpired men ;—who
omit, or but flightly and fuperficially difcufs the peculiar truths of divine revelation, and who do not
enjoin thofe graces of the heart and thofe moral virtues which diftinguifh the Chriftian religion from all
others, do not imitate the apoftle Paul, and are not
faithful ftewards of the myfteries of the kingdom of
God.

But referring to the next general head of difcourfe feveral particulars which it might feem proper
to introduce under this head, I pafs on to obferve,

II. It is the duty of Chriftian minifters to " teach
thofe things which concern the Lord Jefus Chrift."

To preach Chrift is to have a general reference to
him in all religious fubjects ; in conformity with the
fcope of divine revelation, and with the preaching of
the primitive apoftles.—The work of redemption is
the moft glorious of all God's works ; indeed the
others are but appendages of this.   The true character of God is feen only as it fhines in the face
of Jefus Chrift ; and thofe truths and doctrines
which have been already mentioned cannot be rightly
underftood and explained without reference to Chrift.
" We preach Chrift crucified," fays St. Paul, " to
the Jews a ftumbling block, and to the Greeks foolifhnefs ; but to them that are called, both Jews and

Greeks, Chrift the power of God and the wifdom of
God.   I determined not to know any thing among
you fave Jefus Chrift and him crucified." In Chrift
as a central point, all the lines of evangelical truth
meet and are united.   Suffer me, to afk your attention to a quotation from an elegant writer on this
fubject.

" Jesus Chrift, far fuperior to all human glory,
" was known and celebrated long before he came
" into the world.   His magnificence is of all ages.
" The foundations of his religion were laid with
" thofe of the world ; and tho he did not appear
" on earth till four thoufand years after the creation,
" yet his hiftory begins with that of the world.   He
" was firft preached in Paradife ; the fubject was
" continued down to Mofes ; and revealed ftill more
" frequently and more clearly during the reign of
" the law and the prophets.   For four thoufand
" years Jefus Chrift was the object of the promifes of
" heaven, and the defires of the earth ; he was ty-
" pified by righteous men and by the worfhip of the
" law ; he was proclaimed by a long train of pro-
" phets, and his way prepared by the whole chain
" of political events.

" Jesus, above all, Jefus crucified, throws the
" brighteft light upon the old teftament.   Without
" him what can we comprehend in the multitude of
" ceremonies and facrifices of the law ? What ima-
" ges without him do the lives of the patriarchs offer ?
" What can we find in the prophecies but impene-
" trable enigmas ? The law would be a fealed book,
" and Judaifm a confufed heap of precepts and cere-
" monies, piled up without meaning.   On the con-
" trary, how beautiful is the hiftory of the people of
" God and all their worfhip when the crofs is the
" key !—What order !—What defign !—What
" plan !—What an admirable economy !—It is one
" whole, the different parts of which relate to the
" fame end.   It is an edifice which God himfelf

12   AN ORDINATION SERMON.

" founded, and infenfibly raifed, with a defign of
" placing upon the top the crofs of his Son. It is a
" long allegory which divine wifdom contrived and
" conducted during many ages, and of which, at
" length, the crofs has given the true fenfe."

So full are the holy fcriptures of Jefus Chrift, and
fo important is it that his minifters have an ultimate
reference to him in all their difcourfes.   Having
made thefe general remarks refpecting preaching
Chrift, I proceed to mention feveral particulars concerning him which faithful minifters of the gofpel
will inculcate.

THEY will infift upon the original dignity and
glory of his nature, as one with the Father in every
adorable attribute of divinity ; as the fecond perfon
in the holy trinity ; and as mediator uniting in himfelf the divine and human natures, being God and
man in two diftinct natures and one perfon.   They
will mention the various circumftances of his incarnation, his birth, life, fufferings, death, refurrection
and afcenfion; together with the offices which as mediator he fuftained.   And they will explain all thofe
doctrines which relate to the way of falvation through
him.

WERE I at this time to go into a particular detail
of all the Chriftian doctrines, and attempt to illuftrate and prove them, I fhould far exceed the proper limits of a fingle difcourfe, I fhall therefore only
mention a few leading fundamental doctrines.

1. IN the firft place, the univerfal and total depravity of mankind.   The whole fyftem of Chriftianity is evidently grounded on this idea, that mankind are in a fallen, degraded, depraved ftate ; to
recover an elect number of whom from which was
the defign of the miffion of Chrift.   The more
deeply we feel our depravity, the greater fenfe we
have of our exceeding finfulnefs, and the confe-

482

quent mifery to which we are expofed, the higher will our ideas rife of the importance and worth of the Chriftian falvation.   While thofe who do not believe mankind to be totally depraved, can never thoroughly underftand nor duly appreciate the way of redemption through Chrift.   " In fuch as have " never felt their fins as any incumbrance, it would " be mere affectation to pretend to very exalted con- " ceptions of the value and acceptablenefs of the " proffered deliverance."

2. ANOTHER effential doctrine of the gofpel, which faithful minifters will preach, is, that Chrift by his fufferings and death expiated the fins of the world; that he fuffered and died not as a martyr to the truth, but to make a vicarious atonement for fin; and that this atonement confifted not in obedience to the divine law but in fuffering its penalty in the finner's ftead.

IN the death of Chrift there was an infinite value and merit.   It afforded a difplay of the moral per- fections of God, and difcovered the evil nature and confequences of fin more ftrikingly than if the whole human race had been left to fuffer the pen- alty of God's righteous law.   This is the uniform language of the new teftament, in which the doc- trine of the crofs is reprefented as the grand pecu- liarity of Chriftianity.   This doctrine is defcribed as being not merely an important branch of the gof- pel but the gofpel itfelf; and it is reprefented as fo effential that the final falvation of the Corinthians was declared by the apoftle to be fufpended upon their adherence to it.

THOSE who deny or explain away the doctrine of human depravity, and thofe who, from inattention to the fubject, or from not examining themfelves, have faint ideas of their finful and miferable condi- tion, fee no neceffity of fuch an atonement, and therefore do not really believe the doctrine as explained in the holy fcriptures.   The confequence is, their whole fyftem of fentiments as regards falvation by Chrift is erroneous.   To counteract fuch errors and inculcate the truth, the idea that Jefus Chrift, by his death and fufferings, purchafed falvation for finners, and that falvation is in no other way to be obtained, fhould be often held up to view.

3. AGAIN, the neceffity of divine influences to renew and fanctify the heart, is another effential doctrine of the gofpel.   This neceffity arifes from the depravity of the human heart, which is fo great that if left to himfelf man never would become holy. A great variety of expreffions are ufed in the fcriptures on this fubject, and the idea inculcated by them is, that a moral change muft take place in man to fit him for the happinefs purchafed by the death of Chrift ; and that this change is effected not by any power in man, but by the operation of the holy fpirit of God ; who, in this refpect, acts as a fovereign, having mercy on whom he will have mercy.

CHRIST, by his death, has expiated fin ; he has fatisfied the law of God, and made it confiftent with the honor of the divine government to pardon the finner.   But notwithftanding this, no one of the human race could be happy were not God, in his fovereign mercy, to change the heart, and thus fit the finner to receive a pardon and to enjoy happinefs, which can refult only from the exercife of a holy temper.

THE different parts of the gofpel fcheme harmonize with each other.   Chriftianity views man as a finful and as a guilty being.   As finful it holds forth the idea of divine influences to renew him and make him holy ; as guilty it directs him to a Saviour who has died for him, and fuffered the penalty of fin on his account.   Thus is the gofpel, what the word itfelf imports, a meffage of glad tidings.

THE doctrines which have been mentioned as fundamental and effential to the Chriftian fcheme, may
be confidered as comprifing the whole fyftem. In
difcuffing thefe points, faithful minifters will bring
up to view the various ideas neceffarily connected
with them. They will defcribe the nature of fin
and wherein the depravity of the heart confifts.
They will often fpeak of the various bleffings purchafed by Chrift, and particularly defcribe that faith
by which believers are united to Chrift, and made
to participate of the bleffings purchafed by him, and
that repentance towards God which is faid to be unto life. They will dwell much upon experimental
religion, defcribing the progrefs of the divine operation in awakening, convincing and converting the
finner, and carrying on a progreffive work of fanctification in thofe who are ordained to eternal life.
This will lead them frequently to explain and inculcate the various graces of the Chriftian life ; to hold
up to view the character and privileges of believers,
and thus to lead them to felf examination, that they
may not deceive themfelves with a falfe hope.

THEY will alfo exhort their hearers to the practice of every moral virtue ; and enforce the idea that
the law of God, tho no longer a covenant of works,
is ftill binding as a rule of life ; and that any pretenfions to faith without fincere repentance for fin,
real holinefs in the heart, and an external conformity
to the moral precepts of the fcriptures, are falla-
cious.

TIME will not permit me to go into a further detail of the doctrines and precepts of our holy religion.
I have endeavored briefly to hold up to view that fyftem of truths which appears to me to be contained
in the word of God, and which therefore I think it
the duty of Chriftian minifters to explain and inculcate. I may have omitted fome things which many
of my hearers may deem effential and important
truths ; and I may have noticed others which may

16   AN ORDINATION SERMON.

be thought lefs important.   All religious truth muſt
be examined by the word of God.   What will not
bear that teſt muſt be given up.   To the volume of
divine revelation let a candid appeal be made.

On the general ſubject of preaching Chriſt, I
would further obſerve, that faithful miniſters will
make the advancement of his kingdom and the ſalvation of men the great aim of their preaching.   " We
preach not ourſelves," ſays our apoſtle, " but Chriſt
Jeſus the Lord, and ourſelves your ſervants for his
ſake."   All ſelfiſh, private conſiderations muſt be
ſacrificed, to the promotion of that glorious cauſe
for which the bleſſed redeemer quitted the boſom of
his father, ſuffered, bled and died.   The miniſters of
Chriſt muſt not ſeek their own glory, but the glory
of him who ſent them.   " The glory of God, and
" the ſalvation of man are the great and good ends
" of the paſtoral office ; and he who loſeth ſight of
" theſe, may acquire the reputation of a learned, an
" ingenious, or an eloquent orator, but cannot be
" ſtiled a preacher of Chriſt."

Finally, my brethren, to recur back to an idea
mentioned in a preceding part of this diſcourſe, thoſe
miniſters who take the apoſtle Paul for an example,
will have a continual reference to Chriſt in all their
preaching.   In every age thus to preach Chriſt hath
been the means of convincing and converting ſinners,
and of building them up in holineſs and comfort
through faith unto ſalvation.   It was the obſervation
of a judicious and pious writer on this ſubject,
" That where a great and univerſal neglect of preaching Chriſt hath prevailed in a Chriſtian nation, it
hath given a fatal occaſion to the growth of infidelity : for when people have heard the ſermons of their
miniſters for many years together, and find little of
Chriſt in them, they have taken it into their heads
that men may be very good, and go ſafe to heaven
without Chriſtianity ; and therefore though they
dwell in a land where the goſpel is profeſſed, they

486

AN ORDINATION SERMON. 17

imagine there is no need they fhould be Chriftians. To which I may add, that it is no lefs obfervable on the other hand, that wherever there has been any revival of religion, it has uniformly been introduced and carried on, through the blefling of God, by preaching the peculiar doctrines of Chriftianity. Thefe, and thefe alone, have been, and ever will be, the wifdom and power of God unto falvation."

A few remarks will be made upon the third general idea fuggefted in our text :

III. It is the duty of Chriftian minifters to preach the kingdom of God and to teach the things concerning the Lord Jefus Chrift, " with all confidence."

The apoftle Paul, tho a prifoner in Rome, and fent there on account of his preaching the truth, boldly perfifted in teaching the fame fyftem of doctrines. Feeling the force of divine truth on his own mind, he refolutely determined to inculcate this upon others, whatever might be the confequences as refpected himfelf. No danger deterred him, no perfecution reftrained him, no ridicule difcouraged him. He knew he had been called to preach Chrift, and looking to his great mafter for grace to help him, he, " with all confidence," went on in the difcharge of his duty.—Thofe who fucceed him, as difpenfers of the everlafting gofpel, fhould imitate him not only in the fubject of their preaching, but in their zeal and boldnefs in the caufe of the Redeemer. Though not like him expofed to open perfecution, yet many temptations will be thrown in their way to induce them to fupprefs truths fo mortifying to the pride, fo thwarting to the corrupt propenfities of finners as are many doctrines and precepts of the gofpel. Againft fuch temptations they muft be on their guard, and not fhun to declare the whole counfel of God, whether people will hear or forbear. They muft contend earneftly for the faith once delivered to the

C

18   AN ORDINATION SERMON.

faints, and boldly and refolutely inculcate the truth, unawed by the fcoffs of the libertine or the cavils of the fceptic. The caufe in which they are engaged is the caufe of God, and he that is for them is greater than thofe that are againft them.

In the difcuffion of points which are rather fpeculative than effential, or of thofe intricate and myfterious fubjects which are not to be fully comprehended by the human underftanding, a prudent care fhould be taken not to give needlefs offence. That harfhnefs of expreffion and feverity of recrimination, which tend to irritate the minds of men, and prejudice them againft the truth, fhould be carefully avoided. Our bleffed Saviour, when he firft gave a commiffion to the twelve difciples to preach the kingdom of heaven, told them not only to be harmlefs as doves, but alfo to be wife as ferpents. There is fuch a thing as minifterial prudence, which is not at all incompatible with a bold, manly and open avowal of effential truths. Thefe truths are never to be facrificed to gain temporary applaufe from men who love darknefs rather than light becaufe their deeds are evil.—Let Chrift, let the doctrines and duties of his religion be preached " with all confidence," at the fame time, in that difcreet manner which fhall be beft calculated to win men over to the belief of the one and the practice of the other.

Having finifhed what I propofed by way of illuftration of the text, I fhall now proceed to apply the fubject.

1. From that view of fcripture truth which we have now taken we learn the fuperior excellency of the Chriftian religion.

Well might St. Paul fay, he counted all things but lofs for the excellency of the knowledge of Chrift Jefus ; and well might he declare that he was not afhamed of the gofpel of Chrift.—No other fyftem

AN ORDINATION SERMON. 19

of religion gives fuch juft and rational ideas of the divine character; no other fo truly defcribes the character of man, his prefent condition and the connection between the prefent and a future ftate of exiftence;—no other teaches on what terms God can pardon fin, nor are any intimations given of fuch a Saviour as man needs except in that volume which, tho defpifed by many, contains the only knowledge which can make man wife to falvation. All the truths of the bible are important, becaufe they relate to the happinefs of our eternal exiftence. If we give up thefe truths we fhall wander like blind men without a guide till our feet ftumble on the dark mountains and plunge us into endlefs and remedilefs woe. " Lord Jefus, to whom fhall we go? Thou haft the words of eternal life."

2. WE learn from our fubject what great obligations of gratitude we are under to the Father of lights for bleffing us with the light of divine revelation.

How different is our fituation from that of a great part of mankind, who are ftill wrapped in midnight darknefs with regard to religion? They know not the God who made them; they are ignorant of a Saviour and of a future ftate of exiftence: While on all thefe deeply interefting fubjects, we have the means of acquiring information. Let us remember who hath made us to differ; let us be truly grateful to God for his goodnefs to us, and be careful to improve the privileges we enjoy that it may not hereafter be our condemnation that light came into the world and that we loved darknefs rather than light, becaufe our deeds were evil.

3. THE fubject to which we have been attending is particularly applicable to the folemn yet joyful fervices of this day.

WE have affembled in the fanctuary of the Lord for the purpofe of confecrating his young fervant to

20   AN ORDINATION SERMON.

the work of the gofpel miniftry, and of ordaining him to the paftoral care of this church and fociety. Important is the work to which he is to be feparated; arduous are its duties; yet great are the encouragements to the faithful difcharge of thefe duties. Deeply interefting alfo are the tranfactions of this day to this people. They are to have fet over them in the Lord a fpiritual guide to preach to them the truths of the everlafting gofpel, and adminifter to them in holy things. May he be made a favor of life unto life to each individual, and not of death unto death to any one.

MY DEAR BROTHER,

You are about to be confecrated to the work of the evangelical miniftry, by prayer and the impofition of the hands of the prefbytery. To this work I truft you are alfo called of God, elfe thefe public ceremonies will be of no avail. We can give only an external commiffion; the real qualifications for the work muft come from a power infinitely fuperior to man. Your duty, as regards the fubjects on which you are to preach, together with the general manner of your preaching has been, tho in a very imperfect manner, fet before you. Permit me again to turn your attention to it. You are to preach the religion of the bible in diftinction from the fyftems of uninfpired men. You are to preach Chrift, to have a general reference to him in the difcuffion of all religious fubjects; to inculcate the peculiar doctrines and duties of his religion; and to make the advancement of his caufe your great aim. You are to proclaim the truth with all confidence, at the fame time with prudence, that you may be faithful to your own foul, and the fouls committed to your care. In the difcharge of your office you muft expect to meet with many trials and difficulties; remember that your fufficiency is not of yourfelf but of God, and that he hath promifed his grace fhall be fufficient for you. Look therefore to him; be a man of prayer; afk for wifdom from above; and as a faithful foldier of Jefus

AN ORDINATION SERMON.

Chriſt, ſeek directions from your great captain ; obey his orders, and exert yourſelf boldly in his cauſe. May your days be many and proſperous ; your labors ſuccefsful ; your improvements conſpicuous and perpetual ; your uſefulnefs extenſive ; and your reward glorious in the kingdom of your Father where they that be wiſe ſhall ſhine as the brightnefs of the firmament, and they that have turned many to righteouſnefs as the ſtars for ever and ever !

BRETHREN OF THIS CHURCH AND SOCIETY,

As it will be the duty of him who is about to be ordained your paſtor, with all confidence, to preach to you the ſyſtem of divine truth revealed in the holy ſcriptures, ſo it will be your duty to hear that ſyſtem and to receive it in the love of it. Permit me to remind you, that the condemnation of thoſe to whom the truth is preached, who yet will not receive it, will be deſervedly greater than that of thoſe who do not enjoy ſuch privileges. We truſt that he whom you have choſen to take the over-ſight of you in the Lord, will endeavour faithfully to diſpenſe to you the goſpel of Chriſt. May you long rejoice in his light, and be profited and edified by his miniſtry. Eſteem him highly in love for his work's ſake ; conſtantly and diligently attend upon his miniſtry, with minds open to conviction, and with hearts diſpoſed to receive inſtruction. Aſſiſt him by your prayers ; comfort him under his trials ; give him every encouragement and ſupport in your power, and may you be each other's crown of joy and rejoicing in the preſence of our Lord Jeſus at his coming !

MY HEARERS,

WHAT hath been at this time delivered may ſerve to teach us what kind of preaching we ought moſtly to value. By many, at the preſent day, the great and eſſential truths of the goſpel are too little regarded. Like the Athenians of old they require ſomething new, ſomething that may gratify an itching ear, and

22   AN ORDINATION SERMON.

furnifh matter for a vain imagination to work upon.
Would you be made wife unto falvation ? Then cordially embrace the doctrines of Chrift. Be not
merely nominal Chriftians, believing, in a vague, in-
diftinct fenfe in Chriftianity, becaufe it is the religion
of the country in which you happen to live ; but be
the real followers of a crucified Saviour. Look to
him as a prophet for inftruction ; look to him as a
prieft to make atonement for you ; look to him as a
king to rule in your hearts by his fpirit, and as entitled to the fervice of your lives. And may he be
made of God to each one of us, wifdom, righteoufnefs, fanctification and redemption. AMEN.

CHAPTER 19

THE CHARGE,

By the Rev. CYPRIAN STRONG,
OF CHATHAM.

DEAR SIR,

YOU being now feparated to the work
of the evangelical miniftry, by PRAYER and the
laying on of the hands of the PRESBYTERY, and ordained the Paftor of the Church of Chrift in this
place : And, being authorized to preach the everlafting gofpel, to perifhing men—to adminifter the
ordinances of *Baptifm* and the *Lord's Supper*—to
affift in ordaining Elders—to difpenfe difcipline, and
to take the lead in the Church of Chrift ;—and, in
in a word, to perform the whole work of a gofpel
minifter :

WE would now charge thee, before GOD and the
Lord Jefus Chrift—before the holy Angels and this
affembly, that thou be faithful in the difcharge of
all the duties of your facred office, as a minifter of
Jefus Chrift.

PARTICULARLY, we charge thee, to " take heed
unto thyfelf," and keep thy foul diligently." Look
well to the ftate of your foul, and fee thou to it,
that it be adorned with all the graces of the Divine
Spirit—that the love of God, of Chrift and the fouls
of men, be the governing principle of all your conduct. Feel thy dependance on the grace of God ;
and give thyfelf much unto prayer.—Study the facred fcriptures with great diligence and conftancy ;
and make them your directory in your private walks
and public adminiftrations, as well as the fource of
your comforts and confolations. On the one
hand, be very zealous in maintaining and fupporting the important truths of the gofpel ; and, on the
other, be careful to exercife a due degree of meeknefs and benevolence, towards fuch as oppofe it. In
a word, be an example to the flock of Chrift ; and

exhibit that zeal and benevolence which fhone fo confpicuoufly in the conduct of our bleffed Redeemer ; that others may take knowledge of you, *that you have been with Jefus.*

AGAIN : *Neglect not the gift that is in thee, which was given thee by prayer, with the laying on of the hands of the prefbytery. That thy profiting may appear unto all. Take heed to thy* DOCTRINE. Let it be pure, uncorrupted and expreffive of the plain truths which are recorded in the gofpel. Ufe great *plainnefs of fpeech ;* and avoid the *enticing words* of man's wifdom. Preach and explain, with great plainnefs, not only the gracious *promifes* which Chrift has made, for the comfort of his own people ; but enforce the awful and dreadful *threatenings* which he hath denounced, for the awakening of finners.

IN the adminiftration of the ordinances of BAPTISM and the LORD's SUPPER, fee to it, that it be to fuch only as are the proper fubjects. Making a diftinction between the *holy* and *profane,* that the temple of God be not defiled.

IN the exercife of thy minifterial truft, in ordaining Elders over the Churches, fee to it that thou art faithful, and exercife the greateft wifdom and care. *Lay hands fuddenly on no man.* Commit the miniftry to fuch men only, as in a judgment of charity, are men of knowledge, experience, a holy life, and are the lovers of Jefus and the fouls of men.

IN the exercife of difcipline in Chrift's houfe, do thou manifeft a moft facred *impartiality ;* not *prefering one to another,* nor *lording it over God's heritage.*—Be thou in all things, *an example to the believers, in word, in converfation, in charity, in fpirit, in faith, in purity.* In doing thefe things, *thou fhalt both fave thyfelf and them that hear thee.*

A CHARGE.

WE, efpecially, charge thee, *to take heed to the flock over which the Holy Ghoft hath made thee an overfeer.* Watch over it with diligence, feed it with the fincere milk of the word ; and in all things, be thou an example to it. Exhort *the aged to be grave, fober, temperate, found in the faith, in charity, in patience. Young men, likewife, exhort to be fober minded.*

DEAR BROTHER, remember that you muft render a moft folemn account to the Chief Bifhop of fouls, for the improvement you make of the miniftry, which you have now received of the Lord. Prepare to meet Him with exceeding joy. The important defigns of your miniftry, the influence it will eventually have on the concerns of your own foul, and the confequences which will follow, refpecting the fouls of this flock, are worthy of your conftant and moft ferious confideration. It will be but a little while, before the connexion between you and this people will be diffolved, by death ; and every thing prepared for a moft folemn meeting at the bar of Jefus Chrift.—Be thou faithful unto death. If thou keepeft this charge, which we commit unto you, unrebukable unto the end ; when the Chief Shepherd fhall appear, you may be affured, that you fhall then receive a crown of glory, which fhall never fade away.

Now unto Him, who is able to keep you from falling, and to do exceeding abundantly, above all that we afk or think ; unto Him be glory in the Church, by CHRIST JESUS, throughout all ages, world without end. AMEN.

D

RIGHT HAND OF FELLOWSHIP, &c.

BY THE REV. DAVID SELDEN.

T H A T the Minifters of the bleffed Jefus may advance the glorious defign of their divine miffion, it is highly neceffary, that they cultivate Chriftian love and unity ;—that they live in fellowfhip with one other, and with the whole houfehold of faith ; that thus they may ftrengthen each other's hands, and encourage each other's hearts, and do honor to their Divine Mafter.   As a teftimony of their Chrif-tian fellowfhip, the fcriptural practice of giving the right hand, hath ever been obferved at folemnities like the prefent—a practice in its own nature of friendly import, and expreffive of the greateft cor-diality and affection.   Therefore, in compliance with the defire of the Ordaining Council, I   now wel-come this our Brother into the vineyard of Chrift. Reverend Sir, *Is thine heart right, as my heart is with thy heart ? If fo, give me thine hand.*   By this token, we receive you into the chariot of the gof-pel miniftry ; and certify our cordial approbation of you, as a fellow laborer in the vineyard of our great Lord.—We affure you of our readinefs to affift you, and to be affifted by you in our common employ-ment.   We commit and commend you, dear bro-ther, with the Church over which the Holy Ghoft hath made you overfeer, to the allwife care and pro-tection of the great head of the Church.   We pray that you may be ftrong in the grace, that is in Chrift Jefus ; that you may be perfect, thoroughly furnifh-ed unto all good works, and abundantly fuccefsful, that when your faithful labors fhall terminate on earth, you may receive a crown of glory that fadeth not away.

WE rejoice with you, brethren of this Church, in the bleffings of this aufpicious day.   Rejoice in this man of God, whom you have chofen, and who has been folemnly fet over you in the Lord.   Efteem him highly in love, for his work's fake.—Affift, encourage, and ftrengthen him in the important duties of his office.—Under his faithful miniftry, may your fouls profper and be in health.—May you be fed with fpiritual knowledge and underftanding.—May the houfhold of God grow in purity and holinefs.— May finners be awakened, convinced, and converted to the Chriftian faith and practice.   And at laft, *may you all come unto Mount Zion and unto the city of the living God, the heavenly Jerufalem, and to an innumerable company of Angels : to the general affembly and church of the firft born, which are written in heaven, and to God the Judge of all, and to Jefus the mediator of the new covenant.*

CHRISTOPHER RORY HOOPS
January 29, 1950–July 17, 2008

Christopher Rory Hoops was born January 29, 1950. He grew up in Southern California with his loving parents, two brothers, and two sisters. For most of his early life, he was surrounded by books, music, and exotic plants from his father's garden.

His teen years were spent entirely during the sixties, which for Chris and his generation was a time of exploration and search for personal identity. Never one to watch the parade pass him by, he decided to join what appeared to him a happy throng of loving young individuals calling themselves "Flower Children."

His trek encompassed many adventures, some exciting and some just frightening. Relationships formed during that time ultimately proved to be the means through which God made effectual His Electing Grace for Christopher Hoops, who subsequently confessed his faith in Jesus Christ as his Savior. Chris then experienced that Purest and Highest Love, found only in God, that most of his peers had vainly sought in profligate dissipation; he turned his entire quest for enlightenment God-ward.

Throughout his late teens and early twenties, he studied voraciously, absorbing as much wisdom as he could from God's Word, from volumes of Theology and of Church History, and gleaning whatever he could from various Mentors, Pastors, and Teachers at San Bernardino Bible College. By his mid twenties he was involved heavily in Christian ministry, teaching full time, and attending college.

When he was twenty-seven, he married Gail Melinda Turner, whom he met while teaching a Bible class. They had a daughter, Erin Christine, and two sons, Christopher Rory, and Michael Charles. Eventually the family settled in Camarillo, California, where Chris co-founded American Heritage Christian Church.

In 1989, Chris was diagnosed with a liver disease. Doctors told him that his lifestyle must slow down, and that he must find a quieter place to live out the few years he had remaining. In 1991, Chris left the Congregation he had pastored since 1983, and moved his family to Colville, Washington.

Washington held blessings and many trials for Chris and his family. His health continued to degrade, but eventually a transplant liver was found for him, which subsequently blessed him with fourteen additional years of relative health. Returning health allowed Chris to run a Christian bookstore, return to Pastoral Ministry, and co-found two additional congregations. Enjoying country life, he raised impressive gardens, ran a small farm, taught school, and became an innovative cook. One winter evening in 1995, the Hoops' daughter Erin, aged sixteen, was returning from a Church outing with some friends, and was killed in a tragic automobile accident. A profound grief settled over the Hoops household. It was not until Chris and Gail were able to adopt three young daughters, that a full sense of purpose and mission returned to Chris. He rallied, and devoted himself with renewed passion to the upbringing and education of his young children.

Late in 2001, Chris moved his family back to California and took a teaching job in Santa Cruz. In 2003, his health beginning to decline again, the Hoops relocated once more, this time to Sacramento. By late 2006, trips to the hospital had become routine, and Chris was once again on the Transplant List awaiting another liver. By March of 2008 damage to his kidneys necessitated removal of Chris' name from the transplant list and his health continued to degrade. The end was imminent.

Many people were able to visit him in those remaining days, and he was happy to share their company. They talked of faith, politics, old classic movies, and, of course, Bob Dylan. Chris had a profound sense that the consequences of past sin had brought him to this place, but he never protested his providence. Sure of his eternal destination in Glory, and anxious to be re-united with loved ones lost, he nevertheless was saddened at the prospect of leaving his loving wife and children behind. Struck with a sense that the Church Militant in the Earth had work remaining that he might yet be able to accomplish, he continued his work until his declining health forbade it. He cried with some friends and laughed with most.

On July 17, at 2:35 P.M. the Rev. Christopher Rory Hoops heard his Savior's voice call him home. He breathed his last with his loving wife by his side and yielded up his spirit. His earthly pains, cares, and worries have all been rolled up and laid aside like a used garment, and Chris gathered to the bosom of his Lord.

Obituary of Christopher R. Hoops

Chris was preceded in death by his parents Wilbert and Elizabeth, and by daughter Erin. He is survived by his wife Gail, sons Christopher and Michael, daughters Bridgette, Tia, and Katie, brothers Bill and Jon, and by sisters Averil and Priscilla. Countless friends will mourn who loved him, and not a few who called him "Pastor" will profoundly miss the one who shepherded them most faithfully. All who knew him will honor his memory.

This obituary first appeared on the website of Inland Christian Center Church at www.inlandchristiancenterchurch.org/christopher_hoops.htm